American Culture in the 1950s

Twentieth-Century American Culture
Series editor: Martin Halliwell, University of Leicester.

This series provides accessible but challenging studies of American culture in the twentieth century. Each title covers a specific decade and offers a clear overview of its dominant cultural forms and influential texts, discussing their historical impact and cultural legacy. Collectively the series reframes the notion of 'decade studies' through the prism of cultural production and rethinks the ways in which decades are usually periodized. Broad contextual approaches to the particular decade are combined with focused case studies, dealing with themes of modernity, commerce, freedom, power, resistance, community, race, class, gender, sexuality, internationalism, technology, war and popular culture.

American Culture in the 1910s
Mark Whalan

American Culture in the 1920s
Susan Currell

American Culture in the 1930s
David Eldridge

American Culture in the 1940s
Jacqueline Foertsch

American Culture in the 1950s
Martin Halliwell

American Culture in the 1960s
Sharon Monteith

American Culture in the 1970s
Will Kaufman

American Culture in the 1980s
Graham Thompson

American Culture in the 1990s
Colin Harrison

American Culture in the 1950s

Martin Halliwell

Edinburgh University Press

For Mum and Dad

© Martin Halliwell, 2007

Edinburgh University Press Ltd
22 George Square, Edinburgh

Typeset in 11/13 pt Stempel Garamond by
Servis Filmsetting Ltd, Manchester, and
printed and bound in Great Britain by
Cromwell Press, Trowbridge, Wilts

A CIP record for this book is available from the British Library

ISBN 978 0 7486 1884 2 (hardback)
ISBN 978 0 7486 1885 9 (paperback)

The right of Martin Halliwell to be identified as author of this work
has been asserted in accordance with the Copyright, Designs and Patents Act 1988.

Published with the support of the Edinburgh University Scholarly Publishing Initiatives Fund.

Contents

Figures

Case Studies

Acknowledgements

I have been very lucky that during the writing of this book the 1950s has once again come into full view, with fifty-year commemorations and renewed interest in the decade reenergising a period that has been put to rest many times over. When Warren Susman explored the idea of a 'usable past' in the mid-1960s, he could not have predicted the number of occasions since then that the 1950s has been read, reread and misread. This book is just one attempt among others to revive interest in the cultural vitality of a decade that is often written off as anodyne and one-dimensional.

My first debt is to the students at the University of Leicester who have taken my final-year module Containment and Resistance in 1950s and 1960s American Culture over the last seven years, and who have helped me realize that when it comes to direct comparison the 1960s does not hold all the cultural aces. I am thankful for their lively discussions and for making me return with fresh eyes to aspects of the decade I thought I knew well. Secondly, I would like to thank colleagues at Leicester, particularly my Heads of Department Elaine Treharne and Richard Foulkes, for supporting my research, and Guy Barefoot, Nick Everett, Sarah Graham, George Lewis, Paul Marygold, Andy Mousley, Mark Rawlinson and Annette Saddik for valuable comments on sections of the manuscript. Thanks also go to the members of the Intellectual History Group at Jesus College, Cambridge; to Bridget Bennett, James Dale, Michael Eaton, Pete Groshl, Michael Hoar, Joel Isaac, Andrew Johnstone, Richard King, Peter Kuryla, Catherine Morley, Sue Porter, Jon Powell, Graham Thompson, Greg Walker and Imelda Whelehan for their interest in the project; and to Nicola Ramsey at Edinburgh University Press for her professionalism and friendship.

My gratitude goes to the British Academy and the Department of English at the University of Leicester for the funding and study leave that enabled me to do much of my research stateside. I am very grateful for the help of the librarians at the Library of Congress and Smithsonian Institution Archives, Washington DC; the New York Public Library and the Schomberg Center for Research in Black Culture; the John M. Flaxman Library, The Art Institute of Chicago; the Wisconsin Center for Film and Television Research, Madison, Wisconsin; the University of Washington, Seattle; and the Biblioteca Renzo Renzi, Bologna. Thanks are due to the Scala Archive in Florence for the supply of digital images of Jasper Johns's *Flag* and Robert Frank's 'Parade', reproduced in Chapter 5. I would also like to thank Mary Donovan and Carl Nelson for their generous hospitality during my visits to Capitol Hill.

I am very grateful to have been given the opportunity to present aspects of the book at the following institutions: the American Studies Seminar Series, University of Leeds (December 2004); the Midwest Modern Language Association Conference, Milwaukee, Wisconsin (November 2005); the British Association of American Studies Conference, University of Kent, Canterbury (April 2006); the Inaugural Lecture Series, University of Leicester (May 2006); the American Modernism: Cultural Transactions Conference, Oxford Brookes University (September 2006); and the American Studies Seminar Series, University of Sussex (February 2007).

My last two debts are too great to express in words: to my wife Laraine who continues to amaze me with her energy and commitment, and to my parents David and Jean Halliwell to whom I dedicate this book.

Chronology of
1950s American Culture

Date	Events	Criticism	Literature	Performance
1950	Alger Hiss convicted of perjury (January). Joseph McCarthy begins anticommunist crusade (February). Korean War (June 1950–July 1953). Albert Einstein discovers the general theory of gravitation. Charles Schulz's *Peanuts* comic makes national debut.	Bruno Bettleheim, *Love is not Enough* Erik Erikson, *Childhood and Society* Haywood Patterson, *Scottsboro Boy* David Riesman, *The Lonely Crowd* Lionel Trilling, *The Liberal Imagination*	Paul Bowles, *The Delicate Prey* Ray Bradbury, *The Martian Chronicles* Charles Olson, 'Projective Verse' Conrad Richter, *The Town* Micky Spillane, *My Gun Is Quick*	William Inge, *Come Back, Little Sheba* *Call Me Madam* (644 performances) *Guys and Dolls* (1,200 performances) *The Member of the Wedding* (501 performances) *South Pacific* wins Pulitzer Prize for Drama
1951	American Committee for Cultural Freedom founded. W. E. B. DuBois tried for treason. Julius and Ethel Rosenberg sentenced to death for conspiring to commit espionage (executed 1953). Selective Service Bill lowers draft age to eighteen-and-a-half. Transcontinental television launched (September).	Hannah Arendt, *The Origins of Totalitarianism* Rachel Carson, *The Sea Around Us* George Kennan, *American Diplomacy* Marshall McLuhan, *The Mechanical Bride* C. Wright Mills, *White Collar*	Langston Hughes, *Montage of a Dream Deferred* James Jones, *From Here to Eternity* Carson McCullers, *The Ballad of the Sad Café* Norman Mailer, *Barbary Shore* J. D. Salinger, *The Catcher in the Rye*	*The King and I* (1,246 performances) Merce Cunningham, *Sixteen Dances for Soloist and Company of Three* Lillian Hellman, *The Autumn Garden* Tennessee Williams, *The Rose Tattoo* Public launch of the Living Theatre

Film	Television	Music	Art
All About Eve (Joseph L. Mankiewicz) *The Asphalt Jungle* (John Huston) *The Big Lift* (George Seaton) *I Married a Communist* (Robert Stevenson) *Sunset Boulevard* (Billy Wilder)	*Your Show of Shows* (1950–4) *The Cisco Kid* (1950–6) *Racket Squad* (1950–3) *What's My Line* (1950–7) *Your Hit Parade* (1950–9)	Gordon Jenkins with The Weavers, 'Goodnight Irene' Moon Mulligan, 'I'll Sail My Ship' Muddy Waters, 'Rolling Stone' Hank Williams, 'Cold, Cold Heart' People's Artists launch magazine *Sing Out!*	Franz Klein, *Chief* Willem de Kooning, *Excavation* Rico Lebrun, *Crucifixion Triptych* Jackson Pollock, *Autumn Rhythm*, *Lavender Mist* and *Mural on Indian Red Ground* Barnett Newman's first solo exhibition
An American in Paris (Vincente Minnelli) *The Day the Earth Stood Still* (Robert Wise) *I Was a Communist for the FBI* (Gordon Douglas) *Strangers on a Train* (Alfred Hitchcock) *A Streetcar Named Desire* (Elia Kazan)	*The Amos 'n' Andy Show* (1951–3) *Boston Blackie* (1951–3) *Dragnet* (1951–9) *I Love Lucy* (1951–7) *Red Skelton Show* (1951–71)	Tony Bennett, 'Because of You' and 'Cold, Cold Heart' Jackie Brenston, 'Rocket "88"' Nat King Cole, 'Unforgettable' Perry Como, 'If' The Weavers, 'On Top of Old Smokey'	Barnett Newman, *Adam* Irene Rice Pereira, *Light is Gold* Mark Rothko, *Black, Pink and Yellow over Orange* Hale Woodruff, *The Art of the Negro* (1950–1) Robert Rauschenberg's first solo exhibition

Date	Events	Criticism	Literature	Performance
1952	Dwight D. Eisenhower (Rep) runs against Adlai Stevenson (Dem) in presidential campaign. First US hydrogen bomb detonated, at Eniwetok in the Pacific. Paul Robeson awarded the Stalin Peace Prize. UFO sightings across the country. Hasbro's Mr Potato Head first child's toy advertised on TV.	Aaron Copland, *Music and the Imagination* Reinhold Niebuhr, *The Irony of American History* 'Our Country and Our Culture', *Partisan Review* Norman Vincent Peale, *The Power of Positive Thinking* Paul Tillich, *The Courage to Be*	Ralph Ellison, *Invisible Man* Ernest Hemingway, *The Old Man and the Sea* Flannery O'Connor, *Wise Blood* Micky Spillane, *Kill Me Deadly* John Steinbeck, *East of Eden*	Cage-Rauschenberg Happening in Black Mountain College *Pal Joey* (revival, 542 performances) George Axelrod, *The Seven Year Itch* Tennessee Williams's *Summer and Smoke* revived Off Broadway
1953	Dwight Eisenhower's inauguration as thirty-fourth President (January). Execution of Julius and Ethel Rosenberg for espionage (June). Josef Stalin dies (March). Elizabeth II's coronation (June). Cinemascope and 3-D film introduced. *Playboy* magazine founded; Marilyn Monroe is first centrefold (December).	Daniel Boorstin, *The Genius of American Politics* Sidney Hook, *Heresy, Yes – Conspiracy, No!* Alfred Kinsey, *Sexual Behavior in the Human Female* B. F. Skinner, *Science and Human Behavior* Leo Strauss, *Natural Right and History*	James Baldwin, *Go Tell It On the Mountain* Saul Bellow, *The Adventures of Augie March* William Burroughs, *Junkie* (republished as *Junky*, 1964) Richard Wright, *The Outsider* Lawrence Ferlinghetti opens City Lights Bookshop	Robert Anderson, *Tea and Sympathy* William Inge, *Picnic* Arthur Miller, *The Crucible* Tennessee Williams, *Casino Real* Can-Can (892 performances)

Film	Television	Music	Art
The Bad and the Beautiful (Vincente Minnelli) *High Noon* (Fred Zinnemann) *Limelight* (Charles Chaplin) *My Son John* (Leo McCarey) *Singin' in the Rain* (Gene Kelly and Stanley Donan)	*The Adventures of Ozzie and Harriet* (1952–66) *Dragnet* (1952–9) *Four Star Playhouse* (1952–6) *Our Miss Brooks* (1952–6) *This is Your Life* (1952–61)	Karen Chandler, 'Hold Me, Thrill Me, Kiss Me' Lloyd Price, 'Lawdy, Miss Clawdy' Johnnie Ray, 'Cry' Harry Smith's *Folkways Anthology* Sun label launched by Sam Phillips	Willem de Kooning, *Woman I* (1950–2) Robert Rosenberg, *American Action Painting* Andy Warhol's first solo exhibition The photographic quarterly *Aperture* established 'Diogenes with a Camera' exhibition, MoMA
All I Desire (Douglas Sirk) *House of Wax* (André De Toth) *Niagara* (Henry Hathaway) *Pickup on South Street* (Sam Fuller) *The Wild One* (Laslo Benedek)	*The Liberace Show* (1953–6) *The Life of Riley* (1953–8) *Marty* (Goodyear Television Playhouse) *Person to Person* (1953–6) *Private Secretary* (1953–7)	Tony Bennett, 'Rags to Riches' Bill Haley, 'Crazy Man Crazy' Big Mama Thornton, 'Hound Dog' Lawrence Welk, 'Oh Happy Day' Hank Williams, 'Your Cheatin' Heart'	Robert Rauschenberg, *Erased de Kooning Drawing* Larry Rivers repaints *Washington Crossing the Delaware* Richard Stankiewicz, *Warrior* (1952–3) *Life* magazine starts using colour Stacked and stiletto heels in fashion

Date	Events	Criticism	Literature	Performance
1954	Senate censures McCarthy following Army–McCarthy hearings (April–June) televised live on ABC. US Supreme Court rules school segregation unconstitutional following *Brown* v. *the Board of Education*. Eisenhower signs bill outlawing the Communist Party. US tests hydrogen bomb at Bikini Atoll in the Pacific. Comics Code set up after the publication of Frederic Wertham's *Seduction of the Innocent*.	Malcolm Cowley, *The Literary Situation* David Potter, *People of Plenty* David Riesman, *Individualism Reconsidered* Irving Howe founds political magazine *Dissent* W. K. Wimsatt, *The Verbal Icon*	Raymond Chandler, *The Long Goodbye* Allen Ginsberg, *The Green Automobile* Evan Hunter, *The Blackboard Jungle* Anais Nin, *A Spy in the House of Love* Theodore Roethke, *Collected Poems*	John Cage's happening at Black Mountain College *House of Flowers* (Truman Capote and Harold Arlen) *The Pajama Game* (1,063 performances) *Peter Pan* (Edwin Lester and Jerome Robbins) Revival of Brecht and Weill's *The Threepenny Opera*
1955	First McDonald's hamburger outlet, Illinois (April). Warsaw Pact (May). Disneyland opens in Anaheim, California (17 July). Montgomery Bus Boycott (December 1955–December 1956). Joe DiMaggio elected to the Baseball Hall of Fame. Deaths of Albert Einstein (18 April) and James Dean (30 September).	James Baldwin, *Notes of a Native Son* Leslie Fiedler, *An End of Innocence* Erich Fromm, *The Sane Society* Louis Hartz, *The Liberal Tradition in America* Herbert Marcuse, *Eros and Civilization*	W. H. Auden, *The Shield of Achilles* William Gaddis, *The Recognitions* Lawrence Ferlinghetti, *Pictures of the Gone World* Flannery O'Connor, *A Good Man is Hard to Find* Sloane Wilson, *The Man in the Gray Flannel Suit*	Michael Vincente Gazzo, *A Hatful of Rain* Paul Goodman's *The Young Disciple* produced by the Living Theatre Off Broadway William Inge, *Bus Stop* Arthur Miller, *A View from a Bridge* (revised 1956) Tennessee Williams, *Cat on a Hot Tin Roof*

Film	Television	Music	Art
From Here to Eternity (Fred Zinnemann) *On the Waterfront* (Elia Kazan) *Rear Window* (Alfred Hitchcock) *Roman Holiday* (William Wyler) *Them!* (Gordon Douglas)	*Disneyland* (1954–8) *The Adventures of Rin Tin Tin* (1954–9) *Father Knows Best* (1954–3) *Lassie* (1954–71) CBS *See It Now* documentary on McCarthy (March)	Rosemary Clooney, 'Mambo Italiano' Doris Day, 'Secret Love' Elvis Presley, 'That's All Right (Mama)' Frank Sinatra, *Songs for Young Lovers* Newport Jazz Festival established, Rhode Island	Stan Brakhage, *Desistfilm* Mark Rothko, *Ochre and Red on Red* Richard Stankiewicz, *Middle-Aged Couple* Esther Bubley first female recipient of *Photography Magazine* grand prize Six Gallery opens in San Francisco
All That Heaven Allows (Douglas Sirk) *The Blackboard Jungle* (Richard Brooks) *Invasion of the Body Snatchers* (Don Siegel) *The Man with the Golden Arm* (Otto Preminger) *Rebel Without a Cause* (Nicholas Ray)	*Alfred Hitchcock Presents* (1955–65) *Cheyenne* (1955–63) *Ed Sullivan Show* (1955–71) *The Honeymooners* (1955–6) *The Mickey Mouse Club* (1955–9)	Chuck Berry, 'Maybelline' Fats Domino, 'Ain't That A Shame' Bill Haley and his Comets, 'Rock Around the Clock' Alan Freed's first Rock 'n' Roll Party stage show Following performance of 'Around Midnight' at Newport, Miles Davis joins quintet with John Coltrane	Ray Johnson, *Elvis* collages Jasper Johns, *Flag* and *White Flag* Franz Kline, *White Forms* Robert Rauschenberg, *Rebus* 'The Family of Man' exhibition, MoMA

Date	Events	Criticism	Literature	Performance
1956	Eisenhower elected for second term (beating Stevenson). Suez crisis in Egypt. Soviet Union invades Hungary (October). Antineutron discovered at the University of California. Federal and Interstate Highway Act authorizes construction of interstate highways.	Felix Frankfurter, *Law and Men* Dwight Macdonald, *The Ford Foundation* C. Wright Mills, *The Power Elite* William Whyte, *The Organization Man*	James Baldwin, *Giovanni's Room* Saul Bellow, *Seize the Day* Elizabeth Bishop, *North and South* and *A Cold Spring* Allen Ginsberg, *Howl and Other Poems* Grace Metalious, *Peyton Place*	*Bells are Ringing* (924 performances) *My Fair Lady* (2,717 performances) Samuel Beckett, *Waiting for Godot* (from Paris) Eugene O'Neill, *Long Day's Journey into Night* performed Tennessee Williams, *Sweet Bird of Youth*
1957	School desegregation enforced in Little Rock, Arkansas. Martin Luther King Jr elected as first leader of Southern Christian Leadership Conference (SCLC). Civil Rights Act (first successful civil rights bill since 1875). USSR launches Sputnik 1 (October) and Sputnik 2 (November). US Surgeon General reports link between cigarette-smoking and lung cancer.	Irving Howe, *Politics and the Novel* Dwight Macdonald, *Memoirs of a Revolutionist* Norman Mailer, 'The White Negro' Richard Wright, *White Man Listen!* Vance Packard, *The Hidden Persuaders*	Jack Kerouac, *On the Road* Bernard Malamud, *The Assistant* Vladimir Nabokov, *Pnin* Frank O'Hara, *Meditations in an Emergency* Dr Seuss, *The Cat in the Hat*	William Inge, *The Dark at the Top of the Stairs* Eugene O'Neill, *A Moon for Misbegotten* first performed John Osborne, *Look Back in Anger* (from London) *West Side Story* (732 performances)

Film	Television	Music	Art
Bus Stop (Joshua Logan) *The Man in the Gray Flannel Suit* (Nunnelly Johnson) *Moby Dick* (John Huston) *The Searchers* (John Ford) *The Ten Commandments* (Cecil B. DeMille)	*Steve Allen Show* (1956–60) *The Price is Right* (1956–65) *To Tell the Truth* (1956–68) *Twenty-One* (1956–8) Mass release of pre-1948 films to television	*American Banjo – Three-Finger and Scruggs Style* Johnny Cash, 'I Walk the Line' and *Folsom Prison Blues* Elvis Presley, 'Heartbreak Hotel' and *Elvis Presley* Little Richard, 'Tutti Frutti' Gene Vincent, 'Be Bop a Lula'	William Klein, *New York* Gordon Parks, *Black Graveyard* Jackson Pollock killed in car crash (August) Marcel Breuer designs Whitney Museum of American Art
The Incredible Shrinking Man (Jack Arnold) *Peyton Place* (Mark Robson) *Raintree County* (Edward Dmytryk) *The Three Faces of Eve* (Nunnally Johnson) *12 Angry Men* (Sidney Lumet)	Dick Clark's *American Bandstand* (1957–89) *Leave It to Beaver* (1957–63) *Perry Mason* (1957–66) *The Real McCoys* (1957–63) *Richard Diamond, Private Detective* (1957–60)	Fats Domino, 'Blueberry Hill' Sam Cooke, 'You Send Me' Buddy Holly, 'Peggy Sue' Jerry Lee Lewis, 'Great Balls of Fire' Elvis Presley, 'All Shook Up' and 'Jailhouse Rock'	Robert Rauschenberg, *Factor I* and *Factor II* W. Eugene Smith's major photographic study of Pittsburgh Aaron Siskind photographs human feet Wallace Berman opens Ferus Gallery, Los Angeles Leo Castelli's Gallery opens in New York

Date	Events	Criticism	Literature	Performance
1958	US launch Explorer 1 (February) and Vanguard 1 (March) satellites into orbit. Elvis Presley drafted into the US Army. Worst recession since World War II. Wham-O's $1.98 Hula-Hoop was the summer craze. First skateboard, invented in Dana Point, California.	Hannah Arendt, *The Human Condition* John Kenneth Galbraith, *The Affluent Society* Martin Luther King Jr, *Stride Toward Freedom* Martin Mayer, *Madison Avenue U.S.A.* Paul Robeson, *Here I Stand*	Truman Capote, *Breakfast at Tiffany's* Lawrence Ferlinghetti, *A Coney Island of the Mind* Jack Kerouac, *The Subterraneans* and *The Dharma Bums* Bernard Malamud, *The Magic Barrel* Vladimir Nabokov, *Lolita* (US publication; France 1955)	*Flower Drum Song* (600 performances) Archibald McLeish, *J.B.* Eugene O'Neill, *Hughie* first performed Tennessee Williams, *Suddenly Last Summer*
1959	Nikita Krushchev and Richard Nixon in live televised 'kitchen debate' from Moscow. IBM put first transistorised computer on the market. Soviet spacecraft photographs far side of the moon. Buddy Holly and Ritchie Valens die in plane crash. Frank Lloyd Wright's Guggenheim Museum completed.	William J. Buckley Jr, *Up From Liberalism* Norman O. Brown, *Life Against Death* Norman Mailer, *Advertisements for Myself* C. Wright Mills, *The Sociological Imagination* Paul Tillich, *Theology of Culture*	Saul Bellow, *Henderson the Rain King* William Burroughs, *Naked Lunch* Philip Roth, *Goodbye, Columbus* Jack Kerouac, *Mexico City Blues* Robert Lowell, *Life Studies*	Edward Albee, *The Zoo Story* (performed in West Berlin) Lorraine Hansberry, *A Raisin in the Sun* Allan Kaprow, *18 Happenings in 6 Parts*, Reuben Gallery Tennessee Williams, *Sweet Bird of Youth* *The Sound of Music* (1,443 performances)

Film	Television	Music	Art
Cat on a Hot Tin Roof (Richard Brooks)	*The Donna Reed Show* (1958–66)	Chuck Berry, 'Sweet Little Sixteen'	Robert Frank, *The Americans*
The Defiant Ones (Stanley Kramer)	*Naked City* (1958–63)	Phil Spector, 'To Know Him Is to Love Him'	Louise Nevelson, *Sky Cathedral*
Imitation of Life (Douglas Sirk)	*Peter Gunn* (1958–61) *77 Sunset Strip* (1958–64)	*South Pacific* and *Gigi* soundtracks top sellers	Bruce Conner, *A Movie*
The Naked and the Dead (Raoul Walsh)	*Twenty-One* scandal and end of high-jackpot quiz shows	First commercial stereo recordings released	Jasper John's first solo exhibition, Leo Castelli Gallery
Vertigo (Alfred Hitchcock)		Newport Jazz Festival filmed and released in 1959 as *Jazz on a Summer's Day*	Mark Rothko paints murals for the new Seagram Building
Anatomy of a Murder (Otto Preminger)	*Bonanza* (1959–73) *Hawaiian Eye* (1959–63)	John Cage, *Indeterminacy*	Robert Frank, *Pull My Daisy*
The Manchurian Candidate (Richard Condon)	*Rocky and His Friends* (1959–61)	Ray Charles, 'What'd I Say'	Edward Kienholz, *John Doe* (1959) and *Jane Doe* (1960)
North By Northwest (Alfred Hitchcock)	*The Twilight Zone* (1959–65)	Lloyd Price, 'Stagger Lee'	Frank Stella begins his Black Paintings
Pillow Talk (Michael Gordon)	*The Untouchables* (1959–63)	*Mountain Music Bluegrass Style*	Harold Rosenberg, *The Tradition of the New*
Some Like It Hot (Billy Wilder)		Star and Motown labels make their debut	'New Images of Man' exhibition, MoMA

The Intellectual Context

At a *Variety* magazine conference at the Cannes Film Festival in May 2004, film producer Lawrence Bender responded dramatically to a question about media censorship in the United States. Censorship had increased suddenly in February 2004 after the inopportune exposure of singer Janet Jackson's breast at the live televised Superbowl from Houston, Texas, and Bender's response was biting: 'I feel like I'm going back to the fifties here ... the conservatives are taking over the country'.[1] This unease about censorship was shared by many directors, writers and producers in Cannes 2004, with the rise of the Right on American network television and talk radio, and the threat of the Federal Communications Commission imposing large fines on networks, making it increasingly difficult to debate issues freely or to offer oppositional views to George W. Bush's Republican administration.

Given the widespread dissent from the film industry to Bush's presidency, it was not surprising that in the last year of Bush's first term the satirist and filmmaker Michael Moore won the Palme d'Or for *Fahrenheit 9/11*, his documentary attempt to topple the Republicans. The film received rapturous applause at its Cannes premiere, was seen by over 20 million people in 2004, and was the most discussed film of the year. *Fahrenheit 9/11* argued polemically for the existence of a global conspiracy in which the US government and big corporations did little to prevent the attacks on the World Trade Center and the Pentagon in September 2001. It makes the claim that the government had hoodwinked the American public into believing that the pre-emptive strikes on Iraq represented a just war when the underlying motives were economic ones. Moore champions ordinary people – grieving mothers, reluctant young soldiers, and peace-loving citizens – against the greed of power groups, in his attempt to loosen what liberals see as the corporate stranglehold over the American media.

Bender's reference to the 1950s as a conservative age in this context evokes a decade half a century earlier in which no one asked too many questions of the government. Although the deeply ingrained deception that Moore was keen to expose is in part the legacy of conspiracy theories that emerged following the assassination of John F. Kennedy in 1963, the ideological warfare that *Fahrenheit 9/11* documents, between 'freedom-loving Americans' (to use Bush's phrase) and hateful Middle East terrorists, is the direct legacy of the early cold war years, with the target now projected onto a different enemy. The fear that the Soviet Union had the capability and the inclination to launch attacks on the United States in the late 1940s and 1950s led not only to the development of the atom and hydrogen bombs in the West, but also to the fear that communists were working to disintegrate American society from within. That physicist Klaus Fuchs and State Department official Alger Hiss were routed out of government circles for being Soviet spies (Hiss was exposed in the famous trial of 1949, Fuchs in 1950) and that Julius and Ethel Rosenberg were executed in 1953 on conspiracy charges (without full substantiation) are indications of the political paranoia that grew steadily after 1946. The looming presence of the Director of the FBI, J. Edgar Hoover, and the Wisconsin Senator Joseph McCarthy's infamous list of fifty-seven 'card-carrying Communists' that he claimed in February 1950 to be working within the Department of State (a number scaled down two days before from 205) inflamed the anticommunist hysteria that burnt strongly for eight years.

Cold war ideology is central to understanding 1950s culture but it was also a period in which the economic prosperity that began during World War II started to have tangible effects on middle-class life. Ex-First Lady and New York Senator Hillary Clinton recalled this aspect in her memoir *Living History* (2003). Reflecting on her sheltered midwestern childhood in the 1950s, she remembered 'middle-class America was flush with emerging prosperity and all that comes with it – new houses, fine schools, neighborhood parks and safe communities'.[2] For Clinton it was a decade of rising expectations, the emergence of youth culture, and the unprecedented availability of cultural products. But prospects in the 1950s came at a price: rather than questioning political decisions that contributed to the nation's rise to global eminence, the growth of mass media encouraged consumers to simply enjoy the material comforts that international prestige brought.

Historian Lizabeth Cohen shared a similar upbringing to Hillary Clinton as children of 'the Consumers' Republic', which Cohen describes as defining 'many more dimensions of life than most of us recognized at the time'.[3] Although liberal and conservative currents blurred in the anticommunist climate of the early 1950s, as Lawrence Bender emphasizes, the decade is remembered for its conservatism. This is evident in the case of Hillary Clinton. Although a moderate liberal in her adult life, Clinton adopted the conservatism of her father in the 1950s, was an active Young Republican and supported the right-wing Senator Barry Goldwater in the early 1960s, and did not find her liberal voice until the Vietnam War in the mid-1960s when she was a student at Wellesley College, Massachusetts. Clinton's story of political re-education is by no means an isolated case, reflecting the transition from inward-looking conservatism of the 1950s to the political activism of the mid-1960s.

Decades, of course, rarely add up to consistent wholes. The 1920s is much more complex than 'the Jazz Age' suggests and the 1930s more culturally varied than its 'Depression Era' tag. The 1950s is one decade that looks flat and uncomplicated, dominated by Joe McCarthy's anti-communist accusations in the early decade and the benign face of Dwight D. Eisenhower in the mid- to late 1950s. For left-liberals the decade is often written off as a low point for oppositional politics, whereas for conservatives, especially since the 1980s, it is a decade of consensus worthy of celebration. Whatever political perspective is adopted it is difficult to evade the shadow of the cold war. But, while it is tempting to read the cold war into all cultural products of the 1950s, this can be a reductive exercise. Art critic Fred Orton claims that 'the Cold War is a constraining notion, a closure, which conditions us not to probe deeper the real determinations of foreign and domestic policy' and he urges us to ask harder questions about the relationship between art and politics.[4]

Although books such as Douglas Field's collection *American Cold War Culture* (2005) continue to frame the 1950s in terms of the cold war, on closer inspection the decade reveals a number of political, social and cultural currents that cannot easily be expressed as 'cold war culture'. In popular memory the decade gave rise to Elvis, high-school romances, Tupperware, the *Peanuts* comic strip, Hollywood blondes, 3-D cinema, and black baseball star Jackie Robinson helping the Brooklyn Dodgers to six World Series finals. No overarching or static notion of culture can do justice to these parallel emergences, a realization that has led recent cultural historians to focus on 1950s culture as a site of dualities, tensions and contradictions. This book develops the idea of American culture in the 1950s in this broader sense, where a notion of national culture – with 'One nation under God' added to the Pledge of Allegiance in 1954 – jostles with a range of other cultural expressions and practices.

Periodizing the 1950s

One of the earliest periodizing accounts by the historian Eric Goldman takes 1945 to 1955 as 'the crucial decade', whereas philosopher Hannah Arendt characterized the postwar period as one caught 'between past and future'.[5] More recently, in 1986, J. Ronald Oakley described the 1950s as 'a period of puzzling paradoxes': it was 'an age of great optimism along with the gnawing fear of doomsday bombs, of great poverty in the midst of unprecedented prosperity, and of flowery rhetoric about equality along with the practice of rampant racism and sexism'.[6] And, writing in 2004, historian Richard Fried suggests that at first it seems 'a unique era that we think we know and often recall fondly', but it was, in fact, 'a fidgety mix of anxiety and relaxation, sloth and achievement, complacency and self-criticism'.[7]

Looking beyond memories, myths and nostalgia helps to unearth historical tensions that cannot easily be slotted into a unified narrative. The 1950s – or what is often confused with a half-remembered and half-mythical period called 'the fifties' – is no exception. It was the decade of popular and avant-garde music; of abstract and commercial art; of eggheads and dumb blondes; of gray flannel suits and loafer jackets; of ballet and westerns; of bus boycotts and B-52 bombers; and of the growth of big corporations and increased membership of workers' unions. The decade was vilified in the 1960s for its conservatism, particularly by those who saw themselves as its victims: the young, black, female and gay all found collective voices to denounce a decade that promised so much, but delivered little to those on the margins. However, many have claimed that the 1950s was necessary for the social revolution of the next decade to happen; and, while it is important to resist the temptation to read history as teleological (in which everything is a potential foreshadowing of future events), more recent trends suggest that the decade was one of the defining periods of the twentieth century, prefiguring the materialism of the 1980s, the media control of the 1990s, and the ascendancy of the Right in the early twenty-first century.

My intention here is to recover the diversity of cultural forms from the ingrained view that cold war culture is monolithic and one-dimensional, and also to distinguish the historical resonances of the

1950s from the popular memory of 'the fifties'. The theoretical problem, of course, is that any attempt to discuss a period only succeeds in rewriting it in another form – and sometimes with a hidden ideological slant. My agenda here is to examine, as well as look beyond, the 'cold war culture' label to explore the historical, ideological and aesthetic contours of the decade. The purpose of this book, then, is to offer a more nuanced notion of cultural production than suggested by the recycled myths of the decade.

There are various strategies for seeing beyond the mythology of 'the fifties'. One strategy is to focus on 'the facts' as established in historical texts, government documents, economic data and demographic statistics. This is where the 1982 volume *Reshaping America: Society and Institutions, 1945–1960* begins: the US population increased 30 per cent from 139.9 million in 1945 to 180.6 million in 1960; the rural population decreased from 17.5 per cent of the whole in 1945 to 8.7 per cent in 1960 (shifting from 24.4 million to 15.6 million); 31 per cent of children were under 14 in 1960 compared to 24 per cent in 1945; and the non-white population increased by 41 per cent in these fifteen years, from 14.6 million to 20.6 million.[8] Given that suburban development, juvenile delinquency and racial conflict were three hot social issues of the decade (alongside communism), these statistics go some way to characterize its salient features.

A timeline is another indicator of historical trajectory, particularly as the decade began with a new war in Korea and ended with a potent symbol of political détente when Vice-President Richard Nixon travelled to Moscow to engage in a televised 'kitchen debate' with the Soviet premier Nikita Khrushchev, in which the battleground had shifted from bombs to domestic appliances, from the Soviet satellite Sputnik to 'Split-nik' as the model American kitchen was called. There are dangers in pursuing these approaches in isolation, though. The first strategy privileges quantifiable statistics and underplays emerging trends that may not be measurable; and the second strategy often resorts to a top-down version of history in which all cultural expressions are taken under the umbrella of national politics.[9]

Another way of analyzing the decade is to identify hotspots or turning points, the hottest spot being the explosion of the H-bomb in the Pacific on 1 November 1952, generating nine times more heat than the sun. Hannah Arendt claimed that the Soviet launch of the first earth satellite Sputnik 1 on 4 October 1957 was another hotspot, an event like no other that heralded the economic slump of 1958 and the advent of the space race which preoccupied the cold war adversaries for the next fifteen years. Sometimes turning points do not focus on historic events but on personalities; the deaths of actor James Dean in September 1955 and painter Jackson Pollock in August 1956 – both through car crashes – are often cited as dramatic moments that altered the direction of film and art culture in the second half of the decade.

In terms of vital moments in the decade it is significant that two historians – Lisle Rose and Robert Ellwood – both choose 1950 as the year in which 'the cold war [came] to main street' and the 'crossroad of American religious life' (to quote the subtitles of their two books). Rose focuses primarily on foreign policy and Ellwood on religion, but both accounts identify 1950 as a crucial year – the penultimate year of Truman's Democratic administration which saw the start of two years of conflict in Korea with strong prospects of another world war. Sandwiched between World War II and Vietnam, the Korean War is often overlooked as a fairly short skirmish without a strong war narrative to hold it together. But in many ways the conflict was key to understanding national fears in the 1950s; whereas World War II was an honourable war the reasons for Korea were not as clear cut, with soldiers 'dumbly follow[ing] / leaders whose careers / hung on victory', in the words of poet William Childress.[10]

The Korean War began with the invasion of South Korea by communist North Korea, a potent symbol to the West of the ideological menace that was creeping through East Asia. The US had committed itself to supporting non-communist forces in Asia in 1949, as well as advancing its own national interests on the Asian subcontinent. The promise was of swift military action under the command of the dependable face of World War II: General Douglas MacArthur. But the reality was a war in an unknown land, where geography, language and a new enemy quickly eroded the triumphalism of 1945. Much of the war revolved around the 39th Parallel which separated North from South Korea, without any major long-term gains by either side.

Although the Korean War film *One Minute to Zero* (1952) claimed that 'the American Army does not make our foreign policy it only backs it up', the politics of the war were actually very complex. MacArthur seemed to be making key decisions, but the offensive against the North Koreans was actually directed from Washington by the liberal Secretary of State Dean Acheson; MacArthur blamed the stalemate in Korea on Truman for not letting him take full command; and Truman dismissed MacArthur in April 1951 for his arrogant and bullish military tactics. William Childress's bitter poem 'The Long March' attacks 'the General' for stealing victory from the soldiers, but two-thirds of the public actually took MacArthur's side in the dispute with Truman. This sway of public opinion and the attacks by Joseph McCarthy on the Democratic administration (he famously called the President a 'son of a bitch') were major reasons why, at the end of Truman's second term in 1952, the guardianship of the country was entrusted to a Republican: the World War II veteran Dwight Eisenhower who had commanded the Normandy invasion of 1944 and accepted German surrender in 1945.

Ike and his fashion-conscious wife Mamie were iconic faces of the decade, and Eisenhower's 1953 inauguration was a major media event, only to be upstaged by the birth of television star Lucille Ball's baby. Eisenhower was not just a golf-loving president and fiscal conservative, but also the benign patriarch that Sylvia Plath satirized in her novel *The Bell Jar* (1963) for having features that were reflected in the face of all the 'Eisenhower-faced babies' born in mid-decade.[11] But, despite Plath's view, early-decade worries receded during Eisenhower's presidency. The temporary waning of cold war fears has led some critics to focus on 1954 to 1958 as a defining period of the consumer boom. In 1954 *Life* magazine proclaimed that never before had the nation achieved so much social abundance and 1955 was described as 'the most frantic year of car buying America had yet experienced'.[12] Nixon and Khrushchev's live 'kitchen debate' at the American National Exhibition in Moscow in June 1959 signalled a possible end to the cold war, which did not fully re-ignite until the Cuban Missile crisis of autumn 1962.

There were key moments in the mid-1950s when cold war fears re-emerged: in 1956 when the Soviet Union invaded Hungary after the Hungarian withdrawal from the Warsaw Pact and in 1957 when the Soviet satellite Sputnik 1 was launched into space. Even though the anti-communist presence of J. Edgar Hoover continued to loom in American public life through the 1950s and 1960s, with the public demise of McCarthy in 1954 following his hubristic attempt to indict the Army, the paranoia and Red-baiting of the early decade ebbed. Three years later McCarthy was prematurely dead from alcohol poisoning and the 1962 film *The Manchurian Candidate* depicted him as a crazed careerist, echoing the *New York Post*'s description of him as a 'buffoon assassin'. This transition has led critic Alice Jardine to divide the decade at its mid-point (the 'First American Fifties' covering 1945 to 1955; the 'Second Fifties' spanning 1955 to 1965), while Mark Hamilton Lytle has argued that the historical phase after 1955 is actually part of the 'uncivil wars' of the long 1960s.[13]

But how could a decade be at once 'secure and hopeful', as Hillary Clinton describes it, and also be plagued by such profound ideological and atomic fears? Historian Lisle Rose brings together two such contradictory images in the title of his book, *The Cold War Comes to Main Street* (1999), as two shifting lenses that critics must look through to view the decade clearly. It was at once a period of optimism and high expectations but also the beginning of half a century of 'profound, embittered malaise' that has taught us that we cannot trust 'our neighbors, our workplace colleagues, our sources of information, or our institutions and leadership'.[14] Main Street was the symbol of wholesome Middle America and the central thoroughfare of Walt Disney's new adventure park Disneyland when it opened in Anaheim, California, in 1955. But Main Street was a symbol of a previous era: Disney's was a nostalgic Main Street, *circa* 1900, and it had been usurped in popular imagination by the threatening alleys of film noir, the suburban drives of Levittown, and the interstate highways that were snaking across the land by the late 1950s. While Rose's account is engaging he largely ignores the decade's cultural dynamics; only the parallax view of politics and culture – cold war and Main Street – can hope to do justice to its complexities.

Rose focuses on 1950 as a watershed year in Truman's last term, but a broader perspective of 'containment' is often adopted to explore the contradictions of the decade. Deployed by statesman George F. Kennan, head of Truman's Policy Planning Unit in 1947, as part of his recommendation that the nation should try to stem the communist threat in East Europe and South East Asia, the term 'containment' has since been used more widely to characterize the general climate of the 1950s.[15] Rather than dealing with it in the precise way that Kennan and the cold war policymakers had intended, cultural historians Stephen Whitfield, Lary May, Margot Henrikson, Alan Nadel and Mary Dudziak all treat containment as a general metaphor of social restriction in cold war America. It was central to Kennan's philosophy of political realism in the late 1940s and his warning that the nation must be watchful and vigilant against security threats, particularly from an ambitious Soviet Union. But postwar containment also had negative connotations, suggesting that classified information was being withheld or that citizens were being duped into believing the official line from Washington. The rise of the secret service and the CIA was important for garnering intelligence but also fed fears that a culture of secrecy was developing and that the destiny of the country was controlled by a power elite. To contain external communist threats was seen by many as a Herculean task (the journalist Walter Lippmann warned that it might well turn into a wild-goose chase across the globe), but to eliminate threats from within was virtually impossible: everyone was potentially a suspect within a global communist conspiracy.

Focusing on political history and foreign policy offers one account of the decade, but the danger is that critics either ignore the broad sweep of American culture to focus on government (as Rose does) or read all cultural forms through the filter of international relations. This top-down reading has its benefits in revealing a subtext to cold war culture, but the danger is that everything becomes an allegory of political events or an embodiment of the Manichean struggle in which the forces of American democracy are pitted against the godless tyranny of communism. This reading has validity when approaching some cultural texts: for example, Arthur Miller's play *The Crucible* (1953) draws parallels between McCarthyite America and the seventeenth-century Salem witch trials, and the first Twentieth Century-Fox film to use the new widescreen format of CinemaScope, *The Robe* (1953), depicts the clash between Christian and Roman values, in which allegories of McCarthyism (some characters are betrayed and others asked to name names) are juxtaposed with the liberal belief in the possibility of alliances between races, with Rome depicted as the prototype of the modern superpower. *The Robe* was part of the cycle of biblical epics that began with *Quo Vadis* in 1951; director Cecil B. DeMille even appeared in person for the prologue of *The Ten Commandments* (1956) to make explicit parallels to the contemporary climate in which he contrasts the 'freedom of man under God' to the man-made tyranny of the state. It is also possible to mount an argument to suggest that the 'soft power' of cold war culture fulfilled the job of promoting values of democracy and freedom of expression abroad in such organizations as the International Congress for Cultural Freedom, where the 'hard power' of politics, coercion and warfare might have had the opposite effect.

It is the legacy of the 1960s to search for conspiracies and subtexts where they may not exist; from this perspective containment is evident in almost every aspect of domestic, political and cultural life in the 1950s. In contrast, the ideological battle-lines of cold war America were laid out clearly by President Truman's proclamation in March 1947 that 'at the present moment nearly every nation must choose between alternative ways of life', and Eisenhower echoed this in his Inaugural Address of January 1953 by claiming that 'we sense with all our faculties that forces of good and evil are massed and armed and opposed as rarely before in history'.[16] As Allen Hunter detects, it was very difficult in the 1950s 'to secure standpoints outside its paradigm of neatly aligned binary oppositions: United States/Soviet Union, West/East, capitalism/communism, freedom/tyranny, good/evil'.[17]

However, these presidential statements do not lead the critic to the realm of facts but towards a set of mythic statements and rhetorical half-truths that only add to the sense that historical realities are not as simple as they seem. Were the drip paintings of Jackson Pollock or the colour abstractions of Mark Rothko in the late 1940s an embodiment of free expression or did they hide subversive messages? In the science-fiction film *The Day the Earth Stood Still* (1951) does the spaceman Klaatu's long closing speech reassert US defence policy or suggest the communist way is ideologically superior to a weak democratic system? Did the religious revival of the early 1950s suggest that the nation was moving towards spiritual enlightenment or to a self-righteousness that was blind to the need to forge international alliances? Was Norman Vincent Peale's *The Power of Positive Thinking* (the bestselling book of 1954 behind the Bible) a genuine attempt to help individuals achieve autonomy or was it a form of cheap commer-cialism with Peale the master salesman? Of course, none of these ques-tions has a straight answer. But, taking a cue from the popular cold war television series *I Led Three Lives* (1953–6), it seemed that in the 1950s all univocal statements were open to subversion – a reading that strains against the 'right and wrong', 'good and bad' logic of Truman's and Eisenhower's statements.

One of the strongest themes of the decade was that of authenticity, the difficulty of preserving genuine experience in the face of commer-cial and ideological pressures. The hard economic experiences of the Depression and close-range combat of World War II soldiers fighting for a just cause were favourably contrasted to shallow suburban lifestyles, television quiz shows and the easy musical sentiments of the *Billboard* charts. The image of the 'phoney' runs through 1950s liter-ature: from Holden Caulfield's concerns about the lack of authentic-ity in *The Catcher in the Rye* (1951) and Norman Mailer's exposure of shallow Hollywood culture in *The Deer Park* (1955), to the hidden identity of the carefree socialite Holly Golightly in Truman Capote's *Breakfast at Tiffany's* (1958) and the lack of authentic religion in the South as portrayed by Flannery O'Connor's *Wise Blood* (1952). Other texts such as Jack Kerouac's *On the Road* (1957) and Robert Frank's photographic study *The Americans* (1958) attempted to rediscover the possibility of genuine experience in a decade where everything was open to salesman's spin and Madison Avenue repackaging. And it was this search for authentic experience that led Beat writer Lawrence Ferlinghetti to began his iconic poem 'I Am Waiting' (1958) with the lines: 'I am waiting for my case to come up / and I am waiting / for a rebirth of wonder / and I am waiting for someone / to really discover America / and wail'.

'Experience' has never been a simple concept in American cultural life. At times it has been associated with corruption against the simplicities of an innocent life; at others it has represented the rugged frontier sensibility of the West in contrast to the enclosed patrician communities of the East; and at others has been associated with bitter encounters with economic hardship. Quite what happened to experience in the 1950s is one of the concerns of this book, when the expansion of culture to include commercial television, a popular music industry and the dramatic increase of consumables complicated any idea of 'raw' or 'unmediated' experience. The hankering in Ferlinghetti's poem for a lost America is also a waiting for a rejuvenating experience that would give him a 'rebirth of wonder'. Following a Romantic precedent, Ferlinghetti places experience outside the cultural domain in a realm of spiritual vitality as something pure yet elusive. Ferlinghetti's vision was shared by many writers and artists, and foreshadows the spirit of the New Left and the counterculture of the mid-1960s. But, although thinkers such as Norman Mailer, C. Wright Mills and Erich Fromm were arguing that courage was needed to break through the constraints of conventionality and the 'slow mechanical determinations of society' (as Mailer called them in 1961), it is perhaps more valid to claim that experience in the 1950s could only be found within the cultural sphere.[18] The rhetorical power of Ferlinghetti's poem should not be underestimated, but perhaps one reason he had to wait for a rebirth of wonder is that he is looking in the wrong places for what experience was, or could be, in the 1950s.

In order to explore the theme of experience in and of the 1950s, this introduction will revolve around four primary frames of reference – culture, ideas, spaces and identities – which are discussed in turn and then resurface in the following chapters. Discussion of these reference points help to demonstrate the ways in which American culture, ideas, spaces and identities were all contested in the 1950s, with the view that the decade is best characterized as a struggle between conflicting forces. From a Marxist perspective this conflict is true of all historical periods, but the pull of opposing forces – economic, ideological, political, cultural and experiential – intensified after World War II and in the Consumers' Republic transformations and contradictions arose at every turn.

In the following discussion, each of the four frames of reference is accompanied by a focused case study which exemplifies key points and gives shape to the broader outlines. The inclusion of case studies is consistent through the five chapters across a range of cultural forms. Their purpose is to demonstrate the diversity of American culture in the 1950s, and to balance broad commentary with detailed analysis of some of the decade's most important texts.

Culture

The concept of culture in 1950s America was not very clearly defined. There was a much sharper sense of what culture meant in Britain, where traditionally it was linked to class identity and the shaping influence of economics. This British tradition goes back at least as far as the Victorian encounter with the forces of industrialization. Although the US Labor Movement had grown apace since the late nineteenth century, and had made real steps forward in achieving workers' rights during the 1930s, it had never shaped the direction of culture to the extent of in Britain. American culture at mid-century was seen variously as everything that people do, but also a special sphere of creative activity for artists, writers, musicians and performers. Culture in the widest sense fed into some of most potent myths about American collective identity. The popular myth of the American Dream, for example, suggested that fame could be achieved in the arts, and the movie industry was particularly keen to exploit this in the studio 'dream factories' of the 1930s. But the American Dream was only a slightly different version of Horatio Alger's rags-to-riches stories in the 1890s which ultimately emphasized social recognition and wealth. On this view, artistic excellence and cultural achievement are only stepping stones in the search for social status.

The word 'culture' figured frequently in postwar writings, but was a slippery term, which can be approached from at least four different perspectives. Firstly, it was often used as a marker of national identity. This view was consolidated by the first wave of scholars that helped form American Studies as an academic discipline after the war: the so-called 'Myth and Symbol School'. Enquiries into the American 'character' and 'mind' in an attempt to identify dominant national traits began before the war with Perry Miller's *The New England Mind*

(1939) and F. O. Matthiessen's *The American Renaissance* (1941), and continued afterwards with exceptionalist accounts of American national origins such as Henry Nash Smith's *Virgin Land* (1950) and R. W. B. Lewis's *The American Adam* (1955). This school of critics did not disregard historical complexity, but rarely commented on the contemporary moment. Instead of discerning a turbulent past feeding into a complex present, these critics created a mythic framework within which concepts of 'the virgin land', 'the errand in the wilderness', and 'the American Dream' were affirmed as founding myths.

A second view of culture was an experience that ennobles individuals by providing values, skills and social accomplishments. The historian Henry May in *The End of American Innocence* (1959) looked back to the early twentieth century as a time when culture, rightly conceived, showed people how to behave, teaching them 'polite manners, respect for traditional learning, appreciation of the arts, and above all an informed and devoted love of standard [usually British] literature'.[19] On May's model innocent nineteenth-century traditions fell away in the turbulent 1910s with the experience of war and a loss of old confidences. The linking of culture to high art forms re-emerged periodically, particularly in the late 1920s with the revival of interest in the Victorian writer Matthew Arnold's distinction between 'culture' and 'anarchy', and was often linked to ideas of social betterment. The 'new humanists' Irving Babbit and Paul Elmer More were keen to affirm Arnold's high cultural standards to rescue America from what they perceived as moral bankruptcy, particularly with the wave of East European immigrants coming to the US in the mid-1910s. Vestiges of this position were still evident in the 1950s: the emergence of 'mass culture' after the war stimulated some critics to affirm high art as a means for educating readers and securing social order, while for others it helped to ward off foreign threats, expressed most dramatically by J. Edgar Hoover's claim in 1958 that communist culture was spreading through the country 'as an indoctrinal spray seeking to control every part of the member's heart, mind, and soul'.[20]

A third view of culture in the 1950s was a privileged realm of activity at a remove from everyday life. This view locates culture as a specialist activity in which the talented few engage: Jack Kerouac lost in his spontaneous 'typewriter jazz' or Jackson Pollock surrendering his artistic intentions to his semi-autonomous drip paintings. But many of the debates in the 1950s revolved around different levels of culture, with the term 'mass culture' suggesting that 'consumption' had replaced 'activity' as the dominant mode of cultural behaviour. 'Films, radio, and magazines make up a system which is uniform as a whole and in every part' German émigré thinkers Theodore Adorno and Max Horkheimer claimed as early as 1944, and they worried about the tendency of American culture to sink to the lowest level in turning out standardized products to consumers: 'under monopoly all mass culture is identical, and the lines of its artificial framework begin to show through'.[21] On this model, mass culture is the product of the 'entertainment business', which grew dramatically with the development of television, popular music, and paperback book industries. In essence, Adorno and Horkheimer wanted to resuscitate high culture with all its complexities as an antidote to the bland uniformity of mass culture.

The fourth perspective on culture was reflected in the work of the historian David Potter, particularly in his book *People of Plenty* (1954). Potter was unhappy with received notions of 'national character' that tended to be riddled with generalizations, folding many different elements into a harmonious whole:

> We [are] told in the same breath that Americans are optimistic (a trait of temperament), that they attach great value to productive activity (a trait of character), that they are fond of jazz music (a cultural trait), and that they are remarkably prone to join organized groups (a behavioural trait which may provide overt evidence of some underlying trait of character).[22]

For Potter, not only do critics often overlook the meaning of 'character', 'nation', 'group' and 'tradition', but they also underestimate the economic, historical and environmental forces that underpin them. Reacting against vulgar materialist notions of culture in which the economic base determines everything else, Potter adopted a flexible view of culture: at times it represents personal expression, at others an interface between individuals and society, and at others an integrative force that enables individuals to communicate, to reach a consensus, or to cohere around symbols of national unity or group loyalty. This is a very different perspective to Adorno and Horkheimer's pessimism, suggesting that consensus and assent are linked closely to 'abundance' as the overriding trait of 1950s American culture.

Potter's particular concern was to identify the complexion of America's culture of abundance, and in *People of Plenty* he discusses equality, democracy and the national mission to emphasize the historical nature of these themes. He returns at the end of the book to the relationship between abundance and identity in light of the growth of national advertising. Potter called postwar advertising the new 'institution of social control', which Lizabeth Cohen has more recently argued was instrumental in reinforcing the 'postwar ideal of the purchaser as citizen who simultaneously fulfilled personal desire and civic obligation in consuming'.[23] Although *People of Plenty* can be read as an exceptionalist view of an abundant nation, Potter was one of the first critics to understand the power of advertising, which had surpassed the government, school and church after the war as a major social force, particularly through its new powerful outlet of television. Charting the development of the advertising industry, Potter estimated that the amount spent on print advertising alone grew six-fold between 1929 and 1951. This statistic suggests not only that supply consistently outstripped demand, but also that individuals had been transformed into consumers; in Cohen's words 'the good purchaser devoted to "more, newer and better" was the good citizen'.[24] Fifty years before Cohen's *A Consumer's Republic*, Potter concluded *People of Plenty* by claiming the economics of advertising are less interesting than the way that it shapes values, serving 'to enforce already existing attitudes, to diminish the range and variety of choices, and, in terms of abundance, to exalt the materialistic virtues of consumption'.[25]

Potter's focus on advertising as a medium of social control is not quite as bleak as Adorno and Horkheimer's theory of a production-line culture industry, but it does suggest that individuals are ill-equipped to challenge the power of advertising to shape choices and values. It was possible to go against the grain of cultural expectations – a businessman choosing to go the bowling alley when the golf club is his cultural metier, for example – but these cross-class activities were rare, particularly in a decade when advertising encouraged the working class to aspire to middle-class values. We shall see in this book that culture in the 1950s was sometimes used agonistically as a tool to challenge authority, but with the lure of advertising it was difficult for many to resist the pleasures of consumption.

It is important not to underestimate the growth of advertising after World War II for instructing the public in their cultural tastes and aspirations. Potter sketched in the outlines for understanding culture at mid-century, but it was the sociologist Vance Packard who helped more than any other thinker to refine a theory of advertising and assess its impact on American life in the 1950s.

The Hidden Persuaders (1957)

The Pennsylvania-born journalist Vance Packard is often dismissed as a 'pop sociologist', but in *The Hidden Persuaders* (1957) Packard wrote one of the first sustained studies of the psychological techniques used by advertisers, and the ways in which 'many of us are being influenced and manipulated – far more than we realize – in the patterns of our everyday lives'.[26] The growth of mass culture after the war, the surplus in disposable income (five times as much in 1955 as 1940) and the fact that by the mid-1950s many families owned basic domestic appliances and at least one car meant that advertising strategies had to become more subtle to convince consumers to replace products on a regular basis. With increased standardization of products, rather than concentrating on durability or sustainability, marketing in the 1950s tried to tap into consumers' desires about prestige, style and the desire to be contemporary. Taking the lead from the postwar boom in fashion, in which the vogue for particular styles of clothing changed much more rapidly than in previous decades (for example, Dior's New Look range from the late 1940s), domestic appliances such as cookers, televisions, showers and refrigerators had begun to be similarly marketed.

The popularization of Freudian psychoanalysis in the 1950s and investment in 'motivation research' led firms to invest money in consulting advertising agencies and employing what Packard calls 'symbol manipulators' and 'probers' to feel out 'our hidden weaknesses and frailties in the hope that they can more efficiently influence our behaviour'.[27] A far cry from the depressed and doomed salesman Willy Loman in Arthur Miller's play *Death of a Salesmen* (1949), these jobs seemed in tune with an upwardly mobile mid-1950s, in which the threat of over-productivity encouraged companies to invest heavily in advertising and market research ($53 was spent on targeting each individual in 1955). Although Packard saw something amusing about some research carried out in the name of effective advertising (such as a psychiatric study of menstrual cycles to increase the appeal of certain food items to women), he also believed the trend to have 'seriously antihumanistic implications' putting the consumer at the mercy of invisible manipulative forces.[28] One of the most significant discoveries for companies was that many of the reasons for consuming products are often irrational – such as buying products in a particular colour of packaging – and they realized that only depth-advertising could discover the appropriate psychological hook to tap into these deeper impulses.

In adopting a version of the Freudian model of the mind, advertising linked itself closely to psychological profiling and behavioural research in an attempt to appeal to deeper levels of consciousness. The major points of vulnerability, as Packard described them, were commonly identified as 'the drive to conformity, need for oral stimulation, [and] yearning for security', but ego-gratification and love objects also awakened deep emotional reflexes.[29] Because the desire for social status often works in tension with these vulnerabilities, advertising strategies had to be varied and subtle to appeal to a range of consumers, so as not to draw attention to the fact that many products were actually superfluous to requirement.

It is worth comparing a 1948 advertisement for the new Hudson automobile, described as 'A Sensation Coast to Coast', with that for the 1953 Roadmaster from Buick, the 'Star of the Silky Way', to see how depth-psychology affected advertising.[30] In the 1948 advertisement, a monochrome drawing of a large black Hudson with a driver and five passengers passes by a large house and well-manicured lawn, presumably on a weekend drive. The copy reads: 'There's something really new in the motor-car world – a daringly designed, gorgeously finished Hudson . . . a new kind of car that fires interest wherever it's seen'. Focusing on the late-1940s vogue for low-framed cars that 'you step down into' and 'a rugged, box-steel foundation frame' that 'gives you a sensation of snug safety and serene smooth going', its appeal to comfort and security is obvious. But compared to the advert for the 'custom built' 1953 Buick Roadmaster with its large colour image of a sleek, aerodynamic and space-age vehicle (gleaming chrome bodywork and bright red upholstery) driven through the milky way by a handsome tuxedoed driver, the 1948 Hudson looks like a bulky funeral car.

Promoting the golden anniversary of the Roadmaster, Buick mention their reputation in manufacturing, but the advert focuses centrally on the power, acceleration, 'velvety luxury' and 'the great and gorgeous going of the swiftest, the smoothest, the silkiest, the most silent automobile' they had yet produced. Attention is directed to the starry image of the car, the promise of luxury, and the possibilities of the future (Buick's logo is accompanied by the tagline 'Then – Now – Tomorrow'), rather than the everyday pleasures associated with the Hudson.[31] Packard argues that these desires are linked not only to childhood memories and fantasies, but also to the search for status in the 1950s. Taking his lead from sociologist Thorstein Veblen's study of 'conspicuous consumption' in the late nineteenth century, Packard considered in *The Status Seekers* (1959) the reasons why consumers 'constantly striv[e] to surround themselves with visible evidence of the superior rank they are claiming'.[32]

There are a number of criticisms that can be made of Packard's analysis, most notably that women, particularly housewives, were among the most vulnerable consumers and easily duped by manipulative advertising. But the fact that some household products became very popular in the early 1950s, such as toasters and time-saving devices, give some, if inadequate, weight to his argument.[33] Packard goes too far in claiming that all advertising is brainwashing, and he rarely credits individuals with the capacity to resist the lure of marketing campaigns. However, Packard was not alone in his position, with critics like C. Wright Mills in *The Power Elite* (1956) warning against the invisible channels of power in postwar America and Theodor Adorno blaming 'organized culture' for cutting off 'people's last possibility of experiencing themselves'.[34] Some commentators have called Packard a conspiracy theorist in his deep suspicion of advertising, but certain aspects of his work, such as adverts targeting children, political campaigning and subliminal advertising, predate the interest in the growth of corporate control of the media in the 1980s and 1990s.

Ideas

If the 1950s was a decade of new American experiences, then at first glance it also seems to be a decade lacking in any major ideas – certainly in comparison to the more radical politics of the 1960s. While the group of New York Intellectuals from the late 1940s (among them Lionel Trilling, Clement Greenberg, Dwight Macdonald and Philip Rahv) continued to find outlets for their ideas in mainstream publications and émigrés connected with the Frankfurt School (Adorno, Horkheimer, Paul Tillich and Erich Fromm) found North America a much safer placer to live than Central Europe, there was nevertheless a widespread suspicion of the intellectual's social role. There was a general mistrust of ideas in the 1950s and a reluctance to speak out on controversial issues. CBS broadcaster Edward Murrow worried that television entertainment would erode public debate: as he claimed in October 1958 in a speech to the Radio-Television News Directors Association, 'just once in a while let us exalt the importance of ideas and information'.[35] This mistrust was, in large part, stimulated by Joseph McCarthy's accusations that the enemy had already infiltrated deeply into public institutions, and right-wing publications such as *Red Channels* emerged with the intention of naming subversives within the broadcasting industry. One contributor to the liberal magazine *The Nation* noted that in 1952 'the fear of speaking out is the most ominous fact of life in America today. The virus of McCarthyism chills the heart and stills the tongue . . . and destroys its victims' resistance'.[36]

Writing as late as 1967, Michael Paul Rogin noted the ongoing effect of McCarthyism on the intellectual community. Rogin argued that it is feasible to claim either that McCarthyism 'symbolized the death of radical protest in America', or that it was itself a manifestation of the radical Right, with the knock-on effect of making intellectuals in the 1950s and early 1960s wary of any form of radicalism.[37] It is also possible, as Rogin notes (although it is not his opinion), to argue that McCarthyism was a brand of populism that pitted 'a democratic revolt of dispossessed groups against the educated, eastern elite' of intellectuals and academics.[38] The cold war consensus, as it is often

Figure I.1 Senator Joseph McCarthy on CBS Television in 1954.

termed, brought together liberals, moderates and conservatives in an alliance against the excesses of communism on the one hand and the reckless accusations of McCarthy on the other. To affirm the socially cohesive qualities of American culture, or its 'vital center' as the liberal intellectual Arthur Schlesinger Jr called it in his 1949 book, was a way of offsetting forces that undermined the vitality of culture. But the danger was that, as C. Wright Mills detected in 1954, there was no viable opposition to the consensus of the centre: disappointed radicals, tired liberals 'living off the worn-out rubble of [their] rhetoric' and conservatives who had 'no connection with the fountainhead of modern conservative thought' all seemed to accept the status quo, while 'political decisions' were being made 'without the benefit of political ideas'.[39]

Rogin's study *The Intellectuals and McCarthy* suggests that, whether or not McCarthyism was itself a 'radical specter' (as Rogin's subtitle calls it), McCarthy tapped into widespread 'feelings of uneasiness over a sophisticated, cosmopolitan, urban, industrial society' by appealing across the political spectrum.[40] Until he was discredited in the live broadcast of the Army hearings in spring 1954, McCarthy was approved by between 30 and 40 per cent of the population, suggesting a widening gulf between the public and intellectuals. To be an intellectual in the 1950s was usually to be part of the eastern patrician world that McCarthy's midwestern populism attacked. McCarthy's aim was to purge institutions of those deemed to be holding subversive ideas, but it was his ability to manipulate anticommunist sentiments, particularly during the Korean War, which explains his widespread appeal in the early decade. While many liberals were afraid to oppose McCarthy for fear of being recast as radicals, the newspapers helped to inflame matters by reporting unfounded claims as facts. Straight intellectual discussion could not compete with the dramatic assertions of Tail Gunner Joe and public polemic against him was in danger of being seen as un-American.

Although television quiz shows in the 1950s revealed a widespread desire for factual knowledge (see Chapter 4), another aspect of the bad press that intellectuals received was the sense that there were, it seemed, few connections between academic life and mainstream culture. The mass media helped to widen the perceived gulf between the two arenas, often pushing intellectuals like Trilling and Adorno into defending high culture in strong moralistic tones. In 1953 art critic Clement Greenberg revised his early opposition between 'avant-garde' and 'kitsch' from 1939, claiming that middlebrow culture (including fiction, concerts and museums) provides a bridge between the elites and the masses to reveal a more variegated culture than suggested by the 'high culture v. mass culture' model. But others such as Dwight Macdonald disagreed, arguing that 'Midcult' was little better than mass culture in preventing consumers from thinking clearly about the reasons behind their chosen pursuits; indeed 'Midcult' offered a 'special threat' to Macdonald in exploiting 'the discoveries of the avant-garde' and in degrading modernist culture.[41]

The intellectual community's distrust of the masses was mirrored by unease among the general public concerning intellectuals. Even thinkers who made links between different spheres of American life were either ignored or treated with scepticism. Sociologist C. Wright Mills, religious thinker Reinhold Niebuhr and physicist Albert Einstein were among other public figures that stepped out of the academy to address pressing social issues, but in moving outside their specialist fields they aroused the suspicion of those that guarded those specialisms. Public intellectuals were often unfavourably contrasted to experts – particularly technical experts – working within the fields of science, law or business, and the culture of technical expertise and big business was particularly worrisome for them.

Primarily due to this anti-intellectual climate, one of the major reasons that the Democrat candidate Adlai Stevenson lost twice to Eisenhower in the 1952 and 1956 presidential campaigns is that he came across as too cerebral and serious. Where Stevenson received support from voters in 1952 for his intellectual acuity, in 1956 Eisenhower had greater popular appeal across the political divide as head of state and successful military leader in World War II. One journalist, John Alsop, described Stevenson in the first election clash as having a 'large oval head, smooth, faceless, unemotional, but a little bit haughty and condescending'; he coined the word 'egghead' to describe Stevenson and his supporters: 'all the eggheads are for Stevenson', Alsop commented, 'but how many eggheads are there?' [42] In 1952 the anticommunist film *My Son John* did nothing to challenge this distrust of intellectuals, suggesting that too much education is responsible for leading John Jefferson (Robert Walker), the son of honest church-going parents, into an un-American world of atheism, espionage and treason. In this climate it was no surprise that Eisenhower won the election that year, leading Arthur Schlesinger to declare that the intellectual 'is on the run today in American society'.[43]

The flipside was a wariness of 'Madison Avenue packaging', as Stevenson called it, and the popularization of ideas at the expense of rigorous debate. Popular books of criticism had been published before the war. For example, Philip Wylie's *Generation of Vipers* (1942) examined the phenomenon of 'momism' by applying psychoanalytic ideas to a perceived malaise in family life. Wylie's book was selected in 1950 as The American Library Association's nomination for one of the major works of non-fiction in the first half of the century, and was re-released in paperback in 1955. Wylie saw his jeremiad as perfectly suited to 1955, 'a year more threatening to American freedom, American security and even to American existence than the year 1942' in the aftermath of Pearl Harbor.[44] But, while some of Wylie's ideas are unfounded and others unpalatable (such as his claim that 'mom' is 'cinderella . . . the shining-haired, the starry-eyed, the ruby-lipped virgo aeternis'), *Generation of Vipers* is actually anti-Madison Avenue in the respect that it is a noisy book lacking the polish of many cultural products in the mid-1950s.[45]

Advertising culture and the bright surfaces of 1950s commodities were, for most, more attractive than thoughtful discussion about labour value, overproduction and regulating markets. Ideas seemed much more appealing when given the Madison Avenue treatment, particularly religious ideas at a time when church-going had risen dramatically. Norman Vincent Peale's spiritual improvement manual *The Power of Positive Thinking* was one of the bestsellers of the decade, and the Catholic priest Fulton Sheen was a regular on television to hand out spiritual advice.[46] Lone voices such as Reinhold Niebuhr spoke out against Peale's evangelism as a product of the Eisenhower era with its 'techniques of modern salesmanship', and he dismissed popular preachers like Billy Graham for ignoring pressing economic and racial issues, with Graham trying to convert his audience into good Christians through oratory.[47]

Perhaps it was unfair (and much too easy) to blame the popularization of ideas on advertising, as even Eisenhower was accused of selling out to Madison Avenue and key members of his administration John Foster Dulles and Richard Nixon were criticized for indulging in 'double-talk and word-magic'.[48] In an attempt to dispel the myths of advertising, Martin Mayer provided an insider's view of the industry in *Madison Avenue U.S.A.* (1958), noting that many workers are faced with 'brutal hours' and dogged by 'psychological insecurity'.[49] But Mayer's description of the advertising industry is telling: he compares it to a complex game of chess with the ad man 'a cog in a little wheel that runs by faith inside a big wheel that runs by the grace of God'.[50] These metaphors actually help to reinforce the theory that advertising quickly became a culture of deception where no one really knew the rules of the game except executive elites. It was this point that really worried critics: the postwar promise of self-determination often degenerated into subservience to a technocratic society run by a power elite intent on hoodwinking consumers.

In one of the defining postwar studies, *The Affluent Society* (1958), the economist John Kenneth Galbraith characterized the decade as representing a high point for free enterprise and a widespread faith that all 'social ills can be cured by more production'.[51] It could be argued that the emphasis on productivity was itself a potent idea, but Galbraith argued that this emphasis goes back to John Maynard Keynes immediately after World War I and had only recently become 'the *summum bonum* of liberal economic policy'.[52] It was the passive absorption of these ideas that worried Galbraith, leading him to write a chapter of *The Affluent Society* on 'conventional wisdom' and the general acceptance of the belief that increased productivity was the marker of social achievement. Whereas in the communist world doctrine and dogma were regulated by the state, Galbraith noted an informal – but nevertheless endemic – enforcement of American social values through the promulgation of 'conventional wisdom'. In Marxist terms, whereas the economic base was readily discernible in the Soviet Union (at least up to Stalin's death in 1953) or in Red China (following Mao Tse-tung's overthrow of Chiang Kai-shek in 1949), the complex superstructure of postwar US society often hid economic realities behind the veil of entertainment. Galbraith thought that ideas were often at odds with ingrained values, claiming that to have currency, ideas 'need to be tested by their ability, in combination with events, to overcome inertia and resistance'.[53] More radical critics of 1950s America, such as Norman Mailer and C. Wright Mills, would have agreed with Galbraith that there was too much coming 'to good terms with life' in postwar America, and not enough questioning of what is at stake when the vast majority of citizens concur with conventional wisdom.

It may seem that Galbraith was intent simply on combating conventional wisdom, but he was, in fact, suspicious of ideas as a whole, perhaps because they were too easily co-opted for ideological ends. While Robert Oppenheimer was arguing in 1955 that 'the integrity of communication' and free exchange of ideas across national boundaries was vital to ensure the health of the country, four years later Richard Nixon in his kitchen debate with Khrushchev came very close to downgrading international communication to the gimmickry of colour television.[54] Galbraith, though, believed that ideas are only powerful 'in a world that does not change', and he had a suspicion that the opposite of ideas is not conventional wisdom at all, but 'the massive onslaught of circumstance with which they cannot contend'; if the mantra of the 1950s was the pursuit of happiness, it was not an exact idea but more 'a profound instinctive union with the stream of life'.[55] Galbraith was worried by the instinctual acceptance of 'the social good' in times of prosperity, particularly when accompanied by only a vague sense of the rules of the game. For this reason, *The Affluent Society* ends with an urgent call for 'resources of ability, intelligence, and education' to overcome the passive acceptance of conventional wisdom and the 'grandiose generalizations' of the day.[56]

Galbraith's study touches on two of the central nerves of 1950s America: first, the mistrust of intellectuals and, second, the idea of consensus bound up with the myth that the whole nation was moving in the same direction 'in union with the stream of life'. Public scepticism for ideas runs through the decade: from the ridiculing of Adlai Stevenson as an egghead, to the shift from Abstract Expressionism to an aesthetic interest in manufactured goods in the mid-1950s, to a film like MGM's *The Band Wagon* (1953) in which Fred Astaire's song-and-dance routine is portrayed as more authentic than a theatrical revival of Faust. One argument would be that the democratization of culture facilitated a shift from highbrow to middlebrow and increased the accessibility of cultural products. But there was still a mistrust of intellectuals, which the historian Richard Hofstadter formalized in 1962 with the publication of his Pulitzer Prize-winning book *Anti-Intellectualism in American Life*.

Hofstadter contended that the 1950s was one of the peaks of American anti-intellectualism, in which 'men of culture' and 'intellectual accomplishment' were treated unfavourably as the Stevenson versus Eisenhower election contests demonstrated. Hofstadter argued passionately that to preserve the critic's 'freely speculative and critical function' intellectuals must separate themselves from government, business and science. However, the danger in operating outside institutions was a 'state of powerlessness', leaving the running of the country to businessmen such as Charles Wilson, Chairman of General Motors and Eisenhower's Defense Secretary from 1953.[57] Critical distance is vital for illuminating matters to which business leaders and government advisors are blind, but it can also lead to a failure to tap into channels of power or to be heard in the cultural mainstream.

Whichever perspective is adopted, the intellectual posture was all but excluded by the centripetal pull of the postwar consensus. Hofstadter's claim that 'the critical mind was at a ruinous discount' in the early 1950s mirrored Philip Wylie's assertion in his 1955 introduction to *Generation of Vipers* that 'the critical attitude . . . is mistrusted in America' because it is 'thought by millions to border on subversion especially when it becomes criticism . . . of popular American attitudes'.[58] Wylie believed that advertising, business and censorship were responsible for a narrow consensus of acceptable views that had replaced a critical stance: '"Boost, don't knock," has replaced the Golden Rule as the allegedly proper means to the American Way of Life'.[59] Underlying Wylie's rhetoric is the suspicion that consensus is less about informed agreement and more about fears that differing views would arouse censure or punishment. Even critics who applauded the pluralism of American society against the narrow materialism of communist countries only tolerated diversity within a fixed range; as Michael Rogin argues, pluralists championed individualism over group pressure but also feared 'the unattached individual' and the potential disruption of social order that radical behaviour brings.[60] It was for this reason that communism, juvenile delinquency and race relations were the hotly debated topics of the decade. We will come back to these fears in the next section, but it is first worth dwelling on one of the defining documents of the early 1950s consensus.

'Our Country and Our Culture' (1952)

A handful of liberal and left-wing intellectuals in the early 1950s continued to position themselves as critics of modernity. The architect and social critic Lewis Mumford, for example, bemoaned the shift towards consumption, arguing that individuals were becoming imbalanced and increasingly mechanised in their habits. 'Like a drunken locomotive engineer on a streamlined train, plunging through the darkness at a hundred miles an hour', Mumford suggested in 1952, 'we have been going past the danger signals without realizing that our speed, which springs from our mechanical facility, only increases our danger and will make more fatal the crash'.[61] But Mumford differed from the widespread opinion that US culture in the 1950s was much more affirmative than it had been before World War II.

The key document that signalled this trend was the symposium 'Our Country and Our Culture' published over four issues of *Partisan Review* in 1952. *Partisan Review* was closely connected with the Communist Party when it was founded in 1933, but it was re-launched in 1937 under the editorship of Philip Rahv and William Phillips, shifting away from communism whilst keeping its leftist agenda into the 1940s. In 1946 literary critic Lionel Trilling was claiming that the purpose of *Partisan Review* was 'to organize a new union between our political ideas and our imagination', and by the late 1940s the journal was publishing social commentary alongside fiction and reviews and was more moderate in its politics.[62] *Partisan Review* had its most influential phase from 1946 to 1955, moving from quarterly publication to bimonthly, and briefly to monthly in 1948–50. The editors sensed that 'the ideal reader' believed that 'what happens in literature and the arts has a direct effect on the quality of his own life'.[63] Although it remained opposed to 'all varieties of know-nothingism' and Mumford's critique was echoed by other contributors, many in the 'Our Country and Our Culture' symposium agreed that the adversarial stance of the modernists had given way to a general affirmation of national culture.[64]

Perhaps because the country had become a haven for European émigré intellectuals in the face of political hostility in Europe, most of the twenty-five contributors felt more at ease with American culture than they would have done thirty years earlier. But it is misleading to think that the contributors were entirely uncritical. They argued that the intellectual has a crucial role for ensuring national balance and contributing to the country's international prestige. Some contributors shared Trilling's view that the national situation had vastly improved over thirty years and that American culture was no longer inferior to Europe: not since before the Depression, Trilling claimed, has the public thinker had 'a whole skin, a full stomach, and the right to wag his tongue as he pleases'.[65] Other critics such as David Riesman, Arthur Schlesinger and Leslie Fiedler offered more modulated responses. Fiedler claimed that the separation of affirmative and oppositional currents was actually a false distinction: Americans have always held these two views at the same time.

Despite the general consensus, there were some outright rejections of the editors' premise, with some arguing that the critic's role is always to oppose the cultural establishment. Irving Howe, Norman Mailer and C. Wright Mills (all three to become important figures in the New Left in the early 1960s) stood firm as nonconformists suspicious of the lures of American culture, believing that to give up a critical stance would be to surrender to the reckless course of postwar capitalism. All three writers discussed what Mills termed 'social drift' and the barely visible changes that most citizens could not detect, and Irving Howe followed up his critique with another *Partisan Review* article in 1954, arguing that intellectuals had been tamed by returning to 'the bosom of the nation'.[66]

While these dissenting critics were far outweighed by accepting voices, there were others such as the poet Delmore Schwartz and religious thinker Reinhold Niebuhr who occupied the middle ground that Leslie Fiedler had identified. For example, Niebuhr disliked mass culture and the marriage of business and technology, but he argued that as a young nation the United States could not hope to possess the spiritual treasures of much older ones. Instead, he discerned that the country had cultured 'qualities of robustness' and he was proud of the way in which American social criticism had developed without becoming weighed down by dogma. However, Niebuhr worried about whether this kind of criticism was actually helpful for the nation in its new role as global leader, claiming that the 'ruthless and intransigent foe' of communism forces 'even the most critical and sophisticated patriot' in an 'uncritical' stance towards America.[67] Niebuhr thought that the stand-off with the Soviet Union had closed down intellectual possibilities – it was now a matter of deciding whose side you were on rather than exploring the complex political and cultural terrain between opposing worldviews. While he claimed patriotism was right and necessary, Niebuhr went on to warn against flag-waving, arguing that the 'foes within America' (including McCarthy) offer greater danger than 'the foe without', adding that one must be vigilant against 'hysteria, hatred, mistrust, and pride'. The nation's cultural legacy, for Niebuhr, was no defence against the potential 'destruction of the spirit of democratic liberty' in the face of communist hysteria or foreign policies 'frozen into inflexible rigidity'.[68]

The title of the 1952 symposium 'Our Culture and Our Country' suggests inclusivity – what Norman Podhoretz has described as 'a radical declaration' and 'a major turning point in American intellectual life'.[69] However, while the symposium presented a mixture of Jewish and Christian opinion, the contributors were mainly white men; only two women (poet Louise Bogan and anthropologist Margaret Mead) and no black critics were involved. It is clear that the 'our' of the title was intended to suggest a generosity of spirit, but the group of contributors reveals that intellectual culture in 1952 was far from inclusive, with black and female public thinkers a rarity into the late decade.

Partisan Review organized a fifty-year conference in 2002 to assess the historical impact and the theoretical limitations of the original symposium, with speakers noting that the 1952 contributors were unsure about what to do with mass culture and that their liberal politics and cultural conservatism did not sit easily. But the prominence of right-wing voices in the early 1950s, epitomized by William F. Buckley's argument in *God and Man at Yale* (1951) that Ivy League alumni should determine university syllabi to ward against dissent being taught in the classroom, was a major reason why 'Our Country and Our Culture' was so important as a public document promoting intellectual freedom and the open discussion of ideas.

Spaces

By the end of the decade the spatial configuration of the United States altered when the forty-ninth and fiftieth states Alaska and Hawaii joined in 1959 after a long struggle for statehood. Although it had been an official territory since 1912, the strategic addition of Alaska, the 'great northern and western citadel', during the cold war brought the nation closer geographically to the other global superpower and the nation's most feared postwar neighbour: the Soviet Union. The narrow Bering Straits was all that separated the USA from the USSR, with the frozen lands of Alaska virtually a continuation of the wastes of Siberia. CBS broadcaster Edward Murrow tried to start a public debate on the issue of statehood, given that there were strategic reasons to either include or omit Alaksa and Hawaii from the Union, with some claiming that they should be excluded because they were non-contiguous states and the inhabitants had 'no direct knowledge of life in the United States'.[70]

Both Alaska and Hawaii were strategic military bases after Pearl Harbor, but one theory for the delay in granting statehood was that Eisenhower, in 1954, feared that Alaska would vote Democrat in the next presidential election despite its huge military contingent. The outcome was a joint statehood bill: Alaska entered the Union on 3 January 1959 and Hawaii followed on 21 August. Racial prejudice also played a part in arguments against the statehood bill, as segregationists in the South were fearful of the mixture of races and nationalities in both states. On the positive side, in May 1959 the popular magazine *Look* ran a feature on racial mixing in Hawaii, with one nineteen-year-old Hawaiian claiming 'I'm Filipino, Chinese, Hawaiian, North American Indian, English and Spanish. I'm all mixed up' and the

Governor of Hawaii promoting the island as a microcosm of democracy: 'the Hawaiian is the man of the Pacific, bearing the seeds and fruits of the cultures of East and West. In the age of the H-bomb, the East and West must live in peace'.[71] Whatever the underlying reasons for delay and eventual admission, these debates concerning American territory are crucial for understanding social and political developments in the postwar years.

The mid-1940s had seen an almost complete reversal of the alliances of World War II: the Germans and Japanese were no longer the sworn enemy, even though West Coast Japanese Americans had been interned and relocated *en masse* in the late 1940s, causing widespread resentment. Now Red China and the Soviet Union were perceived as grave threats with a combined land mass that dwarfed the US. When George Kennan and the State Department called for the containment of communism in 1947, it was born out of the fear that other countries in Asia and East Europe would succumb to communism and that, in time, the world's democracies would be outnumbered. While some feared that Kennan's recommendation to hold back the spread of communism would be a wild-goose chase, containment policy informed many of the political decisions in the late 1940s: the Marshall Plan to bring aid to war-torn Europe; the formation of NATO in 1949; and the decision in 1950 to help the South Koreans push back the advancing armies of North Korea and China, leading to over two years of skirmishing on the 39th Parallel.

Fears of an attack close to home did not come to a head until the Cuban Missile crisis of 1962, but the sense that spies and informers had already secreted themselves into influential institutions fed anticommunist fears through the first half of the decade. For this reason, spaces and international travel were policed vigilantly, even if it meant the denial of civil liberties. The black singer Paul Robeson had his passport confiscated in 1950 for being a Russophile, warning that blacks would not fight for the United States against the Soviet Union, and during the previous summer in Paris speaking favourably about the absence of discrimination in the Soviet Union; the passport of activist W. E. B. DuBois was cancelled in 1952; the Caribbean intellectual C. L. R. James was deported in 1953; and the 'father of the atom bomb' physicist Robert Oppenheimer lost his security clearance in 1954 for casting doubts over the wisdom of developing the H-bomb. There were others as well, such as left-liberal playwright Arthur Miller who, although never a communist, was refused a visa in 1954 that prevented him from seeing a performance of his own play *The Crucible* in Brussels. Paradoxically Europe was much closer for many Americans with the development of air travel and the extension of the GI Bill for veterans wanting to study abroad, but it was also further away for perceived subversives like Miller, whose marriage to Marilyn Monroe in 1956 conveniently shifted the media spotlight away from his politics.

Paris had been a haven for a generation of writers and artists in the 1920s and after World War II became a strategic American entry point into Europe and the most important site for the transfer of artistic ideas to and from the US. France was vigorously promoted in tourist brochures in the early 1950s, and the favourable exchange rate encouraged many Americans to sojourn in Europe. The iron curtain that the British Prime Minister Winston Churchill detected was moving steadily west across Europe was blocked by the divided city of Berlin, but also halted by the spread of American culture across the Atlantic. There was European opposition though. Anti-American sentiments and French cultural superiority were rife. The French writer and statesman André Malraux claimed that there was no such thing as 'American culture'; a Sorbonne literature professor René Etiemble claimed that France was being corrupted by American exports and by the bastardised language 'franglais'; and many agreed with President Charles de Gaulle that France should embody a third way between the political alternatives of the two superpowers.[72]

Nevertheless, many Americans saw Paris as their point of connection to Europe, both geographically and culturally. It is significant that the reason why ex-GI and wannabe painter Jerry Mulligan, played by Gene Kelly in *An American in Paris* (1951), is befriended by Parisian boys is that he brings bubble-gum and optimism to the war-torn city. Other musicals such as *April in Paris*, *Gentlemen Prefer Blondes* and *Funny Face* use a Parisian setting to emphasize romance and glamour, but the city was also used for more strategic reasons as the gateway for American culture into Europe. For example, Paris was not merely the setting but also a strategic site in the MGM musical *Silk Stockings* (1957), the retelling of Ernst Lubitsch's film *Ninotchka* (1939), in which the carefree optimism of the American producer Steve Canfield (Fred Astaire) is thrown into conflict with the iron discipline of the Russian emissary Nina Yoshenka (Cyd Charisse). Sent to Paris to bring back three commissars and a deserting pianist who has sold out to Western decadence, Nina Yoshenka embodies the will of the Party, only to find her discipline slowly eroded by a metropolis combining American free enterprise with French elegance.

Figure I.2 Fred Astaire and Cyd Charisse act out the cold war in *Silk Stockings* (MGM 1957). Wisconsin Center for Film and Theater Research.

Paris was also one of the strategic sites for the International Congress for Cultural Freedom (CCF), which worked against censorship to promote cultural expression across the globe, epitomized by a festival of arts held in Paris in May 1952. Leading American thinkers were allied to the US branch of the Congress, including Lionel Trilling and Reinhold Niebuhr who spoke out when the Russian writer Boris Pasternak was barred from receiving the Nobel Prize for Literature in 1958 and condemned the discrimination of Jews in the Soviet Union in autumn 1960.

One of the directives of the American Committee for Cultural Freedom was to promote American values in Europe, but that did not mean that the American Committee saw eye to eye with the international organization. In 1951 the secretary of the CCF Nicolas Nabokov was worried that the American branch was out of touch with the central international principles; he realized that a lot of work needed to be done to prevent Europeans from simply thinking Coca-Cola and Hollywood when they thought of Americans.[73] The political complexities of the CCF and the fact that the CIA later turned out to be a hidden benefactor of the Committee have been well documented. However, while Richard Pells argues that during the 1950s members of CCF 'believed they were engaged in a project that was politically necessary, morally ennobling, and entirely theirs to superintend', more recent critics like David Caute and Penny von Eschen argue that culture did not always behave in the way that its political advocates wanted it to.[74] For example, von Eschen claims that while the jazz tours of the mid- to late 1950s in Europe, the Middle East and Asia were encouraged by the government for promoting Americanness, 'jazz musicians didn't simply accept the way they were deployed by the State Department'; rather, 'they slipped into the breaks and looked around, intervening in official narratives and playing their own changes on Cold War perspectives'.[75]

If Paris and Moscow provide important international sites for viewing American culture from afar, back at home the development of cities was heavily influenced by the International Style of modernist architecture. This was widely in evidence through the building of high-rise office blocks and epitomized by the German émigré Ludwig Mies van der Rohe's thirty-eight-storey Seagram Building on Park Avenue, New York City. The Seagram Building followed the twenty-four-storey Lever House (completed in 1952) in making use of new zoning laws in the city that permitted high-rises to no longer be set back (as had been the previous law), provided that the building did not cover more than a quarter of the lot. Completed in 1958 the Seagram Building was a classic example of all-glass office high-rise with simple clean lines and a plaza front. Some critics (including the editor of the magazine *House Beautiful* in 1953) were concerned that the International Style was linked to communist ideology, but the Seagram Building was widely copied as the template of corporate modernism and a symbol of a well-ordered nation.

There were variations on corporate architecture such as the futuristic Alcoa Building, Pittsburgh, with its aluminium skin (completed in 1953) and the multi-cellular Price Tower in Bartlesville, Oklahoma (1956). Price Tower was architect Frank Lloyd Wright's only skyscraper, using glass and copper – Wright's attempt to bring back organicism to the postwar built environment (even though the tower's small cells were not very practical). Some grand building projects never came to fruition like the planned new headquarters for the World Trade Center on the waterfront in San Francisco, which had a projected cost of $750 million.[76] But other completed buildings, such as the Lincoln Center for the Performing Arts (for which Eisenhower

Figure I.3 Lever House, 390 Park Avenue (Skidmore, Owings and Merrill, 1952).

broke the ground in May 1959), were seen as architectural symbols of an upwardly-mobile and culturally vibrant nation, in this case helping to regenerate a slum area around Columbus Circle in Manhattan.

Figure I.4 Seagram Building, 375 Park Avenue (Ludwig Mies van der Rohe, 1958).

While some public spaces in the 1950s, particularly in the segregated Deep South, were slow to change even after the *Brown* v. *the
Board of Education* ruling of 1954 (see the following section), the new
geography of the decade is best viewed by focusing on the built environment in the Northeast. A changing demography was linked closely

to shifts in living spaces in the 1950s, with many Puerto Ricans and African Americans migrating to northern cities in search of work (over 5 million blacks migrated to the urban North and West between 1950 and 1965), at the same time that many white middle-class city dwellers were moving out to the suburbs. The Federal Housing Administration Program (FHA) was established in the mid-1930s, but after World War II it went into overdrive to re-house families and returning veterans, concentrating on the growth of the suburbs in the second half of the 1940s to prevent city centres becoming overcrowded. The lure of newly created suburbs such as Park Forest, Illinois, and the three Levittowns in Long Island, Pennsylvania and New Jersey (named after planner William Levitt) was particularly strong for parents wanting to bring up children in a clean and safe environment.

The safety of surburbia was promoted by property investors and glossy ads, stressing that new Levitt houses were 'out of the radiation zone' beyond the reach of atom bombs.[77] Low prices and favourable interest rates enticed many lower middle-class families to purchase homes rather than rent, but moving to the suburbs meant almost total reliance on a car because public transport links were poor and general services often a drive away from housing areas. The zoning of suburban areas tended to push economic groups closer together, with the middle class moving to medium- and low-density housing and the working class to high-density dwellings. This created homogenized environments marked by identikit houses and similar lifestyles, with television drawing the family into the home where a diet of sitcoms provided 'how-to lessons' for 'organizing marriage and child raising'.[78]

In many ways the homogeneity of Levittown's population was planned, with African Americans barred from renting or buying property in certain areas up to (and even after) the Brown v. the Board of Education ruling. Before this, integrated neighbourhoods did exist, but they were rare in the early 1950s and many banks resisted making large loans to finance integrated housing. Although Levittown was often described as the largest all-white community in the country, Look magazine ran an article in August 1958 of the first black couple, William and Daisy Myers, to move into Dogwood Hollow (a section of Levittown, Pennsylvania); they were subject to vandalism, physical threats, a flaming cross on the lawn, and 'KKK' painted on their friendly neighbour's house before state authorities could intervene.[79] The FHA actually encouraged the zoning of neighbourhoods along class and race lines, arguing that 'if a neighbourhood is to retain stability . . . it is necessary that properties shall continue to be occupied by the same social and racial classes'.[80]

Urban problems in inner cities and grey-belt areas were masked by firms wishing to encourage young couples to suburbs like Levittown, such as in magazines like *Redbook* that focused on the need to balance the responsibilities of home and work. In 1957 *Redbook* produced a short promotional film *In the Suburbs* dealing with the pleasures of a suburban lifestyle and its suitability for starting new families.[81] Because around 2.5 million new families were involved in this social trend it was not surprising that there were initially few negative voices about the downside of suburbia, which Lizabeth Cohen argues 'became the distinctive residential landscape of the Consumers' Republic'.[82] Civic pride in city centres was also high in the mid-decade, with *Look* running a long feature in February 1958 on New York as a city of 'incredible contrasts', although behind the façade of Manhattan were slums and segregation that ran 'the length of the island'.[83] Several concerned reports on city centres were published in 1959, followed by the critical study *Anatomy of a Metropolis* in 1960 and Jane Jacobs' *The Death and Life of Great American Cities* in 1961, and a scandal arose when the city developer Robert Moses turned over many Manhattan tenement areas to private developers, forcing poor families to live in derelict buildings.[84] A watchful eye was also turned on suburbs: the critic John Keats satirized the lifestyles of John and Mary Drone in *The Crack in the Picture Window* (1956); in *The Split-Level Trap* (1960) Richard Gordon renamed the suburbs 'Disturbia'; and Richard Yates offered a harsh critique of a typical Connecticut suburb in his satirical novel *Revolutionary Road* (1961).

There were some alternatives to suburbia such as modernist designer Joseph Eichler's designs for innovative homes for the Californian middle class, but the options were more limited in the Northeast. Lewis Mumford was particularly scathing of suburban developments, coining the phrase 'anti-city' to describe areas of sub-urbanization. Back in the 1920s Mumford had looked upon the suburb favourably for renewing the natural environment that the modern city had swallowed up, but his early dream of an organic regional commun-ity (or garden city) conflicted with the homogenized topographies after World War II. Mumford was horrified that suburban dwellers were heavily reliant on car transport to commute to cities, making sub-urbia into a 'bedroom community' that lacked any kind of organic coherence.[85] In his major work *The City in History* (1961) Mumford described contemporary suburbia as:

A multitude of uniform, unidentifiable houses, lined up inflexibly, at uniform distances, on uniform roads, in a treeless communal waste, inhabited by people of the same class, the same income, the same age group, witnessing the same television performances, eating the same tasteless prefabricated foods, from the same freezers, conforming in every inward and outward respect to a common mould, manufactured in the central metropolis.[86]

It was not the growth of suburbia that worried Mumford, but the low-grade unimaginative lifestyles that it encouraged, with the promise of freedom ('the open basket-work texture of the suburb') being replaced by a contained environment ('the solid stone container of late neolithic culture').[87] Rather than finding a mixed culture in suburbia, Mumford discerned only an 'over-specialized community' where 'compulsive play' became the natural analogue of 'compulsive work', reinforcing 'a standardized and denatured environment' bereft of self-sustaining resources.[88]

Sociologist Herbert Gans argued in *The Levittowners* (1967) that Mumford's reading of suburbia was too critical, reducing all postwar developments to an abstract model that contrasts unfavourably with his ideal of a garden city, whereas Keats' *The Crack in the Picture Mirror* and Yates' novel *Revolutionary Road* were too cynical in suggesting that there can be no escape from the low-grade life of suburbia. It is, of course, the exact opposite of the happy and optimistic images of the *Redbook* promotional film *In the Suburbs*, but provides another example of the ways in which popular culture and intellectuals (with a streak of urban snobbery) were going their separate ways. If culture was on the move in the mid-1950s, it was moving against the direction that many intellectuals wished to see. It was, in fact, a triumph for popular culture that commerce and imagination came together to give rise to the decade's most distinctive new geography on the West Coast: Disneyland.

Disneyland 1955

The most iconic manufactured space in the 1950s was Disneyland, built in 160 acres of orange grove in Anaheim, California. The creator of the new theme park was Walt Disney, the animator and self-styled uncle of all young Americans. Disney had designs for a theme park before World War II and originally planned to use an eight-acre site adjacent to Burbank

Studios which he initially intended to call Fantasia after his 1941 musical animation and then, later, Mickey Mouse Park. Disney was disappointed with other amusement parks and wanted to create 'a place that's as clean as anything could ever be' that would appeal to both children and adults.[89] This emphasis on the cleanliness of the park is itself significant given that Eisenhower and Nixon used the image of the 'clean house' in their presidential campaign of 1952 (to eradicate suspected subversion in the government), but the specific idea that Disney could transform the dreamlike worlds of his animation into spatial forms was almost unthinkable. But the war halted his initial plans and it was not until August 1953 that the Anaheim site was found, twenty-seven miles from Los Angeles. Much of the finance for the theme park (which exceeded $17 million) came from the ABC network, and was given in exchange for Disney's commitment to the eight-year television show *Disneyland*. He made good promotional use of the ABC show, premiering with 'The Disneyland Story' (17 October 1954) which pulled in over 30 million viewers, and he followed this with regular bulletins as the site developed.

Disney's passion was to bring to life characters and experiences that existed only in the imagination. Although Disneyland is often seen as the epitome of mass culture, as a 2006 exhibition on Walt Disney at the Grand Palais in Paris suggests, Disney can be seen as a pioneering figure in breaking down the boundaries between fact and fiction and between high and low culture (he even collaborated with Salvador Dali in 1946). In his first television show Disney expressed his hope that Disneyland would be 'unlike anything else on this earth: a fair, an amusement park, an exhibition, a city from Arabian Nights, a metropolis from the future . . . of hopes and dreams, facts and fancy, all in one'.[90]

Even though he had relied for many years on his co-animator and one-time partner Ub Iwerks for the success of his animations, Disney prided himself on 'gathering pollen' and stimulating everybody to work towards the same goals. One *National Geographic* writer recalled Disney's admission that 'I certainly don't consider myself a businessman, and I never did believe I was worth anything as an artist'.[91] Nor was Disney an architect or planner, but he had an ear for folklore and a cinematic vision of his theme park split into four realms that radiated like 'cardinal points of the compass' from a main access route, Main Street, USA. Main Street was deliberately nostalgic in recreating a typical Midwestern main street circa 1900 that Disney hoped would bring back 'happy memories' for those that had lived through the innocent years (as historian Henry May called them), and for children it would be 'an adventure in turning back the calendar to the days of grandfather's youth'. When Disneyland opened on 17 July 1955, Main Street was filled with recreated buildings five-eighths full size, a fire wagon and horse-drawn streetcars; it housed a city hall, kinetoscope, shooting gallery, and fire station; and connected up to the old-style Santa Fe and Disneyland Railroad.

Radiating from Main Street were four lands with their own identity. Each land was familiar to viewers of the television show – with Disney careful to theme his shows from the start. Frontierland took visitors back to pioneering America complete with wagons, a stagecoach, an Indian village and the Mark Twain riverboat; Adventureland was 'nature's own realm' in which was to be found a jungle cruise and (in the early 1960s) the pioneering animatronics of the exotic birds in the Tiki Room; in Fantasyland were recreations of Disney's animations: Casey Jr's Circus Train, Dumbo's Flying Elephants, Alice's Mad Tea Party and Mr Toad's Wild Ride; and Tomorrowland brought to life the science of the future in Autopia, Rocket to the Moon, Space Station X-1 and 20,000 Leagues Under the Sea, which tied in with Disney's Cinemascope live-action film of that year. The four lands promised adventures into the past (Frontierland), to elsewhere (Adventureland), into dreams (Fantasyland), and into space (Tomorrowland), all within '160 acres of fantasy'.[92]

Eighteen rides were showcased to nearly 30,000 visitors on the opening day, virtually half of whom had been sold counterfeit tickets at $15 each. The ninety-minute ABC show of the opening celebrations, 'Dateline Disneyland', projected the dreamlike space of the park into the homes of 90 million viewers. The excited hosts Bob Cummings, Art Linkletter and a young Ronald Reagan mingled with the invited celebrities – Frank Sinatra, Sammy Davis Jr, Debbie Reynolds, Eve Arden, Kirk Douglas – and with Disney himself, who introduced some of the attractions. But the reality of the opening is hard to gauge by watching the show, which is slightly chaotic but portrays a day of jubilation. In reality Tomorrowland was incomplete; Fantasyland had to be shut down after a gas leak; some rides did not work; cafés ran out of food; high-heeled shoes stuck in the newly-laid asphalt; paint was still wet; trees were still being planted; and water fountains did not work, which was especially disastrous given that temperatures had risen to 110°F. Disney was not aware of all this at the time, but he later referred to the opening day as 'Black Sunday'.

Disney was very careful in the first six months to ensure that the problems of the opening day did not recur, and he was rewarded by the public's unprecedented excitement for Disneyland: it took only seven weeks to receive its millionth guest and less than two-and-a-half years to reach ten million visitors. To many the park epitomized everything good about the nation: it demonstrated Disney's resourcefulness and vision; it rewarded ABC's sound investment, virtually rescuing the network from bankruptcy; it provided a clean and wholesome place for children to pursue their imaginations; and mixed entertainment with education in its exploration of past and future. Disney's major features *Cinderella* (1950), *20,000 Leagues under the Sea* (1955), *Lady and the Tramp* (1955) and *Sleeping Beauty* (1959) all had box office success, *The Mickey Mouse Club* and the Davy Crockett television shows were very popular, and the Disneyland project developed swiftly.

Some critics have looked to Disneyland with a much more jaundiced eye, though: one critic in 1977 called it a 'degenerate utopia'; for years Uncle Walt had been at odds with his workforce, demanding rigid and consistent performances from his Disneyland workers; and Disney's anticommunist sentiments seep into the moral polarities of his postwar ani-mations.[93] While Disneyland offered a space for new experiences – one could move between Davy Crockett's frontier and a rocket launch within half an hour – visitors and critics offered polar views of the magic kingdom, with the French sociologist Jean Baudrillard arguing in the 1980s that Disneyland only offers simulated experiences that throw into doubt the whole notion of 'reality' in America.[94] Karal Ann Marling sums up this double vision of Disneyland: 'the tension between perfection and reality, between the real and more or less real, was the primary source of the visitor's delight' whereas critics saw 'only plastics and profits in a society hopelessly corrupted by TV, suburbia, tail fins, and too few distinctions of caste and class'.[95]

Figure I.5 The Sleeping Beauty Castle, Disneyland, Anaheim CA. © David Halliwell, 1974.

Identities

Just as corporate architecture and suburban developments dominated
the built environment in the 1950s, so have standardized versions of
gender and class come to epitomize the decade. This standardization
has not been helped by satirical portraits of middle-class lives: the long
commute to work in the city for the 'organization man' and a day per-
fecting the home for housewives 'smiling at they ran the new electric
waxer over the spotless kitchen floor', as Betty Friedan mocked in *The
Feminine Mystique*.[96] Rigorous advertising campaigns promoted this
suburban ideal and it was not until late in the decade that rigid gender
roles were widely questioned.

As the following chapters will explore in more depth, there was
some unrest in the mid-1950s as can be gauged by uneasy representations of gender roles in film and fiction: in Jack Arnold's film *The
Incredible Shrinking Man* (1957) domesticity becomes an oppressive
prison for the shrinking white-collar protagonist Scott Carey, while in
Sloan Wilson's novel *The Man in the Gray Flannel Suit* (1955) the
organization man, Tom Rath, feels uncomfortably caught between the
demands of work and the home; he cannot ever fully settle down to
suburban life, with memories of active combat and a wartime affair
dragging him back into the past.

The figure of the returning war veteran feeling uncomfortable in his
new 'gray flannel' life became a stock character. The general sense at
the time was that too much domesticity would make returning soldiers
soft and erode their masculinity. This is a thesis that Steven Cohan
develops in his book *Masked Men: Masculinity and the Movies in the
Fifties* (1997), in which he argues that threats to masculinity reached its
apogee in the 1959 poster of Alfred Hitchcock's film *North By
Northwest*. Cohan interprets the image of Cary Grant falling help-
lessly through space as a prime symbol of emasculation during a period
of loss of national confidence late in the decade.[97]

Despite the popularity of Mickey Spillane's cycle of crime novels
featuring the tough, fast-living and, at times, brutish detective Mike
Hammer, from the mid-1950s onwards the American male was seen to
become increasingly complex. Following articles such as 'Uncertain
Hero: The Paradox of the American Male' in a November 1956 issue
of the *Woman's Home Companion*, in which the gray flannel male is
pictured leading a beleaguered life of 'quiet desperation', *Look* magazine published a series in 1958 on new pressures facing American
men.[98] One contributor claimed that the nation was in danger of

becoming 'too soft, too complacent and too home-oriented to meet the challenge of dynamic nations like China and the Soviet Union'.[99] Cohan argues that these fears of 'going soft' in peace-time suburbia were linked to cultural fantasies of remasculinization, particularly evident in the cycle of film epics which displayed the manliness of Moses and Rameses (Charlton Heston and Yul Brynner) in *The Ten Commandments* and made spectacles of the broad chests of William Holden and Rock Hudson. Despite the boom in television westerns in 1957–8, that masculine identity was in crisis late in the decade, or was not all that it purported to be, is given weight by the fact that Rock Hudson, the epitome of strong masculinity, was confirmed as gay following his AIDS-related death in 1985; that James Dean and Marlon Brando had homosexual inclinations; that the moralistic J. Edgar Hoover later turned out to be a cross-dresser; and that the gay subject matter of Robert Anderson's play *Tea and Sympathy* (1953) was drastically toned done in Vincente Minnelli's MGM film version of 1956.[100]

If masculinity was contained in the early 1950s, then American women suffered even more from gender standardization, with most of the important sociological texts – *The Lonely Crowd*, *White Collar* and *The Organization Man* – largely ignoring women's experiences. The likes of anthropologist Margaret Mead, writer Mary McCarthy, and civil rights activist Jo Ann Gibson Robinson were busy in the public sphere, but the fact that the phrase 'public woman' in the 1950s was more likely to be associated with prostitution than intellect is one marker that the home became the naturalized habitat for many women.[101] Recent historians have challenged the theory that women were simply victims of the decade, but widespread college engagements and falling marriage ages were sure signs that motherhood and housework had become sanctified.[102] Standardization was not linked only to the domestic sphere but also to class, region and ethnicity; advertisers focused almost exclusively on the white middle-class ideal: the housewife in the suburban Northeast and the 'golden-haired girl of plantation mythology' in the South.[103]

While many magazines were portraying the domestic housewife as stylish and glamorous, issues of sexuality were often implicit in discourses on women. This was underlined by the outcry on the publication of Alfred Kinsey's *Report on Sexual Behavior in the Human Female* (1953), which claimed that sexual relationships outside marriage were much more frequent than was commonly thought. Kinsey's report on male sexuality in 1948 had led to many negative responses, but the female volume outraged those that associated femininity with

moral purity and thought sex was the exclusive domain of marital relationships. But, although the Church was particularly outraged by
Kinsey's findings, other sectors of American culture seemed to change
around 1953 following Kinsey's 'atom bomb' publication.

Sex was everywhere. Hollywood blondes Marilyn Monroe and
Jayne Mansfield and the growth of male magazines *Playboy* and *Esquire*
offered a model of ostentatious sexuality, epitomized by New York-
based Bettie Page, 'the pin-up queen of the universe', whose explicit pictures led to the anti-pornographic hearings of 1955.[104] This double
image of women – the devoted housewife and glamorous diva – is less a
paradox than a duality in the 1950s. Media interest in body shape found
its way into films such as the neo-noir *Niagara* (1953) in which
Monroe's dangerous and hyper-sexualised character is contrasted to the
modest and sensible Polly Cutler (Jean Peters), and *Vertigo* (1957) in
which the homely Midge (Barbara Bel Geddes) survives while the
shape-shifting femme fatale Madeleine (Kim Novak) eventually per-
ishes. The film industry realized that displays of female sexuality gave
Technicolor movies an edge over small-scale television, but many films
concluded with a reassertion of traditional feminine modesty against
glamorous and superficial figures. The MGM musical *Singin' in the
Rain* (1952), for example, harks back to the beginning of sound film in
the late 1920s and ends with the swanky movie star Lina Lamont (Jean
Hagen) exposed as a fraudster while the demure and faithful Kathy
Selden (Debbie Reynolds) is revealed as the true musical talent.

Hollywood was keen to exploit female sexuality but was also
worried by it and repeatedly drawn to plots in which dangerous sexu-
alities led to death or dissolution, such as the beauty-obsessed fading
movie star played by Gloria Swanson in *Sunset Boulevard* (1950).
Monroe's sexualised image was contrasted to the more wholesome
Doris Day whose comedies with Rock Hudson pictured a world of
girl-next-door romances, notwithstanding the fact that bedrooms
often came into play in films such as *Pillow Talk* (1959). Even
Monroe's roles after *Niagara* moved away from threatening sexuality
to the more 'innocent' dumb blonde characters of *The Seven Year Itch*
(1955) and *Some Like It Hot* (1959).

But when it came to lifting the veil off gender roles, it was down to
the first-time writer Grace Metalious in the notorious bestseller
Peyton Place (1956) to suggest that what went on behind closed doors
revealed female sexuality to be more complex than many thought.
While critics dubbed the book sordid and filthy, and Canada banned
its exportation into Commonwealth countries, sales were phenomenal

with many readers commenting that the fictional Peyton Place was just like their home town. In *Peyton Place* Metalious succeeds in turning the mythologies of New England into a story of 'female sexual agency, hypocrisy, social inequities, and class privilege' that many conservatives could not accept as truthful.[105] But, despite the novel's assault on the assumed moral purity of womanhood, it was not until 1963 that Friedan's *The Feminine Mystique* and novels such as Mary McCarthy's *The Group* and Sylvia Plath's *The Bell Jar* fully explored the postwar experience of women.

This is not to suggest that the historical reality of women in the 1950s can be reduced to film representations, but that more challenging acting roles at the turn of the 1960s reveal that female identity was changing during a decade in which it looks inert. Gender identity is inflected in different ways when linked to issues of class and race: as Joanne Meyerowitz argues, women were not just mothers or entertainers but also workers and activists, while unwed mothers, abortionists and lesbians offered different female experiences even though many were socially disenfranchised. These 'uncontained women' suggest a variety of subcultures 'beyond the feminine mystique' that are often neglected when focusing on white middle-class identity.

Wini Breines asserts that these 'other' women were restless and sometimes dissident, inspired by the Beat writing of Jack Kerouac but aware that women were often excluded from bohemian lifestyles as they are in Kerouac's *On the Road* (1957), or from radical studies of youth culture such as Paul Goodman's book *Growing Up Absurd* (1960).[106] It is perhaps no surprise that, in 1955, J. D. Salinger's heroine Franny Glass comments that 'if you go bohemian or something crazy like that, you're conforming just as much as everybody else, only in a different way', as more women were looking for subtle ways to bend or subvert constraints of class and ethnicity to find creative outlets.[107] Gender identity was being widely questioned by the time artist Ed Kienholz used bloody doll's heads to satirize male and female American archetypes in his assemblages *John Doe* (1959) and *Jane Doe* (1960).

If women's identity was 'the problem that had no name', as Betty Friedan called it in 1963, then an articulation of class identity also disappeared off the national radar. The labour disputes in Hollywood in the mid-1940s were diffused by the anti-union Taft-Hartley Act of 1947 which outlawed picketing, sympathy strikes and boycotts, with the growing fear that all union activities were a shield for communist conspiracy. The main initiative was the merging of the two main union organizations, the American Federation of Labor (AFL) and the Congress of Industrial Organization (CIO) in December 1955 to form the AFL-CIO which at the time had 16 million members, about 30 per cent of all employees (although this figure dipped in 1957 after evidence of union corruption). The AFL-CIO produced numerous public-service films, particularly through the newly formed Committee on Political Education (COPE) which encouraged the working-class vote and called for the donation of $1 from all members to fund aid to schools, health care and pensions.

The very beginning of the decade also saw workers' films in cinemas, such as the leftist *With These Hands* (1950) which deals with union activity since the 1910s and *Salt of the Earth* (1954) based on a miners' strike in New Mexico and using blacklisted actors. But contemporary representations of activism were rare, with two instructional films for schools, *The Labor Movement* (1959) and *The Rise of Labor* (1968), ending their narratives in 1914 and 1932 respectively: 1914 saw the emergence of company unions that prevented unlawful monopolies and restraints against workers and 1935 saw the passing of the Wagner Act during President Roosevelt's first term that granted the right to organize and join a union.[108] The truncated narratives of these documentaries are two indications that the 1950s was an uncomfortable decade for the working class.

The 'disappearance' of working-class identity was in part due to the rigorous promotional campaign to encourage workers to aspire to the same consumer lifestyle as middle-class Americans, with traditional working-class consciousness undermined by the Taft-Hartley Act. Working-class families in television sitcoms such as *The Goldbergs* (an immigrant Jewish family that moves from New York City to the New Jersey suburbs) and *The Honeymooners* (with Jackie Gleason playing a working-class New York bus driver) both illustrate this trend of status aspiration. But Lizabeth Cohen argues that while the mass media (and Eisenhower himself) promoted the benefits of middle-class lifestyles, other legislation reinforced 'class distinctiveness', including zoning laws for new housing, the difficulties of working-class war veterans gaining the same benefits from the GI Bill as their middle-class compatriots, and an uneven tax structure discriminating against working-class families.[109]

The disappearance of the working class was only apparent, though (the middle class only rose from 37 per cent to 44 per cent from 1952 to 1964); it was just that working-class issues were rarely dealt with in any depth by the mass media. Even Betty Friedan had to play down her leftist sympathies; in the early 1950s she had fought against wage discrimination, but in *The Feminine Mystique* she focuses almost exclusively on the problems of the suburban housewife. Years of writing for middle-class magazines *Mademoiselle, McCall's* and *Ladies Home Journal* led Friedan to deal with 'the feminine mystique' as a national issue, with class distinctiveness fading from view, alongside race and regional identity.[110] This was also true of much 1950s fiction and cinema, with authors and filmmakers much less ready to deal with class conflict than in previous decades, mainly for fear of reprisals from the government investigating body, the House Un-American Activities Committee (HUAC), which became a standing committee in 1946 initially to investigate labour disputes in Hollywood. The result was that Elia Kazan's Oscar-winning film *On the Waterfront* (1954) focuses less on the travails of Hoboken dockers and more closely on mob rule, which the testimony of Terry Molloy (Marlon Brando) helps to break up. The fact that *On the Waterfront* is often read as a thinly veiled allegory of Kazan's and screenwriter Budd Schulberg's testimonies in front of HUAC (in which they named names, although Kazan initially refused) suggests that the film dealt with the anticommunist climate rather than focusing closely on workers' lives.[111]

If working-class life was all but absent in popular cultural representations then African Americans were even more marginalized. After the National Association for the Advancement of Colored People (NAACP) lobbied in 1953 for the removal of 'racist' sit-coms *The Amos 'n' Andy Show* (1951–3) and *Beulah* (1950–3) there was almost a complete absence of African American representations on television (see Chapter 4). In the film industry the presence of black actors was very limited, with only Sidney Poitier, Harry Belafonte and Dorothy Dandridge breaking through to mainstream success. And although Harlem gave rise to some young black dramatists in the mid-decade, not until 1959 with Lorraine Hansberry's groundbreaking play on Broadway *A Raisin in the Sun* did the Black Arts Movement find momentum (see Chapter 2). But this is only a partial picture. We find a quite different story when we turn to regional music and local radio, revealing that African American culture was very influential in moulding broader musical and performance styles through the decade. The importance of black music in the 1950s has led music critic Ben Sidran to claim that it ushered in a 'new visibility' for African American culture which

counters the lasting image in the title of Ralph Ellison's 1952 novel
Invisible Man.[112]

Some very interesting studies of postwar black cultural forms have
emerged since the early 1990s.[113] But the history of African Americans
in the 1950s is less often traced through cultural representations
(which were largely problematic in film, television and national
theatre) and more frequently through major social events, such as
NAACP member Rosa Parks' refusal to give up her bus seat on
1 December 1955 (which sparked off the Montgomery Bus Boycott)
and the formation of the Southern Christian Leadership Conference
in 1957 under the presidency of Martin Luther King Jr (which provided a focus point for the student sit-ins of 1960 and the Freedom
Rides of 1961). There were some historic advances in the struggle for
civil rights, but racial discrimination, abuse and loss of life characterized the decade, most notably in August 1955 when 14-year-old
Emmett Till from Mississippi was brutally beaten and shot in the head
for reputedly whistling at a white woman. The 1950s can be seen as a
germinal time for black activism but, as Richard King discusses,
through the decade many critics, both black and white, were offering
'a largely negative, or at best ambivalent, view of African American
culture', from the sociologist E. Franklin Frazier's attack on the conformity of middle-class blacks in *Black Bourgeoisie* (1957) to tensions
embedded in black identity explored by novelists Richard Wright and
James Baldwin writing in exile from Paris after leaving the US in 1947
and 1948.[114]

Even progressive responses to 'the Negro problem' had faded
from view by the mid-1950s. For example, Trinidadian intellectual
C. L. R. James was calling for a 'revolutionary answer' in 1948 in his
proposal to join together the energies of the proletariat and black
movements, but he became warier a few years later, arguing that the
lure of middle-class lifestyle was eroding the radical edge of the movement.[115] Despite these internal critiques of African American culture,
it is crucial not to underestimate the changes that desegregation
brought about in the second half of the decade, initiated by a truly historic moment in US federal law.

Brown v. *the Board of Education* (1954)

The single most important judicial decision of the decade was the 1954 case *Oliver Brown et al.* v. *the Board of Education of Topeka, Kansas* that made the racial segregation of schools unconstitutional. Following two years of legal cases led by Howard University and the NAACP, the declaration made by the Supreme Court on 17 May 1954 proclaimed 'separate educational facilities are inherently unequal' and called for the desegregation of schools across the country. Led by attorney Thurgood Marshall, *Brown* v. *the Board of Education* turned on an interpretation of the 10th and 14th Amendments, with segregationists arguing that the constitution did not require white and black children to attend the same school, while desegregationists claimed that the 'separate but equal' policy that followed the 1896 *Plessy* v. *Ferguson* case was a misreading of the 14th Amendment and that the government should prohibit states from establishing segregation policies in public places. Given that at the beginning of the decade 70 per cent of African Americans lived in states which had some form of segregation, *Brown* was not just abstract legislation but deeply bound up with the identities of children and students throughout the country.

One important piece of evidence that the desegregationists used in court was the results of research by the New York psychologist Kenneth Clark in the 1940s. Clark tested the different psychological reactions of children aged three and upwards in a range of schools, noting that most children in segregated schools expressed their negativity towards coloured dolls and showed favourable responses to white dolls. Delivered as a conference paper at the White House Mid-Century Conference on Children and Youth in 1950, Clark was sceptical about whether the tests provided scientific proof, but the NAACP realized their worth and Thurgood Marshall used them in the trial as evidence of the psychological harm done in segregated schools.

The response of the court in the *Brown* case was unanimous and elicited much optimism from NAACP members, but the ruling gave rise to far-reaching social and cultural problems. Eisenhower wanted to defer the implementation until the next administration and retaliation arose in many southern states. Questions about how to implement *Brown* led Chief Justice Earl Warren to push through a second court ruling in 1955 (known as *Brown* II), allowing for a transitional period for some states to adjust to full integration. The phrase 'all deliberate speed' was intended to minimize this period of adjustment, but brought an element of uncertainty into the time needed to phase in the changes: deliberation suggested a cautious response, rather than immediate action demanded by NAACP activists. Eisenhower's hesitancy to reinforce *Brown* stemmed from his fear that the consequences of massive resistance – stretching from closing schools and relocating pupils to white supremacist propaganda and the racial purification of beauty pageants – would combine to create more contentious social problems than those that the court ruling sought to redress.

Almost as momentous as *Brown* were the events of September 1957 when Eisenhower was compelled to call in 11,000 federal troops to protect a group of nine black students in Little Rock, Arkansas. The 'Little Rock Nine' had been prevented from entering Little Rock Central High School by state police acting on orders from Governor Orval Faubus on 2 September. After the Mayor took out an injunction against Faubus, on 23 September the students again tried to enter the school only to be met by a thousand embittered townspeople. The use of Federal troops to permit school access to the nine students was a symbolic moment that gave national sanction to *Brown*, but caused even more unrest among white Southerners who read the judicial decision as a direct attack on their traditions.

If *Brown* represented a historical crossroads, then the case was also a crossroads for liberal intellectuals, although signs of immediate change were hard to detect. Historian Walter Jackson argues that discussions of civil rights in national journals such as *The New Republic*, *Partisan Review* and *The Atlantic* tended to 'have an air of unreality, a lack of comprehension of the changes that were building up within black America'.[116] Liberal reactions to *Brown* were almost as hesitant as Eisenhower's response. Rather than concurring with Swedish social scientist Gunnar Myrdal's opinion in 1944 that America's 'moralistic optimism' would solve the race issue, Reinhold Niebuhr and Arthur Schlesinger Jr were advising Democrat candidate Adlai Stevenson in 1956 to take a gradualist approach to desegregation because it was politically prudent in an election year. Niebuhr is an interesting figure to assess the ambivalence of 1950s intellectuals. In 1956 he called *Brown* 'not only a milestone in the history of relations between races in our country, but also in the wholesome interaction between the abstract concept of human rights and the specific rights of the American citizen'.[117] However, Niebuhr worried that *Brown* promoted 'heedless action' instead of allowing the organic development of 'law and custom' to gradually improve race relations. And not until the early 1960s did African American thinkers begin to publish regularly, prompting northern white intellectuals to recognize that race conflict was more than just a problem in the South.

African American writers were also divided on *Brown*. Singer and actor Harry Belafonte was involved centrally in civil rights activism from an early stage and in May 1954 Ralph Ellison applauded the 'wonderful world of possibilities' that biracial classrooms promised. However, James Baldwin was arguing in 1962 that 'white Americans are not simply unwilling to effect these changes' but they have become 'so slothful' that they are 'unable even to envision them'.[118] Sidney Poitier, the most iconic figure of black integration in Hollywood and a prominent figure at Brown's sixth and tenth anniversary celebrations in 1960 and 1964, was also worried that the democratic system was proving hypocritical in its hesitant response to Brown.[119]

Conclusion

As this Introduction has shown, a detailed consideration of race, gender and class reveals that cultural production in the 1950s was much more diverse than is often credited. In order to explore this diversity, the following chapters interlink the four frames of reference discussed in this Introduction: culture, ideas, space and identities. Rather than taking a static notion of culture, the chapters focus on the cultural transitions of the 1950s and are organized to maximize connections between cultural forms, dealing in turn with (1) fiction and poetry; (2) drama and performance; (3) music and radio; (4) film and television; and (5) the visual arts. And, as I begin to discuss in more depth in Chapter 1, the cold war and modernism provide twin lenses for exploring how American experiences and social patterns were themselves changing. While critics such as Daniel Bell were arguing that modernism had become exhausted after World War II, the following chapters demonstrate that modernism actually re-emerged in the 1950s in more diffuse forms, partly in a response to cold war pressures but also partly free from them.[120]

This discussion culminates in the focus of the fifth chapter, in which the visual arts offer the clearest indication that modernism was undergoing a metamorphosis in the 1950s. Sometimes this took the form of the social modernist dream of standardization and at other times reflected a more eclectic genre-bending modernism in which high and popular culture crossed over in complex ways. Together with the Conclusion, the chapters develop the view that the decade was, to recall two earlier descriptions, 'a period of paradoxes' and 'a fidgety mix of anxiety and relaxation, sloth and achievement, complacency and self-criticism'.[121]

Chapter 1

Fiction and Poetry

The early 1950s was a transitional period for American literature. A clear sign of this was the award of the 1949 Nobel Prize for literature to William Faulkner. His middle phase as a novelist from *The Sound and the Fury* (1929) to *Go Down, Moses* (1942) was his most experimental, with stylistic innovation and psychologically troubled characters Faulkner's modernist trademarks. The award of the Nobel Prize can be seen as formal recognition of Faulkner's 'powerful and artistically unique contribution to the modern American novel' (in the words of the Nobel Committee), but he had actually shifted away from experimental fiction and had re-emerged in the 1940s as a more conventional realist. The Snopes trilogy (*The Hamlet*, 1940; *The Town*, 1957; *The Mansion*, 1959) continued his project of working through the historical implications of Southern identity, but the trilogy was not as complex as his earlier fiction and less searching in its exploration of race and genealogy. Rather than acclaiming Faulkner as an experimentalist, then, the Nobel Prize was recognition of his long-term service to literature, as he joined T. S. Eliot (Nobel Prize 1948) and later Ernest Hemingway (Nobel Prize 1954) as grand old men of American letters.

Faulkner did not like formal speeches, but in accepting the Prize in Stockholm on 10 December 1950 he made telling remarks about his own artistic priorities and about wider cold war concerns. He described his writing as 'a life's work in the agony and sweat of the human spirit' and identified himself as an example to young writers struggling with their literary craft. But he worried that younger writers had forgotten that 'the problems of the human heart in conflict with itself' are essential for artistic creation. Instead, he thought they were preoccupied with the pressing question of 'when will I be blown up?'[1] Revealing a conservative streak that grew steadily through his career,

Faulkner suggested that deep-rooted fears had led young authors to write with their 'glands' not their 'heart', and he recommended that they relearn 'the old verities and truths of the heart'. His message was essentially a humanist one. He refused to accept that the atomic threat would bring about the 'end of man', and he wanted to revive the belief that 'the poet's voice' is not simply a lone voice among others, but a social pillar that can help us 'to endure and prevail'.

In 1952 British poet Stephen Spender was noting with regret that the modernist movement had been dead for twenty years, but Faulkner's acceptance speech is helpful for understanding two postwar literary trends: the first, a shift from the high modernism of the inter-war years towards a less easy-to-label literary aesthetic; and the second, a sense that contemporary affairs might provide new subject matter, but with the risk that the writer becomes reactionary and dissuaded from dealing with far-reaching themes.[2] There was a sense among some American authors that international events following World War II had become so significant that they could no longer be ignored, but there were also pressures that prevented writers from looking too deeply: political commitment to social causes which had been strong in the 1930s was now unwelcome in a climate of communist suspicion.

Younger writers such as Norman Mailer concurred with Faulkner that the cold war climate of censorship had created fear among writers, but this did not prompt Mailer to retreat from the contemporary moment. The southern novelist Carson McCullers also documented this tension between cultural introspection and the pull of contemporary events in her novella *The Member of the Wedding* (1946). The androgynous thirteen-year-old girl Frankie Addams cannot even picture Alaska where her brother and his new wife have gone, but radio reports of global events shock her out of her sheltered Georgian world. Frankie senses that the world is spinning too fast to properly understand. She reduces everything to her own personal anxieties and is self-centred in wishing to be the member of her brother's wedding, but by the end of the narrative she understands that world events are only ignored at a high price.

Faulkner was arguably unfair in his assessment of younger writers of McCullers's and Mailer's generation, born two decades after Faulkner in 1917 and 1923. Given that the literary critic Leslie Fiedler later argued that Faulkner and Hemingway both received Nobel Prizes 'posthumously' (in the respect that their best work was behind them), it is poignant that Faulkner wanted to allay current fears that

World War III was imminent.[3] He claimed that if younger writers could 'relearn' the values of 'compassion and sacrifice and endurance' then the artistic spirit would prevail. There is little in the speech, though, that acknowledges younger writers responding to contemporary events in their fiction. The fact that the theatrical version of *The Member of the Wedding* was acclaimed in its New York production at The Empire in early 1950 suggests that Frankie's adolescent concerns – 'looking around hungrily for human companionship and for something that she can join' – were far from unique and, in fact, chimed with Faulkner's own worries.[4]

The tensions evident in Faulkner's speech run through literary culture in the 1950s and strain against Daniel Bell's thesis in his 1960 book *The End of Ideology*. Echoing the general feeling that political ideas had become exhausted by the 1950s (see the Introduction), Bell identified a widespread acceptance of the ideology of liberal democracy and a culture of consensus. However, if ideas revolved around a cultural consensus in the early 1950s, then much of the decade's fiction and poetry reveals a contrary set of impulses: as Morris Dickstein argues, it was 'a moment when outsiders were becoming insiders, when American literature . . . was becoming decentred, or multicentred, feeding on new energies from the periphery'.[5]

This 'multicentred' impulse is particularly relevant for considering the emergence of Jewish American, African American and émigré literary voices. It was in fact the struggle between centre and periphery that characterized literary production, shuttling between an engagement with contemporary events and a disengaged retreat from them. If acquiescence characterized some middlebrow literary responses (a term identified by Russell Lyne in a 1949 *Life* article on 'High-Brow, Low-Brow, Middle-Brow'), then other voices spoke out: poet Robert Lowell claimed that art should maintain an arm's distance from practical affairs and Jack Kerouac privileged personal experience over social responsibility.[6] A closer view of any ten-year period of cultural output will always unearth complexities. However, these trends are perhaps more pronounced in the 1950s because it was such a transitional period full of 'unresolved contradictions' which, as Richard Chase commented, were rarely 'absorbed, reconciled, or transcended'.[7]

It is important not to overplay the role of the 1950s writer as rebel, particularly in the early decade when the climate of censorship made it difficult for writers to offer direct social commentary. With the rise of cold war hostilities toward 'engaged' writers, particularly those having past associations with communism, there was an attempt among some to distance themselves from the committed role of 1930s authors. Those that continued to link literary and political concerns such as the African American novelists Ralph Ellison and Richard Wright set their major 1950s fiction – Ellison's *Invisible Man* (1952) and Wright's *The Outsider* (1956) – back in the 1930s, and Wright and James Baldwin were living in Paris at a remove from national life. This may lead us to view the role of the 1950s writer as compromised, or to suggest that radicalism had been absorbed into liberal culture and that modernism had been neutered to meet the demands of the market.[8] But these same trends might also encourage us to see 1950s writers as 'struggling to maintain their precarious balance when the rules of life and art were being rewritten'.[9]

Literary Forms in the 1950s

Many writers in the 1950s were struggling to throw off the weight of modernist experimentation that characterized the interwar years, and also seeking new literary modes better suited to the changing postwar climate. It could be argued that many writers were searching for a middle way between high modernism and popular tastes.[10] This view is given weight by the fact that both Ernest Hemingway (in 1950 and 1952) and John Steinbeck (in 1952 and 1954) made the top-ten lists of bestsellers, and also tallies with the 'Our Country and Our Culture' symposium from 1952 (see the Introduction), in which many contributors agreed that modernist disaffection had been replaced by a more affirmative response to national culture. But the picture is more complicated than this. Poet Delmore Schwartz argued in 1950 that serious writers were finding it difficult to move beyond modernism and that it is a mistake to think 'that the modern artist does not want and would not like a vast popular audience, if this were possible without the sacrifice of some necessary quality in his work'.[11] Schwartz thought that the serious writer's conscience was a deterrent from simply pandering to popular tastes, but he also detected that negative responses to 'difficult' writing had created a panic about the direction authors should take.[12]

The growth of the mass paperback market after World War II did much to change the relationship between writers and readers. The war contributed to the boom for paperbacks, with many of them produced in Armed Service Editions and targeted specifically at GIs. The taste for hard-boiled crime writing was reflected in Dell's first paperback, Philip Ketchum's murder mystery *Death in the Library* (1943), and a stream of paperback crime fictions up to 1951. The vogue for crime continued well into the 1950s, with Paperback Originals after 1949 enabling crime writer Mickey Spillane to become one of the bestsellers of the decade. The paperback market for new titles provided a platform for other genre-based writers such as science-fiction authors Ray Bradbury, Richard Matheson and Philip K. Dick, and Dell also published a stream of romance titles, although the stories rarely lived up to the salacious pictures on the covers.[13] The industry also benefited from re-issues of fiction by established writers like Steinbeck and Faulkner (New American Library of World Literature's first publication in 1948 was Faulkner's *The Wild Palms*). It also enabled the young William Burroughs and Jack Kerouac to find a readership; Burroughs' first novel about heroin addiction, *Junkie* (1953), was published in a two-novels-in-one Ace edition with a conventional crime narrative by an ex-FBI agent.

To buy a paperback for 25 cents early in the decade one would use mail order or visit the local drugstore, but by the time paperback bestsellers started to be listed in 1955 they could be easily purchased from bookstores. We may think that the postwar paperback industry signalled the triumph of popular over serious literature, but hardback sales were still strong and there were so many independent publishers within the paperback market that it is dangerous to generalize about dominant literary tastes: the bestseller list mixed serious authors (Hemingway, Faulkner and Vladimir Nabokov) with middlebrow writers (Daphne du Maurier, James Michener and Grace Metalious), religious writers (Lloyd Douglas, Fulton Sheen and Billy Graham), and a range of non-fiction titles from cook books and garden manuals to Rachel Carson's environmentalist *The Sea Around Us* (1951) and Alfred Kinsey's controversial *Sexual Behavior in the Human Female* (1953). What the popularity of the Kinsey Report revealed (despite the moral outrage it caused) was an appetite for books like *Peyton Place* and *Lolita* that explored the secret lives of middle-class Americans.

In 1948 the literary critic Leslie Fiedler noted that there were, in fact, not enough new authors to feed consumer demand, leading more publishers towards serious writers to support the paperback market. Fiedler's warning was that the increased 'opportunities for publication' were accompanied by 'pressures toward accommodation' on behalf of writers.[14] We will see in Chapter 4 that this tendency to 'dead centrism' was one of the forces behind television programming in the mid-1950s, but Delmore Schwartz's comments suggest that the decade gave rise to a number of competing literary currents that make this

middle space between highbrow and lowbrow difficult to codify. By
the mid-1950s literary production appeared to correspond with
Dwight Macdonald's conception of 'Midcult' as a deeply middle-class
phenomenon, but some writers were drawn back to modernism as a
way of resisting the lures of commercialism.[15]

Despite Fiedler's warning and the consensus of the 'Our Country
and Our Culture' symposium, the role of the writer as a social critic
was kept alive through the decade, with Robert Lowell famously
calling the decade the 'tranquillized fifties' and rebels like Mailer and
Ginsberg later becoming key figures in the rise of the emerging counterculture in the early 1960s.[16] It is significant that both Mailer and
Ginsberg were Jewish as the contribution of American Jewish writers
was very significant with many writers and critics entering the mainstream of literary life after the war. A variety of Jewish voices emerged
in the 1950s, but two impulses were dominant: the first suggested that
assimilation to mainstream American culture was a desirable option
for many Jews, while the second revealed that other second and third-
generation American Jews were feeling dislocated from their past, particularly for families with relatives back in Europe living in the
aftermath of the Holocaust. This helps to explain why an ambivalent
tone marks many Jewish American narratives, in which the redemp-
tive myth of America is often accompanied by the sense that assimilation only ends up neutralizing ethnic difference.

Sometimes this ambivalence spilt over into open defiance, such as
in Ginsberg's famous diatribe of 1956 when he told America to 'go
fuck yourself with your atom bomb'.[17] For Ginsberg and Mailer only
the figure of the artist can help to check the nation's spiritual decline
in the atomic age, with Mailer arguing in 1955 that the true role of the
artist is 'to be as disturbing, as adventurous, as penetrating, as his
energy and courage make possible'.[18] This quotation predated his
famous essay 'The White Negro' (1957) in which he claimed that the
writer's energy is the only defence against the denial of free speech: 'a
stench of fear has come out of every pore of American life, and we
suffer from a collective failure of nerve'.[19] At the end of the decade
President Eisenhower gave the phrase 'military-industrial complex' to
the growing pressures that Mailer detected. But, whereas Eisenhower
projected into the future this threat to civil liberties, the sociologist C.
Wright Mills argued that this 'complex' was already in place during
Eisenhower's presidency. Mills detected certain symmetries between
US and Soviet systems and he worried that the national agenda was
being set by military leaders, scientists and technocrats.[20]

Although other voices, particularly among the émigré intellectual community, were offering critiques of the prevailing social and political system, it is important to note that Mills' and Mailer's extreme pronouncements were more a prelude to the radical stance towards conformism in the mid-1960s than a touchstone for the 1950s. Writers at the time might have shared Mailer's anxieties, but most were less ready to adopt a stance of outright social and political rebellion. A sense of unease was often modulated by social promise and critiques were guarded or lacked real clarity.

It is often more difficult to link poetic production to the contemporary moment, especially in its more lyrical forms and in decades like the 1950s when it was not overtly political. As Delmore Schwartz noted, American poetry in the 1950s was also trying to shake off the modernist legacy and took on a number of different styles in doing so, some in imitation of erudite poetry and others in a quest for simplicity. The publication of John Ciardi's anthology *Mid-Century American Poets* in 1950 suggested a shift after the war from the noisy poetry of Walt Whitman and Carl Sandburg on the one hand and the high modernism of T. S. Eliot and Wallace Stevens on the other. Ciardi detected a growing interest in poetic craft and asserted that 'the poets writing today are in a better position to write good poetry, in part because some of their ancestors showed them the perils of loud poetry'.[21] Although established poets such as Archibald MacLeish and W. H. Auden revealed routes back to modernism, the incarceration of the modernist poet Ezra Pound in 1945 provided a warning of the dangers of mixing politics and art (after turning to fascism in the 1930s and moving to Italy, Pound was arrested at the end of the war and handed over to the US military for inciting treason in his radio broadcasts). Much postwar verse tried to move beyond modernism, either through the personal poetry of Robert Lowell and Theodore Roethke, or the jazz rhythms of Frank O'Hara and Langston Hughes, or in Allen Ginsberg's adoption of a poetic voice that is at once intimate and prophetic.

Confessional poetry is often upheld as the dominant form of the decade in which poems became tools for self-exploration, but a number of poets like Elizabeth Bishop and Frank O'Hara complicated the confessional mode, while John Ashbery and John Berryman were developing modernist aesthetics in new directions. Many of these younger poets were born in the mid- to late 1920s and formed four distinct groupings: the Beat poets, the San Francisco Renaissance, the Black Mountain poets in North Carolina, and the New York School poets. While some writers found their way into more than one group, these younger voices are often contrasted to the more established poets Lowell, Bishop, Roethke, Schwartz and Richard Wilbur – all of whom featured in Ciardi's *Mid-Century American Poets*.

We will see later in this chapter how these different groups challenged poetic orthodoxy, but it is a mistake to think of younger Beat poets Gary Snyder and Michael McClure as 'destroyers of language' as they were very interested in developing new relationships between poetic form and content as an extension of, but also a break from, modernism. Some critics claim that postwar poets managed to escape the 'giant shadows' of modernism by writing 'diverse, intrepid, spirited and surprising' work, and John Ciardi was worrying that modernism was by 1950 'something slick, plastic, and a bit over-bearing'.[22] Ciardi wanted to cling onto 'modern' to describe the poets in his collection, but he noted that one could only tentatively refer to the new generation of poets as modernists.

The new direction of poetry was formalized in Charles Olson's famous claim in 'Projective Verse' (1950) that a poem 'must, at all points, be a high energy-construct and, at all points, an energy-discharge': taking in and giving out energy.[23] Rather than seeking a closed form which resists the intake of poetic energy or in which energy is entrapped, Olson recommended a 'field composition' which puts the poet 'into the open'. This suggests a movement away from the modernism of Eliot and Pound, and the carefully crafted poem revered by the New Critics; younger poets were rejecting the well-wrought artefact, replacing it with a fusion of form and content and an emphasis on 'process' and 'energy'. On this theory, the line of energy should be untrammelled, the poem acting as a mediator between poet and reader.

But this type of poetic abstraction is characteristic of the early part of the decade rather than developments later in the 1950s. With Olson we move back towards abstraction, in which the poetic energy is more important than anything the poem formally represents. This suggests that personal experience dissolves into an energy field where markers of identity and society are less distinct, such as Olson's poem 'In Cold Hell, in Thicket' (1953) in which the poet muses: 'Who am I but by a fix, and another, / a particle, and the congery of particles carefully picked one by another'. There is an argument to say that Olson's ideal of projective verse was never fully realized, but his interest in breathing found echoes in the poetic performances of Ginsberg and McClure. For example, Michael McClure in *Simple Eyes and Other*

Poems (1994) followed Olson in describing his craft as working 'with a breath line' and listening 'to the syllable as it appears in my voice or on the tip of my pen or on my screen or on my field of energies'.[24] This drew the likes of McClure and Frank O'Hara towards the painterly abstraction of Jackson Pollock; in 'Ode to Jackson Pollock' (1961) McClure describes the artist's craft as: 'Hand swinging the loops of paint – splashes – drips – / chic lavender, duende black, blue and red!'[25]

This emphasis on poetic form was not a retreat into modernist experimentation, but the attempt to discover a new vocal range to speak to the rapidly transforming postwar nation. Within the swirl of poetic styles many critics identified a broad shift from impersonal poetics in the early 1950s towards a poetic interest in the personal realm epitomized by the confessional poetry of Lowell and Plath at the turn of the 1960s. As Chapters 2 and 5 will explore, interesting links can be made between poetry, art, music and performance in the 1950s, suggesting that a 'mixed mode' is the best way to characterize its poetic developments.

The following sections discuss the ways in which 1950s fiction also reveals a mixed mode and a movement beyond rigid oppositions, particularly the 'Paleface and Redskin' dichotomy that Philip Rahv established in 1947 to divide the American literary tradition into camps of intellect and experience. Instead of reinforcing traditional literary modes these opposing influences became fused in the 1950s. If we are looking for a dominant mode then perhaps, as the German modernist Thomas Mann suggested, tragicomedy was more suited to mid-century complexities than a purer literary mode.[26] And such a tragicomic tone is exemplified in the first line of Saul Bellow's 1953 novel *The Adventures of Augie March*:

> I am an American, Chicago born – Chicago, that somber city – and go at things as I have taught myself, free-style, and will make the record in my own way: first to knock, first admitted sometimes an innocent knock, sometimes a not so innocent.[27]

Augie's introduction of himself as possessing a 'free-style' suggests a loosening of literary form and a model for other anti-heroes of 1950s fiction, hovering between an innocent acceptance of life (the 'somber city' of Chicago for Augie) and a streetwise rebellion against it. As a development from Bellow's more solemn 1940s fiction, *Dangling Man* (1944) and *The Victim* (1947), *The Adventures of Augie March* links the protagonist's comic sensibility to fleeting picaresque adventures at college, with union organizers, and in the US Navy. As a modern-day Columbus and Huck Finn, Augie is deeply American and a seeker always on the lookout for something more.

It is too easy to use the label of 'the American Dream' to describe Augie's search. He does not have the rising expectations of Horatio Alger's rags-to-riches stories from the 1890s and nor does he suffer the tragic anonymity of Arthur Miller's Willy Loman in *Death of a Salesman* (1949), despite the tribulations that Augie's family suffers. Instead, Augie experiences a rollercoaster ride with ups and downs following closely on from each other. Mirroring the energy of the young American poets, Augie's adventures are characterized by dynamic movement; Augie claims towards the end of the novel that 'since I never have had any place of rest, it should follow that I have trouble being still'.[28] As the next section discusses, this kind of restlessness is characteristic of many protagonists of 1950s fiction.

Fictions of Unease

If tragicomedy can be seen as the dominant mode of postwar writing, then it can be linked to the appearance of the anti-hero in late 1940s and 1950s fiction. The anti-hero emerged in a number of guises, from J. D. Salinger's Holden Caulfield in *Catcher in the Rye* (1951) through Ralph Ellison's eponymous *Invisible Man* (1952), Hazel Motes in Flannery O'Connor's *Wise Blood* (1952), Cross Damon in Richard Wright's *The Outsider* (1956), Dean Moriarty in Jack Kerouac's *On the Road* (1957) and Humbert Humbert in Vladimir Nabokov's *Lolita* (1958), and continued into early 1960s fiction with John Updike's Harry Angstrom in *Rabbit, Run* (1960) and Norman Mailer's Stephen Rojack in *The American Dream* (1965). Like Bellow's Augie March, these protagonists are marked by restlessness and a rootless identity. In part this is borrowed from the European picaresque tradition of roguish anti-hero (which Mark Twain had given an American slant in the late nineteenth century) and also from a discomfort with the rising middle-class expectations of the decade. Strangely enough, rootlessness and entrapment are closely related themes in 1950s fiction.

The wandering protagonist was also a development of existential currents from the 1940s, finding expression in the travelling characters of Paul Bowles's novel *The Sheltering Sky* (1949) – when Bowles's American characters lose their passports in North Africa they have 'no feeling of being anywhere, of being anyone' – and, later, the spiritually lost characters of Flannery O'Connor's *Wise Blood* surrounded by signs of bogus religion just as they yearn for authenticity.[29] While the comic exuberance of Augie March appears to be the keynote for a body of fiction that deals with the rising expectations of 1950s society, rootlessness is often a sign of loss, without the inner certainties that make travel exciting or productive.

In Bernard Malamud's *The Assistant* (1957), for example, the stasis of the ageing New York Jewish grocer Morris Bober is juxtaposed with the young rootless gentile Frank Alpine. Early in the novel Alpine arrives in Brooklyn from the West Coast to assist Bober in his shop, but unbeknown to the grocer he is also the masked man that has recently robbed him. During the robbery Bober's 'frightened eyes sought the man's but he was looking elsewhere'.[30] This theme of evasive identity is dominant in *The Assistant*, but Malamud also interweaves Jewish and Christian mythologies as the grocer and assistant are strangely drawn to each other. Rather than attempting to deal with contemporary issues directly, Malamud explores social conditions by examining the prosaic demands of everyday life. Paradoxically, the book is a wandering narrative without much physical movement, the undertow of desperation tempered by a sense of possibility. If, as Leslie Fiedler noted, the book is only a little less desperate than 'the more post-apocalyptic fears and hopes of our bland but immensely complex times', then it also suggests that spiritual renewal can emerge through the relationship of two individuals from opposite sides of the tracks.[31]

Friendship is a theme that emerges periodically in 1950s fiction, but protagonists are often isolated in the mode of 1940s existential writing. Notably, the protagonists of 1950s fiction are sometimes black (Ellison, Wright), sometimes Jewish (Bellow, Roth), sometimes of European extraction (Malamud, Nabokov), sometimes southern (Faulkner, O'Connor), but almost always male. The gender bias of fiction speaks to the problematic place of women in the cultural sphere at the time, but also links to one of the recurring figures in 1950s films: the returning World War II veteran and his often frustrated attempt to re-integrate into postwar society. But, while moving from national service to civilian life was a difficult transition for many male vets, it was arguably much more difficult for women. Elaine Tyler May estimates that the employment of women had risen by 60 per cent during the war, but soon after 1945 many found themselves embracing domesticity again with a spate of young marriages, a climbing birth rate, and GIs on the job market.[32]

If we read 1950s fiction as a direct reflection of gender roles, then it would seem that both sexes were uncomfortable with middle-class suburban life; it is just that male characters protested their discomfort more vocally: Kerouac's Sal Paradise fears being tied down to home and a wife and Nabokov's Humbert Humbert projects his disdain for the generic New England suburb of Ramsdale onto the empty bourgeois tastes of Lolita's mother Charlotte Haze. Even though Humbert is a European with a proclivity for young girls, his response was far from untypical. Male fears of entrapment were often projected onto women, leading critic Josephine Hendin to note that this often led to the creation of 'perverse drama[s] of sexual power and victimisation'.[33] This was particularly true for John Updike and Richard Yates who, writing at the turn of the 1960s, had enough critical distance to reflect back on the decade with greater insight into the pressures on the formation of gender roles.

One major cause of the gender rift stemmed from the heart of suburban life. Glossy adverts and new magazines such as *Redbook* were promoting suburbia as the bright new future for young adults and a safe place to raise children, but the temptation to conform to normalized gender roles was evident well before Updike and Yates offered critiques of suburban homogeneity. In one of the bestsellers of 1955, *The Man in the Gray Flannel Suit*, Sloan Wilson focuses on World War II veteran Tom Rath as he tries to balance his corporate job in the Rockefeller Center with the desire for a larger house in suburban Connecticut.[34] The major reason why Tom Rath finds office and suburban life difficult is that combat is in direct contrast to the feminized domesticity of the home and the supportive role Tom is expected to fulfil in the corporate workplace. As Erica Arthur argues in relation to 1950s business culture, Tom constantly tries to 'bolster his self-perception as a tough guy' during his struggles to contend with the demands of civilian life.[35]

By choosing a sociological title for his novel, Wilson positions Tom and Betsy Rath as typical of their generation, region and income bracket: they marry young; Tom is drafted in 1942 as a paratrooper; after he returns from the war in 1946 they try to come to terms with the hiatus in their relationship whilst pursuing their domestic dreams. As the original book jacket makes clear, he is a generic character: 'A few short years back, they were wearing uniforms of olive drab. The central theme of this novel is the struggle of a man to adapt himself from the relative security of O.D. to the insecurity of gray flannel.'[36]

Given the frequency of security threats during the cold war, Wilson's novel can be seen to tackle the problems of postwar insecurity – both in the workplace and at home – with the suggestion that, in some ways, suburbia is riskier than combat. Although the suburban home was touted as a safe haven during the cold war, the crack in the shape of a question mark in Tom's living room ceiling (which he finds 'annoying' rather than symbolic) suggests that it was also a place of insecurity.

Tom harbours a secret wartime affair with an Italian woman, Maria, and later discovers that she has had a child by him. Tom tries to erase his war experiences from his mind, but he is plagued by the uneasy feeling that he is leading a partitioned life: 'there must be some way in which the [different] worlds are related, he thought, but it was easier to think of them as entirely divorced from one another'.[37] Financial pressures encourage him to apply for an executive job at the United Broadcasting Corporation. When asked at the interview to write down the most significant fact about himself, Tom can only reflect on his life as a series of numbers: 'thirty-three years old, making seven thousand dollars a year, owner of a 1939 Ford, a six-room house, and ten thousand dollars' worth of G.I. Life Insurance'; he goes on: 'Six feet one and a half inches tall; weight, 198 pounds . . . served four and a half years in the Army' and he cannot rid himself of the memory of seventeen men he had killed during the war.[38] At the interview he cannot decide which version of himself is his best: his role as father or as soldier, his hatred of 'soap operas, commercials, and yammering studio audiences', his 'cheap' cynicism, or the fact that he can play the mandolin, and in the end he gives up on personal analysis, resorting to statistics and the bland promise that he 'probably would do a good job'.[39]

Although Tom suspects that he is leading an inauthentic life – pursuing an insignificant role in a large corporation and being motivated by money and property – he does little to develop a new set of ethics. In fact, he actively embraces phoniness at times. Walking through Grand Central Station one day he notices the stars painted on the ceiling and he decides to make a 'phony wish' on them: 'he wished he could make a million dollars and add a new wing to his grandmother's house, with a billiard room and a conservatory in which to grow orchids'.[40] Tom is not an anti-intellectual figure, but nor can he analyse deeply the forces that are shaping his aspirations. He also finds it difficult to think outside his own limited worldview. When asked by his boss to devise new ways to market 'mental health' he struggles with the subject, even though he is sensitive enough to realize that the promotion of mental health is in danger of degenerating into a cheap marketing slogan.

This tension between acceptance and unease runs through the novel and is also shared by his wife Betsy, who seems to share Tom's 'gray flannel' aspirations for much of the narrative. Later, though, after finding out about Tom's affair and his love child, Betsy realizes that what they have learnt since the war is wholly inauthentic:

> We've learned to drag along from day to day without any real emotion except worry. We've learned to make love without passion . . . All I know to do nowadays is be responsible and dutiful and deliberately cheerful . . . And all you know how to do is work day and night and worry.[41]

Following this revelation Tom and Betsy have a fight which purges them of their pent-up frustration. Tom is shocked into realizing that, although he thought of himself as being 'on the side lines' observing the corporate parade from a critical distance, he 'too was wearing a gray flannel suit' and had joined the 'frantic parade to nowhere'.[42] In the end, the tragic trajectory of the narrative – stemming from betrayal, ignoble deeds and property wars – is diverted by the couple's fresh understanding of each other and their renewed acceptance of middle-class life.[43]

The sociological tone of Wilson's novel suggests a model experience for many Americans born in the years following 1925, contributing to the notion of a 'silent generation' (a phrase popularized by a *Time* magazine feature of 5 November 1951) that was reaching adulthood without the psychological and moral resources to speak out, let alone act against a system which encouraged acquiescence and conformity. This view was evident in two key works of sociology from the early 1950s: David Riesman's *The Lonely Crowd* (1950), which defined a new character type that emerged after the war, the anxious 'other-directed' individual who struggled to contend with moral certainties, and C. Wright Mills' *White Collar* (1951), which examined the ways in which the middle class had become servants to what he later called the postwar 'power elite'. Some social critics like Daniel Bell and Daniel Boorstin detected a cultural consensus during the cold war, but Mills was arguing that the 'consent of men' was actually being manipulated behind the scenes, leading to an 'inactionary' condition in which individuals felt incapable of acting in any but a routine manner.[44] The inarticulacy of Tom Rath in *The Man in the Gray Flannel Suit* is an example of the disorientation of many workers as cogs in a system, the mechanics of which were much harder to comprehend than before the war.

Another of Mills' key points is that the organic cohesion of society had been lost, replaced by the illusion that mass communications and consumerism create a common culture. In 1958 he argued that the 'top of modern American society is increasingly unified, and often seems wilfully co-ordinated', while the 'middle levels are often a drifting set of stalemated forces' and 'the bottom' is 'politically fragmented' and 'increasingly powerless'.[45] If, according to Mills and the émigré thinkers Theodor Adorno and Max Horkheimer, mass media in the 1950s occluded these changing relationships, then it was perhaps left to literature and drama as 'serious' cultural activities to tackle underlying social relations. It was for this reason that Lionel Trilling, in 1955, described literature being distinct from other cultural forms; at its best literature is 'in advance of what society, or the general culture, can conceive'.[46] Trilling was worried by the rationalist direction of liberal thought and saw writers as being in a unique position to 'recall liberalism to its first essential imagination of variousness and possibility'.[47] Fiction and drama had the potential to cut through the simple antinomies of the cold war to unearth hidden complexities and anticipate new currents. This view fed into Trilling's argument that writers must continue to 'make it new' (echoing the poet Ezra Pound's modernist declaration) to prevent inertia from setting in, tempered by his worry that modernist writers might suspend cultural commitment in favour of wild aesthetic experimentation. What Trilling believed that modern writers have at their disposal, above all, is an 'indignant perception' which can make visible occluded areas of American life.[48]

With this in mind, a text like *The Man in the Gray Flannel Suit* might be seen as a 'bread and butter naturalistic novel' that only brushes over the surface of a series of complex issues about class, power and politics, lacking the seriousness of intent that Trilling would identify in the best modernist literature.[49] But, given that it was published in 1955 and that most serious critiques of suburbia did not begin to emerge until the last third of the decade, Wilson's novel managed to straddle the divide between entertainment and a perceptive study of white middle-class life.

Another literary text poised between the popular and serious, and which also revealed glimpses of underlying power structures, was a short novel that soon became the template of teenage fiction: J. D. Salinger's *The Catcher in the Rye*.

The Catcher in the Rye (1951)

The opening of J. D. Salinger's *The Catcher in the Rye* immediately throws the reader into an intimate relationship with the seventeen-year-old protagonist Holden Caulfield. Written in the first-person, the tone of the first line is impatient, off-hand and disrespectful. Whether or not the reader is interested in 'all that David Copperfield kind of crap' or the details of his 'lousy childhood', Holden's restless voice and his ambivalent feelings towards his family are hard to resist.[50] The reader is told that this will not be his 'whole goddam autobiography or anything'; instead it is a personal reminiscence about 'madman stuff' from the previous Christmas. Although the whole narrative is bound up with Holden's personal motivations ('I sort of needed a little vacation. My nerves were shot. They really were'), he is just as inclined to withhold information about himself: 'I could probably tell you what I did after I went home . . . but I don't feel like it. I really don't'.[51]

The narrative is set the day Holden leaves Pencey Prep school. He quickly establishes himself as an outcast, swift to ridicule the phoniness of the adult world and the hypocrisy that he detects hidden in their empty promise to value individuality. The fact that he resists 'all that David Copperfield kind of crap' reveals that this novel is a departure from the classic tale of self-development to one in which the reader is embroiled in the confusion of Holden's adolescence. Salinger later explored the problems of being a postwar 'teen-ager' (a new term in the mid-1940s and spelt with a hyphen at the time) in his short stories about the Glass family, but Holden stands out as a prototype of the youth culture that was to explode upon the scene in the middle of the decade (see Chapters 3 and 4). It is in the nuances of voice that Holden really comes alive: he can be at turns self-deprecating ('I act quite young for my age sometimes'), cunning (he tells his teacher 'I was a real moron, and all that stuff'), arrogant ('I'm the most terrific liar you ever saw in your life'), and vulnerable ('Then, all of a sudden, I started to cry. I couldn't help it') .[52]

The freshness of Holden's voice and the complexity of his teenage world mark him out from his literary predecessors. Like Saul Bellow's Augie March, Holden absorbs the spirit of Huckleberry Finn, with one early critic claiming that Holden's journey through the New York streets retells Huck's odyssey down the Mississippi.[53] Holden aspires to be a rebel against a system that offers him no more than the most superficial support, especially after he is expelled from his school. In many ways he is a younger version of James Joyce's modernist protagonist Stephen Dedalus, who had earlier in the century tried to shake off the Irish nets that ensnare him by relying on his own cunning. However, although Holden can also see beyond the veneer of middle-class lifestyles, his thoughts are too erratic to develop anything more than a tacit realization that he needs to get away from adult phoniness.

There is not even much consolation in his own generation, with only his ten-year-old sister Phoebe representing a safe haven. Indeed, the teenage world can be just as fake as the adult one; on visiting Ernie's nightclub Holden is perturbed to see so many 'prep school jerks' that go 'mad' when the pianist Ernie finished playing: 'They were exactly the same morons that laugh like hyenas in the movies at stuff that isn't funny'.[54] Holden remains in the club for a while, all the time denigrating the braying crowd, but he can do nothing to prevent himself feeling 'depressed and lousy again' except for leaving.[55] Much of Holden's rebellion stems from the tone of his voice; when it comes to actions he is only a little more rebellious than one of Salinger's later characters, Franny Glass, who realizes that going 'bohemian' is often just as fake as conforming. Holden's frustration can be seen as an example of the impasse of radicalism in the 1950s, but, as Sally Robinson argues, Holden's voice is distinctly gendered as he becomes a spokesman for 'a form of masculine protest that was itself fast becoming part of the post-war consensus'.[56]

It is worth considering the novel with reference to two other common contexts for framing Holden's tangled world: the first is the widespread interest in psychology following the war, and the second is the rise of sociology, epitomized by David Riesman's influential study of personality types, *The Lonely Crowd* (1950).

Although Holden is very suspicious of psychoanalysts in the novel, the rhetoric of self-analysis seeps into the text. Psychoanalysis did not just develop as an institution (the American Psychoanalytic Association grew rapidly between the 1930s and 1955), but the idea of the talking cure pervaded mainstream culture, so much so that it became almost impossible not to draw on psychoanalytic concepts to explore identity. With the likes of Erik Erikson and Benjamin Spock publishing widely read books on child psychology, together with the government's increasing concern about juvenile delinquency, it is perhaps surprising that critics did not start to explore the psychological dimensions of *Catcher in the Rye* until the 1970s. More recently, Peter Shaw develops the child psychologist Anna Freud's insights to read 'Holden's psychologically disturbed state . . . as the source both of his insight and of his lack of insight', in which love and mourning are caught up with his uneasy feelings about the phoniness of the adult world.[57] Holden is deeply affected by the death of his brother Allie from leukaemia and the suicide of his schoolmate James Castle, who was wearing Holden's sweater when he jumped out of a school window. But slips of tongue in Holden's narrative and his desperate attempts to save his sister – to become a saviour for her, a 'catcher in the rye' – can be read as a sublimated working through of these two young deaths, for which he feels partly responsible.

Holden is a survivor despite his hang-ups, but he can also be viewed through the lens of David Riesman's sociological character types. In *The Lonely Crowd* Riesman identifies three types – tradition-directed, inner-directed and other-directed personalities – the latter marked by the kind of anxiety that was frequently experienced by male characters in 1950s fiction as they adjusted to the demands of the postwar workplace. Because Riesman saw other-directed individuals as the end-product of liberal capitalism, it is difficult for them to move beyond a general feeling of uneasiness about their lack of self-determinism. Other-directed characters are often linked to the uneasy compromises of white-collar workers like Tom Rath in *The Man in the Gray Flannel Suit*, but Holden finds himself suffering from the early symptoms of Riesman's anxiety-ridden condition where adjustment or failure seem to be his only options. Riesman thought that the way out of this anxiety trap would be to develop autonomy, to recognize one's own 'feelings', 'potentialities' and 'limitations'.[58] While this recommendation appears to be sound, it is not clear what form this autonomy should take. Holden can only see ahead of him an office job 'reading newspapers and playing bridge all the time', and Norman Mailer dismissed Riesman's idea of autonomy as capitulation to the patriarchal order.[59] This then leaves Holden in a quandary: he would have to align himself with adult autonomy to cut free from his anxieties, but, by the same token, this would be a surrender to the middle-class values that he convinces the reader are irredeemably phoney.

The last paragraph of the novel can be read as an admission that Holden is, in fact, a very vulnerable seventeen-year-old; after failing to run away, he resigns himself to the prospect of a new school. But this same moment presents Holden with a strategy to develop autonomy without capitulating. When asked 'what I thought about all this stuff I just finished telling you about' he does not know 'what the hell to say'; he apologises for talking to so many people and concludes 'Don't ever tell anybody anything. If you do, you start missing everybody'.[60] The ambiguity of the word 'missing' here – which can be read as either a longing for company or a set of psychological misperceptions – provides a possible way out for Holden. The technique of remaining silent, or anti-analysis ('don't ever tell anybody anything'), might provide him with the cunning that Stephen Dedalus had sought much earlier in the century. Silence, rather than talking, might offer Holden a clearer perception of 'everybody' than he currently possesses. This movement beyond his current identity is only a hint, though, and offers little consolation, especially when Lionel Trilling and Reinhold Niebuhr were arguing at the time for the urgent need to find a vantage point which takes note of irresolvable contradictions and complexities.

Poetics of Experience

One of the most obvious qualities of *The Catcher in the Rye* is its confessional tone, which reflects the way in which postwar writers, according to Marcus Cunliffe, 'developed techniques of writing-as-talk (confession, harangue, invective)' that broke from 'the genteel tradition' of the early 1940s.[61] The 1950s are also usually remembered as 'the confessional moment' for poetry, characterized by a first-person voice, emotive tone and autobiographical mode. But this is a slight distortion of 1950s poetry. Christopher Beach reads the more 'relaxed' mood among younger poets as a challenge to 'the decorum of an era marked by its containment of psychic needs and desires'.[62] David Perkins pinpoints 1954 as the moment in which formal poetics were rejected, but looks back to Charles Olson's 'Projective Verse' in 1950 and forward to Robert Lowell's *Life Studies* in 1959 as important moments in the postwar transition of American poetry.[63] And Edward Brunner sees a 'resdistribution of power' in 1950s poetry: it was 'linguistically sophisticated even as it offered accessibility' and it blurred with other cultural forms (music, performance, painting) to challenge traditional distinctions between high and low culture.[64] These readings suggest that confessionalism was itself a development of modernist aesthetics, signalling the freedom to explore emotional frailty, psychic complexity, family separation and personal trauma on cultural and poetic levels.

These concerns can be read autobiographically with alcoholism, depression, divorce and suicide (for Plath, Berryman and Schwartz) marking out the generation of poets that features in the 1950 anthology *Mid-Century American Poets*. This turn towards the life of the poet is the legacy of literary celebrity which developed rapidly through the public profiles of Hemingway and Faulkner and the marriage of Sylvia Plath to English poet Ted Hughes in 1956, followed by the suicide of Plath in 1963 sixth months after the publicity surrounding Marilyn Monroe's death. Plath's and Lowell's intimate poetry encourages an autobiographical reading, but it is more useful to read their poems as strategies for getting beneath the skin (sometimes quite literally) of their poetic personae, tapping into deeper impulses than the more impersonal poetry of W. H. Auden and Archibald MacLeish after the war.

It is wrong to think of the poetic output of the whole decade as being 'confessional' though. Auden was writing some of his most interesting verse in the mid-1950s, exploring the relation between art and history. In Auden's 'Homage to Clio', for example, Clio is the muse of history but also the 'Madonna of silences' who does not give any assistance to the poet. She can be approached for answers to historical questions, but the pictures she provides are of little help and 'no explosion can conquer' her silence.[65] Many of Auden's poems in the mid-1950s dealt with history ('Makers of History', 'The Old Man's Road', 'The Truth of History'), but as the title of his 1955 collection *The Shield of Achilles* suggests, he was drawn to classical mythology to explore the wounds of history. The Librarian of Congress MacLeish was also deeply interested in the impact of history on literature, and in the New *York Times* in 1960 he defended poetry against 'our new, precise, objective, dispassionate observation of the world'.[66] There was a common feeling that science, technology and commerce were rendering poetry defunct, but it was perhaps because history seemed too complex in the 1950s that Lowell, Plath and Ginsberg began to delve into deeper recesses of identity. For these poets, Auden's poetics seemed to lack passion, were too intellectualizing, and did not plumb the depths of experience.[67]

We saw earlier how 1950s poetry can be carved up into poets who tended towards abstraction (Charles Olson and Michael McClure) and those that tried to develop more personal forms of poetry (Robert Lowell and John Berryman), but it is worth dwelling a moment on two poets that fill the middle space between 'formalism' and 'informal art', as Lowell called it.[68] These two poets, Elizabeth Bishop and Frank O'Hara, are quite different from each other: Bishop was drawn to Nova Scotia and Brazil (she lived in South America for much of the 1950s) and the formal craft of poetry, whereas O'Hara was a gay New York poet interested in jazz rhythms and the abstract painting of Jackson Pollock. They each published an important collection of poems in the decade – Bishop's *A Cold Spring* (appearing with her earlier collection *North and South* in 1955) and O'Hara's *Meditations in an Emergency* (1957) – and they resist the common labels used to characterize postwar American poetry.

In many ways Elizabeth Bishop is a late modernist poet: she was interested in surrealist poetics, believed that poetry could move beyond rationalism, and was absorbed by the material qualities of words. But her verse also exemplifies the problems of using modernism as a label for 1950s poets: she was drawn to conventional poetic forms like the sestina but also interested in language that turns in on itself in such lines as 'until a name / and all its connotation are the same' and words that move beyond ideas and emotions: 'It is like what we imagine knowledge to be: / dark, salt, clear, moving utterly free'.[69] It is for these opposing tendencies that the critic David Kalstone calls Bishop 'the most elusive of contemporary poets'.[70]

One could argue that Bishop was striving to achieve something similar to the artists Jasper Johns and Joseph Cornell in visual media (see Chapter 5), to blur the edges of what could be considered a poem. She had written, back in 1934, that what she admired in the Victorian poet Gerard Manley Hopkins was 'a moving, changing idea or series of ideas . . . the boundaries of the poem are set free, and the whole thing is loosened up'.[71] On this level, raw experience often meets artifice in Bishop's poems, such as the opening of 'A Cold Spring': 'A cold spring: / the violet was flawed on the lawn. / For two weeks or more the trees hesitated; / the little leaves waited, / carefully indicating their characteristics'.[72] This simple pastoral is complicated by the internal rhyme of the second line, the hint of neurosis in line three and the intellectualism of line five, leaving the words hovering between a description of an external landscape and a subtle exploration of personal identity.

Just as Bishop strains against the label of confessional poet, so too does Frank O'Hara but for different reasons as he tried to steer between the 'personal removal of the poet' in abstract verse and 'the personality and intimacy' of confessionals. His book on Jackson Pollock and reviews for *Art News* early in the decade reveal his passionate interest in painting. Even though he defended the poet's art in 'Why I Am Not a Painter' (1956), his first two collections *A City Winter and Other Poems* (1952) and *Oranges* (1953) were gallery editions and he worked in New York art circles all his life, developing a hybrid form of poem-painting. His poems read as continuations of each other in their colloquial tone, leading the poet Mark Doty to comment that: 'his language is often casual, relaxed in diction, yet it presses forward with a kind of breathless urgency, a will to celebrate the density and richness of experience'.[73]

In his tongue-in-cheek manifesto, 'Personism' (1959), O'Hara outlined a mode of poetry addressed to a single recipient but without excessive feelings towards that person. 'Personism' goes against pure abstraction and tries to sustain 'the poet's feeling towards the poem', placing it 'squarely between the poet and the person' (as Jasper Johns did in his half-abstract paintings – see Chapter 5).[74] We should be wary of reading his manifesto too seriously though: O'Hara was neither a rebel nor a conformist, realizing that the former may be reactionary and the latter is likely to lead to inertia and cliché. Take O'Hara's statement on poetics:

> I don't think of fame or posterity . . . nor do I care about clarifying experiences for anyone or bettering . . . anyone's state or social relations, nor am I for any particular technical development in the American language . . . What is happening to me, allowing for lies and exaggerations which I try to avoid, goes into my poems.[75]

Very personal poetry for O'Hara does not equate to confession, which is perhaps more prone to 'lies and exaggerations' than abstract expressions of selfhood. His poetic portraits of James Dean ('you take up the thread of my life between your teeth'), Billie Holiday ('I am sweating a lot by now and leaning on the john door') and Lana Turner ('I have been to lots of parties / and acted perfectly disgraceful / but I never actually collapsed') reveal much more about the poet's proclivities than it does about the subject of the poem.[76] And the homoerotic charge of his prose poem 'Meditations in an Emergency' (1957) – 'Heterosexuality! You are inexorably approaching' – reveal links back to the avant-garde experimentalism of the French surrealists in the 1920s as well as moving beyond the horizon of modernism.[77]

If Bishop and O'Hara resist the label of confessional poets (a term first applied to poetry by M. L. Rosenthal in 1959), then Robert Lowell's *Life Studies* (1959) is often cited as the most sustained attempt to develop a confessional mode and a 'turning point' in postwar poetry.[78] His interest in personal experience is acute in a sequence of poems that explore Lowell's family relationships. Whereas Auden begins 'Makers of History' with the line 'Serious historians care for coins and weapons', Lowell had a much more personal way of making history, beginning his 'Life Studies' sequence with the line: ' "I won't go with you. I want to stay with Grandpa!" '.[79] He made a deliberate attempt to move away from the esoteric symbolism of his Pulitzer Prize-winning collection *Lord Weary's Castle* (1946) by focusing on particulars. Lowell's Boston family-line turns out to be as complex as the telescopic forces of history for Auden, and in *Life Studies* he develops a conversational form of free verse akin to spoken rhythms and attuned to personal concerns. Delving into his early boyhood of the 1920s, Lowell recalls his Uncle Devereux Winslow dying of Hogdkin's disease at age twenty-nine. He provides direct expressions of his uncle's dress ('his trousers were solid cream from the top of the bottle') as a child would to hide his fears ('I cowered in terror'), conflicting impulses which are brought together when the poem describes his hands: 'warm, then cool, on the piles / of earth and lime, a black pile and a white pile . . .' as his uncle blends 'to the one colour' in death.[80]

Life Studies introduces the reader to 'the vast number of remembered things' from Lowell's past. 'Each is in its place, each has its function, its history, its drama' Lowell claimed in his prose sketch '91 Revere Street'. He uses poetry to excavate the past and fix memories in the mind without distortion, so that 'things and their owners [could] come back urgent with life and meaning'.[81] The fact that Lowell recounts his early years twice in *Life Studies* – in prose in '91 Revere Street' and in verse in the title sequence – suggests that writing can give narrative shape to the past and also capture the drama of intense experiences. The sequence not only extends the chronological range of the prose piece (taking us forward to the poet's forty-first birthday), but it also uses remnants from the past as a way of exploring the passage of time. In 'Man and Wife', for instance, lying on his mother's bed and holding his wife's hand (while she turns his back on him after an argument) the poet is transported into the past when he was 'too boiled and shy / and poker-faced to make a pass' at her.[82] The long ruminative first stanza is followed by a more concentrated one, in which we fast-forward twelve years to the present. His (unnamed) wife holds her pillow 'like a child' as the more recent memory of her 'tirade – / loving, rapid, merciless – breaks like the Atlantic Ocean' on the poet's head. The shift of register from the mundane (the pillow) to the sublime (the Atlantic Ocean) suggests the oppressive weight of experience, but the description is muted and lacks the excessive emotion that one might expect from a confessional poet.

While Lowell was not as outspoken as the West Coast poets, *Life Studies* can be read as an attempt to weave together disparate experiences – past and present, historical and autobiographical, conscious and unconscious, happy and painful – into complex patterns, which go far beyond the stereotypical identities that were frequent in middlebrow fiction of the 1950s. Like Bishop and O'Hara, Lowell was not interested in finding impersonal Truth (with a capital 'T') but wanted to confront the fleeting experiences of a life in flux.[83] Lowell had greater range than Sylvia Plath, whose first collection *The Colossus* (1960) developed a more deeply personal and domestic poetry. Since her death in 1963 the lionizing of Plath has led to the received wisdom that confessional poets are only interested in the autobiographical self. This view is unfair on Plath and, although not as political as Ginsberg and Mailer, Lowell was a conscientious objector in World War II, wrote anti-racist poems in *For the Union Dead* (1965), including a protest against the Bomb 'Fall 1961', and later participated in Vietnam peace protests in 1967, which make it tempting to read his poetry as a resisting strain within 1950s literary culture.

Much of Lowell's poetry offers a quiet ruminative critique of an emotionally pent-up decade, but a much noisier and dramatic voice found expression in the most controversial postwar American poem: Allen Ginsberg's 'Howl'.

'Howl' (1956)

By the time Allen Ginsberg had delivered the first complete public recitation of 'Howl' at Berkeley's Town Hall Theater in March 1956 it had already stirred up controversy, but no one predicted that the poem and its publisher, City Lights bookstore owner Lawrence Ferlinghetti, would be put on trial a year later. The first (incomplete) reading had been given the previous October in Six Gallery in San Francisco alongside others by Beat poets Gary Snyder, Kenneth Rexroth and Michael McClure. Ginsberg's reading was received passionately (Jack Kerouac reputedly yelled 'Go!' after each line) mainly because it reflected the group's interest in Zen Buddhism and the philosophy of 'mindbody'. Ginsberg was excited by mystical explorations of consciousness, but also fascinated by the lyrical visions of Walt Whitman, William Blake and Arthur Rimbaud that helped him write 'without fear, let [his] imagination go, open secrecy, and scribble magic lines from [his] real mind'.[84] He wanted neither a narrative poem nor a short lyric, but a composition that defied poetic convention while remaining socially and politically potent: 'I wanted to let loose and say what I really had on my mind . . . break my own forms, break my own ideals, ideas, what I was supposed to be like as a poet'.[85] As such, 'Howl' was an intensely personal poem (dedicated to Carl Solomon, whom Ginsberg had met at Rockland, a New York psychiatric hospital), but also a panoramic composition that explores a cross-section of American culture.

In his introduction to *Howl and Other Poems*, the poet William Carlos Williams writes about the 'horrifying experiences' of 'Howl' (which Ginsberg and Solomon had themselves gone through), but also a journey from 'the teeth and excrement of this life' to an affirmation of the ennobling 'spirit of love'.[86] While 'Howl' does not convey a narrative in any traditional sense, the poem shifts from a vision of approaching destruction in the first section and an outcry against Moloch (the Hebrew god of commercialism) in the second, to the consequences of such demoralization for Solomon in part three, and the Whitmanesque celebration of body, mind and soul in the final part 'Footnote to Howl'. There are hints of an elegy as the poet finds consolation for death, but its iconic qualities derive from the powerful images that Ginsberg conjures up and his experiments with breathing and line length.

The poem begins with the most memorable of lines: 'I saw the best minds of my generation destroyed by madness, starving hysterical naked'. Surprisingly, this initial sentence stretches over the first section of the poem, concluding ten pages later with 'the absolute heart of the poem of life butchered out of their own bodies good to eat a thousand years'.[87] The long opening section charts a transition between the contemporary moment ('my generation') and the prolongation of time ('a thousand years'), mixed up with the visceral experience of 'starving hysterical naked' as creativity is 'butchered' out of the body. Most of the lines of this prolonged sentence begin with the word 'who'; Ginsberg asks questions of the perpetrator but also implies that social destruction is inscribed on the bodies of the young. In this opening part there is both subjugation of the self, but also creative energy ('publishing obscene odes of the windows of the skull', 'whole intellects disgorged in total recall for seven days') that cannot be quashed by the 'nightmare of Moloch'. The poet's anger is offset by a lamenting tone for a generation of poets and hipsters whose innocent nakedness is overwhelmed by commercialism and intolerance. The vision of renewal in 'Howl' cannot be achieved by alignment to dominant social values; the poem suggests that only spiritual and artistic nakedness can transform madness, homosexuality and dissolution into creative affirmation.

Ginsberg's interest in the poetic line is reminiscent of Charles Olson's concept of 'projective verse': he viewed each line as a 'breath unit' in which breathing is suspended, and sometimes exhausted, by the extended line length.[88] The attempt to render sense perceptions through words stems from Ginsberg's modernist desire to look directly at an object, creating a set of seemingly spontaneous associated images along the breath-line free from the clutter of punctuation. Thus Ginsberg always stressed the poem's verbal qualities ('the rhythm of actual speech') as well as the capacity of poetry to lead to 'the highest moments of mindbody' by providing 'mystical illumination' in which reality can be peeled away to reveal are forced together true forms.[89] The rhythm of the first part owes a debt to jazz and hipster-speak; compound words are forced together – 'hotrod-Golgotha jail-solitude watch' – both for their unusual verbal rhythms and the complex images they evoke.

The exhaustive line length changes in part two when the destructive aspects of 'Howl' come to the fore, with Moloch (the 'sphinx of cement and aluminum') blamed for eating up the generation's 'brains and imagination'. Moloch is a figure who 'murders to dissect' like William Blake's Newton, but is more demonic than Newton as an agent of dehumanizing civilization 'whose mind is pure machinery!' The questioning tone of the first part is replaced by a series of apostrophes in part two in which the repetition of the name Moloch exposes him as the tyrant of postwar America.[90] The tone shifts again at the beginning of section three, in which the poet expresses friendship for his friend Carl Solomon in Rockwell. This section can be read as a 'talking back' to Moloch, in which the set of negatives (madness, murder, straitjacketing, electric shock treatment and communism) are turned into points of resistance. This ability to turn zones of imprisonment into potential liberation leads to the Whitmanesque celebration of creativity in the concluding 'Footnote to Howl', which in its form (but not its tone) mirrors the exclamations of part two.

Fifty years after publication 'Howl' still reads as a contemporary poem, but it is important not to forget the legal charges against Ginsberg for obscenity. A number of writers, critics and educationalists were called to the San Francisco trial in summer 1957 to speak for and against the poem after the second printing dispatched from the UK had been intercepted by US customs in March. Although some thought the poem was pulp writing with no redeeming qualities, at the trial there were many statements in support of its literary and social merit. The book was endorsed by the American Civil Liberties Union and defended by the writer Kenneth Rexroth, who stated that 'its merit is extraordinarily high . . . it is probably the most remarkable single poem' published since World War II.[91] The outcome of the trial was that the book was cleared of the obscenity charge, the judge concluding that it 'does have some redeeming social import-ance'. Indeed, the case actually worked to the benefit of 'Howl', pushing sales up to over 10,000 by the end of the trial, with Lawrence Ferlinghetti commenting that 'it would have taken years for critics to accomplish what the good collector did in a day, merely by calling the book obscene'.[92]

Resistant Fiction

The character of the *schlemeil* is central to understanding the histori-cal development of Jewish writing and also helps to assess the chal-lenges facing American writers more generally in the 1950s. Emerging from Yiddish folklore in East Europe, the *schlemiel* is a comic charac-ter who responds with humour and endurance to all the injustice and persecution that befalls him, a figure such as the downtrodden grocer Morris Bober in Bernard Malamud's *The Assistant* and 'Gimpel the Fool', a Yiddish story by Isaac Bashevis Singer which Saul Bellow translated for *Partisan Review* in 1953, republished a year later for a broad readership in *A Treasury of Yiddish Stories*. The blurring between Jewish and other literary traditions is given some weight by Malamud's famous claim that the Jewish experience is a universal one.

There was, however, a feeling that the *schlemiel* was a conservative figure that accepted fate and plodded on despite the most taxing cir-cumstances. For those writers who wanted to express more than unease with contemporary events, the *schlemiel* did not offer a radical template. As Frank Alpine muses in *The Assistant*, the stoic Morris Bober shuts himself up 'in an overgrown coffin' and accepts his fate as a 'born prisoner'.[93] Alpine realizes that there is much more to Bober's life than he at first credits, and the novel ends with Alpine literally becoming a Jew. But there is arguably too much suffering and fortitude in the lives of Malamud's Jewish characters, which only added to the growing sense among some writers in the mid-1950s that a defiant atti-tude was needed to break the consumerist shackles of the decade.

Bellow's Augie March is one character who thrives because of his restlessness, and Bellow showed through Augie and Eugene Henderson in *Henderson the Rain King* (1959) that it was possible to step out of the Jewish literary enclave by creating American characters not wholly determined by their ethnicity. But other rootless characters in 1950s fiction do not fare so well: Hazel Motes in Flannery O'Connor's *Wise Blood* is defeated by the cheap commercialism that has bastardized religion in the Deep South and social-climber Neil Klugman in Philip Roth's *Goodbye, Columbus* (1959) eventually realizes that his inability to get over his broken relationship with the Jewish socialite Brenda Patimkin stems from his limited worldview, hemmed in by New Jersey suburbia.[94]

This feeling of entrapment also pervades the opening pages of William Burroughs' first novel *Junkie*, published (with the help of Allen Ginsberg) in the Ace Books' two-in-one paperback line under the pseudonym William Lee (the short novel was later retitled *Junky*). The unnamed autobiographical voice of the book rarely spills into confessional mode, but rather adopts a hard-boiled tone in which his middle-class upbringing is contrasted to his diary of addiction and the underground language of junk (he even provides a glossary of drug slang). The night fears, hallucinations and 'supernatural horror' that the narrator experiences as a young boy seem to predestine him for a life of drug-taking.[95] He echoes Salinger's Holden Caulfield in being alienated by social fakery and, after the Army rejects him on medical grounds (diagnosed as a paranoid schizophrenic), he spends time drifting around Europe, New York and later Mexico. At times *Junky* reads as a how-to manual for becoming a drug addict. It is an existence which certainly has its downside, leading to a life of craving, numbness and dependency, but also has educational benefits: 'junk is a cellular equation that teaches the user facts of general validity . . . I have learnt the cellular stoicism that junk teachers the user'.[96]

What *Junky* presents, arguably for the first time in twentieth-century American fiction, is the underside of national culture: an underworld that connects to criminality, secret languages and diverse forms of sexuality. The reader never really gets to know characters like 'Subway Mike' and the addict Herman (based on Herman Huncke who hung out with the Beat writers in New York), and some figures do not rise above the status of caricature, but they are all manifestations of an underground of which most readers would not be aware. Heroin is shown to inhibit creativity, as it does for the Greenwich Village artist Nick (his paintings 'looked as if they had been concentrated, compressed, misshapen by a tremendous pressure'), and often stimulates nightmarish visions for the narrator: 'I closed my eyes and saw New York in ruins. Huge centipedes and scorpions crawled in and out of empty bars'.[97] But sometimes narcotics lead him to social insights to which he would otherwise be blind, such as the double-dealings of drug pushers/police informers, the misuse of authority and power, and what Timothy Murphy calls the 'black-market economies of the flesh and spirit that implicitly parody the rising American consumer society'.[98] The meandering narrative and the cast of roguish characters are borrowed from picaresque fiction, but what the protagonist seeks more than anything is freedom. At the end of the novel the narrator has been clean from heroin for a while and now fixates on a new drug, yage, a hallucinogen which expands the consciousness rather than narrowing it (even the Soviets are interested in the drug's telepathic powers we are told). The narrator sees yage as being the ultimate fix and he sets off to Columbia in search of 'the uncut kick that opens out instead of narrowing down like junk'.[99]

Junky preceded the other major texts of the Beat Generation – Ginsberg's 'Howl', Kerouac's *On the Road*, Mailer's essay 'The White Negro' and Ferlinghetti's poem collection *Coney Island of the Mind* – by a few years, and suggests that the underlying unease of the decade was close to breaking out into full-scale rebellion. This mood is precisely the one that stimulates Salinger's Holden Caulfield and Franny Glass to escape their suffocating environments. John Clellon Holmes had written the closest thing to a Beat manifesto, 'This Is the Beat Generation', for the *New York Times* in late 1952, claiming that 'its members have an instinctive individuality, needing no bohemianism or imposed eccentricity to express it'.[100] But it was not until the second half of the decade (between 1955 and 1958) that Beat writers were finding full expression and beginning to have an impact on American culture at large.

One common view of Beat writing was a collective attempt to struggle free from the cultural stasis of mid-1950s, but another view aligns it more closely with a new emphasis on individualism. Lizabeth Cohen describes the way in which the last third of the decade saw a move by advertisers away from a 'homogenous mass market' into 'segmenting markets' in which companies' targeted 'consumers with distinctive traits and psychologies'.[101] Where, at the beginning of the decade, David Riesman had identified three distinct character types, with the anxious 'other-directed' personality coming to the fore after the war, the rise of the individual in a broader sense – as both consumer and rebel – marked the later part of the decade. With the economic slump of 1958, this was precisely the time that a number of articles bemoaned the decline of masculinity, suggesting that from a sense of unease might spring the new courage that Mailer sought. It is perhaps no surprise that in *On the Road* Kerouac uses the car to symbolize this resurgence of individual freedom.

What is more surprising is that Kerouac had written the story at the beginning of the decade but had failed to find a publisher until the mid-1950s, by which time many of the Beat writers had left New York: Ferlinghetti and Ginsberg had gone to San Francisco (where Ferlinghetti founded the City Lights bookstore in 1953) and Burroughs to Mexico and then Tangiers. The major reason why Kerouac struggled to find a publisher is that *On the Road* is not structured like a novel, but more like an extended jazz riff inspired by the be-bop jazz of the late 1940s. Long rhythmical sentences are testament to Kerouac's claim that the text was written in a compressed period of three weeks (probably fuelled by amphetamines) and approximates to the Beat philosophy of 'first thought best thought' in its spontaneous use of language.

On the Road consists of four road trips, followed by a short epilogue, which chart the restless journeys across America of Sal Paradise and Dean Moriarty around 1947, loosely based on Kerouac and his Beat friend Neal Cassady's road trips. Sal feels that his 'life hanging around' the Columbia University campus 'had reached the completion of its cycle' and had become 'stultified'; Sal sees a wandering spirit in Dean (who has spent time in prison for stealing cars) and has fraternal feelings for him (there are even hints that Sal's attraction runs deeper than this).[102] His aunt warns that Dean will get him into trouble, but Sal is keen for new experiences away from the Northeast, and he senses 'somewhere along the line . . . there'd be girls, visions, everything; somewhere along the line the pearl would be handed to me'.[103] Their first trip is to the West Coast by bus and hitchhiking. The thrill of movement keeps their spirits alive as they 'go mad' together reading, drinking, taking Benzedrine and hanging out. But while Dean immerses himself completely in new experiences, Sal realizes, after the initial excitement of San Francisco has worn off, that 'here I was at the end of America – no more land – and now there was nowhere to go but back'.[104]

The exuberance of travel is complicated by undertones of unease: 'something, someone, some spirit was pursuing all of us across the desert of life and was bound to catch us before we reached heaven'.[105] Existential concerns intertwine with social and cultural themes in *On the Road*, as the pair – who it is increasingly obvious have different priorities – strive to find a place where they can be free. The closest they come to freedom is in the fourth part of the book on their trip to

Mexico, which parallels Burrough's search for the hallucinogen yage at the end of *Junky*: going to Mexico is, what Sal calls, 'the most fabulous' trip of all.[106] But even beyond the American frontier, where the law is more relaxed about the drug subculture and 'life was dense, dark, ancient', there is the feeling that 'the end of the road' only means a return to the start of the journey, back to the Northeast where potential conformity awaits even someone as free-spirited as Dean Moriarty.[107]

Even though Kerouac was trying to recapture the spiritual exuberance of Walt Whitman, it would seem that in the 1950s the only authentic experience 'off the road' was in exile outside the United States. This was certainly true for two African American writers Richard Wright and James Baldwin who migrated to Paris in the late 1940s because they felt that contemporary social pressures gave them no other option. A literary success after his 1940 novel *Native Son*, Wright had been championed by the matriarch of modernism Gertrude Stein shortly before she died in 1946, and he carried forward the torch for American writers in exile on the Left Bank of the Seine after moving to Paris in 1947, tired of feeling pressured for his leftist views, even though he had left the Communist Party five years earlier. Ten years later in 1957, the year that Ghana became the first African country to declare independence from colonial rule, Wright made a call to global responsibility for other national cultures in *White Man Listen!* Here Wright made it plain that he considered rootlessness to be a desirable condition if the alternative was conformity: 'I'm a rootless man, but I'm neither psychologically distraught nor in any wise particularly perturbed because of it . . . I declare unabashedly that I like and even cherish the state of abandonment, of aloneness'.[108]

James Baldwin did not emigrate for the same explicitly political reasons as Wright, but he shared the older author's sense of abandonment because the hostility he faced as a young gay black man was so intense that leaving was his only option. He arrived in an unfashionable area of Paris in 1948 as an unknown writer with only $40 in his pocket. Wright and Baldwin soon fell out, mainly because Baldwin thought Wright too narrowly a protest writer. Baldwin believed that the novelist should explore more deeply the psychological complexion of friendship, desire and hatred, as he did in his first novel *Go Tell It On the Mountain* (1953) and his gay novella *Giovanni's Room* (1956), which explores the reasons why, even though he actively supported the civil rights movement, exile was a permanent condition for Baldwin.[109]

In the eight years leading to the *Brown* v. *the Board of Education* ruling of 1954, it would seem that exile – either internal or external exile – was inevitable for African American writers, particularly those with alternative political priorities. However, as Ralph Ellison demonstrated in his only completed novel, *Invisible Man*, it was still possible to find a critical perspective within the United States.

Invisible Man (1952)

In the introduction to his first collection of essays, *Shadow and Act* (1964), Ralph Ellison identified three themes running through his work: links between literature and folklore, black music, and 'the complex relationship between the Negro American subculture and North American culture as a whole'.[110] Not only did Ellison want to challenge ingrained stereotypes about African Americans, but also the struggle of different cultures that are often elided into a unified notion of 'one nation under God', as the Pledge of Allegiance added in 1954. A left-wing novelist with a similar political education to Richard Wright in the 1930s, Ellison detected that social struggle goes far beyond skin colour. As he wrote in the mid-1940s, the racial conflict between black and white was 'but a part of that larger conflict between older, dominant groups of white Americans . . . and the newer white and non-white groups', particularly 'over the major group's attempt to impose its ideals upon the rest, insisting that its exclusive image be accepted as the image of the American'.[111] The largely Anglo-American national culture had, to Ellison's mind, come about through the subjugation of specific cultures and immigrant groups, neutering them or rendering them invisible. His consolation was that the struggle will continue as part of the democratic process of defining nationhood; fortunately, for Ellison, 'the American himself has not been finally defined'.[112]

The themes of invisibility and identity dominate *Invisible Man*. In taking his lead from the Russian writer Fyodor Dostoevsky's early modernist novel *Notes from Underground* (1864), in the prologue Ellison places his unnamed narrator in a shadowy underground world. Invisible Man is embittered for being ignored and occasionally violent, as he is when an insulting man bumps into him in the dark, but he has inner resolve to 'fight my battle' with the Monopolated Light & Power Company.[113] He manages to cultivate, perhaps due to his invisibility, the cunning that Holden Caulfield cannot quite discover; he tries to sabotage the company by draining power through the 1,369 light bulbs he has wired up in his underground hole. Light and music bring Invisible Man to life: he wants to feel the vibration of music with his 'whole body' and desires light because it 'confirms my reality, gives birth to my form'. Although invisibility has its benefits (one can go unnoticed through life) and sometimes shapelessness can be useful (as it proves for Bellow's Augie March), Ellison's protagonist exclaims that 'to be unaware of one's form is to live a death'.[114]

The tone of the novel's prologue derives as much from 1940s existentialist fiction as it does from the rebellious tones of Dostoevsky's underground protagonist railing against social injustices. It is not as obviously a protest novel as *Native Son*, but does explore the psychological effects of race prejudice and class conflict.[115] The novel adopts the mode of a confessional memoir ('one long, loud rant, howl and laugh' as Ellison describes it), but it is also a picaresque narrative that explores the 'restlessness of spirit' which 'transcends geography, sociology and past condition of servitude'.[116] For this reason, the book is very much part of American folklore. For example, in the opening line Invisible Man compares himself to a spook in an Edgar Allan Poe tale and a little later he is a 'tinker' in the tradition of Franklin and Edison. One way of reading the novel is as a demand for inclusion in national history that has marginalized African Americans, but also a fighting back to be acknowledged and respected. Invisible Man resists standard labels that have often been pinned on African Americans: he is neither subservient nor consistently aggressive, neither socially passive nor sexually voracious. He revels in his irresponsibility, claiming 'to whom can I be responsible, and why should I be, when you refuse to see me?'[117]

It is significant that Ellison wrote the novel in the second half of the 1940s (after he had returned from serving in the US Coast Guard) and that it was published two years before the *Brown* v. *the Board of Education* decision, given that the injustices that Invisible Man experiences were ingrained on both psychological and institutional levels. What is more surprising is that Ellison chose to set the novel back in the 1930s, rather than dealing directly with cold war concerns. The narrative explanation for this is that Invisible Man traces his life over twenty years, charting what critic Irving Howe called 'a Negro's journey through contemporary America, from South to North, province to city, naïve faith to disenchantment and perhaps beyond'.[118] The journey that he takes is not unlike other migrating African Americans in the 1930s and 1940s and his experiences are not extraordinary, leading Saul Bellow to claim in 1952 that the novel's 'balance for instinct and culture' is not just applicable to all Americans, but also to all nationalities and races.[119] However, Ellison keeps incidents specific through the novel and he resists the temptation to write naturalistic fiction by refusing to make Invisible Man merely the victim of circumstances outside his control.

If Invisible Man is the representative of a social and racial type, then his instability is a major reason why he is so bothered about lacking form. This worry is deeply rooted on many different levels. His picaresque wanderings (expelled from his southern college for ignoring racial protocol he journeys to New York where he works in a paint factory, joins the Communist Party and gets involved in a Harlem riot), his idiosyncratic insights ('if only all the contradictory voices shouting inside my head would calm down . . . and sing without dissonance'), and Ellison's mixed mode (fusing realistic, symbolic and expressionistic techniques) all suggest a movement beyond the representative personality type epitomized in *The Man in the Gray Flannel*

Suit. If Ellison's primary focus was on national concerns, he also had an eye on broader global issues, tapping into a modernist tradition of writing on race and nationhood (the novel cites James Joyce's *Portrait of the Artist as a Young Man*) and different political systems (such as the communist Brotherhood in Harlem).

Irving Howe's criticism that 'Ellison cannot establish ironic distance between his hero and himself' is an easy one to make about first-person narratives. Ellison responded by arguing that protest writing comes in many different shapes and that Howe was overly prescriptive about what he expected of black writers.[120] What Howe missed were the subtleties of Ellison's novel; what Saul Bellow detected in 1952 as its 'tragi-comic, poetic' qualities.[121] The filter of fiction enabled Ellison to explore the ways in which taxing experiences sometimes enable individuals to learn responsive strategies rather than forcing them to retreat into the shadows. Although Invisible Man finishes the novel where it begins, in his underground hole, he is not defeated and is able to use his experiences to devise resisting strategies to race prejudice.

Late in the novel, Invisible Man realizes that his younger self was deluded in believing in solidity: 'now I know that men are different and that all life is divided and that only in division is there true health'.[122] What he learns is that the dissonant voices in his head can be advantageous, especially if the alternative is conformity. He does not advocate a colour-blind or grey society, where blacks struggle to emulate whites and white writers like Norman Mailer adopt romantic notions of 'The White Negro'. Instead, Invisible Man understands that many strands of society are equally necessary and that realism rather than cynicism represents the best way forward: as he says, 'humanity is to be won by continuing to play in face of certain defeat'.[123]

Conclusion

In a 1955 interview Ralph Ellison claimed that the search for identity is 'the American theme', running from Washington Irving, Frederick Douglass and Mark Twain in the nineteenth century through post-World War II fiction. The reason why this theme has such longevity for Ellison is that 'the nature of our society is such that we are prevented from knowing who we are'.[124] This lack of self-knowledge chimes with Faulkner's claim in his 1949 Nobel Prize speech that younger writers are too ready to write with their 'glands' and not their 'heart'. Many of the writers discussed in this chapter would have argued in return that too much emphasis on 'the heart' can lead to unhelpful sentimentality: glands are necessary for a healthy bodily life and the intellect is equally important in the search for honest and clear-sighted responses to social pressures. Fiction and poetry in the

1950s might have focused on personal experience, but there were many orientations which marked out the search for identity as complex, restless and sometimes rootless. As we will see, if 'postwar culture looks more edgy and unsettling' than it at first seems, then novelists and poets in the 1950s were encountering similar pressures to those faced by other artists.[125]

Chapter 2

Drama and Performance

In a 1952 article 'Many Writers: Few Plays' for the *New York Times*, Arthur Miller proclaimed that 'our theatre has struck a seemingly endless' low point, 'a lizardic dormancy seems to be upon us; the creative mind seems to have lost its heart'.[1] Miller thought that this had been brought about by the timidity of American dramatists who were willing to toe 'the party line' rather than challenging conventions. He bemoaned the fact that theatrical rebels had given way to showmen and turned their back on 'the soul-racking, deeply unseating questions that are inwardly asked on the street, in the living room, on the subways'.[2] Miller's response derived from his unease at the conservative climate of the early decade, particularly as it paralyzed the energy and non-conformity that he believed to be at the core of the dramatist's art; as he later wrote: 'with remarkable speed conformity became the new style of the hour'.[3]

Another reason for this sense of decline was the changing status of the theatre. Broadway was still the showcase of all major productions in the early 1950s, but the area around Times Square in midtown Manhattan was not as inviting as it had been before the war. While the three major playwrights of the 1950s – Arthur Miller, Tennessee Williams and William Inge – could work on the fine line between critical approval and box office success, Broadway became the victim of cold war conservatism and 'grew more cautious in its cultural diet'.[4] The blacklists did not hit theatre as directly as the broadcasting industry and certain topics could be broached in drama that could not be in film or television. Nevertheless, safe options were often taken, most prominently with musicals which flourished on Broadway in the mid-1950s, with the writing teams of Rodgers and Hammerstein, and Lerner and Loewe, having major successes and inspiring a vogue for film musicals. This chapter will discuss the high profile of musicals, but also the ways that Broadway became the victim of its own conservatism in the 1950s with its impulse for entertainment smothering much of its creativity. This drive was fuelled by the fear that theatre-goers might be lost to television, particularly with white middle-class couples moving out of inner cities to nearby suburbs to raise families. Manhattan's theatre district was seedier than before the war, and Columbus Circle on the southwest corner of Central Park was full of slums, until the controversial urban planner Robert Moses initiated its regeneration late in the decade by designing the Lincoln Center for Performing Arts.

In fact, although recent critics look back at theatre in the mid-1950s with the sense that 'the corrupt old institutions of the business, vulgar commercial Broadway, vulgar commercial Hollywood, could not long endure in their present state', it was not until the last third of the decade that a sustained challenge to Broadway emerged.[5] Some regional companies were established (such as the Alley Theatre in Houston, Texas in 1947 and the Arena Stage in Washington DC in 1950) and black revues were thriving at Apollo Theater in Harlem, but most audiences had to wait until 1959 and 1960 to watch plays that challenged the classical three-act or five-act structure.

Arnold Aronson notes that there were two cultural impulses against mainstream theatre in the 1950s that did not find full expression until the end of the decade: the emergence of Off Broadway 'as a response to the economic restrictions and increasingly narrow repertoire of Broadway' and a series of avant-garde experiments that brought together 'trends in the visual and plastic arts, new music, Beat writing, and historical and contemporary European innovations in theatre'.[6] While Off Broadway productions often included plays by major figures such as Tennessee Williams and Eugene O'Neill it also provided a showcase for European dramatists Samuel Beckett and Eugene Ionesco and the American absurdist Edward Albee, who were all keen to transform modernist energies. And while more radical avant-garde performances were happening in small venues far away from Manhattan, such as the Black Mountain College in North Carolina, a radical company like The Living Theatre (which began in New York in 1951) shared with Off Broadway productions the desire to challenge theatrical narrowness and conservatism.

Forms of 1950s Drama

One way of periodizing American drama is to take the end of World War II as marking a new phase, with Tennessee Williams and Arthur

Miller the two prominent names to emerge in the postwar years, and Lee Strasberg and Elia Kazan influential for a generation of actors in their school of method acting. It is certainly tempting to take 1945 as a turning point, although the real shift was a couple of years later when union disputes, the presidential election of 1948, and the Hollywood blacklist were clearer indications that national insecurities had intensified. As such, 'Cold War drama' is a tag most readily associated with plays written in the late 1940s and early 1950s, even if they did not have an explicitly ideological context. The drama critic John Elsom in *Cold War Theatre* (1992) takes the cold war as the dominant horizon of American theatre and also British, Continental European and Russian drama – extending well beyond the anticommunist hysteria of the early 1950s and even beyond the death of Joseph McCarthy in 1957. The cold war is certainly an important context for Arthur Miller whose leftist sympathies are discernible through his plays, but there is a danger of taking the cold war as the only horizon of postwar drama, even for playwrights whose dramatic interests were not explicitly political.

There is also a tendency to be nostalgic for the late 1940s and early 1950s as a renaissance in American drama, a time which Thomas Adler calls 'the classic period' that 'had a lasting contribution to world drama and literature'.[7] Certainly it was a period during which Williams and Miller emerged with their first plays in 1944 and 1947 and, although Eugene O'Neill had written his most experimental work in the 1920s and 1930s, one of his most challenging plays *The Iceman Cometh* (1939) was not produced on Broadway until 1946. The opening of the Actors Studio on West 44th Street, Manhattan in October 1947 (co-founded by Elia Kazan, Cheryl Crawford and Robert Lewis) also marked a transitional moment in theatre and film acting, with two generations of actors – Marlon Brando, James Dean, Shelley Winters, Anne Bancroft, Steve McQueen, Paul Newman, Al Pacino and Warren Beatty – coached in the school of 'method acting' by the enigmatic Lee Strasberg. The discipline of 'method' – the careful control of emotions, the ability to improvise, and the public display of a private inner world – gave new intensity to acting and lent aesthetic weight to the profession.[8] Emerging out of the leftist Group Theater (co-founded by Strasberg, Crawford, and Harold Clurman in 1931) the Actors Studio put into practice the dramatic techniques of Constantin Stanislavski. That the dramaturgical thought of a famous Russian director was being used to train American actors at the height of the cold war is full of irony, particularly as Kazan was himself to come under scrutiny from HUAC in the early 1950s for his youthful communist sympathies.

However, it is easy to think of Miller, Williams and the Actors Studio as the sum total of American drama at this time. In his autobiography *Timebends* (1987), Miller challenged the tendency in the 1960s to consider the late 1940s and early 1950s as a highpoint, arguing that New York theatre had become 'rotted out with commercialized junk' with only the occasional glimmer of something more challenging.[9] Miller detected in Europe a more stimulating environment, with the intensities of war and class conflict, particularly in Britain, sparking into life European playwrights. According to Miller, only he and Williams were asking 'great questions' and striving for 'real theatre' that attacked social inertia and challenged received wisdom about morality, propriety and sexuality.[10]

The most important year for English theatre is often cited as 1956, with the emergence of 'kitchen sink drama', most notably John Osborne's *Look Back in Anger* performed by the English Stage Society at the Royal Court, London.[11] While censorship was still commonly practised in London (homosexual elements of Miller's *A View from the Bridge* (1955) had to be toned down), it is tempting to view 1956 as a year when drama was undergoing a revolution on both sides of the Atlantic, with the first glimmerings of a challenge to the hegemony of Broadway, together with the American premiere of O'Neill's late modernist work *A Long Day's Journey Into Night* (1940) which was not performed (against his wishes) on Broadway until November 1956, three years after his death. Its intense family conflict and candid references to morphine addiction and alcoholism prompted the *New York Times* to announce that at last 'American theatre [has] acquire[d] size and stature.'[12] The conventional five-act play structure had been earlier tested by Williams and Miller in experimental plays such as Williams's *Camino Real* (1953) and Miller's one-act *A Memory of Two Mondays* (1955), but the greater challenge to dramatic orthodoxy came from the emergence of African American dramatists and avant-garde performances away from the bright lights of Time Square. When Miller described *A Memory of Two Mondays* as a 'letter to that sub-culture where the sinews of the economy are rooted, that darkest Africa of our society from whose interior only the sketchiest messages ever reach our literature or our stage' he was opening the door to more radical theatrical challenges.[13]

If one view of theatre in the 1950s is of a largely apolitical cultural form, then it was also a decade of dramatic explorations of alienation and marginality. Arthur Miller is the clearest example of a political dramatist, but other plays were exploring taboo subjects of homosexuality and drug addiction, and the revival of Lillian Hellman's play *The Children's Hour* in 1952 gave a cold war spin to the original 1934 text concerning a schoolgirl spreading malicious rumours about the 'friendship' between her two female teachers. The revival of *The Children's Hour* (made into its second film incarnation in 1961) suggested that the pernicious ideological forces of the early 1950s had been long buried in the national unconscious, but during the cold war came out into the open and were given institutional weight. Hellman's leftist politics were not a secret; when she was called before HUAC in 1952 it was no surprise that she refused to name names.

As with other cultural forms considered in this book, discussing drama with exclusive reference to the cold war or tracing its linear development oversimplifies the ways in which its forms criss-crossed through the decade. For example, while musical revues were phased out in the 1950s (the Apollo Theater in Harlem was a rare venue for vibrant evenings of music, dance and comedy) musical theatre was in the ascendancy. The demise of the revue was largely down to the rise of the narrative musical which could deal better with character interaction and sustained stories than revues did with their loose vaudeville structure. Cultural parallels can be drawn between the rivalry between radio and television and between revues and musicals, but the story is more complex than that.

Gerald Bordman defines a period between 1942 and 1965, from World War II to the Vietnam War, in which the musical became a 'conscious art form'. Within this period musicals turned away from the comic forms of the 1920s and 1930s and entered a 'sober, sentimental era' dominated by 'older Broadway hands' Irving Berlin, Cole Porter, Richard Rodgers and Oscar Hammerstein II.[14] In many ways this period was a high point for musical theatre, but Bordman notes that 320 musicals premiered in these 23 years compared to 426 between 1930 and 1942, indicating that the musical was experiencing its own rivalry, particularly from film and television. Bordman also subdivides the period into two scenes: (1) the 'new seriousness' of World War II and the cold war from 1942 to 1951; and (2) a more problematic phase from 1951 to 1965 – suggesting that musical theatre was at its peak in the late 1940s with its most creative moments being Oscar and Hammerstein's *Oklahoma!* (1943) and *South Pacific* (1949).

This chapter will discuss these conflicting accounts of the development of 1950s drama by focusing on three main topics: the work of major dramatists; musical theatre; and new theatre. Mirroring the first chapter, each section is followed by a case study of a specific dramatic text to ground the broader commentary: Arthur Miller's *The Crucible* (1953); the Broadway production of *West Side Story* (1957); and Lorraine Hansberry's *A Raisin in the Sun* (1959).

The Big Three: Miller, Williams, Inge

Most critics view 1950s drama through the twin lenses of Arthur Miller and Tennessee Williams, often dubbed respectively the decade's political and poetic playwright. Both dramatists had their first success in the late 1940s – Miller with *All Our Sons* (1947) and *Death of a Salesman* (1949) and Williams with *The Glass Menagerie* (1944) and *A Streetcar Named Desire* (1947) – and they began the 1950s with a strong critical following. Modernist currents run through their plays, but also a commitment to intense forms of realism that recall the psychological interest of the early modernists and also (particularly for Miller) an echo of the social realism of the 1930s. Some critics detect in their work 'a voice for the many discontented American men and women living under the postwar settlement', but the differences between the pair were exacerbated by the fact that one was a New York urbanite and the other a Mississippi-born artist drawn to the bohemian areas of the South (New Orleans and Mexico), and that one married the symbol of Hollywood, Marilyn Monroe, in 1956 and the other became well known for his homosexuality.[15] A third figure, William Inge, should also be added to this pair: Inge's reputation has suffered in the face of Miller's and Williams's ascendancy, but his name was linked closely to both Broadway and Hollywood in the 1950s.

Inge had four major successes on Broadway, beginning with *Come Back, Little Sheba* (1949–50) and running through *Picnic* (1953), *Bus Stop* (1955) and *The Dark at the Top of the Stairs* (1957) – published collectively in 1958. He continued to work as a dramatist into the late 1960s, notably writing the screenplay for Elia Kazan's film *Splendor in the Grass* (1961), but he is best known for his quartet of 1950s plays, all of which were adapted in Hollywood between 1953 and 1960. A Midwesterner, born in Kansas, Inge divides the sensibilities of Miller and Williams, drawn to small-town and prairie locations that are informed by his personal experience. Inge was friends with Williams (although Williams later became jealous of his success); both worked with Elia Kazan; and they were particularly interested in the dramatic clash between romance and reality. Critics at the time favoured Inge's

interest in unremarkable characters whose everyday situations give
rise to personal problems such as alcoholism, sexual neurosis and adolescent insecurity; in most of his plays the moment of crisis leads to an
'acceptance of life as it is, followed [by] a willingness to face life on less
romantic terms than before'.[16]

This theme of adaptation to life's realities is the focus of his most
famous play *The Dark at the Top of the Stairs*, set near Oklahoma City
in the early 1920s and depicting the tense relationships within the
working-class Flood family. In the three-act drama Rubin and Cora
Flood face difficulties seventeen years into their marriage, problems
that are heightened by their excruciatingly shy daughter, Reenie, and
their boisterous son, Sonny, whose closeness to his mother pushes the
wedge more deeply between Rubin and Cora. The key symbol of the
play is the dark space at the top of the Flood's staircase, inaccessible 'to
windows and sunlight' and representing fears of the future for all four
family members: Sonny proclaims at the end of Act Two that his fear
of the dark stems from his sense that 'you can't see what's in front of
you. And it might be something awful'.[17] The darkness is symbolically
linked to the Jewish boy Sammy Goldenbaum, who accompanies
Reenie to a party, only later to commit suicide after experiencing racial
slurs and Reenie's small-minded rejection of him. Sammy's suicide
comes rather suddenly in Act Three; the death can be read either as a
loss of innocence or the need to be more worldly-wise to prevent self-
destructive impulses taking over. Inge's other three major plays do
not invest heavily in symbolism, but in *The Dark at the Top of the
Stairs* Sammy's suicide is a clear example of symbolic and realistic
levels interlocking.

The play is essentially a family romance about the children's fears
of growing up, but also a mother's reluctance to let go; as Cora comments to Rubin: 'I've always felt I could give them life like a present,
all wrapped in white, with every promise of happiness inside'.[18]
Rubin's neglect of his children is mirrored, to his mind, by Cora's
insensitivity to her husband's physical needs, a state of affairs which is
not reversed until the end as the pair resume traditional gender roles
when Rubin beckons Cora to the bedroom. Inge wrote the play as a
call for love and mutual respect, exemplified by Cora berating her
children early on: 'when you can't even get along with people in
your own family, how can you expect to get along with people out in
the world?'[19] The dramatic tension between the family members is
finally resolved by the reassertion of patriarchy. Cora resumes her pre-
motherly role by responding to Rubin's needs, while Sonny makes

a stand against his mother by defiantly smashing his piggy bank to fund his and Reenie's visit to the cinema.

Although Inge can be seen as a more conservative playwright than either Williams or Miller, in the mid-1960s he joined Miller in his critical appraisal of the drive on Broadway and Hollywood towards commercial entertainment rather than challenging drama. Inge's run of success continued in the 1950s when he benefited from the realization on Broadway that new drama was needed to connect with the everyday experiences of audiences. However, Inge sensed that the 'personal contribution' of drama is nearly always in tension with 'theatrical enterprise': 'commercial theatre only builds on what has been created [whereas] creative theatre brings something of life itself . . . New life doesn't always survive on Broadway. It's considered risky'.[20] That is not to say that Inge was a closet experimentalist (only *The Dark at the Top of the Stairs* could be considered mildly experimental), but to indicate that he never believed that popular and critical acclaim actually had much to do with the drama itself. It does say quite a lot about Inge as a creative writer who was suspicious that the machinery of fame serves only to erode talent.

Two elements in Inge's work find resonance in Williams's and Miller's plays: the exploration of the deeper recesses of love in the face of social pressures, and the interest in 'the little man' fighting against forces too overwhelming to entirely comprehend. What Inge achieved in his quiet domestic plays, Tennessee Williams dramatized in heightened forms giving new expression to love and desire, particularly in situations when they blur with conflicting emotions. Williams had explored three-way relationships in the 1940s (Tom-Laura-Jim in *The Glass Menagerie* and Blanche-Stella-Stanley in *A Streetcar Named Desire*) which depict passionate liaisons fraught with problems and, whereas Inge focused on everydayness, in his series of 1950s plays – *The Rose Tattoo* (1951), *Camino Real* (1953), *Cat on a Hot Tin Roof* (1955), *Suddenly Last Summer* (1958) and *Sweet Bird of Youth* (1959) – Williams examined relationships under extreme stress. Madness, homosexuality, megalomania, alcoholism, greed and spiritual crises reach a more intense pitch than in Inge, suggesting that love is always bound up with power, obsession and destructive impulses. The relationship between Brick and Maggie in *Cat on a Hot Tin Roof*, for example, is one of mutual dependency but also slow-burning recrimination and guilty accusations. The iron-control over the family of the wealthy Mississippi landowner 'Big Daddy' Pollitt is only one reason why Brick and Maggie's childless marriage is so fraught. All the characters are trapped by relationships, by sins of the past and by personal obsessions – such as Brick's guilt over the suicide of his friend Skipper (after Brick ignored Skipper's declaration of love for him) and Maggie's cat-like erotic urges – which in Brick and Maggie's case leads to a relationship that is paradoxically both loveless and deeply passionate.

Figure 2.1 Barbara Bel Geddes and Ben Gazzara in *Cat on a Hot Tin Roof*, directed by Elia Kazan. Original Broadway production (1955–6). Wisconsin Center for Film and Theater Research.

The relationship between Brick and Maggie echoes Stanley and Blanche in *A Streetcar Named Desire*, but the power differential between the pair is less stable. Barbara Bel Geddes played Maggie in the original Broadway production (directed by Elia Kazan) quite differently from the more sensuous Elizabeth Taylor in the 1958 film

Figure 2.2 Paul Newman and Elizabeth Taylor in *Cat on a Hot Tin Roof* (Richard Brooks, MGM, 1958).

version (directed by Richard Brooks), but they both brought to the character the complex mixture of assertiveness and vulnerability that characterized Williams's most interesting female roles. Whereas Inge's *Dark at the Top of the Stairs* resolves conflicts by the reassertion of patriarchy, Williams was intent in showing that patriarchal structures are often corrupt and tyrannical, as depicted by Big Daddy (played by folk singer Burl Ives) in *Cat on a Hot Tin Roof*.

Williams was preoccupied by the inner life of his characters, such as the widowed Serafina in *The Rose Tattoo*, who lionizes her dead husband only to slowly realize that he had been unfaithful to her. Serafina is simultaneously sensuous, sexually needy, maternal, jealous, neurotic and naïve, wrapped up in her 'special world', as Williams called it in 1955, 'a web of monstrous complexity . . . from the spider-mouth of [her] own singular perceptions'.[21] Williams often shuttled between oppositions that sometimes resolved themselves into dualities (believing she has conceived at the end of the play, Serafina exclaims 'two lives in the body! Two, two lives again, two!'), and at other times break apart into contradictions (Serafina is both pious and animalistic).[22] Throughout his plays and prefaces Williams strove for metaphors to describe this type of 'personal lyricism'. Sometimes this led to densely symbolic language or images that jar with each other.

The intimate world of Williams's drama and his reluctance to give support to social movements has led critics to interpret his plays as a retreat into loneliness. However, there are strong cultural politics in Williams's work and an interest in social outcasts and disenfranchised characters. Other plays, such as the allegorical *Camino Real*, explicitly attempt to subvert the social order. Set in a fascist regime in Latin America, *Camino Real* is a mixed-mode play combining elements of comedy, tragedy, realism, romance and satire. The epigraph from Dante suggests that this is a play 'where the straight way [is] lost', but this offered Williams freedom from theatrical conventions, 'something wild and unrestricted' like 'the continually dissolving and transforming images of a dream'.[23] All escape routes are perilous for the characters entrapped in *Camino Real* and potentially lead straight to death. With its cast of historical characters such as Lord Byron and figures from Miguel de Cervantes's *Don Quixote*, the play appears to be a flight from reality, but it can be reads as an allegory of a cynical decade 'when the romantic ideals of nobility, truth, valor, and honor give way to desperation'.[24]

On this reading, where Miller made historical parallels explicit in *The Crucible*, Williams's allegory was an oblique attack on censorship and intolerance towards those who do not fulfil social expectations. Williams reinforced this idea in his 1945 production notes for *The Glass Menagerie* in his claim that 'when a play employs unconventional techniques it is not, or certainly shouldn't be, trying to escape its responsibility of dealing with reality'.[25] The spatial qualities of *Camino Real* may suggest an isolated topography from which the characters cannot escape, but Kazan's 1953 production followed Williams's instructions by having the actors run in the aisles and speak directly to the spectators – although this created its own problems. The rejection of the fourth-wall conventions of Broadway was one reason that *Camino Real* failed to appeal: it played for only sixty times and many demanded their money back on the first performance in March 1953. For a playwright tempted by allegory it was safer to keep the drama oblique as Williams did in his next play *Cat on a Hot Tin Roof*, which *New York Times* critic Brooks Atkinson applauded for the 'honesty and simplicity of its craftsmanship'.[26] Whereas *Camino Real* brought too many elements together in a surrealist dreamscape, firmer direction can be found in the 'delicately wrought exercise in human communication' of *Cat on a Hot Tin Roof* (as Atkinson described it), Inge's more limited sense of domestic realism, and the quest for class identity that runs through Arthur Miller's plays.

Miller was respectful of Williams's talent as a playwright, but he thought that sometimes Williams indulged in 'verbal adornment for its own sake' and did not clearly examine the economic forces that shape a character's feeling of entrapment, frustration or inadequacy.[27] Rather than Williams's idiosyncratic inner worlds, Miller was drawn towards the 'general condition of men', which often meant his characters are representatives of a particular class or ethnic group such as Willy Loman in *Death of a Salesman* or Eddie Carbone in *A View from the Bridge*. The power of the Old South is a potent myth in Williams's plays, whereas Miller was distrustful of the past, preferring to place his characters in a near contemporary moment such as postwar Red Hook, Brooklyn, which he describes as 'the gullet of New York swallowing the tonnage of the world'.[28] The choric figure Alfieri, the middle-aged lawyer in *A View from the Bridge*, emphasizes the ambit of Miller's play-world: Alfieri introduces the audience to squalid neighbourhoods, 'the petty troubles of the poor', and characters that lack 'elegance' and 'glamour'. Finding tragic potential in everyday situations, Miller found it possible to adapt classical dramatic structure to ordinary life. In Eddie Carbone, for example, Miller creates a repellent figure 'not quite admissible into the human family', even though in the two-act version of the play from 1956, Carbone is nevertheless able to sacrifice himself for greater ends.[29]

Miller believed that profound dramatic realism can only be generated through human passion and he sought ways of preventing his audience from being satisfied with 'the covering of safety' that often masquerades as reality. Miller's primary task was to challenge any system that purported to be natural, necessary or absolute. Whereas he sometimes criticized Williams for indulging in flights of romantic fancy, Miller's conviction (as expressed in 1958) was that the 'will of man' – 'an innate value, an innate will' – survives because 'however closely he is measured and systematically accounted for' a character like Eddie Carbone is 'more than the sum of his stimuli and is unpredictable beyond a certain point'.[30] It is this unpredictability of human behaviour that interested Miller and led him to shift his focus in the early 1950s from the postwar world to a dramatic moment in early American history.

The Crucible (1953)

Miller's four-act play *The Crucible* stands as the most distinctive dramatic response to cold war censorship and anticommunist hysteria. It does so by establishing parallels between the early 1950s and the Salem Witch Trials of 1692. Nathaniel Hawthorne had used Puritan New England a century earlier in his novel *The Scarlet Letter* (1850) as a means to examine religious and social impediments to a creative life, and Miller returned to seventeenth-century Massachusetts as 'a petri dish', as he called it, 'a sort of embalmed stasis with its principal forces caught in stillness'.[31] He carried out extensive research into the history of Salem to ensure that the play was historically accurate, but focused on the negative elements of Puritanism, depicting Salem Puritans as 'a sect of fanatics' as likely to 'cry witch against one's neighbour and feel perfectly justified in the bargain'.[32]

The play opened at the Martin Beck Theatre in New York on 22 January 1953 and ran for 197 performances, closing on 11 July. Although it won Antoinette Perry and Donaldson awards in 1953, audiences and reviewers responded harshly, with only one early review, by Brooks Atkinson for the *New York Times*, offering a more positive inflection of the general criticism that the characters were wooden and Miller's play was a fall from grace after the success of *Death of a Salesman*. More critically, Walter Kerr wrote in the *New York Herald Tribune* that it was a 'mechanical parable' that appeals only to the head and not the heart, with Miller's characters little more than 'props to his theme'.[33] There is some truth that the theme of social intolerance is privileged over character study, but the negative

responses to the play seem to stem from its topicality and the uncomfortable parallels it draws between past and present.

In between the two plays Miller had adapted Henrik Ibsen's *An Enemy
of the People* in 1950, which rehearsed the way in which *The Crucible* deals
with the persecution of liberally minded characters by social conservatism.
In Ibsen's play the respectable Dr Stockman is dubbed 'the enemy of the
people' because he argues that the polluted town baths should be shut
down, while in *The Crucible* it is the honest farmer John Proctor who makes
a stand against the accusations of witchcraft which spread like wildfire
through Salem.

So worried was Miller that very few public figures were responding
positively to the 'knuckleheadness of McCarthyism' (as Miller called it),
that he devised *The Crucible* as an extended allegory of what happens to
an ordinary farmer when forced to compromise his values in the face of
intransigent social forces.[34] Miller discussed his intentions in *The Crucible*
at length, arguing that McCarthyism was the most obvious sign of an
'official piety' that had emerged at the end of the 1940s with the intent of
paralyzing free thought.[35] The historical parallels between communist
hysteria and the Puritan witch hunts are all but explicit in the opening
description of 'prevailing theocracy', the function of which is 'to prevent
any kind of disunity that might open it to destruction by material and ideological enemies'. Miller elaborated on this point later in life, claiming that
the play was 'more than a political metaphor, more than a moral tale' in its
exploration of 'the awesome evidence of the power of the inflamed human
imagination' and 'the tragedy of heroic resistance to a society possessed
to the point of ruin'.[36] His interest in 'heroic resistance' is dramatized
through the figure of John Proctor. Previously a 'sinner' in his brief affair
with Abigail Williams, Proctor's integrity and honesty is tested to breaking
point by a religious and legal system more intent on collecting the names
of those accused of being in league with the devil than on guaranteeing
social justice.

Proctor's family is positioned squarely between the hysteria of the girls
that infects the whole village and the iron law of the court that prohibits
ambiguity and personal freedom. In one of the central statements of the
play, Deputy-Governor Danforth proclaims: 'a person is either with this
court or he must be counted against it, there be no road between. This is a
sharp time, now, a precise time – we live no longer in the dusky afternoon
when evil mixed itself with good and befuddled the world'.[37] Not only does
the play demonstrate that the befuddlement of the world is actually
exacerbated by a corrupt theocracy, but also that human compassion and
solidarity have been banished in the name of precision. Proctor's complexity is a counterpoint to the narrow logic of the court. He is a flawed man
but tries to lead a good life; he is 'somewhat bewildered' (as his wife
Elizabeth berates him); he fails to recite all Ten Commandments (he
'forgets' adultery); and he cannot decide what the right course of action is
in the court – to deny his affair with Abigail to protect his family or to tell
the truth at the risk of fuelling the hysterical accusations.

Deciding to tell the truth of his affair, Proctor is jailed at the end of Act Three in the face of mounting hysteria. The play reaches its climax soon after, when Proctor is asked to declare his allegiance with the devil – a charade he is willing to play along with to prevent the accusations spreading further. He is also nearly coerced into testifying that he saw other Salemites in league 'with the Devil'; at the last, though, he refuses, claiming 'I speak my own sins; I cannot judge another.'[38] On being asked to sign his name to the declaration Proctor refuses; he then relents, but just before Danforth can take away the signed declaration, Proctor snatches it back and tears it up, exclaiming that the officials may have taken his soul but he will retain his name so that his family will not be cursed throughout history. At the close of the play Proctor sacrifices his own life, but retains his family name and 'some shred of goodness', as he describes it in his final speech.[39]

Despite the intensity of the last scene, there is a textual quality to *The Crucible* that pushes it closer to a play to be read rather than performed. This is signalled by the long descriptive passages that open many of the scenes and the narrative parallels between the contemporary climate and historical play-world. Ironically, given the cold war context and Miller's emphasis on human passions, *The Crucible* can be seen as a 'cold' play that, as Walter Kerr argued in 1953, engages with the intellect rather than the heart. Unsurprisingly, Miller has argued against this criticism, claiming that the play is infused with a dramatic 'heat', not as a cathartic expending of emotion, but in its attempt to find a wider field of vision than most other plays of the time.

This cold/hot polarity often arises in discussions of *The Crucible*, and contributed to Miller's decision to heat up the play in his 1996 screen adaptation, directed by Nicholas Hytner, starring Daniel Day Lewis as Proctor and Winona Ryder as Abigail. Critics even responded to the fifty-year revival by British director Richard Eyre in 2002 at the Virginia Theater on Broadway in a similar way to the original production. Eyre saw Proctor as a version of Miller (based on Miller's refusal to name names at his HUAC subpoena in 1956), but some critics argued that Eyre's revival was too mannered and was rescued only by the set and sound design – the very elements that redeemed the 1953 production for Walter Kerr – while other critics praised Eyre's production, particularly the 'sizzling' performances and 'transfixing heat' of Liam Neeson as Proctor and Laura Linney as Elizabeth.

Musical Theatre

The 1950s was undoubtedly one of the high points for the Broadway musical, but also a time when other forms of music-based performance flourished that had an impact on experimental practices in the 1960s. Musical theatre by definition is a mixed art form that grew out of vaudeville and popular performance in the US, but also incorporates elements of classical music, opera and ballet. This is one of the reasons that musical theatre historically has attracted middle-class audiences that find classical theatre highbrow and the vaudeville too working class. The libretto provides a loose plot structure, without the thematic and symbolic complexity of much straight theatre. This also explains why the 1920s and 1950s were high points for musicals, when the middle classes were looking for serious entertainment without the theatrical intensity of O'Neill or Williams. It is also easy to argue that musical theatre is often escapist, which explains its popularity during the Depression and World War II. There are examples of 1950s musicals which address contemporary issues – *Call Me Madam* (1950) deals light-heartedly with foreign policy and electoral politics, *The Pajama Game* (1954) engages with working practices, and *West Side Story* (1957) explores the dynamics of urban gang culture – but many of the decade's major commercial shows contained within them more than an element of escapism, transporting the audience into other times and places, where heightened emotions reign and social conflicts can be resolved through the transcendent power of love.

Such escapism was a sign that Broadway musicals were thoroughly commercialized in the 1950s. This did not stop audiences flocking to see them, particularly in the first two years of the decade, but by 1952, as Gerald Bordman estimates, musical theatre had sunk 'to an abysmal state'.[40] Only nine new musicals were produced during 1951–2, most of which resorted to formulae. But Bordman also notes that the decade revealed a pattern of 'feast and famine' on Broadway, with bad years often followed by successful ones. The following year, for example, saw success with *South Pacific*, *Guys and Dolls* and *Pal Joey* (all enjoying long runs) as well as new musicals such as *Wonderful Town* and *Can-Can*, in between some flops.

A number of musicals stand out in the decade. Book-ended by Rodgers and Hammerstein's *The King and I* (1951) and *The Sound of Music* (1959), the decade also saw the revival of Bertolt Brecht and Kurt Weill's *The Threepenny Opera* and the adaptation of *Peter Pan* (both 1954), followed by the cold war musical *Silk Stockings* (1955), Leonard Bernstein's operetta *Candide* and the phenomenally popular *My Fair Lady* (1956), the Caribbean-based musical *Jamaica* (1957), and the burlesque *Gypsy* (1959). One reason why the decade is often viewed as the heyday of musical theatre is that Hollywood spin-offs became standard fare, often integrating one or more star actors into the theatrical cast, while major recording companies such as CBS were

investing large sums in shows such as *My Fair Lady*. Musical films
were big business, with MGM particularly adept in linking old and
new stars such as Fred Astaire and Cyd Charisse in *The Band Wagon*
(1953) and *Silk Stockings* (1957) and Ethel Merman and Donald
O'Connor in *Call Me Madam* (1953), while young teams such as
Gene Kelly and Debbie Reynolds had success with *Singin' in the
Rain* (1952).[41]

However, Broadway musicals were not all about commerce or
providing material for the film industry, as old and new writing
teams advanced the cause of musical theatre as a serious cultural
form. Oscar Hammerstein II and Richard Rodgers were the most
successful musical pairing to emerge in the 1940s, with the successes
of *Oklahoma!* (1943), *Carousel* (1945) and *South Pacific* (1949) propelling the musical away from its comic roots into a mode that contained elements of naturalistic and tragic theatre. Rodgers had begun
his Broadway career in the 1920s writing music with Lorenz Hart,
moving to work with Hammerstein in 1943 on *Oklahoma!*, by which
time Hart had become a chronic alcoholic. Whereas Rodgers and Hart
tended to write in comic mode, Rodgers and Hammerstein's work was
more serious, sentimental and theatrical, a shift which indicates where
musicals were heading in the 1940s. After the major successes of the
1940s, the pair entered the new decade on the crest of a wave, and
wrote in the *New York Times* about their allergy to tried and tested
formulae when writing new musicals.[42] Despite this declaration from
1951, critics have argued that Hammerstein's librettos became more
predictable following the war and after *Oklahoma!* his plotting
became very episodic, with narrative development subordinated to
musical spectacle.

Despite these reservations, many critics have praised Rodgers and
Hammerstein's first big hit of the 1950s, *The King and I*, for dealing
'forthrightly with the problem of combining dramatic and musical
theatre'.[43] Following the success of the exotic island location of *South
Pacific* two years earlier, *The King and I* is set in Siam in the mid-
nineteenth century. The show was a rarity in being adapted from a
novel, Margaret Landon's *Anna and the King of Siam* (1946), which
had been made into a film with the same title, also in 1946. The story
concerns the appointment of Anna Leonowens, the widow of a British
Army officer, as governess for the King of Siam's children. Rodgers
and Hammerstein were drawn to the narrative because they thought
that 'stories of the East have seldom reached the Western stage with
any semblance of reality', while the diary format of Landon's novel

meant that they were forced to attend closely to details rather than grand lavish gestures.[44] The show deals interestingly with the clash between two characters with very different ideologies, social positions and cultural values that 'indulge themselves only in oblique expressions of their feelings for each other'. *The King and I* focuses on the respect and love that grows steadily (although is rarely expressed) between Anna and the King, played by Gertrude Lawrence and Yul Brynner when it opened at St James Theater on 29 March 1951, where it ran for three years (the first year with Lawrence before her death) and for 1,246 performances.

Rodgers and Hammerstein had to change their priorities slightly to write the play for Gertrude Lawrence, and worried that their creative freedom might have to be sacrificed. But critic David Lewis praises *The King and I* for being 'one of the two or three best integrated musicals ever mounted on a New York stage', primarily because the dramatic and musical elements work together seamlessly without the episodic pattern of some musicals.[45] Other critics have commented that whereas the Rodgers and Hammerstein shows from the 1940s had been musically challenging, the limited singing abilities of Lawrence and Brynner meant that much of the music for *The King and I* was 'vocally truncated', with the lyrics having more of a dramatic function compared to the grand spectacles of *Oklahoma!* and *Carousel.*[46] The dancing was also more limited than previously, but the strengths lay in the evocative eastern setting, the costumes, scenery and some of Jerome Robbins's choreography, with the King's fourteen children and their ensemble song 'March of the Siamese Children' paving the way for the von Trapp family in *The Sound of Music* at the end of the decade. The show is realistic in exploring the exercise of power in relationships and also succeeds in integrating tragic elements: the cruel King orders the death of his concubine Tuptim and her Burmese lover when he learns of their affair, but Anna's influence tempers his cruelty to such an extent that when he dies Anna promises to remain to look after his eldest son, hoping that this rule will not be as despotic.

The question has to be asked: why open a show dealing with East–West relationships at the height of the Korean War, particularly when its historical setting is almost a century removed from the present? Unlike some of the grand film epics of the early 1950s, there is little obvious allegorical matter, except for the general theme that western good sense can temper eastern despotism and the shifting geopolitics of ancient and modern world maps that Anna and the King show to the royal children (Siam is the enlarged centre of the world on

Figure 2.3 Gertrude Lawrence and Yul Brynner in *The King and I*. Original Broadway production (1951–4). Photograph by Vandamm. Wisconsin Center for Film and Theater Research.

the King's map). It may just be historical coincidence, but the inset ballet in which Tuptim introduces an easternized production of *Uncle Tom's Cabin* is very suggestive and the emphasis on the supremacy of western science is obvious enough.

This has led critics to examine the intertwining of gender and colonial discourses in the 1951 play and 1956 film. Caren Kaplan, for example, discusses the manner in which national concerns are displaced onto the Siamese drama, particularly parallels between American slavery and Asian concubinage. Kaplan argues that Tuptim's tragic story is played out as a 'primary allegory for the story of cross-cultural contact'; Tuptim is portrayed as a liminal character who neither fits in with the King's harem mentality nor Anna's role as 'western liberator' and therefore must be sacrificed to secure Anna's freedom.[47] Although these resonances were lost on reviewers at the time, it is striking that the focus of *The King and I* is upon the difficulties of communicating across cultures. It is also possible to read the play as a broadly liberal attempt to break down boundaries between the East and West: for all of the King's absolutism and his emphasis on modern science he is often uncertain and left in a state of 'puzzlement' as his musical soliloquy stresses.

It was no surprise that Twentieth Century-Fox turned to the musical in 1956 to extend its interest in Oscar and Hammerstein's back catalogue of 1940s musicals. Brynner retained the role of the King for the film and was partnered by Deborah Kerr, who made Anna even more arch and inflexible than in the Broadway performances (Kerr's songs were dubbed for the film). Reviewers such as Brooks Atkinson were full of praise for the 'fine and touching drama'; only later did younger critics like the composer and lyricist Stephen Sondheim speak out against the old-fashioned qualities of *The King and I*, arguing that it failed to do justice to historical and geographic specifics.[48]

Many critics see *The King and I* as Rodgers and Hammerstein's last great musical, but their Broadway career continued up to Hammerstein's death in 1960. Their collaborations in the 1950s were uneven, though, including *Me and Juliet* (1953), *Pipe Dream* (1955) and *Flower Drum Song* (1958), the latter which was the most successful of the three with 600 performances. As Martin Gottfried comments, when it came to their last musical together, *The Sound of Music*, the pair were working from reflex and the product is 'entirely devoid of artistic merit' despite being a major Broadway success with 1,443 performances and a movie sensation in 1962.[49] In reality the balance of power on Broadway had begun to shift by the middle of the decade, and it was a more dynamic type of musical that symbolized this shift.

West Side Story (1957)

Adapted from Shakespeare's *Romeo and Juliet* to the contemporary urban setting of Manhattan, *West Side Story* stands as one of the pinnacles of Broadway musical theatre. It was also an example of musicals pushing the conventional boundaries that remained in evidence in Rodgers and Hammerstein productions in the 1950s. The idea derived from three sources: composer Leonard Bernstein, author Arthur Laurents, and choreographer Jerome Robbins, to which the young lyricist Stephen Sondheim was later added. Bernstein and Robbins conceived the musical originally as 'East Side Story' in which a battle was fought 'between Jewish and Italian or Irish gangs over a budding romance between the young boy and girl in two of the families'.[50] But the idea changed, primarily because the social mobility of New York Jews after the war was in tension with the story, and instead it was projected onto two rival Puerto Rican gangs: the Sharks and the Jets. Like many of the most interesting cultural products of the decade, *West Side Story* was a hybrid product which, in the words of Bernstein, attempted 'to tread the fine line between opera and Broadway, between realism and poetry, ballet and "just dancing", abstract and representational'.[51] Bernstein had attempted this balancing act the previous year with his comic operetta of Voltaire's *Candide*, but the combination was more organic in *West Side Story* with classical and contemporary elements complementing each other.

The story falls into two acts. Act One depicts Tony (Larry Kert) trying to make a new respectable life for himself away from his former gang the Jets. Despite his resolve, Tony is drawn back to the gang, where he meets Maria (Carol Lawrence), the sister of Bernardo (Ken Le Roy), leader of the rival gang the Sharks. A gang rumble leads to the death of Jets leader Riff (Mickey Calin) and in vengeance Tony kills Bernardo to leave two dead bodies on stage as Act One closes. The tragic trajectory is much clearer in the Act Two, which is full of double-crossings as Tony and Maria try vainly to flee the city together. Temporarily separated, Tony is informed that Maria is dead and he wildly runs out into the street only to be shot down by Chico, a Shark that the former leader Bernardo had intended Maria to marry. The play ends with Maria singing 'somewhere there's a place for us' over the dead body of Tony as the Jets and Sharks agree that the bloodbath cannot continue.

Taking its lead from *Romeo and Juliet*, the plot is less interesting than Bernstein and Sondheim's musical partnership and Jerome Robbins' choreography, which blends ballet with contemporary dance within the context of the two gangs. The songs fall into three categories: gang songs such as 'Cool' that transforms juvenile delinquency into urban energy and 'America' which deals with the assimilation of Puerto Ricans; comic songs such as 'Gee, Officer Krupke' sung by The Jets; and love songs between Tony and Maria such as the balladic 'Maria' and the elegiac 'Somewhere'.

West Side Story deliberately avoided using star actors, but not so the film version which was released in 1961, directed by Robert Wise and Jerome Robbins, and featuring Richard Beymer as Tony and Natalie Wood as Maria (Wood's singing was dubbed). All the gang members were younger than thirty and Anita (Bernardo's sister) played by Chita Rivera, a Hispanic actress, was retained for the film. The portrayal of Puerto Ricans is one of the most interesting aspects, given that there was a major influx into the city in the early 1950s. Poet Langston Hughes commented in 1953 that many New Yorkers were complaining that Puerto Ricans were exacerbating the 'terrible housing problems' in areas around Columbus Circle, but the reality was that many were living in slums 'ten to a room'.[52] While the musical was very far from a sociological tract on urban conditions, by using actors like Chita Rivera it was attuned to the changing ethnic cityscape of Manhattan – the slum area of Columbus Circle disappeared at the end of the decade in a move to regenerate the area.

Following some regional performances, *West Side Story* premiered at the National Theater in Washington DC and then moved to the Winter

Garden on Broadway on 26 September 1957 to acclaim by both audiences and press, where it ran for 732 performances and over 1,000 performances in London. The musical also found eager audiences in Continental Europe and Australia and was revived on Broadway in 1968. Writing about the first run on Broadway, Brooks Atkinson proclaimed that through *West Side Story* the musical had not only matured but had rescued beauty and tragedy out of the mediocre fare that had dominated Broadway in 1956. Some publications such as *Time* thought the show clichéd; some considered the portrayal of Puerto Ricans and lyrical references to Hispanic culture problematic; and others thought that it glorified teenage delinquency and gang fighting. Nevertheless most critics agreed that *West Side Story* represents a high point in 1950s musical theatre, while Ethan Mordden notes that it has a liminal space in the history of the musical, seen by some as the 'culmination of an era' and by others ushering in a new phase on Broadway.[53]

Figure 2.4 Bernado (Ken Le Roy, left) and Riff (Mickey Calin) fight during the rumble in *West Side Story*. Original Broadway production (1957–9). Wisconsin Center for Film and Theater Research.

New Theatre

Towards the end of the decade there was a general shift in theatrical style from naturalistic drama to more experimental forms in which standard play structures were either challenged or abandoned. Many of these innovative styles were not thought suitable for Broadway, particularly as they did not conform to conventional three- or five-act structures. With a nod to the conservatism of Broadway, William Inge commented in 1958 that 'you can't get anyone on Broadway interested in one-acts'.[54] But the end of the decade saw some interesting new talents with a social conscience emerging both on and off Broadway. Writing at the end of the 1960s, Michael Rutenberg linked this new awareness of dramatic possibility to the launch of Sputnik in 1957 (the same year as *West Side Story* premiered) and a renewed social commitment that had been scarce in mid-decade theatre.

Drama critic Richard Kostelantz identified in the late 1950s a shift towards what he calls a 'theatre of mixed-means' in which 'new mixtures' were appearing and dramatic space was liberated from the fourth-wall convention to become more fluid and dynamic.[55] The indeterminacy that composer John Cage had been exploring in his music and the 'total art' that Allan Kaprow had called for in 1958 ('as open and fluid as the shapes of our everyday experience') were starting to have an impact on performance modes, as was the mixed mode that Langston Hughes had identified as early as 1951 in African American culture: 'conflicting changes, sudden nuances, sharp and impudent interjections, broken rhythms'.[56] Although Kaprow's Happenings and the avant-garde performance of Fluxus artists did not come to the fore until the 1960s (see Chapter 5), the emergence of a playwright like Edward Albee at the end of the 1950s was a sign of future trends, in which questions were posed about the subject matter of American drama. As Michael Rutenberg argues, Albee's plays 'unflinchingly reveal the pustulous sores of a society plagued with social ills'.[57]

Albee had been encouraged to write drama by the playwright Thornton Wilder in the early 1950s when he was concentrating on poetry. Stimulated by the European Theatre of the Absurd practised in France by Samuel Beckett, Eugene Ionesco and Jean Genet, Albee wrote his first one-act play *The Zoo Story* in 1958 at the age of thirty. Although the play is set in Central Park and involves a prolonged exchange between two New Yorkers, given Albee's European influences it was fitting that the play was premiered at the Schiller Theatre in Berlin on 28 September 1959 alongside Beckett's *Krapp's Last Tape* (it must have been bizarre for Albee to witness as the production was in German, a language he did not speak). By the time *The Zoo Story* reached New York in an Off Broadway production in January 1960, the play had a cult reputation and was offering a challenge to the 'lazy public' which Albee blamed for creating 'slothful and irresponsible theatre' on Broadway.[58]

Although the Theatre of the Absurd had a prominent place in continental drama as an apt response to war-torn Europe, Albee pioneered a version of it in the United States to provoke middle-class theatre audiences to 'face up to the human condition as it really is'.[59] Martin Esslin was to provide the clearest expression of this dramatic mode in his groundbreaking study *The Theatre of the Absurd* from 1961. Esslin focused primarily on European drama but credited Albee's second play *The American Dream* (1961) as the most distinctive example of absurdist American drama, although other critics argued that Albee's early plays 'retreat from the full implications of the absurd' because they contain identifiable themes and meanings.[60]

Albee himself was critical of his early plays (calling them 'novice work'), but his interest was in portraying characters as abstractions, placing them in realistic situations that fray at the edges as the action unfolds.[61] In this mode *The Zoo Story* involves an exchange between Peter and Jerry, men of similar ages (in their early forties and late thirties), sitting on two Central Park benches on Sunday afternoon. Jerry disrupts Peter's peaceful sojourn with a set of seemingly random remarks about his visit to the New York Zoo. Although Peter tries to ignore Jerry without seeming rude, he is made increasingly uncomfortable by Jerry's prying into his family life and his rather bizarre comments about animals, particularly a long monologue about his landlady's dog. Not only does Jerry disturb Peter, but he also introduces uncomfortable subjects – violence, homosexuality and bestiality – into his bourgeois world (Peter is an executive with two daughters, two parakeets and two TV sets), challenging his belief system as well as the middle-class affluence of theatre audiences.

Jerry never makes his intentions clear, but juxtaposes Peter's family circle with his own life as 'a permanent transient' and then goes on to insult Peter, calling him 'slow-witted', an 'imbecile' and a 'vegetable'.[62] The fractured conversation soon leads into a verbal tussle for Peter's bench, in which Jerry deliberately enrages Peter and provokes him to fight with knives. Albee thought that it was important that no actual contact happens before the knife scene, because the gulf between the two characters is intensified by their physical proximity on the bench.[63] Peter's senses are all disorientated – he does not know whether to call the police or run away – and he picks up Jerry's knife moments before Jerry lunges and deliberately impales himself on it. Immediately the mood changes: Jerry thanks Peter using religious language ('I came unto you . . . and you have comforted me. Dear Peter'), but also judges Peter ('You've been dis-

Figure 2.5 Mark Richman and William Daniels in *The Zoo Story*, Provincetown Playhouse (14 January 1960). Photograph by Edward Judice. Wisconsin Center for Film and Theater Research.

possessed. You've lost your bench . . . You're an animal too'), before exonerating him by cleaning Peter's fingerprints off the knife.[64] However, the play ends with Peter not knowing what to do: he staggers, retreats, hesitates and eventually runs off stage uttering a 'pitiful howl' as Jerry dies.[65]

The American Dream and Albee's signature play *Who's Afraid of Virginia Woolf?* (1962) follow a similar mode to *The Zoo Story*: characters' intentions are not made clear, thoughts and actions are disjointed, and loneliness and the inability to communicate divides characters from one another even more intensely than in Tennessee Williams's drama. But these two plays deal more explicitly with themes of national decline, whereas the absurdism of *The Zoo Story* has a universal ambit. It introduces the classical theme of honour, but twists it into something absurd (the honour of fighting for a park bench when there are other benches to sit on) before re-engaging in the high tragic theatre of the individual attempting to combat uncontrollable forces.[66] The play includes religious language but in an uncanny way that disturbs more than it pacifies. In drawing from classical and biblical elements within the naturalistic setting of Central Park, together with disjointed conversation and a minimalist set, *The Zoo Story* is presented as a mixed-mode play, displaying the existential themes of the Theatre of the Absurd, but also foreshadowing postmodern drama with its flat surfaces and layering of performance styles.[67]

Albee's plays gave new outward form to the fugitive internal worlds of Tennessee Williams's drama, linking with other Off Broadway productions in 1959 such as the Beat writer Jack Gelber's *The Connection* (dealing candidly with drug addicts), but he was not alone in marking new theatrical trends in the late 1950s.

African American theatre had a patchy history since the flowering of black cultural forms in Harlem in the late 1920s and 1930s. There had been around forty black theatres in the Northeast in the 1940s, but this had been reduced to two by 1952: Apollo Theater in New York and Howard Theater in Washington DC. The Apollo had taken over from the Lafayette Theater in 1935 as the premier venue for black performance in New York, combining music, comedy and light drama, and in 1953 it appointed a permanent band leader, Reuben Phillips. Outside of Harlem, cities such as Cleveland, Ohio could only offer black venues in small night clubs in the early decade, until local DJ Alan Freed realized that there was a new taste for rhythm and blues music that crossed the racial communities of Cleveland (see Chapter 3).[68]

Langston Hughes was very excited by the vibrancy of black drama in the early 1950s but the reality was far from promising: black repertory companies were few and far between, audience segregation was common (even the National Theater in Washington DC had segregated audiences) and there were hardly any black actors, stage managers, authors, composers, directors or stagehands on Broadway.[69] Whereas the 1940s had seen formal integration of cast and crews, institutional segregation in the theatre industry was very common in the 1950s: the Stagehands Union was not integrated until 1955 and 'integration showcases' for combating employment inequities only began to emerge late in the decade.[70] When black stars did emerge they were usually better known for their musical talents, such as Lena Horne, Harry Belafonte and Sammy Davis Jr, while serious black actors were hardly ever considered for traditionally white roles until the early 1960s.

However, Harlem was one place aspiring black writers and actors could venture for developing their careers. Black comedians Nipsey Russell and Timmie Rogers thrived at the Apollo, as did singers Eartha Kitt and Johnny Mathis, while the *Live at the Apollo* programmes opened up revues to a television audience in the mid-1950s. Two important committees were formed in Harlem in the late 1940s that were to lay the foundation for the flowering of black drama a decade later: the Committee for the Negro in the Arts formed an alliance with the Council on Harlem Theatres in 1950 as an organized forum for black dramatic productions. This alliance helped young black dramatists such as William Branch to find a venue for two early plays. Branch's first play was *A Medal for Willie* (1951), in which the parents of a young black soldier who had died in World War II are presented ceremonially with an award for his bravery. The play explores the theme of personal loss, but also the intolerance and bigotry among both whites and blacks in a southern community. His second play *In Splendid Error* (1954) looks back to the eve of the Civil War, and was even more daring in exploring the rift that arose between abolitionists Frederick Douglass and John Brown just before Brown made his famous raid on Harpers Ferry in 1859.

Both of Branch's plays offered challenging subject matter and received strong reviews in the *New York Times*, although their unusual dramatic structure was criticized, as well as the difficulty of recreating historical incidents accurately on stage. Branch had observed the hounding of the black actor Canada Lee for being a communist fellow traveller in 1949 and, like Arthur Miller in *The Crucible*, he was searching *In Splendid Failure* for a way of examining what he felt was a historical precedent to the political climate of the early 1950s. 'Like [Frederick] Douglass', he claimed, 'I found it hard to discard the ingrained belief that change could somehow take place without the necessity of outright overthrow of the government'. If theatre was not quite an agent of revolution for Branch, then it provided a means for exploring the cultural energies that nourish radical social movements: 'I believed then, and believe now, that society needs both its fiery souls [Brown] and its more reasoned thinkers [Douglass], both its id and its super-ego'.[71]

Another important Harlem organization was the American Negro Theatre, which was formed in a basement as a small amateur theatre group at the end of the 1930s, and moved to a larger performance space in 1946 to help in its production of plays. The group established a theatre school for black actors, attracting Harry Belafonte, Ruby Dee and a sixteen-year-old Sidney Poitier after his spell in the US Army. Poitier's early days with the theatre were anything but auspicious: he failed his first audition and made very hesitant progress with his acting. His lucky break came as understudy to Belafonte for the lead role of *Days of Our Youth* when Belafonte was taken ill. Poitier was talent-spotted during the run of *Days of Our Youth*, but stayed with the American Negro Theatre for three years, starring in *Anna Lucasta* when it toured in 1944. After an unsuccessful attempt to find a company to produce *Anna Lucasta* on Broadway, the writer Philip Yordan changed the ethnicity of the Lucasta family from Polish American to African American in a challenging play which deals candidly with prostitution, class conflict and the psychodynamics of an aspiring middle-class family. Such was its success on tour that Columbia filmed *Anna Lucasta* in 1949, but not before changing the racial dynamics once again, with white actress Paulette Goddard starring as Anna. However, mainly due to its theatrical success among African American audiences, *Anna Lucasta* was filmed for the second time in 1959 with black central characters played by Eartha Kitt and Sammy Davis Jr.

Although the film was not well received, the remaking of *Anna Lucasta* was particularly important for marking a moment of possibility for black performance. Whereas Harlem in the 1920s and 1930s had provided limited opportunities for creative women (except for the odd exception like Zora Neale Hurston and Nella Larson), in the 1950s it was a magnet not just for female singers, but also for progressive female writers such as Alice Childress and Lorraine Hansberry.

The American Negro Theatre welcomed Childress as an actor and nurtured her talents as a writer of Off Broadway plays such as *Trouble in Mind* (1955), about black actors working on an anti-lynching play under a racist white director. Childress was the first African American woman to have a play professionally produced in New York in 1956, with her 1952 musical play about the black struggle, *Gold Through the Trees*. However, her success was limited: institutional pressures made advancing a dramatic career difficult for women – especially black women – and some of her drama, including *Trouble in Mind*, missed out on Broadway. Although she was keen to find public outlets for amplifying her interracial themes, these institutional pressures were a major reason why Childress turned to writing fiction.[72] It was left to a younger black dramatist,

Lorraine Hansberry (who wrote a critical review of *Gold Through the Trees*), to lead the way forward for women playwrights in the late 1950s and to open the door for the Black Arts Movement of the early 1960s.

A Raisin in the Sun (1959)

If Arthur Miller was the foremost ethical playwright of the 1950s and Tennessee Williams the decade's poetic playwright, Lorraine Hansberry has a strong claim to being its most important political dramatist. She wrote only one play in the 1950s, *A Raisin in the Sun*, and saw only one other performed, *The Sign in Sidney Brustein's Window*. But, before her premature death from cancer in 1964 (at the age of thirty-four), she did more than any other dramatist to pave the way for the Black Theater Movement. *A Raisin in the Sun* is often taught in high schools, mainly because it reflects the social aspirations of the postwar nation in its portrayal of the Younger family and their desire to move into a more affluent neighbourhood of Chicago. On this level the play invites comparison with *Death of a Salesman*, with Hansberry herself detecting similarities between Miller's Willy Loman and her protagonist Walter Lee Younger, noting that they share 'the acute awareness that something is obstructing some abstract progress that they feel they should be making; that something is in the way of their 'ascendancy'', but it does not occur to either of them to 'question the nature of this desired "ascendency"'.[73] While it is possible to interpret the play as a racial inflection of the American Dream, Hansberry was more interested in the inability of most individuals to clearly perceive the 'something' that shapes social aspiration. Whereas Miller's Willy Loman – the 'last great hero in American drama' as Hansberry calls him – is an isolated figure, the Younger family relationships reveal a more complex series of 'somethings' that shape their lives.[74]

It is not always beneficial to look to a writer's biography to explain their fiction, but the subject-matter of *A Raisin in the Sun* is closely bound up with Hansberry's own childhood in racially segregated Chicago, where she suffered prejudice at school and within the largely white district where her family moved in 1938 when she was eight. Such was the resentment among white neighbours that her father, Carl Hansberry (a migrant from Mississippi), took the grievance to the Supreme Court in 1940; he won the case, but this did not prevent neighbourhood hostility. Lorraine's own political identity was directly shaped by her father's legal stand, as well as his forthright support of the NAACP and Carl's connections to composer Duke Ellington and athlete Jesse Owens. After studying literature, drama and painting at university, Hansberry became firmly committed to left-wing causes: she was made President of the student organization Young Progressives of America in 1949; in 1950 she began writing for Paul

Robeson's magazine *Freedom* (associate editor by 1952); and she fought for local causes in pre-civil rights Harlem.

Her writing career began as a student, but she moved from short stories to drafting the play *A Raisin in the Sun* in 1956, which detailed a similar experience to her own growing up in Chicago. That she saw herself as part of a politicized black community is evident in the play's title, which she took from a poem by Langston Hughes, 'Harlem' (1951). Hughes's poem answers the question 'What happens to a dream deferred?' by posing a further series of questions: 'Does it dry up / Like a raisin in the sun? / Or fester like a sore . . . / Does it stink like rotten meat? . . . / Or does it explode?' Hansberry took this theme of the consequences of deferred dreams, but also works it into the form of her three-act play, which is precisely about the deferral and frustration of aspirations, but also about possibility.

In the play the Younger family wish to move from their small oppressive Southside apartment into a more affluent neighbourhood. Act One revolves around a $10,000 insurance cheque that Walter's mother, Lena, expects to receive following the death of her husband. The younger members of the family have different expectations of how the money can best be spent: Walter dreams of his own liquor store; Beneatha (Walter's strong-willed intellectual sister) wants the money to pay for her university education; and Ruth (Walter's pregnant wife) dislikes Walter's plans for a liquor store and is herself contemplating an abortion, as they barely have enough to raise their son Travis. It is Lena's choice to put the money towards a new house with a garden which will allow the family to thrive unlike the wilting plant she tends in her kitchen 'that ain't never had enough sunshine or nothing'.[75]

She gives over half the money to Walter, sets aside a portion for Beneatha's education and puts a down-payment on a house in Clybourne Park, a white district of Chicago, mainly because black housing facilities are worsening by the day. She hopes the move will prevent her family 'falling apart': Walter drinks too much, Beneatha postures in African dress (inspired by her Nigerian college friend Joseph Asagai), and Ruth is on the verge of an abortion; as Lena says: 'When it gets like that in life – you just got to do something different, push on out and do something bigger'.[76]

But the news that the Youngers intend to move into a white neighbourhood travels fast, and it is not long before a white spokesman from Clybourne Park, Karl Lindner, arrives to bribe them not to move to his area. An incensed Walter orders Lindner to leave, but the family is driven into greater strife when they hear news that Walter's liquor store partner has disappeared with a large share of the inheritance. This causes Walter to agree to Lindner's bribe, only to change his mind again when Beneatha insults him and he remembers his dead father's rage when faced by a racial attack. The play ends with the family about to move to Clybourne Park. Walter has grown in stature, but he is still motivated by wealth and argues that Beneatha should marry for money and not for love. Walter is the central and most complex character, but Hansberry's real focus is on the tensions between family members, and the way in which key decisions can lead to the affirmation or disintegration of kinship bonds.

In terms of the representation of black characters, the play is realistic in its portrayal of psychologically torn characters: Walter is likened to Prometheus, but he does not recognize the name; Beneatha is aloof and self-centred; and Lena does not fully understand her children or anticipate the racial hostilities of moving to a white neighbourhood. Hansberry's realistic instinct was partly born out of the influence of the leading black writer of the 1940s, Richard Wright, and his attempt to expose the racial conflicts of interwar Chicago in *Native Son* (1940), but it was also stimulated by real-life issues, with the play's theme of housing tapping into one of the main causes of concern for civil rights activists, particularly when Martin Luther King Jr marched on Chicago in 1966. Hansberry's realism was also stimulated by her despair about the roles available to black actors: in a public letter on the Gershwin musical *Porgy and Bess* (which had in 1959 just been turned into a film starring Sidney Poitier and Dorothy Dandridge) she expressed her dismay about 'the hip-swinging, finger snapping race of prostitutes and pimps which people the imagination of white writers of musical comedy "Negro" shows'.[77] The portrayal of serious characters deeply immersed in their own lives and without the insight to see clearly their circumstances is precisely the metier of writers like Miller and Wright, but Hansberry added an intense examination of family relationships at their most loving and destructive.[78] It was her passionate desire to refute the theory that art, and particularly the theatre, was useful only for exploring emotions at the expense of social commitment – a realization that fuelled much of her work from the late 1950s and early 1960s, posthumously collected in *To Be Young, Gifted and Black* (1971).[79]

A Raisin in the Sun opened at the Ethel Barrymore Theatre on 11 March 1959, directed by Lloyd Richards, the first black theatre director on Broadway since the 1920s. It ran for 530 performances (switching to Belasco Theatre in the autumn) and won the New York Drama Critics Award for the best play of 1959, beating a trio of established male playwrights: Williams, O'Neill and Archibald MacLeish. The strong performances of Sidney Poitier as Walter Lee and Claudia McNeil as Lena and the reception of the play by enthusiastic black and white audiences were the major reasons why Hollywood became interested in adapting it, with the Broadway cast retained for the 1961 Columbia release, directed by Daniel Petrie. Hansberry insisted on writing the screenplay for the film, but certain aspects of the play were cut for both Broadway and Hollywood, particularly the links that Jospeh Asagai makes between civil rights and the African liberation movement.[80]

Many critics applauded the play, including James Baldwin and Kenneth Tynan, but not all were enthusiastic. Some criticized the fact that the play only had one white character (and a stereotypically bigoted one with a Germanic name), while others, like the black theatre critic Harold Cruse, thought its focus was too middle class and did little to make theatre audiences uncomfortable. LeRoi Jones was also critical of the play in the mid-1960s, when it seemed passive, tame and domesticated alongside radical plays like Jones's *Dutchman* (1964), with its protagonist Clay's violent realization that white America will 'murder you, and have very rational explanations'.[81] However, Jones changed his assessment of the play's importance in the mid-1980s, and when the theatre producer Woodie King Jr directed his three-part documentary on the Black Theater Movement in 1978 he chose to begin with *A Raisin in the Sun* as the play that made the Movement possible.[82]

Figure 2.6 Claudia McNeil as Lena Younger in *A Raisin in the Sun* (1960–1 stage tour). Wisconsin Center for Film and Theater Research.

Conclusion

To a large extent the development of postwar drama mirrors the transitions in fiction, as the impact of Beat writing between 1955 and 1958 coincided with the development of forms of new theatre which challenged the dominance of Broadway. This phase also saw the emergence of other voices, particularly African American drama in an industry in which hard and soft forms of segregation continued even after the *Brown* v. *the Board of Education* ruling of 1954. While New York remained the epicentre of theatre through the decade, there were signs of the re-emergence of non-standard and regional venues which helped to broaden the possibilities of performance.

As I have argued, fiction, poetry and drama in the 1950s all reveal a complex set of negotiations between modernist culture and the mainstream, leading Lionel Trilling to argue that as cultural forms they have a privileged role in society in exploring newly emerging currents that would otherwise be invisible. The danger with this stance is that it reinforces a 'high culture v. mass culture' model which the discussion of drama and performance in this chapter problematises, particularly as regards the business of theatre. The common prejudice among intellectuals about the rapid growth of mass media was one of the major fault-lines in postwar America, an exploration developed further in the next two chapters on popular cultural forms.

Chapter 3

Music and Radio

Whereas theatre and performance styles developed slowly in the 1950s and did not really diversify until late in the decade, the rapid growth of the music industry marked a decade of changing consumer tastes and an expanding market for records and live events. The record industry was prevented from expansion during the war because of production restrictions but grew quickly afterwards with 400 record labels in existence by 1949, just one year after the launch of the 33 rpm twelve-inch disc and the 45 rpm single. Many labels did not exist very long and five main companies – Decca, Capitol, RCA-Victor, Columbia and ABC-Paramount – were quick to capitalize on the increase in disposable income, particularly among middle-class teenagers. The launch of the *Billboard* Top 40 in 1951 changed the way in which music was played on radio. Formulaic programming was common among the four major radio networks – NBC, CBS, ABC and MBS – with many channels playing only hit songs which listeners could be confident they would hear regularly.

Before the Top 40, *Billboard* did produce lists (such as 'the hit parade', most radio plays, and most popular jukebox songs), but beginning in Omaha, Nebraska and expanding through the prairie towns the new format of repeated plays meant that 'announcers' (newly dubbed disc jockeys or DJs) did not need to have specialist musical knowledge. Some critics were appalled that the diversity of radio shows was being sacrificed in the name of repetition, but in the 1950s the Top 40 'became a crucial conduit for giving people what they wanted to hear – particularly when what they wanted to hear was not what the guardians of cultural taste supposed'.[1]

Musical tastes were not alone in changing. The whole dynamic of the music and broadcasting industry was in transition, as Detroit, Memphis, Nashville and New Orleans became important regional sites in the 1950s. The cultural diversity of two other musical centres, Chicago and New York City, had also increased after the war with the migration of many African Americans from the South, but the Top 40 tended to elide regional differences in favour of a standardized format. Producers, musical arrangers and promoters took heed of the rapidly changing tastes for postwar fashion and began marketing new styles that would appeal to an ever-renewing audience of teenagers and young adults eager to discover their own sound. The aim for producers was to make music accessible, instantly recognizable, and played as frequently as possible across the continent.

But while the record industry was growing, radio was suffering a fierce challenge from the emergence of television. Popular memory suggests that radio listening went into freefall with talent defecting to television where comedies and westerns could attract bigger audiences, but the reality was quite different. Although radio audiences had dipped by 1953 and the threat of HUAC made experimental radio drama almost taboo, radio was still the major source of news and music for most people through the 1950s, it was just that the listening patterns had changed, dipping during prime time but peaking during drive time and late in the evening.[2] Portable transistor radios and car radios meant that listening was no longer confined to the home, which was one of the reasons why automobiles and rock 'n' roll were often linked closely as cultural symbols of the decade. The emergence of the DJ as a personality enabled listeners to bond with the radio, and symbolically with other local and regional listeners, in ways that centralized television programming did not permit. This is quite a different story to that of musical standardization. Mainly due to the fact that small radio stations proliferated in the late 1940s and became regionally specific, radio could be (and at times was) much more socially progressive than television.[3]

As the next chapter discusses, hardly any black writers were regularly employed in broadcasting; African American presence on television shows was minimal after 1953 and was largely demeaning in the roles available in radio drama. In contrast, music radio offered greater possibility for black stations such as WDIA which began in 1947 in Memphis, and the number of stations devoting time to black radio grew from four in 1943, to 270 in 1953, to 400 in 1956.[4] Listeners could not always be sure of the colour of the musicians they were listening to as racial styles began to blur. For this reason Susan Douglas calls 1950s radio a 'trading zone' between white and black culture revealing as much 'about the emptiness and forced conformity of white culture' as it did 'about the new ambitions of blacks'.[5]

This chapter analyses these tensions in music and radio in the 1950s, examining emergent musical currents, and focusing on three forms in particular – folk, rock 'n' roll and jazz – that offer different perspectives on the decade. Folk and jazz were older forms undergoing transitions after the war, while rock 'n' roll was a new trend that emerged out of rhythm and blues, a strain of black music (called 'race music' in the 1940s) which later became the sound of the 1950s. Commercial imperatives and major labels dominated the second half of the decade but, particularly between 1956 and 1958, creative musical energies were in full flow in a manner not repeated until the mid-1960s. Popular music in the 1950s might have been the epitome of a 'mass culture' of consumption (as Adorno and Horkheimer sneeringly called it), but this chapter highlights that musicians and performers were never far away from politicized discourses about region, race, sexuality and class.

Forms of 1950s Music

At a 1956 music seminar in Cooperstown, New York critic Carlton Sprague Smith divided American music into three primary forms: folk, urban and art music. There was a general consensus that folk music was predominantly a rural form, whereas the growth of commercial music in the 1950s occurred primarily in major cities. The standard narrative of the growth of postwar music is a movement from a regionally diverse set of musical currents to more standardized urban patterns that legitimated certain sounds and marginalized others. Charlie Gillett in *The Sound of the City* (1970) documents the rise of urban music along these lines, noting that the two musical impulses of 'standardization' and 'hybridity' were in tension throughout the decade. While the music industry and the emergence of the Top 40 standardized recording and radio output, the ways in which different musical styles overlapped, merged and developed out of each other underlines the fact that popular music is intrinsically hybrid. Some forms of musical hybridity were organic, while others were pushed by record labels or artists looking for fresh success. For example, the sequence of Elvis Presley's releases had become predictable by 1958 (the despairing loner followed by the tough beatnik, the tender lover, and the balladeer) and after moving from the niche label Atlantic to the major Paramount, Ray Charles experimented with rhythm and blues, gospel, country and soul in the search for new audiences, epitomized by the title of his 1961 album *Genius + Soul = Jazz*.

Another way of framing musical developments in the 1950s is to see the growth of popular music as an ever-widening middle space between 'traditional' music (taking in folk, country, vaudeville and Broadway) and 'serious' composition (ranging between classical and avant-garde music). This model is helpful, but it is not possible to map the rise of popular music onto the space that defined middlebrow culture for critics such as Dwight Macdonald (or 'Midcult' to use Macdonald's term). In this respect rock 'n' roll and its variants were very much part of lowbrow culture, which was rarely seen as possessing artistic merit until the mid-1960s.

A better model would be what African Americanist Houston Baker Jr calls a cultural 'matrix', defined as a 'point of ceaseless input and output, a web of intersecting, crisscrossing impulses always in productive transit'.[6] The fact that Baker takes his metaphor jointly from the industrial image of locomotives and the black vernacular form of blues is testament to the fact that music in the 1950s was as valid a response to modernity as fiction, poetry and theatre were. It is difficult to apply this model if modernism is taken as a periodizing term linked to early-century culture, especially as popular/commercial music was so new after the war. But, as this chapter will explore, the modernist impulse was integral to the growth of the music industry as a bridge between artistic and commercial energies. Baker's metaphor can be taken as a celebration of postwar cultural exuberance – 'vast dimensions of experience' and 'vibrantly polyvalent interpretations' as he describes it – but also the drive of postwar capitalism to find new products to sell back to the consumer.[7] And, whereas Baker followed writers Ralph Ellison and Langston Hughes in reserving his discussion for blues, Baker's description works equally well for other musical forms, particularly the three primary forms discussed here: folk, rock 'n' roll and jazz.

There is always the danger of looking to periodize music by 'cutting time up into unjustifiably neat slices', as former editor of the magazine *Jazz Hot* André Hodeir argued in the mid-1950s.[8] In his pioneering book *Jazz: Its Evolution and Essence*, first translated in 1956, Hodeir was wary about dividing jazz into historical slices and simply taking the model of 'growth, maturity, decline' to explain the trajectory of musical forms.[9] Instead he looked at the ways in which classical, primitive and modern styles interconnect and have historically given rise to surprising new forms, meaning the debate will never be resolved 'between those who believe that jazz is about to disappear and those who think it has a practically limitless future'.[10]

What is often overlooked in a discussion of postwar music is that it was not just about the marketplace or the release of the increasingly familiar three-minute-long 45 rpm singles. Band leader and composer Duke Ellington was still working hard, celebrating twenty-five years in the business in 1952 and outperforming all other acts at the 1956 Newport Jazz Festival; the decade was the heyday for the bastion of country music the Grand Ole Opry (which had been broadcast on radio since 1925 but was televised from September 1950); Frank Sinatra was turning his hand to concept albums with his 1958 release *Come Fly With Me*; Bernard Hermann was composing a series of signatures pieces for the films *The Day the Earth Stood Still* (1951), *Vertigo* (1958) and *North By Northwest* (1959); the songwriting teams of Rodgers and Hammerstein and Lerner and Loewe were having hits on Broadway; Leonard Bernstein was fusing popular and serious music in Hollywood and on Broadway; French-born Edgard Varèse had been innovating with classical and electronic musical forms in the US for decades, culminating in his *Poème électronique* for 400 loudspeakers in 1958; and John Cage was experimenting with pieces such as the chaotic *Music of Changes* (1951) and the ultra-minimalist *4'33"* (1952) that took him into the realms of performance, poetry and art – cross-cultural experiments which were to inspire a new wave of avant-garde practice later in the decade (see Chapter 5).

In addition to these different strains, two of the most important musical figures of the pre-World War Two years, classical composer Aaron Copland and jazz performer Louis Armstrong, published books in the 1950s that offered very different perspectives on the American musical landscape.

Copland's study *Music and Imagination* (1952) evolved out of lectures given at Harvard University, in which he made links between poetic and musical composition and between imaginative listening and writing, arguing that 'interaction' is the primary condition of 'a healthily functioning musical community'.[11] In contrast, Armstrong's *Satchmo: My Life in New Orleans* (1954) is written as a colloquial memoir tracing his early years in early-century 'Back o' Town' New Orleans, where he was exposed to street music and the 'toughest characters in town . . . would shoot and fight'.[12] Armstrong traces his early musical career up to his decision to leave for Chicago in 1922, at the same time other black musicians such as Big Bill Broonzy and Muddy Waters were migrating from the South. *Satchmo* is a portrait of the jazz musician as a young man, far removed from the commercial imperatives propelling music in the mid-1950s, by which time Armstrong's star had risen so high that he appeared as the official face of jazz in the film musical *High Society* (1956). Written on the eve of the explosion of rock 'n' roll, these two books were out of kilter with a commercial environment in which the creative interaction of musical communities had been usurped by the cult of individualism, star performers and teenage fans. We will come back to rock 'n' roll later in this chapter, and return to jazz as well, but first it is worth focusing on folk music – the most communal of musical forms, that found life in the 1950s far from comfortable.

Bringing It All Back Home

Folk music is often thought to emerge out of regionally distinct environments that possess 'a uniformity of character and disposition'.[13] This description derives from a 1958 issue of the jazz magazine *The Second Line* which developed the theory of 'folk' from William Graham Sumner's classic book *Folkways* (first published in 1907; reprinted in 1940 and 1959) as signalling a traditional and oral culture 'bound together by the single tie of long common ownership'. Burl Ives commented that folk music was 'an honest musical expression taken up by many', evoking an unchanging culture in the remote past, epitomized by *The Burl Ives Song Book* which contains a variety of traditional songs going up to 1850.[14]

Ethnologists and music collectors John and Alan Lomax (father and son) offered a more nuanced interpretation of folk during their sponsorship by the Library of Congress to collect folk songs from across the country. In 1937 the Archive of American Folk Song received money from the government as part of Roosevelt's New Deal and the Lomaxes were encouraged to journey to remote parts of the country to collect regional music. Alan Lomax went to the Appalachians, Indiana and Ohio and John Lomax to the South, focusing particularly on folk cultures in transition.[15] In the song collection *Folk Song U.S.A.* (1947) Alan Lomax describes American folk song as:

> Homemade hand-me-downs in words and music, songs accepted by whole communities, songs voted good by generations of singers and passed on by word of mouth to succeeding generations, a tradition quite distinct from popular song (made to sell and sell quickly) and cultivated art (made, so much of it, to conform to prestige patterns).[16]

Rather than suggesting something static and unchanging, the Lomaxes emphasized the malleability of folk music, in which balladeers 'change an old song slightly to fit a new situation', making emendations in tone and content, 'reweaving old materials to create new versions, much as an old lady creates a new quilt out of an old by adding, year by year, new scraps and patches'.[17] The Lomaxes were sometimes criticized for being pillagers of folk material, but this commitment to explore far-flung communities was part of their project to rescue a disappearing America.[18]

The field recordings were made for the Archive of American Folk Song at the Library of Congress from 1937 onwards, and Alan Lomax's contribution was later released as the thirteen-volume *Southern Journey* on the Folkways label. Recording was carried out in the 1940s and very early 1950s using microgroove technology for portable recording which, in their words, gave 'a voice to the voiceless'.

Although the Lomaxes had a functionalist approach to classifying folk styles, this claim suggests that folk music for them was not unchanging and completely resistant to modernity. As cultural historian JoAnne Mancini argues, the development and use of recording equipment 'for the inscription' of authentic songs can be seen to mark 'a key moment within a longer modernist trajectory' of ethnology and regional sensitivity, from Zora Neale Hurston's field recordings and the WPA Depression photographs of the 1930s to the ecological movement that began with Henry David Thoreau and John Muir in the nineteenth century.[19] This was not an anti-modern impulse but a committed response to the centripetal pressure of urban modernity, preserving regional cultures but also, to quote Mancini, using 'the past to make a future that was better than the past'.[20] The Lomaxes were not interested in an insular culture, but one reflecting the American cultural patchwork with connections to 'kinfolk in Russia, China, Spain, Ireland', linking 'the races and the nation into the big family of humanity'.[21] Far from traditional music being culturally conservative, for the Lomaxes it was at root a 'democratic art' with deep political convictions.

But it was precisely the politics of folk music that were under attack in the early 1950s when political activism in the music industry found itself quelled. A year before the major workers' strikes of 1946, folksinger Pete Seeger founded People's Songs: an organization of singers, musicians and union educationalists to promote the folk tradition through such publications as *Song Book* and *People's Songs*

Bulletin. Robert Cantwell notes that People's Songs was the first stage in the folksong movement, appealing particularly to listeners with left-wing sympathies that may have encountered such music in summer camps.[22] The organization did not just focus on workers' songs, but also promoted a variety of musicians from jazz and classical back-grounds, with Pete Seeger, Paul Robeson, Woody Guthrie and Alan Lomax prominent figures in Henry Wallace's (failed) political cam-paign of 1948 as Progressive Party candidate, representing one phalanx of the politicized 'cultural front' with roots in the 1930s. However, by 1949 People's Songs had disbanded; by 1952, with the war in Korea and HUAC investigations, the movement seemed to be all but over. This was symbolized by Alan Lomax's eight-year trip to Europe which followed soon after his abrasive politics had been publicly criticized and he had been named in the right-wing paper *Red Channels*.[23] In this climate of suspicion, the rise of the music industry and the impact of television pushed folk music further from the main-stream. As suggested by the American folk boxed-set *Songs for Political Action* (1996), the period 1949–53 can be considered the end of an era when the leftist impulses from the 1930s were quashed by cold war anticommunism.[24]

A counter-narrative tells a slightly different story in which social protest never entirely disappeared in the 1950s. The independent Folkways label was founded in 1947 by Moses Asch and Marian Distler as a means to distribute a wide range of aural material, from folk songs and stories to children's and educational songs. Alan Lomax followed his father John in collecting regional folk music at home and abroad, promoting the likes of Woody Guthrie, Muddy Waters and Jelly Roll Morton. At the same time The Weavers (comprising Pete Seeger, Lee Hayes, Fred Hellerman and Ronnie Gilbert) became the first commercial folk band when they formed in 1948. The Weavers' major commercial success came with the 1950 recording 'Goodnight Irene', a new version of a Huddie Ledbetter song from the mid-1930s. With its catchy chorus 'Goodnight Irene' became the best-selling song of the year and led Decca to sign up the quartet with the promise of a weekly network television show. Seen by some as the primary channel 'for genuine expressions of people's culture', The Weavers were a major success, but there was also a suspicion among the folk commu-nity that the industry would serve only to diminish 'the artistic quality' of their songs.[25] The group had a three-year run of recording, but the intolerant political climate made it difficult for them to func-tion as a left-wing group: Seeger (a member of the Communist Party until 1950) recalls that the group's television contract was 'torn up' soon after they were named in *Red Channels*.[26] Following early success with 'On Top of Old Smokey' (1951) life became much harder for The Weavers. Their Christmas 1952 concert was almost devoid of social protest songs (except for a few non-English-language ones) and the quartet took an enforced sabbatical in 1953.

Although he was dead by December 1949, another important presence in the folk music of the 1950s was the twelve-string-guitar player Huddie Ledbetter (or Leadbelly as he was popularly known). With John Lomax as his manager Leadbelly recorded three volumes of songs in Moses Asch's New York studio between 1941 and 1947, including 'Bourgeois Blues' and 'Rock Island Line' (later a hit in 1956 for the British skiffle singer Lonnie Donegan) and he featured regularly on radio shows. Some critics argued that the Lomaxes wrongly lionized Leadbelly, pointing out that he was an exhibitionist with a violent streak (he spent seven years in a Texas jail on assault charges and even threatened John Lomax with a knife), but for the Lomaxes, along with black folksinger Josh White, Leadbelly was a powerful conduit of the folk and blues spirit. It is significant that some commentators see his death as the end of the activist period in folk music: Robert Cantwell argues that 'the last expression of the progressive spirit behind the folksong movement' occurred in January 1950 at a memorial event for Leadbelly.[27] But Cantwell also notes that even after The Weavers' demise in 1953, the popularity of 'Goodnight Irene' (Frank Sinatra recorded a successful version) kept the door open for other folk acts in an increasingly commercial environment.[28]

The ongoing presence of the Peoples' Artists Publication *Sing Out!* is a case in point. *Sing Out!* began as a sixteen-page monthly magazine in May 1950 as an attempt to reconnect music to 'the hopes and fears and lives of common people'.[29] Seeger noted that in the first few years the magazine 'barely stayed alive', but under editor Irwin Silber it expanded to a quarterly thirty-six page publication in 1954–55, reverting to a much longer bimonthly format in the early 1960s.[30] The aim of *Sing Out!* was to chart any form of music – 'folk song, concert song, dance, symphony, jazz' – that made the connection to 'common humanity'. Presiding over the magazine was the figure of Benjamin Franklin, who featured in the first issue as the 'advocate of people's music' because of his claim that the spirit of music was more important than the formal rules of composition. In the first year *Sing Out!* featured lyrics and music for work songs (such as 'Bread and Butter Blues'), ballads ('The Dying Sargent'), spirituals ('Scandalize My

Name'), children's songs ('Old Aunt Kate'), union songs ('We Are American Labor'), choral pieces ('When Jesus Wept'), world music ('Basta Ya!') and peace songs ('Peace, It's Wonderful'), with pacifist tunes particularly prevalent during the Korean War. The whole publication was given over to collective activity and encouraging readers to play and sing along. One article 'How to Write a Song' stressed that the first impulse is 'to feel strongly about something' using 'simple easy words' that are 'pointed, catching, easy for a people to identify with'.[31] The article coaxed readers not only to write songs in which 'the words and music fit together', but also to sing them aloud.[32]

Some issues of Sing Out! had an overriding theme, such as the February 1951 issue celebrating Negro History Week, with the 'voice of thunder' Paul Robeson a regular contributor and figurehead for civil liberties. The message of peace was linked to strident articles encouraging the social fight against racism and chauvinism, including a report on the formation of an interracial St Louis Neighborhood Folk Chorus and a 1953 column urging support of the Rosenbergs (later noting the 'barbaric sacrifice' of their death).[33] In winter 1956–7 Sing Out! ran an article on women's suffrage and dedicated a special issue commemorating forty years since the murder of union activist Joe Hill. More than anything, the dedication to other cultures – Polish, Czech, Hungarian, Creole, Brazilian and Korean – stands out in a period when many eyes were looking inwards and television was moving towards the dead centrism that characterized programming in the mid-1950s.

The magazine was also highly politicized and attuned to Red-baiting, exposing Burl Ives in 1952 as a turncoat and noting that former People's Artists folk singer Oscar Brand had turned to '200% Americanism' by spuriously attacking 'the use of folk music by the Communists'.[34] Sing Out! took the HUAC subpoenas as 'testament to the growing effectiveness of the work of our organization'; in spring 1952 the magazine urged readers to renew their fight for free speech; and in early 1954 Irwin Silber positioned Sing Out! against the 'vulgarity, chauvinism and sadism' of 'our film, radios and other commercial mass media' which he associated with the same 'anti-human culture' as the blacklists.[35] Perhaps this sentiment arose from the fact that folk music did not receive its share of radio or television airplay, but the magazine's political stance was boldly described as a fight against 'all lists' that attempt 'to tell American citizens to what organizations they may or may not belong'.[36] The editorial columns shrank in the mid-decade when the magazine moved to a quarterly format, but

Silber continued to highlight the stultifying presence of HUAC. When HUAC investigated Pete Seeger and Silber in 1956 they refused to name names.

The survival of folk music in the mid-1950s is illustrated by The Weavers reforming as a band in 1956 on the Vanguard label, together with the release of Pete Seeger's *American Industrial Ballads* on the Folkways label in 1957. Many of these songs had earlier featured on Lomax's collection *Hard-Hitting Songs for Hard-Hit People* in the 1940s (with music by Seeger and commentary by Woody Guthrie; unpublished until 1967), ranging from nineteenth-century industrial songs, Western ballads and union songs to industrial accident songs, workers' blues and Depression songs. The acoustic guitar accompaniment is largely incidental, with Seeger's voice driving the songs and enunciating every lyric. The past comes alive in the working environments of mill, mine and farm and individuals are rescued from historical anonymity. The working-class spirit of songs such as 'Hard Times in the Mill' (1890) and 'Beans, Bacon, and Gravy' (1931) on *American Industrial Ballads* evokes a beleaguered humanity which survives despite hardship, migration and exploitation. *Sing Out!* editor Irwin Silber wrote the original sleeve notes as well as an introduction for the 1992 reissue, in which he emphasized the 'common cultural community', embodying 'hopes, while more often than not at odds with harsh realities' and embracing 'the best in our common human legacy'.[37]

Folk music struggled for direction in the mid-1950s, but by the end of the decade had rediscovered itself. In charting this revival Charlie Gillett identifies the release of two versions of 'The Banana Boat Song' ('Day-O') in 1957: a Calypso version by Harry Belafonte and a harmony folk version by The Tarriers.[38] Both made the top ten and inspired the major labels to recruit a number of old and new folk acts: Belafonte (RCA), Ives (Decca), Seeger (Columbia) and Peter, Paul and Mary (Warner). On his return from Europe at the end of 1958 Alan Lomax also marked this moment by writing about the appearance of young urban 'folkniks' and 'citybillies', while the re-emergence of politicized folk music stemmed from the first Newport Folk Festival in July 1959, featuring The Kingston Trio, Earl Scruggs, Oscar Brand and Pete Seeger (one of the organizers) performing to 15,000 people.[39] An eighteen-year-old Joan Baez was invited to sing with folkie Bob Gibson at Newport. With her distinctive vocal range and melodious timbre Baez was one of the hits of the Festival, and the following year she used the occasion to speak out in support of marginalized ethnic groups. Whereas earlier in the decade this would have been dangerous,

1959 proved to be a very different climate and did not prevent Baez from signing for Vanguard and releasing her first album *Joan Baez* in 1960.

Even though the Newport Folk Festival was suspended for two years in 1961 and 1962 because of crowd disturbance, the 1959 Festival was a sign of what was to come in the early 1960s when Bob Dylan pushed folk music in new directions. Dylan followed in the footsteps of his childhood hero Woody Guthrie on a series of folk-inspired albums, *Bob Dylan* (1962) to *The Times They Are A-Changin'* (1964), at which point Dylan decided to plug in his electric guitar to reveal new musical directions in his 1965 album *Bringing It All Back Home*.[40] However, when Dylan went back to his folk roots much later in his career with the release of his albums *Good as You've Been to Me* (1992) and *World Gone Wrong* (1993) he returned to the music he had grown up with in the 1950s: Harry Smith's Folkways *Anthology*.

Anthology of American Folk Music (1952)

The six-album boxed-set released on the New York Folkways label in 1952 represented the most sustained effort from the American folk fraternity to document the variety of historical musical forms, compiled by music enthusiast Harry Smith from recordings made between 1927 when electronic recording devices became available and the onset of the Depression in 1932. The eighty-four tracks are divided into three categories – Ballads, Social Music and Songs – with illustrations by Smith himself. The six albums were accompanied by a hand-illustrated booklet edited by Smith, with track details, a synopsis of lyrics, general notes and bibliographic references. The boxed-set was not only a historic moment in national folk history, but also an innovative piece of design offering a mixture of music history, folklore and occult symbolism, leading the 1997 CD reissue to describe it as on 'the boundaries of science and art, history and aesthetics, scholarship and commerce'.[41]

Smith grew up in the Northwest in Portland and Seattle in the 1920s and 1930s and was inspired by a different set of impulses to those driving the music industry after the war. Smith's intention was similar to that of John and Alan Lomax in preserving musical traditions that were endangered by the modernist pull towards urban culture. But whereas the Lomaxes made field recordings from the mid-1930s onwards, the songs on Smith's *Anthology* were previously available but had never been collected together in an orderly way. This fact leads JoAnne Mancini to argue that, whereas the Lomaxes used recording technology to preserve folk cultures, Smith's technology was 'the long-playing album, which could convert dozens of solitary songs into a visionary whole that did not itself resemble a commercial product but rather a collection of sacred texts'.[42] Not only does this reanimate regional traditions but also creates a sense of mythical time and space by juxtaposing otherwise isolated tunes with songs from other regions with different ethnic variants. At a time when HUAC and the black-lists were laying down ideological prohibitions, the *Anthology* presented a cultural mosaic in which regions, genders and races are thrown into contact with each other and speak across spatial and temporal borders.

This is a slightly different reading of the *Anthology* from other critics such as Benjamin Filene, who sees the collection as an example of the way in which the folk community adopted 'a less explicitly political agenda for their work' in the early decade.[43] Filene notes that the affiliation with rural African American music gives the *Anthology* a 'decidedly antiestablish-ment bent', but along with other contemporary collectors such as Samuel Charters and Mack McCormick, he argues that Smith approaches black music with a mixture of 'yearning and regret'.[44] A more nuanced reading is offered by Robert Cantwell in his argument that the *Anthology* represented the birth of the counterculture, well before the Beat movement took off. 'At the very moment that a new medium, television was making a spectacle of American life', Cantwell interprets Harry Smith's project as a conduit to 'the unbounded space in which the cultural imagination wants to move': a 'memory theater' partly rooted in Smith's interest in the occult and deeply embedded in American folkways.[45]

This image of a 'memory theater' seems apt given the design features of the box. The colours of green, red and blue for the three albums can be seen to represent water, fire and air; an ancient monochord (a fifteenth-century symbol of harmony) turned by the hand of God illustrates the front cover; and the booklet has interesting typography throughout, with numbers, figures and woodcuts on every page.[46] On opening the box the music seems almost buried in textuality and iconography but this only adds to its exceptional nature; Smith viewed the project as a rescue act for early recordings endangered by a commercial environment.

A different form of roots music – country music based in Nashville, Tennessee – suffered a major blow when the mercurial Hank Williams died on New Year's Day 1953, only two years after his songs had found a national audience helped by Tony Bennett's cover of Williams's song 'Cold, Cold Heart'. The Folkways *Anthology* does not foray into contemporary Nashville music, nor does it trace a single lineage of a distinct regional sound. Instead songs from Illinois, Texas, New York, Tennessee, Georgia, New Jersey, Missouri and Indiana nestle against each other and Smith's notes offer detailed (if idiosyncratic) information about the recording, theme and provenance of the songs. The documentation does not make the *Anthology* a stuffy museum piece, but is a testament to the many con-tours of American roots music. Nor is it entirely an oddity. In many ways it was the culmination of the folk traditions of the 1930s and 1940s and prescient of the folk revival at the end of the 1950s. Even in mid-decade, Elvis Presley and Chuck Berry were recording songs that derived from Smith's collection, while the mixing of styles 'took on a new meaning for younger listeners' with 'unexpected crossovers' between discrete musical styles.[47] Whatever degree of contemporary relevance is attached to the Folkways *Anthology* it remains a unique achievement in music history, sparking Bob Dylan's desire in the second half of the 1950s to search for 'some new kind of template' for his music, 'some philosophical identity that wouldn't burn out'.[48]

The Channels of Rock 'n' Roll

There are three mythical beginnings of rock 'n' roll. The first is 21 March 1952 when WJW radio personality Alan Freed was due to host the Coronation Ball rhythm and blues event in Cleveland, Ohio, although the concert was cancelled when a largely black crowd of upwards of 20,000 tried to squeeze into the old hockey rink with its 10,000 capacity.[49] The second beginning is 18 July 1953 when the nineteen-year-old Elvis Presley, just out of school, walked into the Memphis Recording Studio to record a birthday song for his mother and paid $4 for his two tracks 'My Happiness' and 'That's Where Your Heartaches Begin'. And the third beginning is the opening sequence of Richard Brooks's film *The Blackboard Jungle*, which premiered on 20 March 1955 in New York, for which the driving beat of Bill Haley and His Comets' 'Rock Around the Clock' marked the first rock 'n' roll soundtrack.

All three beginnings are plausible and each serves a different historical function. Alan Freed was one of the most ardent champions of rhythm and blues, but the débâcle in Cleveland revealed that music could unlock restless energies in the young. From 1954 onwards Elvis Presley became a musical star without rival, taking the art of virtuoso performance in new directions. And the use of 'Rock Around the Clock' in *The Blackboard Jungle* opened up a new and sometimes surprising relationship between film and youth culture, dividing young from adult viewers; it was banned in some localities and a government warning was added for film theatres in which it did play (see Chapter 4). 'Rock Around the Clock' sold phenomenally and gave rise to its own film targeted at an adult market, but also excited young working-class audiences when released in Britain in September 1956.[50]

Whichever of the years 1952, 1953 and 1955 is taken as the birth of rock 'n' roll, there is no doubt that it helped to radically transform the musical scene by mid-decade. Its sound drew heavily from twelve-bar blues, but relied on the versatility of electric guitar and bass to create an energetic beat for dancing. Rather than the solo performer singing ballads in the style of Bing Crosby, the four or five-piece rock 'n' roll band was fronted by a charismatic singer whose voice attenuated the jerky staccato rhythm. Lyrics were no longer romantic but much more direct, raw and very often suggestive. And rock 'n' roll did not rely on a speciality audience, unlike rhythm and blues and country music that appealed to regional fan bases in Chicago and Nashville. Instead rock 'n' roll launched itself into the cultural mainstream as an urban sound and the new expression of youth, with Alan Freed's successful shows revealing its popularity with both black and white listeners.

DJs such as Freed were vital in developing an audience for rock music. Record announcers had started back in the 1930s, but increased in numbers in the 1940s when the bar was removed that previously prevented playing phonograph records on air. By the time that Freed entered radio broadcasting in Pennsylvania in 1942 over 75 per cent of broadcast time was music, 55 per cent of it being pre-recorded.[51] These figures rose after the war and it was now possible to become a DJ personality, as Freed realized when blacks and whites in Cleveland started to listen *en masse* to his rhythm and blues shows in 1951. It was not just in Cleveland either. Other radio stations in Nashville, Memphis, Chicago and Los Angeles were hosted by DJs who adopted nicknames such as Moondog, Hot Rod, Dr Jive, Daddy-O-Daylie and Bear Cat. While the journalist Wes Smith labels early DJs 'the pied pipers of rock 'n' roll' more interested in fame than in music, Susan Douglas asserts that the DJ introduced a new vernacular to radio, using 'different vocal registers, slang, tone of voice, even whoops and howls, to give listeners multiple versions of himself to latch on to'.[52] Along with a number of other DJs, Freed's significance was that he helped to dissolve the racial barriers between listeners who had previously only listened to either 'white' or 'black' radio.

It is important to realize that much of Freed's repertoire had been learnt from black radio stations, with the number of radio stations devoted to black subject matter growing from four in 1941 to 270 in 1953, by which time WDIA in Memphis, Tennessee and WEDR in Birmingham, Alabama were pioneering black radio in deeply segregated areas.[53] And by 1952 even a major network such as NBC was trying to tap into a black market, appointing the baseball star Jackie Robinson as director of community activities at New York's WNBC.[54] But these facts do not detract from Freed's achievements, nor do they diminish his celebrity which surpassed that of any other DJ. From 1953 onwards he was not just a presence on local radio but could be heard on WINS in New York City, where he moved to in

1954. He was also hosting shows featuring Fats Domino and Bo Diddley and started to popularize the phrase 'rock 'n' roll' on his shows in early 1955.

The sound of rock 'n' roll was unmistakable, but Charlie Gillett identifies five distinct styles associated with different performers: (1) northern band rock 'n' roll of Bill Haley with 'high-spirited feelings of togetherness' in songs such as 'Crazy Man Crazy' and 'Shake Rattle and Roll'; (2) rhythm and blues for white audiences which usually took the form of covers by white singers such as Pat Boone, who covered 'Ain't That a Shame' and 'Tutti Frutti' from Fats Domino's and Little Richard's New Orleans 'dance blues' repertoire; (3) country rock, or rockabilly, which was a version of the twelve-bar boogie blues emerging out of Memphis; Elvis Presley was the most popular exponent, but the style blurred at times with the country music of Johnny Cash; (4) Chicago rhythm and blues of Chuck Berry and Bo Diddley which had mainstream success, particularly the up-tempo 'jump blues'; and (5) 'vocal group rock 'n' roll' that relied on vocal harmonies rather than electric guitars, but had a fast beat for dancing.[55] These five styles characterized many successful songs on the *Billboard* charts between 1954 and 1956, setting up the ' "ingredients" which were mixed together in slightly varying combinations for the next thirty years'.[56]

It is hard to assess whether rock 'n' roll suggested a new awareness of class consciousness, primarily because it was such a diverse phenomenon, with its variants finding fans in the Northeast, Midwest and South. It is tempting to see in rock 'n' roll as an assault from the margins on the conservative values of the mid-1950s, but this would be a distorted picture as some of its forms were palatable to middle-class audiences: records could be ordered through the mail and bought in suburban supermarkets by 1956.[57] One response from middle-class critics was the type of knee-jerk reaction that followed the release of *The Blackboard Jungle*, but another reaction was to ignore rock music altogether or to focus on high cultural pursuits at the theatre, opera and symphony concert. This response of ignoring popular music was institutionalized by the American Society of Composers, Artists, and Publishers (ASCAP) which controlled all music publishing rights until 1941 and ignored black and regional music in the 1940s. But by 1953 the ASCAP found that the new organization Broadcast Music International (BMI) had licensed as much as 80 per cent of music played on radio that year, by which time it was too late for ASCAP to catch up, even though the Society tried to file an antitrust lawsuit against BMI.[58]

Rock 'n' roll was a strongly masculinized form of music, from its beat, its lyrics, its performance style, and its DJs. All of its major singers and musicians were male, with women usually consigned to the role of backing vocalists. There were some exceptions such as the McGuire Sisters, Ruth McFadden and Dori Anne Gray, the latter two featuring in Freed's Rock 'n' Roll Easter Show of April 1956. But titles such as the McGuire Sisters' 'Sincerely' (1955), Gray's 'Tears for Me' (1956), and McFadden's 'Darling, Listen to the Words of This Song' (1956) sat uncomfortably with the spirit of rock 'n' roll, especially when compared to the suggestive titles of Ray Charles's 'I Got a Woman' (1955) and Fats Domino's 'What's the Reason I'm Not Pleasin' You' (1956). This void stemmed from the general expectation that young women should be demure and respectable – qualities precluded by the performance styles of rock 'n' roll. And it is not surprising so few women were in lead musical roles given the public backlash to the 1953 release of Alfred Kinsey's *Sexual Behavior in the Human Female*. Frank Sinatra and Sammy Davis Jr were mainly worried that rock 'n' roll would mark the end of their careers, but most criticisms touched on sexuality. Even the progressive sociologist Vance Packard claimed in 1958 that rock music has a 'raw savage tone' that brings out 'animal instincts'.[59] Although the black jazz singers Lena Horne, Billie Holiday and Dinah Washington were popular (and the death of Holiday in May 1959 was a huge moment), it was not until the early 1960s that women, particularly black female groups on the Motown label, began to have a broad impact on popular music.

The racial implications of rock 'n' roll were also charged. Some thought that it was a positive force in American culture for dissolving racial barriers, while others were excited by the energies it stirred up in listeners. Alan Freed's shows became increasingly integrated, and in parts of the segregated South semi-integrated live events were permitted (with white and black contingents separated by a rope), much to the chagrin of local authorities.[60] Radio stations began to realize that advertising targeted at black listeners would tap into an upwardly mobile African American population, thought to be worth $11 billion by 1950 and $18 billion by 1960 (up from $3 billion in 1940).[61] However, in 1953 local black DJs in Cleveland were unhappy that Freed was stealing listeners and racial slurs were cast against him for his part in 'a plot to mongrelise America', as Asa Carter of the white supremacist organization the White Citizens Council of Birmingham, Alabama called it.[62] On the other side of the race line, many hard-working black rhythm and blues musicians were disgruntled that their songs were being covered by white singers, usually with more commercial success. The major labels after 1956 blocked out the independent labels with their African American performers to such a degree that the careers of Muddy Waters and Bo Diddley had advanced only slightly by the end of the decade, while the Atlantic label had lost their star talent Ray Charles to ABC-Paramount.

The next section will return to race in relation to blues and jazz, but first it is important to turn to Elvis Presley, the icon of rock 'n' roll, in whose performances the decade's racial tensions were encoded.

Elvis and 1956

The nineteen-year-old Elvis Presley released his first single in 1954 with Sun Records, a company established by the radio engineer Sam Phillips in Memphis at the beginning of the decade. Elvis had initially gone to Sun in 1953 as a nervous young truck driver, but a few months later he was recruited by Phillips and released his first single, a driving rhythm and blues track 'That's All Right (Mama)' on one side and a bluegrass standard 'Blue Moon of Kentucky' on the other. Effectively, one song was black and the other white. Presley's style was born out of Memphis at a time when the city had a thriving country scene (almost exclusively white), but also gave rise to the all-black radio station WDIA in 1947, a station that was to inspire the young Presley.

Despite his first single being pushed on both folk and 'race record' broadcasts and having extensive airplay in Memphis, some radio stations were initially sceptical; many labelled it a 'country' record and others were confused as to whether the singer was white or black.[63] Undeterred Phillips continued to experiment with a combination of blues and country, often dubbed 'country rock' or 'rockabilly', and Elvis soon became Sun's hottest property. Rather than white music dominating the *Billboard* charts, 1955 saw the emergence of Little Richard, Bo Diddley and Chuck Berry out of niche markets and Elvis's physical performance style borrowed heavily from black culture. This leads Michael Bertrand to argue that in Elvis 'the complex issues of race, class, age, region and commerce intersected': a heady mix that had a dynamic effect on his music and listeners.[64] Instead of delivering his songs straight, his live performances became increasingly exuberant; teenagers mobbed and tried to undress Elvis at a concert in Jacksonville, Florida in May 1955.

Elvis's fame grew quickly in 1954 and 1955 as he established a massive teenage following, but very few were prepared for the impact he was to have on American culture in 1956 after Sam Phillips sold Elvis's contract for $35,000 to RCA-Victor in November 1955. Following the re-release of his five Sun singles, Elvis recorded what has been often hailed as his signature track, 'Heartbreak Hotel', in January 1956 at the RCA Studio in

Nashville. Despite poor sound quality, this intimate tale of 'lonely street' is backed only by bass and piano, with Elvis's slurred vocals and breathy delivery turning the hotel for broken hearts into a place of slow-burning sensuality. The release of the single was followed by a series of television performances on CBS's *Stage Show* and ABC's *The Milton Berle Show* in the spring and *The Steve Allen Show* (on NBC) and *The Ed Sullivan Show* (on CBS) in the summer and early autumn. The single 'I Forgot to Remember to Forget' was his first to top the country chart in February and 'Heartbreak Hotel' followed in April, soon to reach number three on the R&B chart and number one on the *Billboard* Chart for eight weeks.

His fame was consolidated by the release of his debut album Elvis Presley, and when 'Hound Dog', which he had performed on *The Milton Berle Show* with his famous pelvic gyrations, was released in July it took only eighteen days to become a million-seller. Along with the numerous television appearances, Elvis spent the year on a nationwide tour and in the studio, breaking only briefly to sign a contract with Paramount Pictures and to start work on his first film *Love Me Tender* in August 1956, premiering in November with a forty-foot statue of Elvis erected outside the Paramount Theater in Manhattan. By the end of the year his second album *Elvis* and the soundtrack for *Love Me Tender* were selling well, Elvis had taken part in the famous Sun jam session in Memphis with Jerry Lee Lewis, Carl Perkins and Johnny Cash, and in December he had ten songs in the top hundred on the *Billboard* chart. He had even appeared by invitation at black radio station WDIA's Goodwill Revue in December which featured black artists such as Ray Charles and B. B. King. Presley's new contract would not permit him to perform for benefits, but his brief appearance created 'spontaneous mass hysteria' among the black audience.[65]

It is easy to be sceptical about Elvis's rise to stardom, particularly after the move to RCA, with record and film contracts and carefully organized publicity appearances feeding the demand for a performer who could harness the energies of southern black music with the popular appeal of a wholesome American white boy.[66] Some newspapers such as the *New York Times* and *Time* magazine were critical of Presley's innuendos and pelvic movements and *Variety* blamed him for the increase in juvenile delinquency that year.[67] However, as Sam Phillips noticed when he first saw Elvis, there was something remarkably original about the way he combined musical influences, developed his own performance and vocal style, and radically transformed covers such as 'Lawdy, Miss Clawdy', 'Hound Dog' and Ray Charles's 'I Got a Woman'. For this reason, Charlie Gillett describes his style as a truly 'personal vision . . . singing high and clear, breathless and impatient, varying his rhythmic emphasis with a confidence and inventiveness that were exceptional for a white singer'.[68] It is also impossible to understate the phenomenon of 1956, which Nik Cohn identifies as the moment when rock music became more than a 'gesture of vague rebellion'; with Elvis 'it immediately became solid, self-contained . . . when those axis hips got moving, there was no more pretence about moonlight and hand-holding; it was hard physical fact'.[69] His ability to appeal across musical genres, across classes, across the racial divide in the South, across the Atlantic, and across genders (from teddy boys to swooning girls) cannot be explained away as just a successful media strategy. This is in line with Michael Bertrand's reading of Elvis in *Race, Rock and Elvis* (2000), whereas other critics argue that Elvis was just as guilty of diluting black music for white audiences as other singers of the decade.

A great deal has been written about the slow decline of Elvis after 1956, with formulaic songs, the backing vocals of The Jordanaires and increasingly dreary movies eroding the fresh talent that was in evidence in the mid-1950s. Increasingly protected by his manager Tom Parker, Elvis had become a mythical presence by the late 1950s. His draft in March 1958 was headline news (as was the cutting of his trademark hair), with RCA and Paramount both eager to maintain public demand during his two years in the US Army.[70] But when Elvis emerged from the Army in 1960 he was more domesticated, soon became swallowed up by Hollywood, and did not perform live again until 1968, when a successful musical comeback from the black leather-clad Elvis on a NBC television special flew in the face of the folk-rock and psychedelic music of the late 1960s.

Whites, Blacks and Blues

Susan Douglas's reading of music radio as a 'trading zone' between two cultures is helpful for exploring the interconnections between black and white music in the 1950s. The blues were popular at the beginning of the decade in Chicago and on the West Coast, with Muddy Waters, Howlin' Wolf and Lightning Hopkins creating a beat that was to galvanize rock 'n' roll. The adoption of black musical styles by white acts may account for the fact that the blues struggled later in the decade, but some black composer-performers such as Duke Ellington and Ray Charles found new ways of exploring racial identity by blending musical styles. Like Louis Armstrong, who appeared without issue in the musical *High Society*, other black musicians found a fan base among both black and white audiences. Music critic Tony Russell argues that these cross-race musical exchanges go back at least to the 1820s (he argues in utopian vein that by singing the blues 'the races almost attained a sort of union'), but in the 1950s these transactions were much more problematic.[71] Douglas's metaphor of 'trading zone' suggests the possibility of breaking down racial boundaries, but musical transactions across race lines were often difficult.

Some musicians who tried to cross the race line found that what was possible in the first half of the 1940s at a time of mixed troops and progressive politics was not possible later on. A case in point is the black bluesman and folksinger Josh White who was very popular in the mid-1940s when he was championed by the likes of Richard Wright, Pete Seeger and Alan Lomax. Back in 1941 White had recorded *Southern Exposure*, an album of songs protesting racial discrimination, but by the early 1950s he had suffered at the hands of cold war intolerance. The reason for White's demise was partly due to his outspoken statements on race issues and his interracial act with white singer Libby Holman in the late 1940s, during which time he expanded his repertoire to draw off jazz, cabaret and other folk traditions. It was no surprise that White was treated with suspicion by the political Right. But when he was listed as a subversive in *Red Channels* in 1950 and decided to voluntarily appear before HUAC, it was the folk community that distanced themselves. White claimed that he had been mistakenly judged a communist because of his former connection with the Café Society cabaret in Greenwich Village, where Billie Holiday first sang the protest song 'Strange Fruit' back in 1939 not long after the venue opened.[72] But in 1950 White's voluntary testimony in front of HUAC was seen by many musicians as a heinous act. The folk community judged him to be a cooperative witness, even though the Committee were really interested in another prominent figure of the cultural front, Paul Robeson, who allegedly advised White to do anything but name names.[73] For the rest of the decade White was a forgotten man. Spurned by *Sing Out!* and out of favour with the Newport Folk Festival organizers, he was largely disenfranchised from his musical roots until he played with Martin Luther King Jr's civil rights march on Washington DC in August 1963.[74]

One response to musicians who blended musical styles too readily, either in the name of progressive politics or in the search for new audiences, was to call for musical purity. On this note, folksinger Oscar Brand closed his 1962 book *The Ballad Mongers* by rehearsing a debate between 'the purists' and 'the popularizers', recalling a similar (and more interesting) debate staged by Pete Seeger in 1957 between 'the purist' and 'the hybridist'. Seeger borrowed these terms from the South African music enthusiast Hugh Tracey to differentiate the even rhythm, loose sense of time and strict melody of European music from the uneven rhythm, strict notion of time and loose melody of African music. Seeger had earlier noted that African American culture borrows elements from both traditions, but in his 1957 piece 'The Purist vs. the Hybridist' he developed this argument. 'The purist' claimed that after the war the nation had been 'swamped' by popular music, whereas 'the hybridist' asserted that 'cultural purity is as much of a myth as racial purity' and that successful hybrids enable different regional and national strains to coexist.[75] Whereas the English folksinger Ewan MacColl (whom Alan Lomax knew in London) was promoting traditional working-class British music, Seeger shared with the Lomaxes the belief that authentic folk is fundamentally dynamic: new arrangements, distinct vocal tones and fresh contexts mean that traditional songs are always in a state of flux.

Other critics were also challenging binaries, particularly the distinction between folk and urban forms of music, arguing that jazz actually combines the two dimensions. In 1958 critic William Cameron claimed that jazz musicians are typically from rural or small-town backgrounds: blues music was originally 'moaned or blown in the cotton fields', but blues players were also drawn to the energy of the city. While its folk roots contributed to the emotional depth of jazz – making 'the music man so unhappy that he had to moan, so bitter that he had to shout' – the city provided working opportunities that allowed the music to get heard.[76] The purpose of Cameron's article 'Is Jazz a Folk Art?' is to argue that jazz does not fall into standard musical categories. His inclination is to celebrate the urban elements of jazz over its grassroots qualities, arguing that jazzmen 'may be refugees from the swamp lands, but their feet are clean and they wear shoes. They are trained, intent, knowledgeable and sophisticated'.[77] For Cameron, the beauty of jazz is that it 'thrives on invention and change'; driven by the dynamism of urban localities, jazz also stems directly from folk melodies 'constructed from bits and snatches of previous ones', adding licks and riffs 'to add sparkle and continuity to . . . personal ideas'.[78]

Cameron's article appeared in early 1958 in the official journal of the New Orleans Jazz Club *The Second Line*. It is worth spending a moment on this magazine as a forum for showcasing regional music. The magazine was started in April 1950 to celebrate individuals 'who have taken up the cudgels for Jazz', including musicians, promoters, teachers and enthusiasts.[79] *The Second Line* was named after the group of fans – young and old, black and white – that traditionally walked in a 'second line' alongside marching bands, while the Jazz Club itself was an attempt to prevent contemporary forces burying jazz in the way that Basin Street in New Orleans had been transformed from a musical hotbed to an eight-lane highway by 1955. The magazine detected that jazz was at a low ebb in the 1940s, but in the early 1950s it saw a renewed interest in jazz history, its relation to other musical forms such as ragtime, Dixieland and swing, and in a range of new jazz styles. The focus of *The Second Line* was centrally on the New Orleans scene and the annual October jazz festival, but it also profiled regional varieties of jazz from southern California to Florida, as well as noting its popularity in Canada, England and Austria. The jazz renaissance was slow to come about, though, with an article in the summer 1951 issue of *The Second Line* claiming that 'America's only original contribution to world culture is rarely heard', and a piece from 1952 dispelling the notion that jazz was necessarily associated with 'squalor and dinginess and bad ventilation'.[80] As late as winter 1955 contributors were still trying to dispel the 'enigma' of jazz, pictured as a 'sorry stepchild who . . . is never allowed out of the cellar'.[81]

The Second Line is just one example of what Ben Sidran has called a phase of 'new visibility' for black music between 1949 and 1969, which counters Ralph Ellison's assertion in *Invisible Man* that Louis Armstrong had 'made poetry out of being invisible'.[82] However, Ellison's description does find an echo in Sidran's assessment that the postwar years were a largely passive phase for black music, with a 'wait-and-see' attitude prevalent until mid-decade. Sidran links this passivity to the wide use of heroin and the 'cool' laid-back styles epitomized by Miles Davis and Gil Evans's 1949 recording *Birth of the Cool*.[83] The wait-and-see attitude could be linked to the cultural conservatism of the early decade, but Sidran detects that the climate shifted in the mid-1950s when a group of young black musicians were pushing jazz away from the appropriation of traditional jazz styles by white musicians. This led to new and 'peculiarly black forms of "deviant" expression', such as the rise of soul music after 1955 and more emotional musical styles such as Miles Davis's album *Kind of Blue* (1958).[84] Sidran interprets this shift, and particularly Davis's tutelage of a young John Coltrane, as a transition from a reliance on 'Western song forms' to create 'new anticipations in the listener' and a sense of musical freedom.[85] The key here is the link to a growing self-consciousness as an indicator of the rise of black activism and a new sense of potentiality of black musical forms.

This new potentiality was encapsulated in a provocative essay on racial identity by Duke Ellington, 'The Race for Space' (1957), which put into words his visionary musical expressions from the 1940s: *Black, Brown and Beige* (1943) and *New World A-Coming* (1945). The 1957 essay is particularly interesting because Ellington was thought to lack race consciousness in some circles, but here he uses jazz as a potent metaphor for creative culture. Rather than responding to the immediate context of the Sputnik launch, Ellington recalls another recent event, the Little Rock Central High School controversy, as an example to support his criticism of the stalling tactics of congressmen and senators to prevent civil rights measures from being passed. His argument is that the government was in such a flap about race relations following the backlash to *Brown v. the Board of Education* that it did not know how to strategically respond to the Sputnik launch.

Ellington argues that jazz is not just an expression of creative freedom, but also the key for facilitating racial harmony. Conjuring up the abstract image of 'the Man with the Different Sound', Ellington asserts that 'we don't care what he looks like, what color he is, what race he belongs to or even what language he speaks best. Music is bigger than all those things'.[86] Instead of focusing exclusively on the individual, he hones in on the jazz band which can only function as a unit by combining talents and creating harmonies out of 'a polyglot of racial elements'. The essay ends with a clarion call for 'a new sound' to pave the way for 'harmony, brotherly love, common respect and consideration for the dignity and freedom of men', a statement which finds an echo in his new recording of *Black, Brown and Beige* in 1958 featuring the gospel singer Mahalia Jackson.[87] Ellington's conclusion is far too utopian, but the use of jazz as a metaphor for freedom of expression and cooperation is significant for 1957, at a moment when black activism was really picking up.

If black music held the aces in the 1950s, it was harder for black producers to find a toehold with the major labels dominating the industry by late decade. However, not all big labels exploited their performers and not all black musicians were disenfranchised by the industry. Sam Cooke and Ray Charles had hits with 'You Send Me' (1957) and 'I Got a Woman' (1955) respectively, but they were also industry players: Cooke owned his own label SAR Records (until his early death in 1964) and Charles demanded that he keep his own masters and created his own Tangerine label when he moved to ABC-Paramount in 1962.[88] At its best music in the 1950s embodied the 'syncretism' of pre-cold war progressive institutions like Manhattan's Café Society cabaret with its aim to blur 'cultural categories, genres, and ethnic groups', but at its worst the rapid succession of musical styles in the 1950s was part of the industry's relentless drive to increase consumption.[89] The tension between these two musical modes was dramatized at the 1958 Newport Jazz Festival, the subject of one of the most important documentaries of the decade.

Jazz on a Summer's Day (1960)

The fifth Annual Jazz Festival in Newport, Rhode Island in July 1958 is seen by many as the high point of the jazz revival. Directed by fashion and advertising photographer Bert Stern (who worked for *Vogue*, *Life*, *The New Yorker* and *Fashion & Travel*) and released in 1960 by Union Films, the use of saturated colours and light in *Jazz on a Summer's Day* distinguishes it from earlier jazz films. Stern used 35mm stock and shot the Festival over several days on a hand-held camera with a 180mm telephoto lens, although it is edited to seem as if all the acts were on a single day. Investing $70,000 of his own money, the film is very much a personal project.[90]

Stern was very interested in the interracial audience, in which enthusiasts and amateurs mixed and the respectable middle-class New Englander found as much enjoyment as the young beatnik. This enhances the sense that the Festival's 10,000 guests in Newport's Freebody Park were participating in one of the moments when many of the creative elements of 1950s culture were on display. Most critics agreed that the virtuosity of the Festival was its strength in bringing together Louis Armstrong, Miles Davis, Mahalia Jackson, Thelonious Monk, Gerry Mulligan and Dinah Washington. However, other critics argued that it was more of a commercial than a musical success, complaining that this was jazz for 'the masses' which diluted regional variations in favour of mainstream appeal.[91]

The Newport Jazz Festival began in 1954 as a non-profit corporation under the directorship of pianist George Wein and has been an annual event except for in 1961 after crowd disturbance the previous year (the Newport Folk Festivals were also suspended in 1961 and 1962). The 1956 Festival featured Duke Ellington with performances from his *Such Sweet Thunder* album, and a year later the Festival was celebrating Louis Armstrong's fifty-seventh birthday on Independence Day. In 1958 Ellington was back again to open proceedings (the *New York Times* reported that his band 'rocked and rode and swung with a firm insistence that had rarely been heard on the Newport platform') and Benny Goodman starred on the second night.[92] Most of the major acts are featured in Stern's film, but some aspects of the Festival such as the whole of Ellington's performance, the International Youth Band (with musicians from seventeen European countries) and the morning sessions were not included. As in the previous year, the Festival coincided with the trials for the American Cup yacht race, shots of which Stern intercut into the musical footage, at one point omitting a substantial chunk of the only recorded song by Thelonius Monk.

Because it adopts the perspective of a single day, beginning with the Saturday morning sunlight falling on the harbour as cars arrive in Newport and ending with the early hours of Sunday morning, the film only gives a partial view of the Festival. The filmed acts range from traditional to experimental jazz and from ensembles such as the George Shearing Quintet and Chico Hamilton Quintet to the charismatic soloists Anita O'Day and Big Maybelle, which reflect Stern's interest in enigmatic women (prefiguring

Stern's famous photo-shoot of Marilyn Monroe in 1962).[93] Not all the performers were jazz musicians: Chuck Berry and Joe Turner showed that rock 'n' roll was far from dead, even though they received a mixed reception.[94]

The film profiles what most reports identified as the star of 1958: the gospel singer Mahalia Jackson, who followed Miles Davis and Dave Brubeck in joining Ellington's band at the end of the first night with a version of 'Keep Your Hand on the Plow' (another number not filmed). Jackson had found an audience on her weekly radio shows in Chicago and garnered international success when she moved from Apollo Records to Columbia in 1954. After her collaboration with Ellington at Newport she returned in the early hours of Sunday morning with a series of classic gospel songs, including 'The Lord's Prayer' which closes the film. Jackson's contralto voice and religious devotion is a powerful spiritual counterpoint to the secular coolness of the Festival's jazz rhythms. She was not to have such a captivated audience again until she performed at President Kennedy's inauguration in January 1961 and on the steps of the Lincoln Memorial in August 1963 prompting Martin Luther King 'to tell 'em about the dream, Martin' during his famous speech. While she did not have the savvy quality of Bessie Smith and Billie Holiday, and she cannot be seen as a precursor of black feminism (as Angela Davis reads into the songs of Smith and Holiday), Mahalia Jackson was to give the civil rights movement a powerful voice in the early 1960s.[95]

New York Times music critic John Wilson commented after the Festival that many jazz festivals of the time were 'content to depend on a relatively pointless grab-bag of names', but in 1958 he thought Newport had taken 'a long step forward'.[96] Stern's film can be approached from both these perspectives. He is as much interested in late 1950s fashion, the yacht trials, and audience interaction as the music itself. The fact that he dedicates a large portion of the footage to four numbers by Louis Armstrong suggests that his interest was in the Festival's popular side. But Stern's drive to record on film the wide variety of acts within a brief time-cycle has helped to preserve one of the most vibrant live music events of the 1950s. Jazz on a Summer's Day not only paved the way for two jazz films in 1961, Too Late Blues and Paris Blues (the latter which explores race relations among the expatriate jazz community of Paris with music by Duke Ellington and Louis Armstrong), but also for the Monterey Jazz Festival documentaries in the late 1960s and the growing interest in musical festivals from the likes of documentary filmmaker D. A. Pennebaker.

Conclusion

Discussion of music and radio brings together a complex set of exchanges between technology, business, fame, region, race, class and gender. The clearest fault-line running through the 1950s is between the organic development of music and the kind of standardization epitomized by the Top 40 format. This can be seen in the conflict between the gradual transitions of folk and jazz idioms and the abrupt changes brought about by the commercial market as it tried to second guess the next popular musical style. This is, at root, a tension between two forms of modernity: the first a moving culture propelled by innovation (even in traditional forms like folk music) and the second a sense that cultural products are always shaped by, and reflect the logic, of the economic forces that drive them.

But this does not mean that traditional music is impervious to social and technological forces; as folk music in the 1950s proved, it was highly attuned to the new recording techniques and to the political climate. To recall Houston Baker Jr's description of a cultural matrix as 'a web of intersecting, crisscrossing impulses always in productive transit', it is clear that industrial and creative forces were deeply entangled in the music and radio of the 1950s.

Chapter 4

Film and Television

The fiercest cultural rivalry of the 1950s was between the established film industry and the emerging medium of television. Film had been a central part of American life for three decades, but the experimental beginnings of television between 1928 and 1947 did little to suggest the dramatic impact it was to have by mid-century. The boom in television sales began in 1948 and had escalated by 1950, a year in which seven million sets were sold. Instead of a trip to the movies, most viewing was now done on the domestic TV set, particularly by the mid-decade when the major broadcasting networks NBC, CBS, ABC and the short-lived DuMont were scheduling shows that appealed to all ages. The meteoric rise of television as the defining cultural form of the decade is often cited as the reason why filmmaking went into freefall, with directors and actors drawn to the immediate commercial gains of the growing small-screen industry, what critics have called 'the decline and fall of an empire, a time of bewilderment in New York boardrooms and panic on Hollywood backlots'.[1]

Although television was often projected as 'the antagonist in the mythic version of Hollywood's postwar crisis' and film actors were prohibited from making television appearances until 1956, that year saw three big film studios – Warner Brothers, Twentieth Century-Fox and MGM – producing their own shows and selling television rights for pre-1948 films.[2] Nearly 90 per cent of homes had at TV set by 1959 and as a cultural artefact it was virtually impossible to avoid.

The main reason why the TV set appeared frequently on television shows was to familiarize viewers with the technology. Two early episodes of Jackie Gleason's show *The Honeymooners* were directly geared to situate the TV set at the heart of domestic life, while one of the regular prizes on the quiz show *The Price is Right* (1956–65) was a colour TV. This did not mean that it was always celebrated as a panacea for home life. In *The Honeymooners* episode 'TV or not TV' (1 October 1955) Ralph and Alice Kramden (Jackie Gleason and Audrey Meadows) argue over the purchase of a new set; the script pokes fun at programming (Ralph proclaims to his Captain Video-obsessed neighbour Ed Norton, played by Art Carney, that 'we've had this set for three nights, and for three nights I've listened to nothing but space shows, westerns, cartoon frolics, and puppet shows'); and late-night viewing destroys Ralph's sleep patterns. In a later episode 'Better Living Through TV' (12 November 1955) and the *I Love Lucy* show 'Lucy Does A TV Commercial' (5 May 1952) the style of television advertising is satirized to the point of ridicule. Nevertheless, television was very clever at affirming itself as a technology affordable to everyone by mid-decade, even to working-class families like *The Honeymooners*' Ralph and Alice Kramden – a show that attracted a large African American audience.

The symbolic function of the TV set in films varied to a greater degree. At the beginning of the decade the science-fiction film *The Day the Earth Stood Still* (1951) presented television as a medium for bringing news directly into the household, taking its place alongside print media and the radio. When the disguised humanoid alien Klaatu arrives at a Washington DC boarding house the lodgers encircle a TV set as they would have done the radio a decade earlier. Five years later it was featuring regularly in films as part of the furniture of suburban life. In Douglas Sirk's melodrama *All That Heaven Allows* (1955) a TV set is the unwanted birthday present that the widowed Cary Scott (Jane Wyman) receives from her adult children with the intention that it will prevent her from dallying with her gardener; the dead channel which Jim Stark (James Dean) faces when he returns home in *Rebel Without a Cause* (1955) signifies the barrenness of his middle-class family life; in *Bigger Than Life* (1956) the schoolteacher Ed Avery (James Mason) berates his son for watching shows in which the same story is told over and over; and in *Will Success Spoil Rock Hunter?* (1957) television is satirized as the medium of cheap advertising. While television lacked the glamour of the Hollywood star system, the force of its rivalry is evident from the negative connotations of the TV set in mid-1950s films.

Form, Ideology and Image

The challenges faced by the film industry in the 1950s were unprecedented. Five years earlier movies were a central part of American life with 100 million people going to the cinema each week in 1946.[3] The war had done much good for the film industry and stimulated a growing market and healthy economy. 1946 was a boom year: the number of dating couples seeking entertainment had risen with servicemen returning from wartime engagements, but this was soon followed by mass movement to the suburbs where marriage and babies distracted many couples from cinema-going.[4] By 1950 weekly attendance at cinemas had dropped to 40 million and cities with television stations lost around 30 per cent of their film audience. In addition, the well-oiled production line of studio films could not be sustained in the late 1940s, with the government intent on loosening the stranglehold of the major studios over film exhibition. A Supreme Court ruling of 1948 demanded the abolition of studio ownership of cinema chains in a move to put distance between the production and exhibition of film. The consequence of this ruling was to create a more disorganized industry than in the classical phase of Hollywood in the 1930s and 1940s.

When the German émigrés Theodore Adorno and Max Horkheimer condemned Hollywood in 1944 for being a bland 'culture industry' in which films were made to order and sold to an unthinking public, they did not anticipate that a decade later film would be seen as a respectable form when compared to television. Formulaic and genre-based films were still produced, but with studios slowing down film production, an increase in independent films (from 1 per cent of Hollywood products in 1950 to 50 per cent in 1958), the rise of auteur directors (many of whom had European sensibilities), and other senior personnel combining roles, such as writer-director Billy Wilder in *Sunset Boulevard* (1950) and *The Apartment* (1960), revealed a more variegated industry than Adorno and Horkheimer's thesis credited.

Although the critic Gilbert Seldes was bemoaning in 1950 that only a 'fraction of the money invested in the movie business goes into the making of pictures' and arguing that real investment in audiences would transform the film industry, the 1950s was marked by a series of experiments with new technologies that ensured the cinematic experience was unique.[5] The experimentation began with the release of the promo *This is Cinerama* (1952) which made the grand claim that: 'We truly believe this is going to revolutionize motion pictures'. *This is Cinemara* was made to show the wonders of the new widescreen format, using three separate but synchronized camera images to create an enveloping picture through an arc of 146 degrees. Most cinemas could not afford to install Cinerama, but a rival

widescreen format – Fox's CinemaScope – was much more successful in establishing an alternative to the academy ratio format.
CinemaScope helped to revolutionize how films were constructed
and dramatically changed the experience of cinema-going. It was
more than twice as wide as the conventional screen and perfectly
suited to the cold war vogue for classical and biblical epics in enhanc-
ing the theatricality of film. When used with a heightened colour
palette such as Technicolor or DeLuxe Color (colour films became
cheaper and increased in number from 115 to 170 per year between
1952 and 1956), CinemaScope encouraged viewers to lose themselves
in the epic spectacle, emphasizing dramatic and symbolic elements
often muted in the academy format.

Critics in 1953 could not agree whether CinemaScope conveyed a
more intense realism or whether it heightened the illusory spectacle
of film, but many concurred with cinematographer Leon Shamroy's
assessment that it liberated the dramatic space by creating 'a new
combination of objective and subjective' cinema.[6] CinemaScope
literally filled the 'spectator's field of peripheral vision' with its broad
horizontal range, but it also intensified the epic parallels between
the contemporary experience of the United States and the fate of
ancient dynasties.[7]

With its 'world of increased vision' (as a 1953 demo film proclaimed), CinemaScope was not just used for epic films like *The Robe*
and *Knights of the Round Table* (both 1953), but also for musicals,
westerns and romantic comedy, and enabled directors like Nicholas
Ray to explore his architectural imagination through its extended horizontal plane.[8] Such was the success of CinemaScope that Fox quickly
licensed it to the other major studios by the end of 1953. It was not just
feature films that were making use of the technology: in 1954 MGM
released the first CinemaScope cartoon, Tom and Jerry in 'Pet Peeve',
and by 1956 all MGM cartoons were using the technology, with 85 per
cent of the 15,000 US cinemas equipped to show CinemaScope by
1957.[9] But while CinemaScope offered clarity, depth of perspective
and smooth camera movements, it also lacked intimacy and tended to
create dead spaces on the screen which often had to be filled in by
observers (in dramas) or dancers (in musicals) and did not always
enhance the spectacle. In fact, by 1962 cinematographers were encouraged to use only the safe area in the middle of the frame to make it compatible with television formats.[10]

CinemaScope was by no means the only technological alternative
to the academy format: Cinerama, VistaVision, Vistarama, Todd-AO

70mm, Technirama and 3-D movies were viewed by some as a series of cinematic gimmicks, while others saw these technologies as attempts to revolutionize filmmaking. VistaVision was the most successful format, giving a much clearer and sharper image than its rivals and allowing cinemas to project onto various sizes of screen. However, it did not enjoy the adoption of CinemaScope across the industry and was used almost exclusively by Paramount, with the odd exception such as the Warner Bros western *The Searchers* (1956). These visual technologies were enhanced by alternative sound systems such as Perspecta Sound and Stereophonic Sound. Together with the rise of drive-in movies in suburban areas and brief forays with 'smellies' such as AromaRama and Smell-O-Vision in 1959, cinema-going in the mid- to late 1950s was a quite different experience than watching domestic television.

It is clear that television had a dramatic impact in its challenge to cinema-going, as well as a negative effect on the attendance of live events, the sale of newspapers and magazines, and the use of lending libraries. It must be remembered, though, that compared to forty or so years of film history, television programming had yet to settle into a fixed pattern. The early decade is often hailed as the Golden Age of television, with quality live dramas shown regularly in the late 1940s and early 1950s.

The critic William Hawes periodizes early commercial television into three phases: 1946–51 was the Golden Age of live television; 1951–8 firmly established television as a mass cultural medium through national broadcasts; and after 1958 programming 'shifted from apprenticeship to sophisticated anthologies to series, from New York to Los Angeles, and from live dramas to recording on film or videotape'.[11] Erik Barnouw divides up the decade slightly differently, stressing that after granting over 100 television licences to stations by 1948 the Federal Communications Commission suddenly put a freeze on licences, which was prolonged by the Korean War into 1952. This 'strange twilight period' meant that television did not really go national until 1953, with major cities such as Houston, Pittsburgh and St Louis only having one station before 1953, and others including Austin, Denver, Little Rock, Milwaukee and Portland, Oregon having none at all.[12]

Hawes's periodization suggests that live television in the early decade was a superior cultural form to the later filmed broadcasts. His narrative also carries two negative connotations: first, that by the mid-1950s television epitomized cultural conservatism which upheld family values and ignored serious attempts to deal with politics or ideas more generally; and, second, that it was an unashamedly commercial form driven by the advertising industry. Advertisers regularly sponsored shows and were particularly keen to target children and housewives with product placement.[13] Although sponsors rarely meddled directly with content, company employees often supervised rehearsals and, as Kenneth Hey points out, the three-act structure of one-hour television drama became a settled form partly because it accommodated three messages from the sponsor, as well as an opening and closing hook.[14] In devising shows which would appeal across economic and regional boundaries, Lynn Spigel argues that television levelled 'class and ethnic differences in order to produce a homogenous public for national advertisers', drawing on 'the image of the white, middle-class family audience when devising programming and promotional strategies'.[15] Television was a more potent medium for advertising than radio and magazines, but sponsors were keen to promote products across different media.

There was also a general agreement to steer clear of controversial matters. Such was the worry that communists and fellow travellers had infiltrated the movie industry that programmers were very cautious in their approach. In 1947–8 HUAC investigated key personnel from the entertainment world, with the consequence that the blacklisted Hollywood Ten were held up as a warning to others who might harbour un-American ideas. But, although CBS was the subject of investigation, television networks escaped largely without blame, with individual producers, directors and writers often used as scapegoats. This was one reason why networks feared dealing with serious issues. Quiz shows, light entertainment, weekly serials and comedy dominated family viewing, while serious issues were the reserve of radio and literary fiction. This kind of 'dead centrist' programming led the liberal journalist Edward R. Murrow to argue in 1958 that television deliberately steered away from unpleasant subjects in order 'to distract, delude, amuse and insulate us'.[16]

But this is only a partial story of 1950s television. On CBS Murrow was pioneering the television documentary series *See It Now*; live drama was a mainstay of evening viewing into mid-decade, including adaptations of Shakespeare, Austen, Dickens, Fitzgerald and Tennessee Williams; and the occasional discussion show such as *The Great Challenge* on CBS in the late 1950s (featuring intellectuals like Schlesinger, Niebuhr and Galbraith) were exceptions to the rule.[17]

Schedules did not become predictable until the end of the decade, with a broad variety of genre products and innovative live shows such as Sid Caesar's *Your Show of Shows* (1950–4) and *The Steve Allen Show* (1956–60) challenging expectations. The appeal of television drama was beyond anything radios could muster, but the anthology format was directly borrowed from radio. Television drama generally lacked the finesse and slick editing techniques of cinema, but did tackle serious issues of poverty, class conflict and racism and 'represented an attempt to establish artistic credentials by making television as much like the theatre as possible'.[18] Series produced in New York early in the 1950s such as NBC's *Kraft Television Theater* and *Philco Television Playhouse*, and CBS's *Ford Theater* and *Studio One* were in direct contrast to the more populist entertainment-based programmes made in Los Angeles.[19] But the vogue for serious live drama had fallen off by the third quarter of the decade: *Kraft Television Theater* wound up in 1958, leaving only *Playhouse 90* as a drama series closely resembling cinematic filmmaking.

Until the mid-1950s television executives and programmers were feeling their way with scheduling and debating television's intermediary role between radio and cinema. Two principles dominated programming: a sense that all audiences shared similar tastes and that aiming for the dead centre was the recipe for success. The result was a tendency to flatten ethnic, class and regional differences and to aim for safe programming that did not offend or stigmatize particular groups.[20] This led to executives searching for a perfect marketing formula.

Even so, up to 1955 the length and frequency of shows was the subject of debate, as were the relative merits of live and filmed performances. Most critics agreed that live broadcasts were preferable to filmed ones because it helped to differentiate television from Hollywood and over 80 per cent of broadcasts were live by 1953. However, the filming of television shows increased as the decade progressed because it allowed syndication and re-runs. In fact, the television and film worlds were more tightly bound than the early-decade rivalry suggests: the Golden Globes inaugurated television awards in 1955; Hollywood stars James Dean, Paul Newman and Sidney Poitier launched careers through television; Charlton Heston and Natalie Wood made successful transitions between the two media; and the writer Paddy Chayevsky's 1953 television drama of working-class ordinariness *Marty* was remade for the cinema to win an Oscar for Best Picture in 1955. Despite these crossovers, the golden age of television was over by the end of the decade: it was felt that the major networks had too much control over the programming, resorting to formulae, turning their backs on live television, and squeezing out shows made outside California.

One debate about the relative merits of television appeared in the pages of the leftist journal *Dissent* in 1956. The German critic Gunther Anders claimed that more than every other cultural form television helped to bring the 'outside world' into the private world of the home: 'this outside world is so unrestrictedly dominant that the reality of the home ... becomes inoperative and phantom-like'.[21] Drawing on the potent metaphor of containment, Anders argued that 'the home tends to become a container, its function to be reduced to containing a video screen for the outside world' with the result that the true privacy of the family 'disintegrates'.[22] His central claim was that television leads to a 'debased, philistinized' experience in which viewers become passive consumers rather than active participants.[23]

In response to Anders' neo-Marxist perspective, Henry Rabassiere wrote an article in 'Defense of Television' for *Dissent* in which he contested the thesis that television is a vehicle of mass deception, arguing that Anders romanticizes the past in order to demonize television. Rabassiere did not dismiss the idea that new technologies can be used for manipulative ends, but he thought that Anders had invented a tyrannical 'Iron Heel' that controls the medium and that he neglected the ways in which television can widen the 'perceptive capacities' of viewers.[24] Rabassiere argued that viewers are not 'helpless, powerless and hopeless in front of inexorable forces unleashed by industry's ingenuity or the Iron Heel's clever scheming'.[25] And he saw Anders's position as common amongst critics who feared the 'narcotic effects' of mass culture that lull to sleep an unwitting public, rather than admitting that television can offer an expanded view of the world.[26]

The different perspectives of Anders and Rabassiere suggest that the new form of television created unease about its possible ideological effects and its blurring of myth and reality. In its early phase television did not rely on star actors to attract audiences, but appealed through its promise of domestic tranquillity for the suburban family. This is the standard view of the birth of television. But, while television brought the world into closer view, it was also arguably moving dangerously close to the realms of business and politics: television could be used for anticommunist propaganda and was often presided over by elite gatherings. The writing seemed on the wall for the close relationship between politics and television when vice-presidential candidate

Richard Nixon wriggled out of a scandal for making improper use of campaign funds that threatened the Republican presidential campaign of 1952. Nixon staged a television broadcast in which he used in his defence his wife's plain coat and his insistence that his children could not give up the family dog Checkers.

Quiz Shows and Television Comedy

Adult viewers in the early 1950s were watching television dramas, *CBS-TV Television News* and *NBC-TV Camel News Caravan* (running for fifteen minutes in the early evening) and factual programmes such as Ed Murrow's documentary series *See It Now*. A development of the radio documentary series *Hear It Now*, CBS's *See It Now* began its seven-year run in 1951. As profiled by the recent film *Good Night, and Good Luck* (2005), the highpoint of *See It Now* as investigative journalism was in late 1953 and early 1954 in a series of broadcasts that investigated Joseph McCarthy's anticommunist claims. These shows helped to set the groundwork for McCarthy's fall from grace during his doomed attempt to indict the Army in the live televised hearings that April.[27] Murrow was skilful at finding appropriate words to capture current events and his terse journalistic style was later to inspire other current-events shows, particularly on CBS which launched the first autonomous news broadcast *CBS News* in 1954 and began its *CBS Reports* series in 1959, including Murrow's report on the plight of migrant farmers in *Harvest of Shame* (25 November 1960). Despite the cultural importance of *See It Now* in the early 1950s (such as the *See It Now* broadcast of 25 May 1954 dealing with the social consequences of *Brown* v. *the Board of Education*), factual programs were pushed later into the evening and remained fairly marginal through the decade as most viewers were turning to television for entertainment.

The development of generic shows was part of the network's attempt to find the perfect formula. Viewers regularly tuned in to episodic detective series such as *Racket Squad* (1950–3) and *Dragnet* (1951–9) and a wide range of westerns such as *Cheyenne* (1955–63) and *Bonanza* (1959–73). Children were watching cartoons (many of them theatrical releases from the 1940s), *The Mickey Mouse Club* (1955–9), the *Gumby* series of clay animations in 1955, and *The Woody Woodpecker Show* in 1957, but also westerns and science-fiction serials, adult matter of which many parents disapproved. The publication of the psychiatrist Fredric Wertham's *Seduction of the Innocent* in 1953 led to wide-ranging debates about what kind of television shows and reading matter were suitable for children. Wertham focused on comic books and other forms of mass media that could corrupt children, with the fear that television would undermine parental authority in the home.[28]

By mid-decade the two most popular genres on television were quiz shows and comedy. Some highbrow critics dismissed popular television for sinking to the lowest common denominator as sponsors strove for mass appeal. While it is important not to overlook the networks' attempt to shape viewing patterns, the popularity of quiz shows and comedy provides an indicator of the tastes of 1950s television audiences. The shift from vaudeville and variety comedy early in the decade to the more contained domestic settings of situation comedy was an attempt to encourage audiences to identify closely with characters, while the popularity of quiz shows was fuelled by the vicarious pleasure of viewers imagining that they were the ones winning prizes. The primary goal may have been escapism but viewing habits reveal a great deal about the national condition, particularly by mid-decade when *I Love Lucy* was number one in the ratings and quiz shows dominated the schedules.

In 1957 five of the top ten television programmes were quiz shows and by summer 1958 over twenty different shows vied for viewers, often in prime-time slots. This vogue started in June 1955 with the *The $64,000 Question* (1955–8), following a Supreme Court ruling in 1954 that exempted jackpot quizzes from any charges of gambling. *The $64,000 Question* began as a replacement programme but quickly won a record 51 million viewers, beating *I Love Lucy* in 1956 with 84.8 per cent of the possible audience for its time slot, while five of the top-ten-rated television programmes in 1957 were quiz shows. They were reasonably inexpensive to produce and could be controlled by a sponsor, such as Revlon cosmetics for *The $64,000 Question*. Low production costs and strong viewing figures meant that prizes could be lavish, while the more colourful the contestants the more likely that viewers would tune in for the drama of head-to-head competition. It was clear that quiz shows tapped into the rising expectations of television audiences, including the working-class Ralph Kramden in *The Honeymooners* who threatens his wife Alice that he will go on *The $64,000 Question* in an early episode 'Funny Money' (8 October 1955). The consumerist appetites of viewers were heightened by an array of cash prizes and commodities, such as domestic appliances and the consolation prize of a Cadillac for reasonably successful contestants who failed to hit the jackpot.

Based on the 1940s radio quiz *Take It or Leave It* with its famous $64 question, the television version *The $64,000 Question* upped the stakes dramatically with contestants having to answer questions in their area of expertise posed by compere Hal March and his female assistant Lynn Dollar (the male compere and female assistant were quickly established as the model hosts for quiz shows). Like rival quiz shows *The Big Surprise*, *Twenty-One* and *High Finance*, the emphasis was on factual knowledge. Successful contestants could win up to $4,000 in each show and were eligible to return the next time when the stakes were higher and isolation booths (also sponsored by Revlon) helped to intensify the drama. Viewers quickly became familiar with the faces of returning contestants – the most successful of whom became household names. The promise of instant fame for winning contestants was capitalized upon by the spin-off show *The $64,000 Challenge* (1956–8), in which contestants from the earlier show with winnings over $8,000 were invited back to go head-to-head with even higher stakes.

There was some variation in quiz show formats. The switch from radio to television of *Truth or Consequences* (1950–88) developed the show's focus on physical games; *Queen for a Day* (1956–64), also a radio show since 1945, gave housewives the chance to win prizes by describing why they needed a specific commodity; and *What's My Line* (1950–67) gave a blindfolded panel the chance to guess the identity of mystery guests such as Bette Davis, Alfred Hitchcock and Ronald Reagan. But big-money quizzes *The $64,000 Question* and *Dotto* dominated schedules from 1955 to 1958, when a major scandal marked the end of high-jackpot shows and the realization that television could be a medium of mass deception.

Twenty-One followed the success and format of *The $64,000 Question*, with its exuberant presenter Jack Barry, its emphasis on factual questions, and use of isolation booths for contestants. The idea was simple: to reach twenty-one points. Contestants could choose to answer questions rated from one to eleven, indicating their level of difficulty, and the winner gained $500 for each point in the winning margin. Capitalizing on the serial format, games were often left hanging with big-money stakes in the offing, and successful contestants invariably returned in the next show to increase their winnings. Ratings were crucial to the show's sponsor Geritol and the producers sought as much high drama as they could pack in to a thirty-minute show.

The scandal emerged when a successful contestant Herbert Stempel was ordered to deliberately lose, which would enable a new contestant

Charles Van Doren (son of Columbia poetry scholar Mark Van Doren) to win as he was thought to have the credentials to maximize viewing figures. Following victory over Stempel, Van Doren was unbeaten on *Twenty-One* from December 1956 through to March 1957, and the show was so popular in early 1957 that it beat *I Love Lucy* in the ratings. Stempel was not disgruntled about Van Doren going on to win $129,000 and a run of fourteen weeks on the show, or that Van Doren was on the cover of *Time* magazine in February 1957, or even that his Ivy League credentials were more palatable to the network than the Jewish working-class Stempel. But he felt cheated because he knew that contestants were being fed answers to the questions in advance of the shows (as he had been) and coached in how to act naturally and how to feign anxiety. Although rumours of fixing were in the air with the rival show *Dotto*, the scandal did not break until another *Twenty-One* contestant James Snodgrass posted himself the answers sent to him two days before he appeared on the show. The allegations of fixing were investigated by the New York Grand Jury, ratings plummeted in 1958, and some shows were cancelled. By the time Van Doren testified in late 1959 the scandal had resolved itself, leading to a law being passed in 1960 to make quiz show fixing a federal crime. As Robert Redford's revisionist film *Quiz Show* (1994) demonstrates, it was individuals whose careers were ruined (Van Doren lost his teaching job at Columbia and producer Dan Enright was fired), whereas networks and sponsors escaped from the scandal without much damage.[29]

Less controversial was the development of television comedy in the 1950s. Like other forms of comedy, early sitcoms tended to deal with stock characters representing certain social types that were often more tightly codified than vaudeville and stage comedy. As Christopher Beach argues, comedy as a cultural form is often used to explore, and sometimes critique, distinctions of class, race and gender, but can also represent an 'escapist and often ideologically conservative response' to social conditions.[30] On this level, sitcoms can be viewed as an escapist pressure valve for cold war tensions, but also, more interestingly, as a relatively safe means to explore the fine line between social norms and their critique. However, the prevalence of middle-class sitcoms like *The Adventures of Ozzie and Harriet*, *Our Miss Brooks* and *Father Knows Best* lend weight to the first view, establishing white middle-class identity as the norm and reinforcing the theory that programming was aimed to appeal to the largest cross-section of viewers. There are other reasons for the rise of the sitcom: the emphasis on domesticity allowed action to occur within a limited space, essential in the early

Figure 4.1 Host Jack Barry questions Herbert Stempel on *Twenty-One* (NBC-TV, 1956). Wisconsin Center for Film and Theater Research.

decade when most comedy was broadcast live. By the mid-1950s the variety comedy of *The Burns and Allen Show*, *Your Show of Shows* and *The Jackie Gleason Show* featuring a range of acts (including a shortened version of *The Honeymooners* on Gleason's show) had given away to the familiar character-led storyline of sitcoms.

Perhaps the most representative of middle-class sitcoms in the 1950s was *The Adventures of Ozzie and Harriet* (1952–66). Adapted from the 1940s radio show starring the Nelson family, Ozzie and Harriet blurred the line between reality and fiction by depicting a

Figure 4.2 Jackie Gleason, Art Carney and Audrey Meadows on *The Jackie Gleason Show* (CBS, 1955). Wisconsin Center for Film and Theater Research.

suburban house modelled on the Nelsons' own home in Hollywood. Ozzie and Harriet and their two sons David and Ricky epitomized the ideal nuclear family without any major worries: they were reasonably affluent, lived in a white neighbourhood, Harriet was an ultra-organized housewife, and Ozzie had enough free time to spend his days with their two clean-cut boys (in fact, it was hard to work out what Ozzie did for a living). Few episodes dealt with social problems, and where serious issues are touched upon – such as in 'The Pills' (17 October 1952) in which Ozzie tries to lose weight by starting a diet and taking pills to help him (only to realize that the pills he is taking actually increase his appetite) – usually ended in mistaken identity, the domestic tribulations of Ozzie, or the playfulness of the boys.

Despite the homogeneity of many sitcoms in the mid-1950s, it was difficult to be subversive given the tight control over broadcasts and the demands of sponsors. But while David Marc is right to point out the conservative form of domestic sitcoms, there were a number of departures from the reinforcement of middle-class norms – even though this was the centripetal force that drove most sitcoms. The suburban sitcom *Leave It to Beaver* (1957–63) is often singled out as an example of the safe format, in which the mischievous eight-year-old Theodore 'Beaver' Cleaver (Jerry Mathers) pokes fun at his parents. In one episode 'Beaver's Poem' (3 October 1958), Beaver's father (Hugh Beaumont) ends up writing a poem for his class assignment. Although the show focuses on the codes of parenting – the moral of the episode is that 'overhelping is better than not helping at all'– Beaver's trickster-like character was often disruptive.[31] Another sitcom appearing to endorse consumerist values, *The Honeymooners*, often depicted Ralph Kramden on the make and looking to improve the domestic environment of his Bronx apartment. However, most of the comedy of *The Honeymooners* revolves around Ralph's working-class life as a Harlem bus driver and the close proximity of his neighbours. Running jokes focus on Alice's upper hand over Ralph, his comic attempts to break out of his world (even though he is deeply wedded to it), Ralph and Ed's buffoonery, and gags levelled at Ralph's corpulence.

Drama critic Frances Gray argues convincingly that the sitcom is 'the only dramatic form that has focused from the outset upon women', estimating that between 1952 and 1973 the proportion of women in prime-time comedy was 40 per cent.[32] But the 1950s is thought of as a low point for women in comedy. Gray argues that female characters usually reinforced stereotypes, with victims, secretaries, mothers, manhunters and dumb blondes the stock female characters of sitcoms. This is also true for many 1950s films – comedienne Judy Holliday could not avoid the role of the dumb blonde despite having an IQ of 174 – but sitcoms rarely escaped routine scripts or the reassertion of male authority. There are exceptions to the rule, though: Alice Kramden in *The Honeymooners* refuses to be pushed around by her domineering husband; the accident-prone teacher Miss Brooks (Eve Arden) in *Our Miss Brooks* is financially independent; and the diminutive and childlike Gracie in *The Burns and Allen Show* was self-assured in her double act with George Burns.[33]

While 1950s sitcoms influenced class aspirations and reinforced gender roles, racial stereotypes on television aroused the ire of the NAACP. One theory for the inclusion of African American characters in sitcoms was the attempt to broaden the television audience, with NBC employing a public relations team to research more realistic representations of African Americans and to scout for new actors.[34] Nevertheless, it is easy to dismiss *The Amos 'n' Andy Show* (1951–3) and *Beulah* (1950–3) as perpetrating negative black stereotypes, featuring the eccentric janitor Kingfish (Tim Moore) and the mammy figure Beulah. Although the actor Spencer Williams (who played Andy) did not think the show was racist, in 1952 the NAACP condemned *Amos 'n' Andy* and *Beulah* for reinforcing popular notions of black inferiority. The film critic Thomas Cripps argues that the shows were 'solidly rooted in a segregated world [which] cast doubt over black social goals' of integration.[35] However, there was irony in the NAACP protest: *Amos 'n' Andy* had not received many negative reviews in its run as a radio serial since 1929, and television comedy in the early 1950s was more diverse than any time again until the late 1960s. Certainly the domestic help Beulah (Hattie McDaniel in the radio series; on television Ethel Waters and Louise Beavers) is a servile character faithful to her white middle-class employers, Harry and Alice Henderson. Beulah and her friends – the slow-witted handyman Bill Jackson and the childlike maid Oriole – do little to challenge black stereotypes, even though Beulah is resourceful and often outthinks the Hendersons.

Another example of a popular ethnic sitcom was *The Goldbergs* (1949–56), also a long-running radio show presided over by Jewish writer, producer and actor Gertrude Berg as Molly Goldberg. Beginning in 1929 as *The Rise of the Goldbergs*, a weekly fifteen-minute radio show, the title reverted to *The Goldbergs* in 1938 and found popularity amongst both Jewish and non-Jewish audiences. The Goldbergs are an immigrant Jewish family newly settled in the Bronx and the comedy focuses on the clash between the European values of the parents and their Americanized offspring. The serial followed the family's life over a decade and their eventual move to the suburb of

Lastonbury, Connecticut in 1939, but the vaudeville elements and Jewish humour complicate the middle-class sitcom pattern. The transition to television in 1949 enabled the show to repeat the early story cycle, with a completely new cast (except for Gertrude Berg) relocated to suburban Haverville, New York. The show suffered network interference when Philip Loeb, who played Jake Goldberg, was blacklisted by the right-wing broadcasting report *Red Channels* for suspected links to communism, but it retained the focus on Molly's Yiddish speech patterns, her folk knowledge, and its cast of idiosyncratic characters.

It is noticeable that the diversity of television comedy of the early 1950s had waned by 1954, to leave a string of middle-class sitcoms which gave the impression of a uniform American experience. Although sitcoms continued to deal with mistaken identities and anarchic encounters, mayhem was almost invariably followed by the restoration of domestic order and the shows seldom dealt with identity politics in any coherent way. Ella Taylor describes this as the 'liberal-conservative dream of a harmonious society in which the conditions for social conflict . . . disappear because there [is] plenty of everything to go around', while Lynn Spigel argues that sitcoms were geared to issues of childrearing and downplayed vaudeville elements in favour of a more naturalistic style.[36] Not only did this comedic form meet audience expectations, but also the domestic tribulations of the suburban characters helped to distract viewers from attending to deeper social divisions.

I Love Lucy

The most popular television show of the 1950s was without doubt the situation comedy *I Love Lucy*. The first weekly episode was aired on CBS on 15 October 1951 and it became a mainstay of American comedy through the decade. The series showcased comedienne Lucille Ball who had appeared in over fifty, largely unsuccessful, films for four different studios in the 1940s; she had become a household name through the CBS radio comedy *My Favorite Husband* (1948–51), in which she played Liz Cooper, a forerunner of her television persona Lucy Ricardo. The transition to television enabled Ball to add slapstick to the observational family comedy of the radio series. Given the paucity of women in comedy on either side of the Atlantic, there were few female comic role models for Ball to follow, and the fact that she was 40 when the series first aired was itself a challenge to Hollywood's emphasis on youth. Ball found her inspiration in vaudeville and silent comedy, particularly Charlie Chaplin's tramp, the mischievous Harpo Marx, and the deadpan physical comedy of Buster Keaton. Ball also filtered the mugging, disguise and grostequerie of female vaudeville comedy into Lucy, the wannabe star and exuberant wife of Ricky Ricardo, band leader at the Tropicana Club, played by real-life Cuban husband Desi Arnaz. The husband-and-wife team and the show's domestic setting encouraged viewers to engage closely with Lucy and Ricky's antics, while Lucy's relentless search for recognition fitted in with the vogue for stardom.

The show was punctuated with song and dance numbers that Ball and Arnaz had performed in vaudeville during the summer of 1950, but it was Lucy's comic capers that stole the show; as Stefan Kafer comments: 'not since Carol Lombard [in the 1930s] had there been a glamorous woman so willing to make a fool of herself in pursuit of laughter'.[37] Ball's physical comedy was framed against the domestic setting of *I Love Lucy*, which strove for familiarity with its audience by focusing on the married life of the Ricardos and their middle-aged neighbours Fred and Ethel Mertz (William Frawley and Vivian Vance). Running for six series from 1951–8 the location shifts from Manhattan in the first three series (1951–4), to California in the fourth season (where all the episodes were shot), to a season charting the Ricardos and Mertzes in Europe (1955–6), and to the suburban setting of Connecticut in season six (1956–7) where the two couples remained together – an element that Lynn Spigel notes was common among shows like *The Honeymooners* for extending 'metaphors of neighbourhood'.[38] Most *Lucy* episodes focused on the Ricardo household, with scripts such as 'The Freezer' (28 April 1952) mining the comic potential of domesticity: when Lucy and Ethel order far too much beef to store in Lucy's new walk-in freezer they decide to go into town to sell the excess meat to unsuspecting housewives before Ricky catches them. The situations become ever more farcical, with Lucy getting into ridiculous scrapes – in the same episode she becomes locked in the freezer and is transformed into a frozen piece of meat.

Preceding the centrality of the TV set in mid-decade shows, some *Lucy* episodes such as 'The Quiz Show' (12 November 1951), 'Ricky and Fred are TV Fans' (22 June 1953) and 'Mr and Mrs TV Show' (1 November 1954) make television the focus, and other episodes in the first series parody the advertising industry, particularly 'Lucy Does A TV Commercial' (5 May 1952). In this episode, Lucy is determined to front a commercial for Vitameatavegamin, a tonic which promises to overcome listlessness but has hidden alcoholic properties. Ricky wants a young 'pretty girl' to do the commercial for his act, and Lucy has to resort to deception and tricks (including an audition literally inside a TV set) to put herself in line for the role. However, Lucy has to do so many takes in the studio before the producer is happy with her performance that she consumes a hefty quantity of the tonic in the process. At first the medicine is repulsive to her, but after several spoonfuls it lives up to its promise of tasting 'just like candy'. Vitameatavegamin's ridiculous name becomes ever more twisted by Lucy's slurred words – degenerating into 'Vita-veeda-vigee-vat' and

'Vita-meedy-mega-meenie-moe-a-mis' – and her handling of the script is ever more farcical as she abandons taking the tonic with a spoon and slugs from the bottle. By the time Ricky appears to perform his musical act, Lucy is blind drunk and completely disruptive.

Episodes of *I Love Lucy* were filmed in front of a live audience using three separate cameras (a technique first devised in 1950) and Ball often improvised on set using Arnaz as her comic foil. Such was the show's popularity that it won two Emmys in its first two years and the episode 'Lucy Goes to the Hospital' (19 January 1953), in which Lucy gives birth the day after Ball had done so, knocked Eisenhower's inauguration off the front page of the papers. But it is important to avoid simply equating *I Love Lucy* with Ball's comic performance: equally vital were writer-producer Jess Oppenheimer and co-writers Madelyn Pugh and Bob Carroll Jr (who had all worked on *My Favorite Husband*), the cinematographer Karl Freud, and the work behind the scenes of Arnaz, particularly in establishing the independent company Desilu in 1950, after buying out RKO.[39]

Desilu was set up to promote the couple's vaudeville act, but the importance of the independent company with its 50 per cent share in *Lucy* was demonstrated in 1953 when Ball's name was connected with communism, an accusation which went back to 1936 when Lucille and her brother Fred registered communists for their grandfather. When Ball's name was cited in *Red Channels*, she was threatened with the blacklist. The FBI had extensive files on Ball and Arnaz, and for most actors it would have been the end of their career. But Ball was cleared of suspicion after testifying as a witness at a HUAC subcommittee in September 1953, and Arnaz began the third series of *I Love Lucy* with an impassioned speech stressing that communists had chased him out of Cuba and that Ball had never been a party member.[40]

The phenomenon of *I Love Lucy* stemmed not just from the viewers' identification with the show's characters and settings, but also the fact that the cultural journey of the Ricardos reflected directly – and even helped to shape – the trajectory of national culture. The visibility of commodities (including the show's sponsor up to 1955, Philip Morris cigarettes), the trappings of suburbia, and the nation's love affair with Europe in the mid-1950s, echoed the lives of many middle-class Americans and gave viewers a sense that their experiences were shared ones. Lori Landay argues that the show was a triumph of commodification, with merchandise (including fanzines, clothes, games, furniture, and dolls after the birth of Little Ricky in 1953) reinforcing *I Love Lucy* as a 'central story cycle' of the 1950s with its narrative of marriage, domesticity, and the desire for a middle-class lifestyle.[41] But while the show became part of cultural commodification, Lucy's exuberant personality and her constant straining against the conventions of marriage (dissatisfied with the role of housewife) and social expectations (with its emphasis on youth and glamour) gave many episodes a more subversive edge. However, although Lucy's adventures and incompetence led her into disastrous scrapes in the public sphere, the episodes often ended with her seeking sanctuary in domesticity and plots resolved themselves with the patriarchal reaffirmation of Ricky as the man of the house.[42]

After the sixth series ended in May 1957 there were thirteen one-hour specials: *The Lucy-Desi Comedy Hour* (2 March 1960) was the last, filmed during the break-up of Ball and Arnaz's marriage. CBS scheduled re-runs of early episodes in the mid-1950s and the persona of Lucy was kept alive into the 1960s, with Ball portraying her as a widow and single mother. But the fact that these later shows – *The Lucy Show* (1962–8, with Vivian Vance as Lucy's sidekick), *Here's Lucy* (1968–74) and the very short-lived *Life with Lucy* (1986) – did not have the impact of *I Love Lucy* suggest that the Lucy phenomenon was deeply wedded to 1950s ideology and culture.

Figure 4.3 Lucille Ball tests Vitameatavegamin in 'Lucy Does a TV Commercial', *I Love Lucy* (CBS, 5 May 1952).

Directors, Studios and Stars

In 1955 French critic Jacques Rivette declared that there was nothing in the American film industry outside Hollywood, while inside the industry he detected two trends: 'the Hollywood of sums and the Hollywood of individuals'.[43] Like other critics writing in the French publication *Cahiers du cinéma* in the 1950s, Rivette championed Nicholas Ray, Richard Brooks, Otto Preminger and Samuel Fuller as filmmakers whose vision remained true despite industry demands. Rivette looked to directors aged around forty as the emerging talent that might rescue Hollywood from the challenge of television and the disorganization that was besetting the studio system. Some of the directors named by Rivette – Anthony Mann, Robert Aldrich and Richard Fleischer – did not have a profound influence on filmmaking in the 1950s, and Sam Fuller was not fully given recognition until the 1960s as the first director to tackle military conflict in Korea and Vietnam. Some important directors like Billy Wilder were neglected by the Cahiers critics, but what linked this group for Rivette was 'a virile anger that comes from the heart' which brings a 'gust of fresh air to filmmaking' with more youthful subjects and skilled cinematography.[44]

Critics tend to focus on three directors – Nicholas Ray, Alfred Hitchcock and Douglas Sirk – as the most distinctive filmmakers of the decade, although Sirk was not really given critical acclaim until the 1970s. European influences were strong for all three directors: Hitchcock arrived in the US from Britain in 1939 and Sirk from Germany in 1940, and Ray's cinematic interests are often thought to be distinctly European. French director François Truffaut noted that all Ray's films from the film noir *In a Lonely Place* (1950) and gangster film *On Dangerous Ground* (1952) to the western *Johnny Guitar* (1954) and the medical tale of middle-class angst *Bigger Than Life* (1956) are marked by ambiguous characters surrounded by 'moral solitude'.

Ray and Preminger were alike in shifting between film genres to explore the interrelationship between character and environment. As Rivette commented, their characters are 'closed in on themselves, turned inward, exactly as a statue can be, presenting themselves without immediately stating an identity'.[45] Hitchcock was equally interested in developing cinematic techniques to explore murder, revenge and psychological uncertainty in his wave of films *Strangers on a Train* (1951), *Dial M for Murder* (1953), *Rear Window* (1954), *Vertigo* (1958) and *North By Northwest* (1959), while Sirk's vivid use of colour and domestic mise-en-scène is a feature of his major melo-dramas: *All That Heaven Allows* (1955), *Written on the Wind* (1956) and *Imitation of Life* (1959).[46] More than anything else, these directors helped to shift the priorities of filmmaking towards an engagement with its visual qualities.

In the late 1940s Truffaut, Rivette and André Bazin were claiming that French filmmakers lacked the more expansive sense of what cinema could achieve as a visual medium of storytelling. What they saw in Ray, Hitchcock and Sirk was a balance between the creative and commercial imperatives of filmmaking. The visual immediacy of their films was attractive to audiences, but also offered a critical focus for exploring cultural and social issues. This balancing act was not easy to maintain: Hitchcock's tense relationship with producer David O. Selznick in the 1940s led to some uneven films before they parted company, while Ray was criticized because audiences and critics felt 'ill at ease' about his blurring of distinct genres.[47] Nevertheless, if Orson Welles was the clearest example of modernism in the American movies during the 1940s, then the mantle was taken over by this triad of filmmakers in the following decade. While Hitchcock, for example, had trained in Britain, he was also very excited by German Expressionism and Soviet montage, and brought modernist experimentalism to bear on the climactic fairground scene in *Strangers on a Train* and the collision of fantasy and obsession in *Vertigo*. Whereas Ray and Preminger were interested in moving between genres to 'reveal the very essence of cinema', one view of Hitchcock's and Sirk's movies in the 1950s is that they were simply updating their earlier films made in Britain and Germany.[48]

All these directors placed emphasis on maintaining autonomy and control over the artistic direction of their films. For example, Sirk was very pleased that his studio Universal 'did not interfere with either my camera work or my cutting' and, although he found the 3-D format unhelpful, he was quite willing to experiment with new technologies to help in his exploration of the 'folklore of American melodrama' and his challenge to postwar expectations about class, race and gender.[49]

The result was that in their films technique and theme became closely entwined. This modernist tendency in filmmaking brought technical experiments with deep focus, lighting and mise-en-scène into close contact with modernist themes of entrapment, psychic confusion and frustrated desire. For example, Ray was often credited for the architectural qualities of his film, with the critic V. F. Perkins noting Ray's use of 'static masses with bold lines – walls, staircases, doors, rocks – which intrude into the frame' and threatening images that close down on characters.[50] Similarly, although Sirk was not a radical exponent of modernism, the colour intensities and his architectural sets reveal as much about the neuroses and conflicts of his characters as they do about Sirk's attention to cinematic detail. As critic Jeremy Butler argues, Sirk developed a style in the 1950s in which visual disequilibrium (involving framing, lighting, movement, camera angle) amplified themes of domestic containment and frustrated aspirations, particularly in *Imitation of Life* in which the chosen profession of Lora Meredith (Lana Turner) as a self-absorbed Broadway actress embodies the 'lifelessness at the centre of the film'.[51]

There is a danger of taking the *Cahiers* view as the sole account of 1950s film, privileging the likes of Hitchcock and Ray while denigrating 'Hollywood film' for being commercially driven. Largely due to the influence of the *Cahiers* group on British and American film critics (such as Andrew Sarris and Robin Wood), the decade is remembered as a time when a handful of creative directors were expressing their personal vision, but the danger is to overlook the ways in which film production was changing. The studio system was increasingly under strain through the decade and B-movies began to tail off with the rise of genre-based television shows leading Warner Bros and Fox to drop B-pictures altogether in 1952. But this was accompanied by the rise of small art-film theaters (226 full-time 'sure-seaters' in 1956 rising to 800 by 1958) and an interest in international products, with 93 foreign films in circulation in 1948 climbing to 532 by 1957.[52]

Two consequences of the Supreme Court ruling of 1948 were that studios were forced to relinquish ownership of cinema chains and that a more complex set of industry negotiations arose, meaning that studios could not always claim sole ownership of a movie. This is often explained as a shift from the 'producer unit' to the 'package unit' system, in which producers were no longer committed to making a requisite number of films for a studio with the same pool of staff. Another way of explaining this is as part of the broader shift from 'Old Hollywood' to 'New Hollywood' and the growth of media corporations in which television broadcasting began to play a significant role. Although job losses resulted from this shift, there were also benefits. Douglas Sirk claimed that Universal gave him more freedom as the studio was content to contribute finance, marketing and distribution; it helped to professionalize some technical roles; provided contracts for talent agencies and location consultants; and contributed to the growth of associations representing the independent sector.[53] But some vital jobs in the industry, such as screenwriting, continued to be undervalued. As industry movies such as *The Bad and the Beautiful* (1952) and *The Barefoot Contessa* (1954) reveal, where directors garnered critical success and producers reaped great financial rewards, screenwriters tended to be treated badly even after a string of successful projects.

Twentieth Century-Fox, Paramount and Universal controlled nearly all studio output in the 1950s and they ploughed money into rigorous promotional campaigns, as well as relying on cross-media advertising, film-related magazines, and the growth of fan clubs to increase the visibility of their major star images. And in the early 1950s the media machine went into overdrive in turning an unknown actress in *The Asphalt Jungle* (1950) into a box office sensation by 1953.

Marilyn Monroe's face and profile outdid any other actress in Hollywood, from the blondes Kim Novak and Jayne Mansfield to brunettes Elizabeth Taylor and Jane Russell. Richard Dyer argues that Monroe's image was so centrally constructed around sexual spectacle that her characters required little biographical depth. Bare details are usually given: we know very little of her character Rose Loomis in the neo-noir *Niagara* (1953); the back-story of *Gentlemen Prefer Blondes* (1953) is about the mistaken love for a drummer; and in some films such as *The Seven Year Itch* (1955) Monroe is simply known as 'the Girl'.[54] Although Monroe was not the first actress to perfect the dumb blonde – Judy Holliday and Jayne Mansfield both worked with the role – she managed to achieve a combination of naturalness and artifice, emphasized by the fact that many of her characters are 'innocents', childlike in their dependency on others and uncorrupted by the affairs of the world.[55] Even her third husband Arthur Miller bought into this 'mass fantasy' of Monroe as the latest in a lineage of screen seductresses; as critic Sarah Churchwell concludes: 'everyone was always looking for the real Marilyn Monroe while insisting that she only did what came naturally'.[56]

One way of reading stardom in the 1950s is that whereas actors received much of the fame, the producer and the studio remained in control, assigning actors to pictures in 'their range – and within the range of the audience's expectations'.[57] Actors had much to gain from studios, but it is easy to see them – especially those who died young or had troubled private lives – as victims of Hollywood. Despite shifts in film production, studios continued to own their actors, such as

Monroe who signed a seven-year contract with Fox in 1950, whereas actors trying to make a career outside the studio system were very vulnerable. For example, Dorothy Dandridge, almost the only black actress in the 1950s to achieve mainstream film success, in the musicals *Carmen Jones* (1954) and *Porgy and Bess* (1959), struggled to find serious roles in a white industry and had to rely on her singing accomplishments to get by. Whereas Ava Gardner and Natalie Wood used industry relationships to enhance their careers, Dandridge lacked a support system (even after signing a three-picture deal with Fox) and had to conceal her affair with Otto Preminger for fear it would ruin both their careers.[58]

Publicity campaigns were carefully constructed to give stars maximum exposure; movies often had exotic locations or musical interludes to justify the extravagant costumes of their female leads; and magazine features introduced future stars to the broader public. However, professional photographers sometimes managed to glimpse behind the cloak of stardom. *Life* photographer Phil Stern's famous peek-a-boo shot of James Dean's head hiding in his sweater in 1955 reveals Dean's vulnerability and discomfort with his star persona just months before his death, while Stern's startled shot of Monroe on set with Jack Benny in 1953 contrasts with Milton Greene's costume shots of her from the same year in which she is transformed into a statuesque Greta Garbo.[59] It was also clear that star images were partly moulded in the public domain. Critic Samantha Barbas notes that fans were outraged that Gloria Swanson did not win an Oscar for her role as the ageing movie star in *Sunset Boulevard* and other fans wrote to Jennifer Jones to plead that the studios do not 'make a vamp out of you' and reminding her not to become 'stereotyped by magazines'.[60] But fans could turn hostile when their star disappointed them, sometimes disbanding fan clubs or withdrawing support as many did towards Ingrid Bergman when she had an affair with filmmaker Roberto Rossellini in 1949.[61]

A key tension in the American film industry was between the actor as artist and the actor as movie star. Actors arriving from theatre such as Marlon Brando, James Dean and Sidney Poitier suggested new possibilities for drama/film crossovers, particularly within the method school of acting (see Chapter 2). Even Monroe wanted to try out classes at the Actors Studio in 1955 to improve her chances of landing serious roles, although many critics thought Monroe's acting aspirations were pretentious and echoed the title of journalist Pete Martin's 1956 book *Will Acting Spoil Marilyn Monroe?* Studios were often cautious with casting: stalwarts of the studio era such as James Stewart, Cary Grant, Fred Astaire and Clark Gable were frequently paired with younger actresses because they were reliable and bankable.

But it was Hollywood glamour and the increased media exposure of award ceremonies that struck a chord with the commercial culture of the decade. The twenty-fifth year of the Academy Awards in March 1953 was televised by NBC for the first time from New York and Los Angeles. Even though it took another five years before the Oscars were fully sponsored by the industry, and many complained about the excessive commercials from the sponsor Oldsmobile, in 1953 one critic claimed that 'instead of finding themselves strange bedfellows, the arch-enemies [of film and television] discovered they were pleasantly compatible'.[62] By mid-decade the religious and classical epics had given way to films about consumption, with characters and audiences indulging in commercial spectacle alike. Even the social problem film *The Man with the Golden Arm* (1955), dealing with heroin addiction in a working-class area of Chicago, depicts the lure of consumables when junkie-drummer Frankie Machine (Frank Sinatra) and Molly (Kim Novak) play out a fantasy of suburban marital bliss as they gaze into a department-store window.

Other films explicitly encouraged consumption. Howard Hawks's 1953 adaptation of Anita Loos's satirical *Gentlemen Prefer Blondes*, for example, was a major box office success, with Monroe replacing the stage star Carol Channing as the flamboyant gold-digging starlet Lorelei Lee, while another Monroe vehicle *How to Marry a Millionaire* (1953) was shot in CinemaScope to emphasize its consumerist themes.[63] With hindsight, the success of MGM and Fox film spectaculars up to the mid-decade did little to disguise the 'last gasp of the studio era', as Thomas Schatz calls it; but, at the time, the combination of star talent and new technologies seemed to offer new potential for mainstream filmmaking.[64] Some directors working in the comic genre such as Frank Tashlin thought seriously about how certain actors (Bob Hope, Jerry Lewis and Danny Kaye) suited particular modes of comedy, but more often than not studio scripts were tailored to star vehicles, with the ageing Fred Astaire and dancer Cyd Charisse returning for MGM's *Silk Stockings* (1957) after their success in *The Band Wagon* (1953). It was perhaps this link between 'stars' and 'consumption' that led Alfred Hitchcock to explore the interrelation between voyeurism and stardom in his most technically accomplished film: *Rear Window*.

Rear Window (1954)

Although Nicholas Ray and Elia Kazan were very interested in method acting and drawn to young theatrically trained actors like James Dean and Marlon Brando, Alfred Hitchcock was notorious for underplaying the role of screen actors. For Hitchcock the actor should follow the command of the director, 'leaving the camera to add most of the accents and emphases', as he commented in 1937.[65] Idiosyncratic or exaggerated acting detracted from his idea of 'pure cinema' in which film editing and the juxtaposition of shots creates a particular subjective effect, in contrast to 'photographs of people talking' as Hitchcock dismissively described conventional filmmaking.[66] He considered the closest he came to pure cinema to be his 1954 film Rear Window, which tells the story of a temporarily immobile character Jeffries (James Stewart) observing his Greenwich Village neighbours from his apartment window. Suffering from a broken leg Jeffries cannot leave the apartment as a regular sleuth would, but is limited to the view from his rear window. On suspecting a murder in a nearby apartment, he is forced to carry out detective work by visual means with a variety of optical equipment he has to hand in his job as photojournalist.

'Looking' is not just a theme in Rear Window but suffuses every aspect of it, leading the critic John Belton to note that the film is ultimately ' "about" spectacle; it explores the fascination with looking'.[67] This theme was earlier noted by the two Cahiers critics, Eric Rohmer and Claude Chabrol, who were very interested in the viewer's invitation to share Jeffries' voyeurism. Although Jeffries begins by observing his neighbours just to pass the day, he soon develops a voyeur's interest in their activities, particularly when one female neighbour Mrs Thorwald disappears following a domestic fight. Although occasionally the viewer has a privileged angle on the apartment block while Jeffries sleeps, because we share his point of view (limited to the block, with only a glimpse of the city outside), his desires become our own. This double operation of 'viewing' led Rohmer and Chabrol to comment that Jeffries and the viewer share the same hopes: 'the crime is desired by the man who expects to make of his discovery . . . the very sense of his life. The crime is desired by us, the spectators, who fear nothing so much as seeing our hopes deceived'.[68] By the time Hitchcock was learning his craft in the 1920s filmmaking had moved on from the 'cinema of attractions' of the early silent era, but the emphasis on visual spectacle remained central to his films. Long sequences in Rear Window are shot with virtually no sound, using close-ups and cutting to emphasize Jeffries' reactions to the story strands that he pieces together from his neighbours' activities.

Hitchcock and screenwriter John Michael Hayes adapted Rear Window from a 1942 short story by the crime writer Cornell Woolrich. The basics of the narrative are retained – an immobile protagonist and an assumed murder – but the film noir mode and first-person narrative voice of Woolrich's story is transformed into a meditation on cinematic viewing and the ethics of becoming a rear-window voyeur.[69] Not only were suspicion of surveillance and fear of the unseen enemy pressing cultural concerns in 1954, but Hitchcock and Hayes also extend the theme of looking into the subplot of *Rear Window* which involves a completely new character: Lisa Fremont played by Grace Kelly. Established as a high-society fashion model, Lisa is constantly trying to attract Jeffries' attention away from his window by wearing an array of seductive costumes, arranging a romantic dinner, and preparing for a night of romance with the enticing words 'preview of coming attractions'. The main conflict in the film concerns Jeffries' desire, caught between his interest in Lisa and his fascination with the rear apartment in which he is convinced a murder has been committed.

The film encourages a psychoanalytic reading, particularly given the currency of Freudian thought in the mid-1950s: Jeffries' refusal to commit to Lisa seems to be bound up with his impotence (symbolized by his immobile leg) and his comfortable relationship with the maternal nurse Stella (Thelma Ritter) who tends to Jeffries' physiotherapy. However, the tensions between Jeffries and Lisa also stem from their class positions, with Lisa moving in high society and Jeffries more comfortable in Stella's unthreatening working-class world. Both themes are linked closely to gender roles, with the dominant reading of the film suggesting that Lisa moulds herself to become the acceptable object of Jeffries' desire. As the film progresses Lisa appears to meet Jeffries on his own terms, abandoning her glamorous evening wear for a more practical dress and literally becoming Jeffries' legs when she agrees to visit Thorwald's apartment (a role carried out by a black servant in Woolrich's story).

However, there is a reversal here. In her active role Lisa literally becomes the film's protagonist, but she unintentionally helps Thorwald to locate the apartment from which he is being observed. Although Thorwald is caught soon after entering Jeffries' apartment, their scuffle ends with Jeffries breaking his other leg when he falls from the window. The film concludes with Jeffries having both legs in plaster and Lisa reading an adventure magazine, only for her to reveal a disguised copy of *Harper's Bazaar* while he sleeps, suggesting that she has retained her fashion interests despite learning the rules of Jeffries' game. As Sarah Street notes, Lisa thus can be seen as a 'double threat to Jeff in her ultrafeminine costumes and her guise as an action-woman: both paralyze him with anxiety about his own masculinity'.[70]

Despite being more consistent than Nicholas Ray in working within the genre of psychological thriller, the unifying elements of Hitchcock's films greatly impressed the *Cahiers* critics. It was not that Hitchcock was drawn to distinctive colour schemes, such as the symbolic colour of Lisa's dresses and the red glare of Jeffries' flash bulb (his only weapon when Thorwald finally enters the apartment) or the use of doubles – subtly in *Rear Window* as Lisa transforms from high-society model to rear-window sleuth, and more explicitly in the double life of the blonde Madelaine and the brunette Judy in *Vertigo* (both played by Kim Novak). It was, rather, the way in which Hitchcock united these elements on moral, psychological, visual and spatial levels, contributing to his notion of 'pure cinema' free from the conventions of literary narrative. Although he was a darling of the *Cahiers* critics, Hitchcock always considered himself a more radical film-maker than he arguably was. While *Rear Window* was technically very accomplished, John Belton notes that its narrative structure conforms to the classical Hollywood pattern, intertwining the mystery or quest story and the romance story 'through the theme of voyeurism', ending in resolution when the two stories are brought together.[71]

Figure 4.4 Alfred Hitchcock on the set of *Rear Window* with James Stewart and Grace Kelly (1954).

Social Problem Films

Even though there was a stream of formulaic films produced in the 1950s, film culture usually did much better in questioning social stereo-types than did television. The NAACP had protested against negative representations of African Americans in Hollywood since the 1930s, but a range of films in the 1940s dealt with class conflict and the effects of economic scarcity. The major reason why social problem films decreased in number was the fear of anticommunist reprisal as HUAC began new hearings in 1951. The subpoenas of the Hollywood Ten in 1947 was a clear indication that the power of film images worried HUAC and the compilers of the industry blacklist *Red Channels*, but films dealing with class and race conflict continued into the early 1950s before giving way, in the main, to spectaculars such as religious epics and consumer films. Movies like *The Men* and *Bright Victory* (both 1951) which dealt with the difficulties faced by war veterans reintegrating into civilian society were slowly phased out (marking the end of the cycle of World War II demobilization films such as *The Best Years of Our Lives*, 1946), while films of working-class life were always in danger of being labelled communist propaganda.

One way of viewing genre-based science-fiction and westerns is as escapist film products, transporting audiences away from cold war anxieties (although these anxieties could easily be reinforced in public-safety films such as *Pattern for Survival*, released in October 1950 to show how civilians should act during an atomic attack). This is the response encouraged by director Robert Wise to his sci-fi film *The Day the Earth Stood Still* (1951), claiming that it was primarily geared towards entertainment. But the whole film is rich with social commentary: the spaceship lands in the centre of a baseball pitch in Washington DC; the humanoid alien Klaatu (Michael Rennie) tries to track down the greatest thinker in the world, Professor Brainard (who closely resembles Albert Einstein) because the government does not listen to him; and Klaatu warns at the end of the film that if world leaders do not mend their ways and reach a peace accord then he will be forced to obliterate the planet. Because *The Day the Earth Stood Still* has the trappings of a sci-fi B-movie and it offers, in part, a child's-eye view of alien landings, it escaped the serious responsibilities that often weighed down social problem films. In fact, science-fiction seemed the perfect vehicle for exploring the complexities of the atomic age without needing a clear-cut moral message, from the apocalyptic warning at the end of *The Thing From Another World* (1951) for citizens to 'watch the skies', the dramatic effects of radiation on the protagonist of *The Incredible Shrinking Man* (1957), and the parallels made between communist and alien invasions in invasion narratives such as *Invaders from Mars* (1953) and *Invasion of the Body Snatchers* (1957).

Westerns were also useful vehicles for exploring issues that could not be addressed directly. The western genre was undergoing changes in the 1950s, with the strong masculinist myths of the West open to challenges and new themes. For example, *The Searchers* (1956),

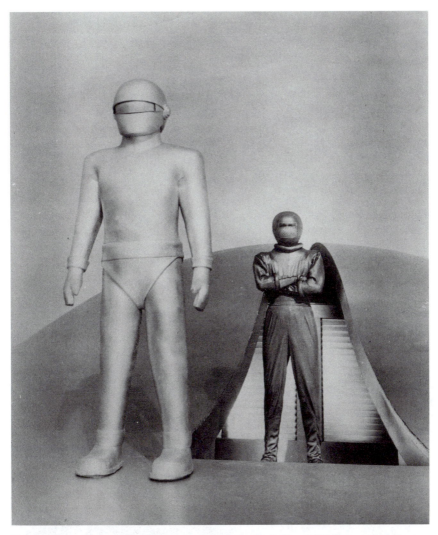

Figure 4.5 Gort the robot and Klaatu in *The Day the Earth Stood Still* (Robert Wise, Fox, 1951). Wisconsin Center for Film and Theater Research.

Gunman's Walk (1958) and *The Unforgiven* (1960) all deal with the problems of miscegenation and white supremacist attitudes to the integration of races. Ethan Edwards (John Wayne) in John Ford's *The Searchers* spends years searching for his lost niece, only to turn on her when he realizes that she has been concubined by a Comanche chief, while the tensions between two brothers, the wild racist Ed Hackett (Tab Hunter) and the progressive liberal Davy Hackett (James Darren)

Figure 4.6 Grant Williams and Randy Stuart in a publicity shot for *The Incredible Shrinking Man* (Jack Arnold, Universal, 1957). Wisconsin Center for Film and Theater Research.

in *Gunman's Walk* are played out when Davy falls in love with the mixed-race Clee Chouard (Kathryn Grant) who is half-French and half-Indian. Their father Lee Hackett (Van Heflin) has a temperament akin to his tough-living elder son and is appalled that his younger son might marry a 'half-breed'. But, in the end, Lee is forced to confront his conscience by killing Ed (when his eldest son is hunted down for committing murder) before reconciling himself to Davy and his fiancée.

These films deal centrally with race, but also the ways in which the rugged masculinity of the West was under siege from 1950s domesticity. The links between racial arrogance and masculine bravado were tackled directly in Norman Mailer's and James Jones's war novels *The Naked and the Dead* and *From Here to Eternity*, but also on a more subtle level in the film musical *The King and I* (1956) and the Hong Kong-based melodramas *Love is a Many-Splendored Thing* (1955) and *The World of Suzie Wong* (1960). The exotic settings of these films possess a degree of fantasy, but Hong Kong also offered a 'place where a postwar American identity can be defined against an emerging Asian communism and the decay of European colonialism'.[72] Gina Marchetti argues that Hong Kong was attractive as a liminal space between the West and the East (the Asian equivalent of the gateway city of Paris in *Silk Stockings*) in which cold war oppositions could be played out in a mixed-race love story without the stigma that would arise if set in the Deep South or the Midwest. But, while patriarchal order is maintained in these Hong Kong films, a spate of magazine articles claimed in 1957–8 that American men were going soft, and films as diverse as *Rear Window*, *Gunman's Walk*, *The King and I*, *Sayonara* and *Home From the Hill* were severely testing traditional forms of masculinity.

It is a fallacy to suggest that social-problem films died out entirely, they just became rarer and were often diluted with directors working strategically within genres. There was a sliding scale of such films, from explicit attacks on prejudice and injustice to more subtle social commentary, and the rise of independent filmmakers later in the decade led to a plethora of competing voices rather than a few worthy message films sponsored by major studios. At the most extreme were films such as *Salt of the Earth* (1954) made by blacklisted artists among the Hollywood Ten focusing on labour strikes in New Mexico and *Storm Center* (1956) which explores the stance of a librarian Alicia Hull (Bette Davis) against the board of governors when they compel her to remove a book on Soviet communism from her school library. More subtle explorations of class consciousness are found in *On the Waterfront*, *The Man with the Golden Arm* and *Tea and Sympathy*, but these are films in which the message about ameliorating class or interpersonal conflict is unclear. Made one year after Elia Kazan's explicitly cold war film *Man on a Tightrope* (1953), *On the Waterfront* – a film that many critics have read as Kazan and screenwriter Budd Schulberg's justification for their decision to testify in front of HUAC – ends with the charismatic figure of Terry Molloy (Marlon Brando) leading the workers forward on 'the lawless frontier' of the industrial waterfront to smash the corrupt power of the mob.[73] Love is often presented as the answer to intractable social problems: Terry is redeemed by the love of Edie Doyle (Eva Marie Saint); *The Man with the Golden Arm* suggests that tough love can reform even the most hardened drug addict; and *Tea and Sympathy* opts for platonic love to offset the bigotry behind school bullying.

Although film censorship was weakening, limits remained about what could be represented. Mental illness was still a tricky subject for film, although a spate of Tennessee Williams adaptations featuring individuals under extreme stress did not prevent *The Three Faces of Eve* (1957) from re-enforcing gender stereotypes, with Joanne Woodward's schizophrenic character involuntarily switching between very stylised gender roles (despite being based on extensive medical reports). One could look to the challenging subject-matter of the Theodore Drieser adaptation *Carrie* (1952), or the dramatization of the famous 1906 murder case in *The Girl in the Red Velvet Swing* (1955), or adapted plays by Williams and Inge for broadening the thematic range of films.[74] Williams even turned his hand to screenwriting for Elia Kazan's film *Baby Doll* (1956), which caused a major stir in its depiction of an older man's sexual relationship with a younger woman. The scrutiny of the censors was closely focused on material dealing with sexual liaisons across race, age and gender lines; even in the early 1960s Stanley Kubrick was forced to cast a sixteen-year-old Sue Lyon as the thirteen-year-old Lolita in his 1961 adaptation of Nabokov's *Lolita*, while the cross-race relationships planned for the jazz film *Paris Blues* (1961) were scotched when the studio, MGM, applied pressure. While novelists and playwrights could push back boundaries, censorship issues meant that directors had to avoid issues of pregnancy outside marriage, same-sex love and interracial relationships – or at least find strategies for sidestepping them.

One film that attempted to grapple with race conflict was the adaptation of South African Alan Paton's 1948 novel *Cry, the Beloved Country*. Directed by Zoltan Korda in 1951 and shot in Africa and England, the film adopts a neo-realist perspective for examining what a *New York Times* review called 'the whole tragedy of hate' at the root of apartheid which was enforced in South Africa in 1948.[75] The film is a clear example of another social trend: that of 'the cultural front', which was much more explicit in its dealing with social and political issues than the modernism of Welles, Hitchcock and Ray, but which, as Paul Robeson found out, was a difficult stance to maintain in the early 1950s. *Cry, the Beloved Country* was historically significant as it featured Canada Lee and Sidney Poitier as black priests at a time when Lee was finding it very difficult to secure acting jobs because of his communist sympathies. This fact was not lost on the *Times* reviewer in making parallels between the situation in South Africa and the United States and bemoaning the fact that most American directors concentrate on 'surface aspects of segregation' rather than digging 'beneath the surface to the human wellsprings'. The reviewer was right that most films dealing with race skirted around tricky issues, even after the *Brown* v. *the Board of Education* ruling of 1954. It is also an indication that the cultural front was struggling against ideological pressures, and did not re-emerge until the late 1950s with the rise of the New Left and the grassroots energies of the civil rights movement.

There were odd exceptions to this failure to engage with race, particularly at the beginning of the decade, in films such as *No Way Out* (1950). Ostensibly a film about postwar medicine, *No Way Out* deals explicitly with race hatred between a wounded gangster Ray Biddle (Richard Widmark) and an African American doctor Dr Luther Brooks (Sidney Poitier), and even goes as far as dramatizing a race riot. There were some forays into dealing directly with race in the second half of the decade, such as interracial love in *Island in the Sun* (1957), racial passing in *Imitation of Life* (1959) and black–white friendship in *The Defiant Ones* (1958). Some contemporary critics thought that this trend was 'a welcome, bold, even enlightened sign of changing times', while others saw it 'as a pathetically inadequate and exploitative response' to racial problems.[76] Whichever view is adopted, directors and studios that broached racial subjects usually had to deal with reprisals: cinemas in South Carolina planning to show the Caribbean-based *Island in the Sun* were threatened with a $5,000 fine, even though there is no direct reference to cross-race love between its two stars Harry Belafonte and Joan Fontaine. Black stereotypes were common (such as in the 1959 film version of Gershwin's *Porgy and Bess*) and white liberal sympathy was regularly identified as the answer to race prejudice.

Because this cycle of race films divided critics, Susan Courtney argues that there were 'no signs of consensus' when it came to racial questions.[77] Nevertheless, many films were forced to compromise, particularly when it came to cross-race relationships and class issues. It was not until the end of the decade with independent director Lionel Rogosin's *Come Back Africa* (1960) that racial themes were tackled in all their complexity. Nominated for an Oscar and gaining awards in Britain and Italy, *Come Back Africa* met resistance in the US State Department, with pressure on European outlets to prevent it being shown, despite its focus on the township of Johannesburg and the fact that Rogosin had never been a communist.[78] Avoiding the seamless construction of classical Hollywood films and the theatrical style of *Cry, the Beloved Country*, Rogosin pointed the way forward for cinema verité filmmakers in the 1960s by using episodic sequences and non-professional actors to emphasize that economic, housing and racial issues are all entwined.

If race films tended to focus on white liberal professionals as having the acumen to find answers to racial conflict, then one general trajectory of the social problem film in the mid-1950s was an emphasis on education. A number of films explored the relationship between teachers and pupils: *The Blackboard Jungle* (1955) and *As Young as We Are* (1958) both tackle intergenerational conflict in the classroom, while *The Wild One* (1953) plays out this conflict in the street. But youth films did not take long to become predictable with the rebellious teenager getting his just deserts or learning to see his parents' point of view. Whereas rites-of-passage novels such as *The Member of the Wedding* and *The Catcher in the Rye* had room to resist straightforward conclusions, teen films often played for kicks or chose to resolve intergenerational conflict through reconciliation or tragic catharsis.[79]

It is a mistake to think that films were not engaging with intellectual sources, though. Sociological books such as educationist Benjamin Fine's *One Million Delinquents* (1956), which claimed delinquency was on a tragic upswing and anticipated two million delinquents in the US by 1960, were behind many of the youth movies.[80] Indeed, it is possible to argue that the mass media in the mid-1950s not only reflected the emergence of youth culture, but also actually intervened in the national debate, with a film like *Rebel Without a Cause* offering a stark dramatization of generational conflict. The film has a very interesting history, not least because rumours were rife that director Nicholas Ray was sleeping with its three protégés, James Dean, Natalie Wood and Sal Mineo, and the fact that the tragic 'chickee run' of Dean's character Jim Stark prefigured the actor's own death in September 1955 (before the film was released), but also because the film stemmed from a number of different sources. Ray had written a short story about a boy wanting to grow up fast, and he was partly responsible for the homoerotic charge that develops between Jim and Plato in the film. But far from *Rebel* simply being Ray's personal project, numerous scriptwriters were used and the main intellectual source was a 1944 book by Robert Lindner, which Warner Bros had bought to rights for back in 1946.

Lindner was a psychologist at the United States Penitentiary and criminologist at Bucknell University, and he was particularly interested in the way in which psychopathology was evident in up to 20 per cent of prison inmates. Psychopaths are the 'truly dangerous, "hard-boiled," "wise guy" and least reformable offenders' Lindner claimed, differing from psychotic patients only in the absence of hallucinations and psychic disorientation.[81] He thought that psychopathology was an infantile response which often arises when personal freedoms are denied: 'the psychopath . . . is a rebel, a religious dis-obeyer of prevailing codes and standards . . . a rebel without a cause, an agitator without a slogan, a revolutionary without a program'.[82]

The central argument is that the rebellious teenager cannot see outside himself: 'all his efforts, hidden under no matter what guise, represent investments designed to satisfy his immediate wishes and desires'.[83] This introspective tendency is a strong aspect of Ray's film, but the answer is not a matter of parents exerting a stronger grip on the rebellious impulses of the adolescent. The movie is clear: if Jim Stark cannot see outside himself, then neither can his parents. The swimming pool scene between Jim, Plato and Judy towards the end represents an alternative space – on both imaginative and cinematic levels – to escape the stifling pressures of growing up in a myopic and intolerant society. This also suggests another intertext for the film: the sociologist David Riesman's influential study *The Lonely Crowd* (1950), in which Riesman describes 'other-directed' individuals caught in the crossfire between moral certainties (see Chapter 1). On one level *Rebel Without a Cause* is a sociological film about juvenile delinquency, but on another level it is a modernist film exploring the ambiguous social, psychic and sexual spaces of the 1950s American teenager.

If *Rebel Without a Cause* is remembered for the iconic presence of James Dean's red jacket and its visually intense mise-en-scène, then this is despite weaknesses in its narrative line. Perhaps a more complete movie that examines similar social pressures, linking youthful rebellion, gang culture, the need for new educational techniques and the issue of racial integration, is *The Blackboard Jungle*.

The Blackboard Jungle (1955)

MGM's *The Blackboard Jungle* was the first movie to contain a rock 'n' roll soundtrack, with the exuberant guitar of Bill Haley and His Comets' hit 'Rock Around the Clock' accompanying the opening sequence. Produced alongside other films in the mid-1950s such as *The Wild One* and *Rebel Without a Cause* which focus on emerging youth culture, *The Blackboard Jungle* deals sensitively with the hot topic of juvenile delinquency. All three films can be interpreted as strong visual challenges to Eisenhower-era conformity, or alternatively as cinematic attempts to suggest that reconciliation between parents and teenage children was still a possibility.

Director Richard Brooks drew on the youthful energy of 'Rock Around the Clock' when he wrote the screenplay for *The Blackboard Jungle*. Despite objections from MGM and the Motion Picture Association of America as to the film's content, Brooks's script takes a broadly adult view on the problems of school delinquency.[84] These criticisms slowed down production, but Glenn Ford was eventually cast as the idealistic teacher Richard Dadier. After completing Army service, Dadier is forced into inner-city high-school teaching, only to be faced with the harsh reality of a New York vocational school where the students are doing time before being released into the urban jungle. The film's mise-en-scène matches Paul Goodman's description in *Growing Up Absurd* (1960), that delinquent behaviour often arises from a combination of 'low verbal intelligence and high manual intelligence, delinquency giving a channel for self-expression where other avenues are blocked by lack of schooling'.[85]

Adapted from the 1954 novel by Evan Hunter (he also wrote crime stories as Ed McBain), the film deals with the clash between educational ideals, the reality of gang life, and conflicts between different ethnic groups. Some critics queried whether real American schools were really this disruptive, a view substantiated by the fact that the class that Dadier teaches has representatives of most ethnic types: the Irish American gang leader, Artie West (Vic Morrow); the African American, Gregory Miller (Sidney Poitier); an Italian American, Belazi (Dan Terranova); Puerto Rican Pete Morales (Rafeal Campos); and Hispanic Santini (Jamie Farr).[86]

The film deals with the urban melting pot throughout, contrasting a private rural New England school with an inner-city New York school that contains the 'blackboard jungle' behind high schoolyard railings. The initial focus is upon Dadier's inability to cope with class rowdiness and the tensions that arise between school and home life. Dadier's frail and pregnant wife Anne (Ann Francis) is threatened by West in an attempt to undermine Dadier's authority in the classroom. When Ann first receives menacing notes she suspects that Dadier is having an affair, but her nerves worsen as the threats mount and she goes into labour prematurely. West's delinquency is not fully explained, apart from the general cold war fear that he will be drafted and get his 'lousy head blowed right off'; his criminal rebellion is offset by the fact that the Dadiers' baby is born on New Year's Eve, symbolizing a liberal lineage which the schoolboys cannot disrupt. The film appears to move towards the adult restoration of order, but its message is far from clear cut, its morals worried mothers and religious leaders, and when it was first released in Britain it caused riots with teddy boys ripping up cinema seats.

The film did very good business grossing $4 million between its New York premiere in March and September 1955, a figure which was to double over two years. But with its depiction of classroom violence, street brawls and sexual assault, the film was banned in several states and the censor in Memphis called it the 'vilest picture I've seen in 26 years'. Even celebrity DJ Alan Freed thought the film was a 'hoodlum-infested movie' that associated rock 'n' roll with delinquency.[87] The Production Code demanded that the film tone down its violence, particularly an assault on the school's only female teacher Lois Hammond (Margaret Hayes); some states reclassified the film as adults only; and the State Department tried to block overseas distribution. It was actually selected as the US entry at the Venice Film Festival, but was pulled by the State Department, followed by the demand that a caption should be shown at the beginning for domestic audiences:

> We in the United States are fortunate to have a school system that is a tribute to our communities and our faith in American youth. Today we are concerned with juvenile delinquency – its causes – its effects. We are especially concerned when this delinquency boils over into our schools. The scenes and incidents here are fictional. However, we believe that public awareness is a first step toward a remedy for any problem. It is with this spirit and with this faith that *The Blackboard Jungle* was produced.

It is difficult to tell how seriously audiences took this warning, but it reveals an exerted attempt to control the audience's response, and perhaps even contributed to a more radical reading of the film as an assault on white patriarchal hegemony.[88]

One of its most interesting aspects is the complex relationship between Miller and Dadier. The film was released only one year after *Brown* v. *the Board of Education* and Miller is singled out by Dadier early on as a potential leader in the class who will help him control the more destructive leadership potential of Artie West. Miller is initially rebellious and disrespectful, but there is also a streak of pride and self-assurance that surprises Dadier. Poitier had already played dignified roles in *Cry, the Beloved Country* and *No Way Out* and he brought to the character of Miller a mixture of defiance and sensitivity to racial issues. HUAC singled out Poitier for his connections to the communist sympathisers Paul Robeson and Canada Lee, and asked him to sign the loyalty oath. Poitier claims that he never signed the oath and Richard Brooks did not press the point, but this incident arguably sharpened the politics of his role. This links to Poitier's biographer Aram Goudsouzian's description of Miller as a version of the 1950s rebel: 'a white T-shirt, its sleeves rolled up to expose his sinewy muscles, offsets his smooth mahogany skin. He moves with an almost feline grace, and he exudes a self-assured calm. Only his eyes reveal an inner fire'.[89]

Dadier tries to strike a pact with Miller early on, only for Miller to turn against him after Dadier informs on the student that attacked Miss Hammond. Their initial emotionally charged meeting in the school bath-room – in which Miller mockingly calls him 'chief' – is mirrored by an encounter on the school stairs after the headmaster has been informed that Dadier has racially insulted the boys in the classroom. The charge is false as Dadier had actually tried to initiate a conversation about racial stereotypes, but his encounter with Miller on the stairs (in which the camera lingers on the pair as they slowly descend locked in each other's gaze) nearly provokes a racial taunt that wells up involuntarily within Dadier.

This moment, ironically, is the turning point in their relationship. Dadier asks Miller to perform in the school play (we see him rehearsing the slave song 'Go Down Moses' with other black students), and Miller comes to Dadier's rescue in a final classroom confrontation, when West pulls a knife on Dadier. Whereas Miller and his gang invent the nickname 'Daddio' for the teacher, suggesting he is a false patriarch, Dadier manages to re-establish classroom authority when the low-IQ student Santini (described as a 'moron' in Evan Hunter's novel) uses the Stars and Stripes as a rapier to put an end to West and Belazi's classroom rumble.

The closing scene of the film depicts Dadier and Miller outside the school: Dadier has learnt what inner-city schools are really like, while Miller agrees to stay on and graduate, rather than dedicate himself to the engi-neering job he does in the evening. The final handshake between the pair, before Bill Haley strikes up again, suggests not only a *rapprochement* between generations but also a liberal understanding between white and black Americans that stems directly from the *Brown* ruling.[90] It is, however, open to interpretation as to whether or not this final scene, as Goudsouzian suggests, transforms Miller from 'cultural threat to loyal citizen' and an emblem of 'polyracial American democracy', or whether he remains a latent political force (he noticeably reverts to calling Dadier 'chief' before switching to his formal title) waiting to erupt outside the confines of the classroom.[91]

Conclusion

Stories of rivalry in the broadcasting industry in the 1950s are often coupled with an account of the film industry going into freefall and the blossoming of the new medium of television (which Richard Nixon emphasized as being the most sophisticated medium of communica-tion in his kitchen debate with Khrushchev). However, these stories are often more to do with the mythology of 'the fifties' than with a his-torical account of the decade. In truth, the close relationship between the two cultural forms grew rapidly in the late 1950s, with actors fre-

Figure 4.7 Glenn Ford and Sidney Poitier in *The Blackboard Jungle* (Richard Brooks, MGM, 1955). Wisconsin Center for Film and Theater Research.

quently crossing over and studios realizing that television was the ideal medium for movie re-runs. A historical account of the industry is vital for charting cultural changes, but so too is discussion of visual representations in which ingrained stereotypes jostle with explorations of characters, ideas and spaces. If dead centrism was one of the controlling principles of television programming by 1955 and some topics remained taboo even after the Hays Code and the threat of blacklisting were on the wane, then this did not prevent social pressure points emerging, sometimes explicitly and at other times against the grain of the filmed images. It is not just the modernist filmmakers Alfred Hitchcock and Nicholas Ray to whom we should turn to explore conflicting accounts of power, ideology, race, gender and adolescence in the 1950s; as this chapter suggests, these conflicts are also evident in genre-based films and formulaic television products such as the domestic sit-com and quiz show.

Chapter 5

The Visual Arts beyond Modernism

Through this book I have argued that modernism and the cold war were equally important as shaping forces on cultural production in the 1950s. Some practitioners were trying to move beyond modernist art and others retreating from it, but it remained the controlling aesthetic paradigm of the decade. As a historical mode modernism became institutionalized in the 1950s as the Nobel Prizes for the trio of modernist writers Faulkner, Eliot and Hemingway suggest. But this did not mean that modernism had lost its contemporary relevance. It was just that many realized that art could never be the same after the Holocaust and the atom bomb.

The art critic Clement Greenberg was worried that modernist and popular styles had become increasingly indistinct from each other in the 1950s. He made this case over a decade earlier in his Marxist essay 'Avant-Garde and Kitsch' (1939), arguing that the economic profits of easily consumable kitsch were a major 'source of temptation' for serious artists. Greenberg claimed that 'ambitious writers and artists will modify their work under the pressure of kitsch, if they do not succumb to it entirely', and by the mid-1950s he was concerned that modernism and kitsch had become deeply entangled.[1] This opinion that modernist artists should be wary of contemporary pressures was largely due to the ubiquity of visual culture in the 1950s.

Visual culture came to dominate the decade more than ever before, with television, widescreen cinema and musical spectacles increasing the opportunity for visual consumption. Karal Ann Marling argues that visuality pervaded 'everyday life', from the picture windows of suburban houses and glossy ads for kitchen gadgetry to the painting-by-numbers craze of the mid-1950s and the rapid turnover of new colours and styles in women's fashion. Mary Caputi explores the ways in which postwar modernity was so 'filled with noise, activity, and change' that it is difficult to view the decade as anything more than a 'commotion' of visual styles.[2]

However, when it comes to considering the visual arts – by which this chapter groups together painting, photography, sculpture, design and multimedia products – modernism was a guiding force that facilitated the production of some forms and discouraged others. Regional painting and overtly politicized art were almost taboo in the early 1950s, when abstraction dominated the agenda: from car and aeronautical design to the clean lines of International Style architecture; from Charles Eames's innovative chairs and sofas to experiments in clay and ceramics on the West Coast; from Ellsworth Kelly's giant murals to the abstract expressionism of Jackson Pollock, Hans Hofmann and Barnett Newman. The emphasis on 'newness' was everywhere, as Pollock noted in his 1950 call for contemporary artists to devise new techniques: 'it seems to me that the modern painter cannot express this age, the airplane, the atom bomb, the radio, in the old forms of the Renaissance or any past culture'.[3] But, while there were many different modernist directions for 'making it new' in the 1920s, by the late 1940s the most interesting experiments were in the realm of abstraction. One approach to abstract art – and modernism more generally – is to see it as a retreat from everyday life into aesthetics, but this chapter will argue that debates about the status of art and the relationship between 'form' and 'function' were crucial for identifying the direction of postwar culture.

The status of art was also central to debates about high and low culture after the war. Greenberg had earlier pondered how a single culture could give birth both to T. S. Eliot's poetry and Tin Pan Alley and after the war he shared the Frankfurt School critics' suspicion of mass culture, particularly its tendency to pull anything innovative into the mainstream, as evident in the Piet Mondrian floor pattern which casually opens *Desk Set* (1957), the Katharine Hepburn and Spencer Tracy film about television office politics. From this perspective, abstract art may well degenerate into 'merely decorative' styles and Pollock be seen as little more than a 'grandiose decorator'.[4] While one of the traits of modernism in the 1950s is that it could no longer be wholly separated from mass culture (as Andreas Huyssen argues in *After the Great Divide*, 1986), Greenberg was caught between his suspicion that middlebrow culture was responsible for promoting standardization by inhibiting 'idiosyncrasy, temperament, and strong-mindedness' and his tacit belief that a strong middle class was necessary for cultural vitality.[5]

These tensions within Greenberg's art criticism are an index of the two standard accounts of postwar art. The first account ran from the 1950s through to the early 1970s and emphasized the aesthetics of form, whereas the second account emerged in the 1970s to place ideology and cultural politics at centre stage. During his career Greenberg wrote criticism of both kinds, but in the immediate postwar period when anticommunist pressures were at their most intense, he focused on painters who refused to be derivative and embodied 'nerve and truth' in their art.[6] Greenberg's postwar essays focused on the artwork itself much more than its consumption. The growth of exhibitions and gallery spaces played an important role in the postwar recognition of abstract art, but the widespread feeling among critics in the 1950s, including Greenberg, was that the public consumption of modernist art might lead to its dilution into the mainstream.

An indication of how far art criticism has come since Greenberg is evident in two retro-films that explore the art scene of the 1950s. *Mona Lisa Smile* (2003) uses abstract expressionist art as an index for personal freedom, as teacher Katherine Ann Watson (played by Julia Roberts) encourages her female students at Wellesley College to broaden the narrow domestic possibilities that life in the 1950s had to offer them. The other film, *Far From Heaven* (2002), is a pastiche of Douglas Sirk's domestic melodramas, but offers a complex response to postwar art by setting one of its most challenging scenes at an abstract art exhibition held in a Connecticut gallery. The improbable love that emerges across class and gender lines between suburban housewife Cathy Whitaker (Julianne Moore) and her black gardener Raymond Deagan (Dennis Haysbert) is brought to a head when Raymond responds sensitively to the abstract painting. Todd Haynes's film is self-consciously revisionist, particularly as few black artists practised abstract art in the 1950s or could find patrons during the cold war. The Harlem artist Norman Lewis is one exception with abstractions such as *Tenement I* and *Blending* (both 1952) and *Harlem Turns White* (1955), but many went into exile in Europe or Mexico, such as Elizabeth Catlett who became professor of sculpture at the National School of Fine Arts in Mexico.[7] Raymond's appreciation of abstract art in *Far From Heaven* is one way in which he avoids the stereotypes of his class and race, creating unease among the Connecticut socialites for whom the paintings just blur with the décor.

In a decade when very few black and women artists were given recognition, Haynes's film explodes the myth that only a class of experts, scholars and art critics could understand modernist art. Of women painters in the 1950s only Lee Krasner (Jackson Pollock's wife) received much recognition and women photographers were also very scarce, with only Dorothea Lange, Margaret Bourke-White and Esther Bubley having public names – Bubley after winning the *Photography* magazine Grand Prize in 1954. But, even though they did not garner the attention of their male contemporaries, others such as Hedda Sterne, Grace Hartigan and Louise Nevelson were practising artists who found an expressive medium in abstract art.[8] Both standard accounts of postwar art – (1) formal innovation and (2) the link with cold war politics – do not do justice to what Ann Gibson calls 'the power of European, male, and heterosexual identity' within the industry.[9] In *Abstract Expressionism: Other Politics* (1997) Gibson offers a rejoinder to discussions of the eight or so white male painters who still dominate discussions of abstract expressionism by focusing on women and ethnic painters. Her argument is that it is 'necessary either to pull "Abstract Expressionism" into a different shape or to admit that its "universality" stops short at the boundaries of race and gender'.[10]

One reason why formalism has inherited a bad name is that the freedom of the artist to immerse him or herself in a realm of 'pure art' can be interpreted as an evasion of contemporary life. But Gibson argues that the historical reality was quite different. Artists, collectors and patrons were engaged in broader cultural currents and undergoing a power struggle which led to a diverse range of forms, some echoing the high modernism of the 1920s, some the politicized modernism of the 1930s, and some hybrid practices that stretched the limits of modernism. For example, Louise Nevelson's experiments *Sky Cathedral* (1958) and *Dawn's Wedding Feast* (1959) were unlike any previous modernist work in challenging gendered constructions (male extrusions and female intrusions) that psychologist Erik Erikson had identified in his popular book *Childhood and Society* (1950).

In order to view the plurality of visual forms in the 1950s it is necessary to broaden the discussion from standard accounts of abstract art. Despite the drive to standardize architecture, early 1950s design was characterized by a plethora of different modes. Manufacturers were leading the game because they saw a buoyant consumer market and thousands of new suburban homes to furnish, but designers were implementing new techniques learnt from industry such as the how to mould plastics, how to spot-weld wood and metal, and how to use lightweight materials such as fibreglass, polyester and foam rubber.[11] The major reason why, from a distance, design in the 1950s looks dull and uninspired is because the federal court prevented designers taking out patents on their furniture designs, allowing manufacturers to churn out cheap imitations. Even though Charles Eames found a new vein of creativity in 1956 after a few uninspired years and the first half of the decade saw many new designs (with showcases such as the annual Good Design Show in Chicago sponsored by the Museum of Modern Art), by 1957 innovative design was jeopardised by the boom in affordable imitations.[12]

As this chapter will discuss in relation to painting, photography and multimedia, abstraction can be seen as either a flight from the social and ideological forces or as an indirect but critical response to the same forces. Sometimes the artist offered an alternative reality beyond advertising and commerce, and at other times plunged the viewer into the very midst of consumer culture.

Abstraction and Ideology

One way of periodizing 1950s art is to take the death of Jackson Pollock in August 1956 as the symbolic end of abstract expressionism which had come to dominate the American art scene in the 1940s and early 1950s. This moment was followed in 1958 by 'a dramatic upheaval' in the art world, marked by solo shows by Jasper Johns and Robert Rauschenberg and the 'Sixteen Americans' exhibition at the Museum of Modern Art (MoMA) in 1959–60 featuring a younger generation of artists: Johns, Rauschenberg, Ellsworth Kelly, Louise Nevelson and Frank Stella.[13] This periodization is helpful, but it not only turns Pollock into a mythical hero, but creates an uncertain hiatus in mid-decade, and sees late 1950s art as a prelude for 1960s pop art. One way of moving beyond this strict periodization is to focus on shifting identity politics as Ann Gibson does, or to position postwar art within the context of cold war culture.

Two key examples of this second trend are a 1974 essay by Jane de Hart Mathews 'Art and Politics in Cold War America' and Serge Guilbaut's 1983 book *How New York Stole the Idea of Modern Art*. Up to the 1970s there was only an implicit sense that cold war politics and abstract art were linked, partly because it was not widely known that the CIA was sponsoring the Committee for Cultural Freedom, an organization which took American ideas to Europe during the Marshall Plan years. Before the mid-1970s, postwar abstract art was seen mainly as a shift from the socially committed art of the 1930s into a realm of 'pure art'. It was also a strategic move for artists with social-ist leanings: abstraction, at least in theory, was beyond reprisal and censor. There was no equivalent of *Red Channels* to threaten artists, and unlike writers, actors and directors, artists could be castigated only by publicly making subversive statements or declaring allegiance to radical groups.

Private patrons based in New York such as Peggy Guggenheim and Samuel Kootz had been showcasing modern art for some time in the Art of This Century Gallery and the Kootz Gallery (which opened in 1942 and 1945). But, in her 1974 essay, Mathews looks closely at public patronage in the 1950s and the efforts of some patrons to recruit abstract art for promoting American ideas abroad. In 1950 Pope Pius XII was condemning abstract art as immoral and others were suspicious that it was actually 'a weapon in the Communist arsenal', but the liberating use of paint and vast canvases could be seen, conversely, as the embodiment of American freedom.[14]

In the late 1940s there was a general suspicion of the term 'modern', though. The Institute of Modern Art in Boston changed its name to the Institute of Contemporary Art and released an anti-modern manifesto in 1948, fuelled by the fear that 'modern' artists were linked to the godless scientism of communism, whereas 'contemporary' and 'new' were more affirmative national signifiers. On this account, public patronage was an attempt to co-opt avant-garde painting during the cold war; painters previously thought to be subversive now were seen as 'the embodiment of the kind of freedom denied their colleagues behind the iron curtain, their works celebrated as quintessentially American'.[15]

Mathews notes that, despite the institutionalization of literary modernism, in the world of painting there was still a suspicion of the term 'modern' until the mid-1960s and the temporary thawing of the cold war. However, Guilbaut sees a more complex series of transactions in which international modernism had been 'stolen' from Paris by New York. Guilbaut's thesis echoes Clement Greenberg's sense that modernism was not working itself out in bohemian Paris, but in the exhibition spaces of Manhattan. As a founding member of the American Committee for Cultural Freedom Greenberg was instrumental in rescuing modern art, aided by the joint manifesto of MoMA and the Whitney Museum in March 1950 which defended modern art against communist charges ('we oppose any attempt to make art or opinion about art conform to a single point of view') and the painters Robert Motherwell and Ad Reinhardt's publication Modern Artists in America which focused on the inherent mutability of abstract art.[16] It is within this cold war context of conflicting ideologies – American diversity versus Soviet dogma – that critics, since the 1970s, have placed postwar abstract art.

Guilbaut detects that the artwork itself and its public patronage need separating out to understand how abstract art 'came to be accepted and used, without their being aware of it, to represent liberal American values, first at home, in the museums, and then abroad'.[17] One problem with Guilbaut's perspective is that it focuses on the struggle between Paris and New York, and neglects other artistic centres such as Warsaw (which recovered its ability to promote abstract art in 1956 after years of Soviet censorship), São Paulo (which hosted a large international exhibition in winter 1953–4), and Mexico City (which held the First Inter-American Biennial of Painting and Graphics in summer 1958). Another problem with Guilbaut's approach is that it empowers patrons and critics and leaves the artist blindly experimenting in a pure medium barely aware of cold war concerns. On this view, the patron and critic frame the artwork and not the artist.

It is dangerous to revive the theory of the artist having sole authority over his or her art, but it is also misleading to divorce process from product. For this reason, French sociologist Jean Baudrillard places abstract art within a cold war framework:

> Abstraction of the 1950s, was not the subtle, analytical, experimental, classical . . . abstractionism of the prewar period. It was a desperate, nervous, pathetic, and explosive abstraction. It was the very abstract image of the Cold War itself, for the Cold War is abstract, it is something suspended, it does not break out, it is simultaneously conflict and deterrence, just as pictorial abstraction is simultaneously forms and forms deferred, a play of signs and a violent dissuasion of the signs of reality.[18]

Baudrillard's theory that abstract painting was the reflection of an abstract war of ideologies is seductively neat, but the problem is that he pays little attention to the diversity of painterly styles in the 1950s in favour of a uniform cold war response. One could perhaps take 1954 (and the demise of McCarthyism) as a moment when 'nervous, pathetic, and explosive abstraction' gave way to a different kind of art more attuned to the consumerist impulses of the mid-1950s. But, even then, abstract artists did not dip into a single paint pot and avant-garde art cannot simply be seen as a reply 'to the Cold War's blackmail threat of annihilation', celebrating 'its own disappearance by an aggravated symbolic gesture', as Baudrillard describes.[19]

With more recent studies exploring the CIA's sponsorship of abstract art such as Frances Stonor Saunders' *The Cultural Cold War* (2000) it is easy to dismiss early formalist art criticism. Greenberg's writings from the 1950s are often criticized for lacking the materialist edge of his earlier essays, and Guilbaut complains that Irving Sandler's influential *The Triumph of American Painting* (1970) was typical of the 'positive, heroic, and optimistic account' of mid-century art.[20] Rather than just accepting the 'cold war patronage' thesis, though, one way of gauging the transitions in abstract art is to focus briefly on two artists who bookend the decade but are often sidelined in a discussion of 1950s painting. The first is German-born painter Hans Hofmann, a contemporary of Picasso, who featured in MoMA's exhibition 'Abstract Painting and Sculpture in America' in early 1951 and had a major retrospective at the Whitney Museum in 1957 at the age of seventy-six, and the second is Frank Stella from Malden, Massachusetts who, only two years out of college, had his first solo show in autumn 1960 at the Leo Castelli Gallery in Manhattan.

Hofmann is a classic example of an abstract artist who focused on process: the texture of the brushstroke, the smear of the palette, and the vibrant field of colour. Leaving behind representational art as a young man, the starting point for Hofmann's paintings from the mid-1930s was a field of forces in which elements and concentrations are held in tension. Greenberg was a great fan of Hofmann because he was a genuine experimentalist and 'a virtuoso of invention' who was very difficult to classify because he transcended national traditions. As one of a generation of émigré artists making the Atlantic crossing in the early 1930s, Hofmann travelled through Germany, France and Italy, before arriving on the East Coast with an avant-garde interest in fractured forms, distorted lines and vibrant colour palettes that lent a 'new liveness of surface' to American painting.[21]

Although he encouraged figurative painting in his art students (one of whom was Robert De Niro's father), Hofmann was particularly interested in complex shapes and an extravagant splurge of colours that characterized his early 1950s paintings such as *Magenta and Blue* (1950), *Scotch and Burgundy* (1951), his *Orchestral Dominance* paintings in yellow, red and green (1954), and *Festive Pink* (1959).[22] Above all, Hofmann's paintings offered viewers the freedom to enter a world of colour and light. He was distinctly modern in his belief that the arts need liberating from 'all the coagulated wisdom of the Academy', and has often been viewed as a synthesist in his fusion of disparate styles and search for new painterly intensities.[23]

Even though he remained prolific through the 1950s, what makes Hofmann's painting more resonant for the late 1940s was his insistence on 'pure painting', in which he sought a 'color complex' emitting 'a multitude of color vibrations'.[24] Critics continued to focus on the 'sheer driving power' of Hofmann's paintings and 'the reckless but assured way with which he tackles complexes of form and color that would bring another artist to his knees'.[25] Although one could use Einstein's theory of relativity as an explanatory framework of Hofmann's art (and for abstract expressionism more generally) or seize upon paintings with titles such as *Holocaust* (1953), *The Ravine* (1954) and even *Towering Spaciousness* (1956) to locate Hofmann's work within a broader social matrix, his statements from the 1950s have little reference to a changing cultural landscape. Rather, he suggested that abstract art has the power to take the viewer beyond the temporal moment into an almost mystical realm where 'inner perception' and 'spiritual projection' prevail.[26]

By the time Frank Stella began painting as a young twenty-two-year-old fresh out of Princeton in 1958, Hofmann's brand of abstract expressionism had, as William Rubin comments, 'run its course'.[27] Given that the movement attracted painters whose styles were both hot (Pollock, Hofmann, Klein) and cool (Newman, Rothko, Reinhardt), the young Stella was left at the end of the 1950s with a feeling of impasse. Although he was excited by the techniques of the abstract expressionists and later said 'I was a Hofmann student without knowing I was one', Stella looked back to the geometrical arrangements of an older painter of Hofmann's generation – Piet Mondrian – for sparking his interest in hard shapes, lines, diagonals and stripes.[28] Stella was also excited by the relationship between object and field that he detected in Jasper Johns's paintings which he first saw in Manhattan in early 1958. Where Pollock and Hofmann were interested in the texture of the paint, Johns's and Stella's interest was in flat objects and mundane patterns. Stella sought simplicity rather than complexity in his early enamel paintings: this can be seen in the series of white horizontal stripes and thin black lines in *Astoria* (1958) and the black cruciform shapes broken by thin white lines in *Die Fahne hoch* (1959) – one of the first in Stella's series of 'black paintings' which he worked on between 1959 and 1964. By focusing on black shapes accented by white lines in the upward diagonals of *Point of Pines*, the concentric black rectangular stripes of *Tomlinson Court Park*, and twin vertical blocks of black stripes of *The Marriage of Reason and Squalor* (all 1959), Stella was striving for a kind of negative or spectral painting that was bold and instantaneous, but also 'generated a glow or shimmer in an ambiguous space'.[29]

Whereas abstract expressionism was recruited as a symbol of American freedom, Stella's paintings seem, like Hofmann's, to be beyond appropriation. At a casual glance the images are no more than decorative patterns. But for the critic tempted by allegory, Stella's early painting can be read as a paradoxical embodiment of 'containment' and 'openness': the spectral forms are bound in relation to other similar forms but open into spaces beyond the picture. Stella called these paintings 'groundwork structures', architectural in their geometric arrangements, but also dynamic as the white lines catch the light, or the eye moves across the pattern in search of somewhere to rest.[30] Because it is difficult to place Stella's work within a wider cultural framework, the temptation is to read him as a pure formalist, but this would be to ignore the way in which his early images break down barriers between decorative and high art and also suggest that cultural monotony (flat lines, sameness, an absence of feature) can itself become new subject matter.

What distinguishes Hofmann's and Stella's work from the more fêted postwar artists – Pollock, Newman, Lichenstein, Warhol – is that they have no signature style, nor the sense that they belong to a particular artistic lineage. As practitioners of abstract art from different generations it is not easy to fit either Hofmann or Stella within a cold war narrative. The 'cold war patronage' thesis is vital for considering the clash of art and politics and the ways in which the painted canvas became an anticommunist weapon, but it is very easy to overlook the painter's craft.[31] On this basis Hofmann and Stella were maverick painters who, to quote William Rubin, seemed for many 'to have come virtually from nowhere, to have no stylistic heritage, and to represent a rejection of everything that painting seemed to be'.[32]

Painting beyond Abstraction

Hofmann and Stella represent two nodal points of 1950s painting, but it is also important to discuss the broader developments in abstract art during the decade. Serge Guilbaut has argued that it is 'difficult to discuss anything in the art culture of the decade but Abstract Expressionism [because] the New York art scene is generally simplified to the point of appearing monolithic'.[33] This tendency to flatten the postwar art scene is quite common and, as Ann Gibson reminds us, it is important to look beyond familiar names to different versions of

mid-century art. A number of tensions are discernible. A painter like
Robert Motherwell, for example, can be claimed either as a pure modernist in his emphasis on 'felt experience – intense, immediate, direct,
subtle, unified, warm, vivid, rhythmic' – or as an eclectic modernist
blending French, German, Italian, Spanish and Mexican styles and
linking poetic, musical, sculptural influences into a uniquely American
idiom. The southern artist Hale Woodruff alternated between abstract
and figurative painting after World War II, but in 1950–1 he fused
together the two aesthetic modes to create the huge six-panel mural
The Art of the Negro (housed at Atlanta University) which traces
African American ancestry, up to the last panel which depicts the
involuntary intermingling of African and European cultures. And,
while the collagist and painter Ellsworth Kelly emphasized the clarity
of pure lines in his huge murals, he was also interested in escaping the
picture frame and creating challenging art for public spaces.

   Some critics celebrated American abstract art through the 1950s,
while others complained that 'extreme abstraction', as it was sometimes
called, was narrow in its range. The *New York Times* critic Howard
Devree cherished the diversity of MoMA's 1951 exhibition 'Abstract
Painting and Sculpture in America', but four years later he complained
that the 1954–5 Whitney show displayed a narrow uniformity:

> One may group certain types of expression within the non-objective field:
> symbols against primarily blank backgrounds; free floating color shapes;
> geometrical use of color forms; an all-over color organization deriving
> frequently from cubism; lyrical use of color frequently suggestive of
> landscape or marine themes; linear mazes from the 'drip' or automatic
> approach . . . But within each of these groups the similarity is pro-
> nounced, the anonymity creeps in . . . there is a dehumanization effected
> which is at the other pole from an artist's individuality of expression.[34]

Artists and critics continued to defend abstraction into the second half
of the decade but, as Devree comments, by 1955 there was a sense that
something more than pure abstraction was needed. But before looking
at the movement beyond abstract art – or what some critics called 'half
abstraction' – it is important to recognize the dominance of the New
York school at the start of the decade.

   The year 1947 is often thought to mark the final transition of
power in the art world from France to America, when Jackson Pollock
completed his first drip paintings in New York and the 'Exposition
internationale du Surréalisme' at the Galerie Maeght in Paris marked

the twilight of the school of European surrealism.[35] Surrealists and abstract expressionists were equally interested in automatic painting as an expression of the unconscious, but by the mid-1940s the abstract painters Pollock, Mark Rothko and Barnett Newman were moving away from all forms of representation. The avant-garde impulse to disrupt conventional ways of seeing was still evident, but now there was no hidden depth beyond the surface of the painting. Instead, abstract expressionism confronted the viewer with 'two dimensionality, fluid space, lack of closed shapes, a deliberately unfinished quality, and an "overall" composition that diffused any notion of focus'.[36] The disruption of the surface/depth opposition led abstract expressionists into a chaotic world beyond meaning and left critics ill-equipped for interpretation. Whereas the surrealists were interested in Freudian ideas, there was no explanatory paradigm for abstract expressionism but rather a profusion of different impulses: Jungian thought, nativism, relativity, the Mediterranean, Japanese prints, nature, religion, commerce, and so on.

Another way in which American abstract painting reframed modernism is the rejection of the easel for vast canvases that filled gallery spaces. The use of massive fields of colour enabled Barnett Newman to give material form to a 'pure idea' in *The Name* (1949) or *The Word II* (1954). Although some of Pollock's paintings have evocative titles suggesting mythical patterns and organic forms – *Full Fathom Five, Cathedral, Lavender Mist* and *Autumn Rhythm* – he preferred non-specific titles such as *Number 3, 1949* and *Number 1, 1950* which give the viewer little help in understanding the painting. His all-over drip technique with its seemingly random lines and interlacing textures had become his signature style by 1950, to such a degree that by 1951 *Vogue* was featuring Pollock's pictures as a backdrop to photographic shots of fashion models.

This was one of the challenges for abstract art: it was easy to appropriate for commercial ends and quickly came to symbolize the 'bad dream of modernism'. There was publicity to be gained, such as the Pollock exposé in *Life* in August 1949, but his art from the late 1940s – 'the wordless, the somatic, the wild, the self-risking, spontaneous, uncontrolled' – was here juxtaposed with contemporary fashion as a symbol of postwar materialism.[37] In fact, although Pollock was at the height of his fame in the early 1950s, arguably his most creative work was behind him by 1951.

The study of Hofmann and Stella in the previous section might suggest that abstraction continued to be the *modus operandi* of 1950s art, but what distinguished it from practices in the late 1940s was a return to 'the figure'. For some artists the shift away from abstraction was marked: for example, the artists in the Bay Area of San Francisco in the early decade used paint in the same way as the abstract expressionists but focused on figurative subject-matter, and even Pollock returned to recognizable objects and figures after 1951.[38]

By the middle of the decade, and especially following the death of Pollock in 1956, it was thought that the aims of abstract artists had become vague and certain styles were becoming hackneyed. One sign of this is Howard Devree's worry in April 1955 that avant-garde art is always at risk:

> the inherent danger of extremism is that, if it is not to solidify as an academy of extremism at some point, it must go on being more extreme to hold attention. This is all too likely to result in novelty rather than true originality.[39]

While certain abstract artists, such as Seattle-based painter Mark Tobey and even the European-influenced Robert Motherwell, were finding fresh influences in Japanese and East Asian art, others were realizing that a new direction was needed. The fact that a six-year-old chimpanzee, Betsy, at Baltimore Zoo had her own one-chimp show of abstract art in spring 1957 is a sign that novelty had taken over from serious experimentation. Strangely enough one of the formative figures in the development of abstract art, Marcel Duchamp, was also behind the wave of artists in the mid-1950s who redefined the terms of painterly abstraction. There were other precedents such as Joseph Cornell's ready-mades in the 1940s, which were more 'object' than 'painting', but it was left to the younger artists Robert Rauschenberg, Jasper Johns and Claes Oldenburg to forge new links between painting and the social environment.

Rauschenberg had shifted away from the pure abstractions of the early 1950s, many of them untitled, towards creating 3-D assemblages such as the vertical wall-hanging *Bed* (1955) and *Monogram* (1959), which consists of a long-horned goat with a tyre around its middle standing on a square base of abstract art.[40] This odd juxtaposition of objects is distinctly modernist, but Rauschenberg's work moved beyond Dadaist jokes and surrealist dreams into an absurd world shot through with the consumerist impulses of the mid-decade. In 1959 Rauschenberg declared in the 'Sixteen Americans' exhibition that he wanted to reduce the gap between art and life by using manufactured objects.[41] His assemblages share with Richard Stankiewicz's junk sculptures such as *Warrior* (1952–3) an interest in the detritus of consumerism; the junk left behind in an expendable society geared to keeping things new.

The beginnings of pop art can be identified as early as 1956 with the 'This is Tomorrow' exhibition at Whitechapel Art Gallery in London as a showcase for British artists Peter Blake and Richard Hamilton, but the late 1950s are often overlooked or just seen as the forerunner to the more obvious pop art products of the early 1960s: Roy Lichenstein's cartoons, James Rosenquist's murals and Andy Warhol's silkscreens. While Clement Greenberg was all for keeping abstract art as a high cultural form, post-abstract art takes as its materials the symbols and artefacts of popular culture, such as the manner in which Claes Oldenburg made collapsing versions of household fixtures or the removal of items from the home to display as art. There were questions over the legitimacy of this practice. The critic Leo Steinberg, for one, only later realized that Rauschenberg's use of a 'flatbed picture plane' in *Bed* was a 'radically new orientation' shifting its focus from 'nature to culture'.[42]

Oldenburg saw that his generation growing up after World War II had 'the great advantage of getting the material of popular culture firsthand . . . having that material makes a huge difference, even if your attitude is objective or ironic'.[43] In a 1959 symposium on 'New Uses of the Human Image in Painting' in Greenwich Village, Oldenburg suggested that the human form could be rescued without needing to turn back the clock to classical portraiture. Even for painters who attempted to transform abstract experimentation, such as Frank Stella, the gap between serious and decorative art could be closed in creative ways. Turning to popular culture was not a 'giving up' to the market for Oldenburg, but a sign of commitment; art did not have to possess the high seriousness of Newman or de Kooning, but could be playful, clownish or ironic without being derivative. As Oldenburg pronounced in 1961:

> I am for an art that embroils itself with the everyday crap & still comes out on top . . . I am for an art that takes its form from the lines of life itself, that twists and extends and accumulates and spits and drips, and is heavy and course and blunt and sweet and stupid as life itself.[44]

This turn from abstraction was a sure sign that artists were thinking for themselves, rather than waiting for critics, curators or patrons to graft meaning onto their art.

It is easy to lump together all post-abstract work under the label of pop art, or to include it within the context of the following decade as Thomas Crow does in his book *The Rise of the Sixties* (1996). But 1960s pop art had a cleaner image than Rauschenberg's rough assemblages and Oldenburg's plaster casts from the late 1950s, and pop artists did not share the collagist's impulse to recompose different substances. This label also ignores the vitality of American art in the second half of the 1950s: a vitality epitomized by the work of Jasper Johns.

Flag (1954–5)

By the time the twenty-eight year old Jasper Johns held his first solo show in early 1958 he had already helped to shift the parameters of what could be considered a work of art. At that exhibition at the Leo Castelli Gallery, New York City, Johns displayed recent pieces such as *Book* (a book in a boxed frame over-painted with wax), *Canvas* (a small canvas glued on a larger one, both painted grey) and *Drawer* (the front panel of a drawer appears in a grey painting). Neither of the major art critics of the 1950s, Clement Greenberg and Harold Rosenberg, had much time for Johns and, even though *Time* was to proclaim a year later that he was 'the brand-new darling of the art world's bright, brittle avant-garde', the general reaction to his 1958 show was that the items on display were humdrum.[45] Some critics could not decide whether his subjects were chosen 'to make them more visible' or more obscure, the pictures evoking 'situations wherein the subjects are constantly found and lost, seen and ignored, submerged and recovered again'.[46] Just as early modernists were interested in making strange commonplace or manufactured objects, so Johns in the second half of the 1950s focused on everyday things which are usually overlooked.

One of Johns's central interests was the way in which objects reveal themselves to have hidden properties if placed in unusual combinations. Sharing similarities with Elizabeth Bishop's poetry (see Chapter 1), Johns's preoccupation was with 'the back' of objects that can only ever be partly revealed in a painting and how straightforward views, on close scrutiny, give way to complexity. These interests stimulated Johns to move away from purely abstract painting to place recognizable objects into peculiar relationship with each other. Johns and Robert Rauschenberg were both accused of creating anti-art because they followed earlier avant-garde artists by trying to reduce the gap between art and life. This technique can also be seen in early surrealist painting and in Marcel Duchamp's Dadaist ready-mades which were to inspire Johns after 1959. But Johns avoided the distortion of the surrealists in favour of a cool and deadpan form of representation which invites the viewer to participate with the painting.

Johns's paintings from the 1950s begin with familiarity, only to leave the viewer feeling puzzled when faced with a series of juxtapositions, fragments and textures that sit uneasily with each other. This is clearly evident in the painting *Target with Plaster Casts* (1955), in which a large target of five bold concentric rings in yellow and blue is set against a bright red field topped with a series of boxes containing plaster casts depicting human remains: a hand, a nose, an ear, and other less distinct parts. Viewers literally had to open the boxes to see the plaster casts, bringing them into an intimate and uncomfortable relationship with what lies within. The obvious contemporary reference point here is war – targets and fragmented bodies – but the painting escapes an allegorical reading, by setting the viewer a puzzle that is impossible to solve. For this reason, Mark Rosenthal argues that 'the spectator may come to feel that a work by Johns cannot be fully understood' because it is likely that 'there is yet more which is beyond our view' behind or beyond the painting.[47]

Johns created a series of paintings involving numbers and other signs in the late 1950s, and also turned his hand to sculptures of everyday objects, but the one commonplace image that Johns returned to most often was the American flag. In an early composition of a long-running series, *Flag* (1954–5), the image of the flag works on a number of levels. First, the flag is a flat object that allowed Johns to work within the plane of the picture; second, it is a unified concept incorporating a complex set of geometric relations; and, third, it has a symbolic dimension that changes depending on the context or environment. Art critic Fred Orton reads Johns's approach to objects such as targets and flags as 'undecidables': the created painting is neither one thing nor another, but sits uncomfortably in a mid-zone between pure abstraction and cultural reference. On this reading the flag is both a series of geometric shapes in which the 'flagness' has been eradicated, but also a representation of the Stars and Stripes with all its symbolic and historical resonances. Johns always maintained that the initial idea for painting the American flag came to him in a dream he had in 1954 and four year later he was claiming that he had no idea 'about what the [flag] paintings imply about the world', simply that he 'intuitively like[d] to paint flags'.[48] But, by 1960, Johns seemed to confirm Orton's reading of his piece as both flag and painting, asserting that 'both positions are implicit in the paintings, so you don't have to choose'.[49]

While Flag works primarily on a two-dimensional plane it is also a highly textured work made out of a painted collage of torn newspaper pasted with hot wax on fabric and then mounted on plywood. Johns was to replicate this collage technique for *Target with Plaster Casts* but, on close inspection, the white stripes of *Flag* reveal the random articles which Johns has torn up to create its texture. None of the pasted newspaper pieces refer directly to contemporary headlines; instead they offer a mosaic of textuality that leads the viewer beyond iconic recognition to conflicting stories that were often overlooked in the cold war climate. As such, the total meaning of the flag is maintained, but the details betray its 'flagness'. As Fred Orton notes, the forty-eight stars are not identical, the red and white stripes do not conform to a standard figure–ground relationship, and 'in some places drips and dribbles of wax cross the edge of stars and stripes and link various areas as surface'.[50]

The initial flag painting led to a series of others running into the 1990s, including in his early phase *Flag above White with Collage* (1955), the massive *White Flag* (1955) in which the stars and stripes lack colour and are only faintly discernible, *Green Flag* (1956), *Flag on Orange Field* (1957), and a year later *Three Flags* with three flags of decreasing size sitting on top of each other. Each of these flags offers surprising juxtapositions of shapes, colours and textures, and force the viewer to approach the national symbol in different ways. *White Flag*, for example, is a ghostly negative of the Stars and Stripes, making the flag itself distinctly non-American, while *Three Flags* (for which the Whitney Museum paid $1 million in 1980) displays eighty-four stars – the inverse of forty-eight states – and three overlapping series of stripes that makes it difficult to find a place for the eye to rest.

It is difficult to know how Johns's early aesthetics developed as he reputedly destroyed all his pre-1955 work. Some critics see his compositions from the late 1950s simply as a series of experiments with shapes and colour fields: Max Kozloff, for instance, in 1973 claimed that it is dubious whether the flag series can be seen as 'derisory in any social sense' because 'the possibilities of the sardonic were limited in a country whose youth . . . was oriented to scientific careerism'.[51] Johns's refusal to make social comment ('I'm interested in things . . . rather than in judgments' Johns claimed) is one of the reasons why Kozloff reads him as a pure formalist, but this is to overlook the context of production.[52] It is no accident that Eisenhower had called for patriotism and loyalty to the American flag in his Flag Day speech of 1954. From this perspective *Flag* provides indirect commentary on the unease that marginalized groups felt towards national symbols – a mode of social critique which Johns revisited with further flags in the series during the 1980s when cold war fears returned.[53]

Photography in Search of America

If 1950s painting is best characterized as a development from the New York school of abstract art, then photography in the 1950s is a more eclectic phenomenon and harder to classify. This is partly because photography had been thoroughly commercialized by mid-century, largely due to the growth of print media during the 1940s. Newspapers like the *Rocky Mountain News* in Denver specialized in hardball journalism and featured regular photographer Morey Engle with his pictures of 'fires, plane crashes, train wrecks, gangland killings, floods, and other natural disasters', as well as more familiar photographs of automobiles, recreation, and celebrities visiting Colorado.[54] While newspaper photography was on the rise, and the emergence of new

Figure 5.1 Jasper Johns, Flag (1954–5), encaustic, oil and collage on fabric mounted on plywood. © DACS, 2005.

magazines like *Ebony* in 1945 provided work for African American photographers, journalistic photography was required to be dramatic and illustrative, but largely at the service of print news. The lowly status of photographers meant the landscape photographer Ansel Adams was forced to earn a living working on portraits, publicity, industrial reports and catalogues, fulfilling assignments for *Life* magazine that took him away from his passion for the natural landscape.

Photojournalism was very much in demand as newspaper and magazine editors tried to entice readers away from the lures of television. There were more immediate ideological implications for photojournalism in the early 1950s though. At a time when Joseph McCarthy was resorting to doctored photographs for propagandist ends, the development of magazine photography by the likes of Robert Capa, Alfred Eisenstaedt and Loomis Dean helped shift the journalistic emphasis from a written to a visual medium, although the powerful exposé *Black Like Me* (1962) by journalist John Howard Griffin, who darkened the colour of his skin in 1959 to investigate race relations in the Deep South, revealed new possibilities for print journalism.[55] But while some photographers specialized in war images and others balanced personal interests and commercial assignments, photography did not have the clear social purpose it had during Depression and World War II.

W. Eugene Smith stands out among magazine journalists for managing to retain individual expressiveness in his photographic essays. Smith had worked for *Life* briefly before the war and he returned again in 1948 where he helped to refine the idea of the photo-essay in *Nurse Midwife* (1951), showing the role of black midwives in South Carolina, and *A Man of Mercy* (1954), which focuses on Albert Schweitzer's humanitarian work in French Equatorial Africa.[56] Smith was never hostile towards *Life* but he found assignments very prescriptive and was unhappy about who owned the images. This led him to resign in 1954 after the Schweitzer story to focus on private projects such as his studies of Pittsburgh and Haiti. But, despite the restrictions of working for a magazine, photojournalism did offer opportunities for travelling to interesting locations, as evidenced by the pictures Smith took of the South Carolina branch of the Ku Klux Klan on a trip there for *Life* in 1951.[57] Similarly, the Budapest-born Robert Capa was known for his combat images during World War II, but he extended his range after the war working for *Life*, by mixing photography of Hollywood icons (Gene Kelly, Gary Cooper and Ingrid Bergman) with location photographs from Paris, Japan and Indochina.[58]

Because the power of images in the 1950s was so intense, it is often easy to conflate photographic event and aesthetic process. For this reason Alan Trachtenberg, writing in 2001 for 'The Tumultuous Fifties' exhibition, focused on 'the relation between raw fact, which photographs are often thought to represent, and some principle of order, some way of cooking the raw into digestible form'.[59] Another way of putting this is that although photography is a powerful means for documenting history, it is itself subject to historical and aesthetic forces beyond its visual range. From this perspective postwar photographers were as much (but perhaps in a more indirect way) influenced by modernist ideas as painters were. Alfred Stieglitz and Paul Strand's interest in form in their 'straight photography' of the 1910s and 1920s was not as evident in the 1950s. Nevertheless, the founding of *Aperture* magazine in 1952 under the editorship of Minor White, who was passionate about developing the art of photography, was one indication that photographers were still interested in formal experimentation. In fact, just as Smith's and Capa's photography documented the changing social climate so they continued to work with strains of abstract modernism, alongside others like the Chicago-based Aaron Siskind who was keen to work in the interstices between abstract and figurative photography, such as in his lyrical study of falling human bodies, the *Pleasures and Terrors of Levitation* series which he began in 1954.[60]

One example of a photographer who tried to negotiate a space beyond modernism is Ansel Adams. He had been introduced to modernist art in the late 1920s, encountering the New York modernism of Stieglitz but also the mix of Indian, Hispanic and Euro-American traditions that had led Stieglitz's partner Georgia O'Keeffe and Paul Strand to test out their urban training in the rural Southwest. Adams found 'raw, elemental nature' in his trips to New Mexico and California which inspired him to move away from a pictorialist technique to seek a 'simplified, geometric graphic organization' of primitive forms.[61] Although the interest in abstraction carried into Adams's postwar photography and took on new aspects as he visited different areas – waterfalls in Yosemite, sand in Oleano, rocks in Big Sur, aspen trees in New Mexico, Buddhist graves in Hawaii – his regionalist sensibility was in tension with the international abstract style. Adams was annoyed by the brash proclamations of the abstract expressionists and depressed by the West Coast school; he could detect only European influences in their work and little evidence of the eclectic cultural mix that he had encountered in the Southwest twenty years earlier.

Despite this distancing from avant-garde painting, Adams continued to work within a modernist tradition. He was always aware that a photographer risks the 'danger of becoming repetitive', and he placed great emphasis on visual perspective for animating 'geometric shapes or faces' that may otherwise be overlooked.[62] He was extremely interested in the process of photography, but was modernist in his emphasis on psychology, beginning all three of his photographic manuals with a section on the technique of 'visualization'. Adams argued that the composition of a photograph begins before the shutter is released; the artist should cultivate an intuitive response to the environment which, given the right conditions, will conjure up 'expressive images' beyond the power of words.[63] This stance is very different from the artisan or newspaper photographer and links Adams's interests to that of the early twentieth-century modernist photographers Stieglitz and Strand.

Where Adams fits uncomfortably in the climate of 1950s photojournalism was his social commitment to conservationism. One could make connections between Adams and Jackson Pollock in their interest in Native American culture, but Adams's ecological sensibility strained against the pure painting that the likes of Pollock and

Hofmann were striving for at the turn of the 1950s.[64] The eco-friendly Sierra Club even published Adams's 1959 exhibition 'This is the American Earth', stimulated by reports that new roads were to open up Yosemite to ever more tourists. Ironically Adams's photographs have often been used to encourage business to Yosemite, but his intention was not that of the tourist photographer. His twin purpose was to capture the sublime aspects of nature and to preserve natural beauty which could only be glimpsed in special moments, early in the morning or when the light fell in a particular way. There is something universal about his images: they are deeply rooted in locality, but echo nineteenth-century landscape painters and the spirituality of Walt Whitman's Romantic poetry (one of Adams's and Paul Strand's favourite poets).

This same impulse to universalize experience was a driving force behind the most famous photography show of the 1950s. 'The Family of Man' exhibition was curated by Director of Photography at MoMA, Edward Steichen, and opened in January 1955 after three years of preparation. Unlike the contemporary trend for photojournalism, the 503 photographs in the exhibition (selected from over 2 million submissions) did not attempt to tell a narrative, but offered vignettes of contemporary life in all its diversity. That the exhibition did not feature a small circle of photographic names, but spanned 274 photographers from 68 countries, was due to Steichen's tendency to theme photographic exhibitions at MoMA (rather than focusing on particular artists) as evident in three exhibitions he curated in 1951 on the Korean War, on abstract photography, and on French photographers, as well as the 'Diogenes with a Camera' exhibitions which ran for four years from 1952.

Steichen was in his seventies when he began working on 'The Family of Man' and represented an older generation of photographers in which the photograph as social document had priority over aesthetics. He was acquainted with Alfred Stieglitz in the 1910s, but had more of a commercial leaning and was less interested in photographic theory than Adams. Others shared Adams's criticism of Steichen's populism, but Steichen had a high social standing following his work on the 'Century of Progress' exhibition at the 1933 Chicago World Fair, producing glamour and fashion shots in the 1930s, and being promoted to captain during armed service in World War II. Steichen was particularly taken by the success of photography to resist becoming ' "frozen" into philosophy or ideology or system of aesthetics'.[65] Although he was of no particular political persuasion, within the cold war context 'The Family of Man' can be read as an anticommunist exhibition, pitting diversity, freedom and creativity against dogma and rigid ideology. These sentiments can be glimpsed through the photographs, collected into groups under the themes of birth, death, justice and peace, and accompanied by texts ranging from Shakespeare, Thomas Paine and James Joyce to the Bible, Maori and Sioux sayings, and the founding statement of the United Nations. The poet Carl Sandburg (Steichen's brother-in-law) amplified Steichen's central theme of human diversity in his evocation of the 'grand canyon of humanity' for the exhibition catalogue.[66]

Critics have seized upon 'The Family of Man' as a symbol of cold war liberal anticommunism: Jonathan Green claims that the exhibition is now generally thought to have been a 'romantic, sententious, and sentimental' form of 'mass-culture spectacle', and feminist thinker Donna Haraway has criticized the way in which it not only universalizes American ideas but turns heterosexuality, monogamy and childrearing into 'essential' experiences.[67] However, these views do not detract from the importance of the exhibition in opening up photography to an international audience, touring in forty-two countries and seen by ten million visitors. It is easy to read the travelling exhibition as an example of the flexing of US cultural muscle abroad, but its diversity and combination of image and text reveals its creative intent in developing the scope of the photo-essay.

As this discussion has suggested, if 1950s photographers had learnt their craft by fusing ideas drawn from the documentary tradition of the 1930s with the formal aesthetic concerns of 1920s modernism, then the end results were not always easy to predict. 'The Family of Man' exhibition can be seen as the triumph of American freedom recast within an international context, but other photographers like Richard Bagley and Mark Sufrin, who collaborated with director Lionel Rogosin in the experimental New York film *On the Bowery* (1956), were interested in exploring the underbelly of 1950s consumerism. The automobile might have been the most photographed image of the decade and a symbol of middle-class aspiration, but that did not prevent isolation and frustration arising as by-products of an economic machine geared to promoting middle-class aspiration. One photographer who epitomized this alternative focus on social fallout was Swiss émigré Robert Frank.

The Americans (1958)

Arguably the most important photographic document of mid-century America was not published in the United States until a year after its first release in 1958, because according to artist Robert Frank it was deemed to be un-American, 'dirty, overexposed, crooked'.[68] *The Americans* was compiled from a series of pictures that Frank took during his journey across the country between 1954 and 1956 in his desire to study the outlying and overlooked corners of the United States. Although photographers were responding to a different set of concerns to painters in the 1950s, Frank shared with Jasper Johns and Robert Rauschenberg a desire to work in the gap between art and life. Rather than seeing photography as a simple record of social habits or a special sphere sealed off from contemporary culture, Frank wanted to create photographs that glimpsed underlying forces beyond the aesthetic frame.

Frank had only been in the United States for eight years following his emigration from Switzerland in 1947 at the age of twenty-two. He initially worked as a fashion photographer for *Harper's Bazaar* at the end of the 1940s (although he admits that fashion was not his forté) and in the early 1950s he spent periods of time taking pictures in West Europe, particularly Paris (1949–53), London (1951–3) and Wales (1953). This strong European attachment gave Frank an outsider's view of his adopted country, but also a perspective that he felt attuned him to individuals living in its hinterlands and outlying regions.[69] His trip across America was sponsored by two Guggenheim fellowships, and he left New York hoping to produce an 'authentic contemporary document' of his new nation: 'it was the first time I had seen this country, and it was the right mood' he later claimed.[70]

When the eighty-three images appeared as *Les Américans* in Paris two years later, the 'hidden violence' that Frank detected in the faces of his subjects as he travelled across the country revealed a dark underside to the consumerist promises of the decade. In the preface to the US edition, Jack Kerouac (who had travelled with Frank) highlighted the 'EVERY-THING-ness and American-ness' of Frank's pictures, yet one reason why *The Americans* was lambasted by critics for being non-American (or even un-American) was that it is hard to find national precedents or direct influences on Frank. He was inspired by the non-conformity of the abstract expressionists, but as a recent immigrant his work did not fit in with any established photographic tradition and, despite links to the Beat writers Kerouac, Ginsberg and Corso, he usually worked alone. This was perhaps the major reason that *Life* turned down Frank's American pictures and why he became increasingly suspicious of magazines that demanded photographs with well-defined styles and clear subjects.

The dignity and courage evident in the Depression photographs of Dorothea Lange and Walker Evans seem to be in stark contrast to the disconsolate figures that Frank captured. Evans did help Frank in gaining his Guggenheim award, but the critical consensus up to the early 1980s was that the two photographers were polar opposites: Frank rejected 'the static, frontal approach' of Evans by focusing on the edge of the photograph and 'the world outside of the picture's limits'.[71] However, in an effort to question this critical consensus, a 1981 exhibition at Yale University juxtaposed images from *The Americans* with Walker Evans's *American Photographs* (1938). Although the mood of the two collections is in sharp contrast, there are some very interesting compositional parallels which support the claim that *American Photographs* provided 'an iconographical sourcebook' for Frank's pictures.[72] Certainly the two can be seen as shadow images of each other; 'Frank's world of the mid-fifties is Walker Evans's world of the mid-thirties stood on end and plunged into the quiet desperation of existential America', as critic Jonathan Green describes.[73]

Frank explained that his interest in moving away from still photography to sequential images stemmed from his modernist desire to push the photographic medium in new directions. The photographic book forces the artist to think in 'long durations' and encourages a blurring of cultural forms: 'the picture that has the television set in it', as Frank claimed in 1977.[74] He was interested in the aesthetics of photography, not just in terms of visualization but also the way in which a single still image fits into a wider cultural pattern. Frank steered away from beautiful compositions because beauty often prevents viewers from thinking about broader social implications; this means that a photograph that may not be perfectly composed can resonate with messages from beyond its frame.[75] As Kerouac did in his prose and Johns in his painting, Frank linked photography to life in all its complexity.

One example of this technique can be found in the opening photograph of *The Americans*. The image 'Parade – Hoboken, New Jersey' (1955) depicts two women in adjacent windows with the American flag flying between them. It is an unremarkable image in many ways, but one which is rich with meaning. Frank's title is ironic as the photograph does not represent a parade. Instead, like Jasper Johns's *Flag* from the same year, 'Parade' defamiliarizes the Stars and Stripes to create a disjunction between the patriotism it is meant to inspire and the isolation of the two women, cut off from each other and the symbol of national pride. One face is mask-like and almost inhuman as the half-closed blind casts it into deep shadow, while the other head is completely obliterated by the fluttering flag. Instead of an uplifting sense of celebration, the American flag here becomes a symbol of division and decapitation.

Reacting to the sentimentality that Frank saw embodied in 'The Family of Man' exhibition, in 'Parade' and other pictures in *The Americans* – empty motel rooms, backyards and gas stations, blank faces turned away in indifference or torment, lost in isolation and inferiority – he displays his interest in what he later called 'disturbing objects which have a tale to tell or just lie low mutely'.[76] *The Americans* does not tell a story, nor is it dramatic as conventional photojournalism was supposed to be, but instead it evokes a series of subdued emotions and troubling environments. Because Frank turned to filmmaking in the late 1950s, many critics see a proto-filmic quality in *The Americans*. This also links with Frank's later sense that a single perspective cannot reach beyond the surface of objects; what he sought was a 'dialogue between the movement of the camera and the freezing of a still image, between the present and the past, inside and outside, front and back'.[77]

Frank was not a political photographer in the 1950s in the sense that he toed a party line, but neither was he a pure formalist. The series of photographs he took of the 1956 Democratic National Convention in Chicago epitomized his belief that the photographer should strive after social truth whatever its ideological implications: the American flag appears casually in a couple of images of the Convention, while others defamiliarize the paraphernalia of party politics. Politics comes in many different forms and *The Americans* turns away from the mystique of Hollywood culture to focus on the low-lying everyday experience of most US citizens.[78] As such, *The Americans* is far from a classically well-crafted photography book; instead in its form and subject matter it highlights regional eclecticism and the different idioms that Frank observed on his travels.

Figure 5.2 Robert Frank, 'Parade – Hoboken, New Jersey', gelatin-silver print (1955). © Robert Frank.

Multimedia and the Avant-Garde

Some of the most interesting practices in 1950s visual culture were hybrid activities, where different media were held in tension with each other – what Susan Sontag has described as the 'recombinant arts'.[79] As we have seen, this tendency was also evident in other forms (music, performance and a certain strain of film culture) in which an experimental tendency kicked against the dead centrism that can be seen to characterize the Top 40 format and mainstream Broadway and Hollywood productions. But it was left to the visual arts to break new ground after the mid-1950s, and a diverse group of artists whose experiments with form and technique were to have a profound influence on the counterculture of the mid-1960s.

In this vein the collaborative book *Cage – Cunningham – Johns: Dancers on a Plane* (1990) focuses on the links between three of the most distinctive mid-century artists: musician John Cage, choreographer Merce Cunningham and painter Jasper Johns. The book is less concerned with their long-lasting friendship than their experiments with music, dance and art that helped to transform postwar culture. Cage and Cunningham (who had met in Seattle in 1938) were eighteen and eleven years older than Johns and frequent visitors to the Black Mountain College in the late 1940s and early 1950s, where artist Robert Rauschenberg encouraged their avant-garde practice in the form of Cage's silent musical piece *4'33"* (1952) and Cunningham's dance work *Suite for Five in Time and Space* (1956).

Even though the generation of Johns, Warhol, Lichenstein, Oldenburg, Rauschenberg, Frank Stella and Edward Ruscha were just beginning their careers in the 1950s, it is reductive to see the decade's avant-gardism merely as a precursor to the flourishing of experimentalism in the 1960s, rather than an entity in its own right. Older artists like Cage and Cunningham were not alone as innovators, with photographer Robert Frank, performer Ken Dewey and filmmakers Stan Brakhage and Bruce Conner creating very imaginative work in the 1950s. Although an artist like Robert Motherwell worked in almost pure abstraction through the decade, his paintings such as the *Elegy to the Spanish Republic* series suggest a social reality beyond the canvas. What these artists have in common is a rejection of the idea that art can be pure and freed from its environment – an idea at the heart of the experiments at Black Mountain College in the early 1950s and in the art department at Rutgers University, New Jersey in the last third of the decade.[80]

'Is our eye dying?' exclaimed Jonas Mekas, champion of underground film and founder of the *Film Culture* journal in 1955. Writing in his movie journal for the *Village Voice* Mekas argued that the emphasis on technical culture and seductive consumer images, linked to the speed of social change since World War II (what Mekas called the 'flash-and-glimpse reality'), prevented many individuals from looking long and attentively.[81] As an antidote Mekas found in short experimental films an expression of the 'total art' which Allan Kaprow had outlined in 1958: the viewers 'enter, are surrounded, and become part of what surrounds us'.[82] Whereas Kaprow focused on perfor-mance art, Mekas looked to the flicker techniques of Stan Brakhage's films from the 1950s to disrupt continuity of vision and leave the viewer feeling disorientated and very often with a headache. Mekas realized that mainstream cinema was also undergoing a period of experimentation, but he detected a major difference: 'the experience of Cinerama' is 'a circus feeling' of being dazzled by technology, Mekas claimed, whereas avant-garde filmmakers were looking to capture 'a new spiritualized language of motion and light'.[83]

By the mid-1960s this 'new spirtualized language' was closely linked to psychedelic culture, but Mekas saw precursors in the Beat movement of the 1950s which gave film a 'new glow' and 'trickle[d] little drops of uncomfortable poison into the fat and plump veins of our commercial cinema'.[84] Some critics have argued that experimental filmmaking was at a low ebb in the 1950s; even Mekas protested in 1959 that short films had become 'sterile' and 'frozen' into generic pat-terns and Dwight Macdonald was complaining in 1962 that 'art film' rarely rises above 'corny avant-gardism'.[85] However, the New York Times was regularly detailing releases on the 16mm film circuit and societies such as the Cinema 16 Club were exhibiting world cinema in New York, as well as hosting events such as the October 1953 sympo-sium on Poetry and the Film (featuring Arthur Miller, Dylan Thomas, Maya Deren and Parker Tyler), showing screenings of group therapy sessions, and showcasing experimental films by the likes of Brakhage, Conner, Kenneth Anger, Joseph Cornell and John Cassavetes which gave new poetic depth to the medium.[86]

Mekas was particularly interested in the way these new forms were born out of cultural exchanges; but rather than from Europe, it was to China, Japan, Indonesia and India that he thought the most creative impulses were stemming. One example of this is a 3-minute animation Dwightiana (1959) by collagist Marie Menken who shared with British-born animator Norman McLaren an interest in the dynamic inner life of objects. In Dwightiana animated objects continually form, dissolve and reform in rhythm to Tokyo-born musician Teiji Ito's Asian score. Mekas detected in Asian cultures holistic practices in which reality and fantasy, arts and sciences, technics and aesthetics, process and product were not held in opposition, but crossed over in

creative ways as exemplified by Menken's cinematic collage.[87] Instead
of rigid cold war dichotomies Mekas looked for border-crossings and
transgressions.

One of these border-crossings can be seen in Robert Frank's first
experiment with film *Pull My Daisy* (1959), made in collaboration with
Alfred Leslie and Jack Kerouac, who wrote the script for the 28-
minute film. Some critics have noted that Frank was thinking as a filmmaker well before he turned to film, and some shots are reminiscent of
The Americans.[88] But Kerouac's narration and the figures of Allen
Ginsberg and Gregory Corso drinking and smoking contrast with the
beginnings of a domestic story about a working couple and their son.
Kerouac starts his narrative: 'Early morning in the universe' – a phrase
that suggests themes which are both exceptional and mundane. Frank's
film is tactile but also cool in its depiction of Greenwich Village
bohemia; it is spontaneous yet strangely staged; it is dynamic in the
poetic range of Kerouac and the peculiar antics of Ginsberg and Corso,
but also frieze-like in its photographic lingering on faces and gestures.
The visual rhythm of the film seems deliberately uneven as it jars with
Kerouac's jazz modulations. *Pull My Daisy* recalls early-century modernist experiments in film, but with an added sense that, like Frank's
The Americans, the search for America lies in everyday activities and
those spaces overlooked by consumer culture.

This avant-garde eclecticism was also exciting for the short-
filmmakers Bruce Conner and Stan Brakhage (the first born in Kansas,
the second Missouri, both in 1933) who began making films in the late
1950s that revolutionized the experience of viewing. Conner and
Brakhage were fascinated with perception and the ways in which a film
can leave the viewer with after-images. 16mm film stock aided their
exploration of subjective viewpoints, montage, discontinuous narratives and the interplay of light and image. As with the painting of
Jasper Johns, their work is both abstract and representational. Shapes,
objects and figures take on new forms which push the viewer beyond
conventional reference points and knowledge of what a particular
image means. It is easy to see them as rebellious artists, but given the
dominant discourse of containment, Conner's and Brakhage's early
work is particularly interesting as it suggests that freedom and containment are closely related: 'free moving changing form isn't free. It's
always contained in something, but every containment is another free
flowing form in another containment'.[89]

Despite having a fairly conventional orchestral score (Ottorino
Respighi's *Pines of Rome*) and the feel of a motion picture, Conner's *A*

Movie (1958, 12 minutes) completely disrupts the narrative sequence of events; 'THE END' flashes up periodically through film and the title 'A MOVIE' and Conner's name also cuts between images. Premiering at the East/West Gallery in San Francisco, *A Movie* has been described as a 'high density narrative' and a pastiche of Hollywood.[90] It is composed piecemeal from old film footage and newsreels, but any sense of narrative pattern soon dissolves as Conner makes fast cuts between high-tempo car crashes, cowboy chases, collapsing bridges, war imagery and atom-bomb footage, punctuated by arresting images of alluring women, urban tightrope walkers, exotic and starving Africans, the death of an elephant, and a diver swimming into an underwater wreck. *A Movie* is the best example of what has been described as Conner's interest in sifting through the junkyard of American history to recombine 'familiar imagery ... into richly provocative puzzles that rhythmically prod the viewer to attempt reconciliations of ambiguity with the obvious and the comic with the horrific'.[91] As with Robert Frank, ambivalence and irony characterize Conner's work, but also an intense subjectivism (aided by Conner's interest in the psychedelic drug peyote) that gives back to the viewer a degree of interpretative freedom and the chance to (metaphorically) swim into the wreck of America.

Inspired by the Soviet filmmaker Sergei Eisenstein, Brakhage was drawn to similar montage techniques as Conner. Many of his films intermingle objects and persons, such as *Window Water Baby Moving* (1959, 12 minutes) which intercuts intimate close-ups of his first wife Jane and the home birth of their child with images taken before the birth, and *Cat's Cradle* (1959, 6 minutes) in which he used a red filter and an accelerating rhythm to convey a family scene – techniques which foreshadow the psychedelic films of the mid-1960s. Although Brakhage's most distinctive films were made in the late 1950s and early 1960s, he started filmmaking earlier in the decade than Conner. In one of his earliest films, *Desistfilm* (1954, 6 minutes), Brakhage foreshadows *Pull My Daisy* in presenting a domestic episode of young adults playing instruments, smoking, drinking and generally enjoying themselves. Like *Cat's Cradle*, but shot in monochrome, *Desistfilm* soon becomes frenetic and the activities more random. The faces of the group flit between joy, pleasure, desire, mania, fear and bewilderment. The group is together in a room, but the individuals are isolated from each other: one is shaken violently in a sheet and then chased outside, while the silhouette of an embracing couple is disturbed by the manic face of a young man. The distorted music works in tandem with the series of cropped images: rarely are faces presented in their entirety, and a number of blurring devices are deployed to disrupt the viewer's continuity of vision.

These films are just a few examples of a number that were made in the 1950s, such as Kenneth Anger's classical/psychedelic fusion *Inauguration of the Pleasure Dome* (1954) and the contemplative 35-minute film *The End* (1953) by San Francisco poet and editor Christopher Maclaine, which uses intercut sequences and an existential voiceover to trace the last days of five despairing individuals, beginning and ending with a nuclear explosion. These examples, and other films by Brakhage, suggest that avant-garde film culture continued strongly from the 1940s, and that the rejection of Hollywood techniques began earlier in the decade than is often credited.

Certainly by end of the 1950s experimental filmmaking had formed a vanguard, as confirmed in 1960 with the inauguration of the (albeit short-lived) New American Cinema Group which aspired to the same status as Off Broadway productions (see Chapter 2).[92] Rather than avant-garde filmmakers working in a pure medium, some like Christopher Maclaine had no formal training and others like Bruce Conner worked among West coast Beat writers and artists, switching between drawing, sculpture and assemblage with a particular interest in manufactured objects and junk. This interest in assemblage was first brought to public attention in William Seitz's exhibition 'The Art of Assemblage' at MoMA in 1961 and also characterized the diverse group of artists that became known as Fluxus in the early 1960s.

Finding inspiration in the transatlantic avant-gardism of Marcel Duchamp, the minimalist experiments of John Cage, and Harold Rosenberg's claim in 1952 that abstract painting is part of a performance ('what was to go on the canvas was not a picture but an event'), Fluxus was a mixed group of artists who moved fluidly between theatre, performance, cinema, music, graphics and poetry.[93] The period 1957–64 was the dominant phase for the thirty or so artists that made up Fluxus, which formally came together at the 'Fluxus Internationale Festspiele Neuester Musik' in Wiesbaden, West Germany, in 1962, with a Fluxus Manifesto released the following year. The American branch of Fluxus was deliberately anti-institutional, performing in small exhibition spaces in Manhattan and San Francisco, but also having bases in Germany and Japan. For them the idea of cultural practice was radically transformed with life and art blurring with each other; on viewing a Fluxus piece, it is impossible to distinguish the object from the viewer's experience of it.

Published material ranged from 'pamphlets and flyers to tablecloths and films; from luxurious, handcrafted furniture to deliberately flimsy throwaways; from vainly ambitious commercial projects to those that held darkly obscure and personal innuendos'.[94] This may suggest a fracturing of the modernist tradition into the ephemera embraced by pop artists, but it is better to read Fluxus as another maverick modernism that both affirms and rejects the modernist experiment.[95] And while Fluxus, like pop art, really belongs to a study of early 1960s culture, it is important to remember that Allan Kaprow was using the terms 'happening' and 'total art' in 1958 and the genesis of Fluxus (often called 'proto-Fluxus') was in the late 1950s.[96]

Some of the Fluxus artists were collected in *An Anthology*, edited by composer La Monte Young in 1963. Young was another artist from the regions (Idaho, before moving to Los Angeles) inspired by John Cage's Zen minimalism and by other traditions: the electronic music of German composer Karlheinz Stockhausen and Gagaku music from India and Japan. *An Anthology*'s title pages were designed by George Maciunas in bold graphic lettering, an indication of the generic hybridity of the book: 'chance operations, concept art, anti-art, indeterminacy, improvisation, meaningless work, natural disasters' in the form of 'plans of action, stories, diagrams, music, dance constructions, poetry, essays, compositions, mathematics'.[97] The anthology is born out of the spirit of eclecticism and genre-bending; many of the pieces defy description and confound any attempt to pigeonhole them.

Much of the work in *An Anthology* is from the early 1960s with entries by John Cage, Yoko Ono and Nam June Paik, but some are from the late 1950s such as the performance pieces George Brecht's 'Card – Piece for Voice' and Dick Higgins's 'Constellation for Five Performers' (both from 1959) – the first is a piece of absurdism and the second printed backwards – together with earlier notebook material by musician Earle Brown from 1952–3 which exemplifies the indeterminate status of the book. Like Brecht's and Higgins's pieces, Brown provides a series of instructions for a musical performance, but the instructions are printed upside down and are explicitly ambiguous: he claims that the performance space can be 'real or illusory' and can 'expand or contract'; the tempo of the music can be 'as fast as possible to as slow as possible'; lines can 'move in either direction'; and the performer can 'either sit and let it move or move through it at all speeds'.[98] Not only is Brown's piece – and *An Anthology* as a whole – an exemplification of what Richard Kostelanetz in his 1968 book calls 'the theatre of mixed means', but it also has a pedagogical element: to re-educate perception in a period of 'perceptual illiteracy'.[99]

Not all mixed-media art was as radical or off-beat as the artists I have been discussing in this section, but there was certainly a sense, beginning in the early decade and growing towards its end, that stable cultural categories no longer had currency. The pastiche of styles later linked to postmodernism finds its germinal moment in the late 1950s, not just in the realm of art, music and performance, but also in the built environment which had been moving away from the standardization of the International Style of architecture since the middle of the decade with buildings such as Frank Lloyd Wright's Guggenheim Museum, finished in 1956 after thirteen years of planning. It was in other regional urban spaces, rather than the modern cities of New York and Chicago, that this more eclectic modernism was most clearly evident, though, and not only in the sprawling postmodern city of Los Angeles.

As a way of examining these changes to the built environment and public art, it is worth concluding this chapter by focusing on one of the most interesting examples to emerge in the postwar period: the collection of structures, buildings and exhibition spaces that made up the 1962 Seattle World's Fair.

Seattle World's Fair (1962)

The planning of the Seattle World's Fair began in 1955, spanned the second half of the decade and became increasingly bound up with cold war politics. Initially conceived as a means for renovating a northwestern city that had been slow to develop in the first half of the century, the Fair grew out of a municipal impulse for a new civic centre in Seattle. A seventy-four-acre plot was eventually found to house the development one mile from the city centre, with the plan to commemorate fifty years since the first World's Fair in the Pacific Northwest: the Pacific-Yukon-Alaskan Exposition of 1909. This Fair was an attempt to consolidate a regional identity for one of the newest corners of the continent, particularly the close relationship between logging companies and the natural environment.

The half-centenary World's Fair was also planned to celebrate the culture of the Northwest, taking in Alaska and Hawaii which had both been recently included in the Union, as well as Pacific Rim cultures. Seattle had long been thought of as the New York of the Northwest, but it needed a way of cementing its relationship with Pacific Asia in the way that New York capitalized on its relationship with Europe. This was helped by the development of the 'sister city' programme in the mid-1950s, when Seattle was paired with Kobe in Japan: the progressive Japanese coastal city featured in the 1957 Marlon Brando film *Sayonara*. But Seattle also needed a media-savvy showcase for demonstrating its ambition to be a world city and 'the gateway to the Orient', as it was called at the time.

One of the reasons that the seven-year planning of the 1962 World's Fair is so interesting is that a cold war narrative overtook the initial plan to celebrate Northwest culture. In large part stimulated by the Soviet launch of Sputnik in 1957, the municipal impulse to regenerate Seattle became increasingly subordinated to the need to present a national vision of the future with science and technology the driving forces.[100] Branded the 'Century 21 Exposition', the Seattle World's Fair was an opportunity to imagine what the country (indeed the world) would be like in the year 2000: 'the Space Age' as it was described in publicity. This is clearly demonstrated in a 1959 book *Century 21 Exposition*, which begins with a rallying cry to 'mark man's progress [in] the years ahead and the miles above'.[101] Although the initial plans were pushed along by city developer Eddie Carlson in 1955, the finances for the Fair were problematic throughout, spiralling up from $15 million to $47 million. Formal sanction for the Fair was not given the official seal until July 1959 by President Eisenhower at the Boeing Flight Center in nearby Boeing Field, when the opening was thought to be only two years away. Although it would be John F. Kennedy who opened the Fair in April 1962, Eisenhower proclaimed that it 'would depict the role of science in modern civilization . . . and contribute to the welfare of all participants by promoting domestic and international commerce and further understanding among peoples through the interchange of scientific and cultural knowledge'. In this statement are echoed the original plans for the Fair, but as the speech goes on the municipal plans are quickly subordinated to a scientific agenda.

As a model the Fair looked to previous Expositions from the 1930s in Chicago, New York City and San Francisco, as well as The Festival of Britain in 1951 which saw the development of the South Bank arts complex on the Thames. Like London, Seattle organizers were keen to represent both high and popular cultural forms at the Fair, but actually the arts were sidelined as publicity focused closely on science and technology. The Fair itself comprised of five main areas: (1) the world of science; (2) the world of Century 21; (3) the world of commerce and industry; (4) the world of entertainment; and (5) the world of art. While the 'worlds' were supposed to be of equal importance, science dominated the agenda, with the primary aim to 'present the role of man in search for truth in science' and to stimulate children's scientific interest.[102] These aims were embodied in the construction of the Pacific Science Center at the centre of the plot. Next to the futuristic 606-foot Space Needle and the Monorail ('the mass transit system of the future' that took visitors on a 90-second ride from the heart of Seattle to the Fair), the gothic architecture of the Science Center, with its six external arched structures surrounded by fountains designed by the Japanese architect Minoru Yamasaki,

epitomized the intention of the Fair to move beyond the corporate architecture that dominated the 1950s.

Together the Science Center and the Space Needle exemplified what the
1962 guidebook called 'the finest of contemporary design' and the embodiment of 'ideas, concepts and materials which may prevail in the 21st
century'.[103] While the Space Needle's innovative design and 360-degree
revolving restaurant was the Fair's most iconic symbol, Yamasaki's architecture was described in the *New York Herald Tribune* as possessing 'infin-
ite grace and delicacy' of structure, combining 'supreme logic, clarity and
order, with incredible elegance and fantasy', and in the *Los Angeles Times*
it was compared to the Taj Mahal, Wells Cathedral, the Piazza San Marco
and Byzantine temples as 'one of the most beautiful buildings of our
time'.[104] Yamasaki's structures were both traditional and modernist, high
art and popular, looking back to classical architectural structures but also
forward to the surfaceless structures that characterized postmodern
architecture in the 1980s.

Compared to Yamasaki's series of intricate architectural structures, the
two major art exhibits drawn from American, Canadian and European
museums were arguably too concerned with looking back to the beginning
of the 1950s; as the journalist Emily Genauer assessed, 'practically everything to be seen in both exhibits is a cliché of the internationally publicized
abstract-expressionist movement'.[105] With aesthetic abstraction suggesting the 'end of man' (to recall William Faulkner's 1949 Nobel Prize
speech – see Chapter 1), rather than the Fair's theme of 'man in the future
reaching for the stars', Genauer was not alone in claiming that the high
profile of abstract expressionism was a 'noisy, already moribund aspect of
present day painting'. Not all the artists on display received such criticism,
though: much praise was lavished on the Seattle-based Mark Tobey's
painterly abstractions, and the local Indian art on display was also well
received. Nevertheless, compared to the attention given to the Century 21
exhibits, the Fair's cultural showcase seemed anachronistic, not least
because film and television were underrepresented, with the exception of
the Cinerama production *Journey to the Stars* showing in the Pacific
Science Center's US-Boeing Spacearium. For a Fair that aspired to the
next century, the cultural sphere seemed to be firmly rooted in the mid-
century, with science seen as the supreme artistic enterprise. A film by
Charles Eames in the Science Center claimed that the scientist has
absorbed the spirit of ennobling art: 'high on the list of perquisites for being
a scientist is a quality that defines the rich human being as much as it does
the scientist: his ability and his desire to reach out with his mind and his
imagination to something outside himself'.[106]

Dubbed in 1987 'The Fair that Made Seattle' by the *Seattle Times*, the
city was transformed from a provincial area of 600,000 in the mid-1950s
into a major North American city and international business centre, which
by the end of the 1980s had been put on the global map with the ongoing
success of the Boeing (despite a dip in the mid-1970s) and the emergence
of Microsoft. The rival paper the *Seattle Post-Intelligencer* used the 1987

celebrations to reassess the World's Fair as marking a closure of 'the age of technological innocence' when the oil crisis and problems of nuclear power were not yet on the horizon.[107] The Seattle World's Fair was deeply rooted in the cultural politics of the 1950s but also marked one of the decade's dramatic closures, ushering in the renewed optimism of the early 1960s (before Kennedy's assassination and the Vietnam War again quashed national optimism) and looking forward to a new frontier beyond modernist culture and technology.

Figure 5.3 Seattle Space Needle and Pacific Science Center. © Martin Halliwell.

Conclusion

In the visual arts we can see most clearly the ways in which popular and modernist cultural currents periodically interlinked and broke apart through the decade to reveal some of its major social and political fault-lines. It is tempting to discuss visual culture primarily in terms of the ephemera of 'everyday life', but for visual artists everyday life was not the stable signifier of white middle-class suburbia that is often remembered. In the work of Jasper Johns and Robert Frank, for example, we see complex critiques of the postwar nation, while other artists were eager to combine different national and transnational conditions to explore America's postwar identity, as the case study of the

Seattle World's Fair demonstrates. And, while it is tempting to link abstract expressionism with the hard abstractions of cold war, by the middle of the decade a much more eclectic and maverick set of practices was emerging in painting, photography, multimedia art and the built environment that were to take the material form of American life in new and unexpected directions.

Rethinking the 1950s

President Eisenhower entered his last year in office by spending New Year's Eve 1959 at the Augusta National Golf Club in the company of William E. Robinson, the Chairman of Coca-Cola, an evening symbolizing the union of politics and business characteristic of Eisenhower's presidency. A Hindu astrologer on Broadway predicted that 1960 would be a 'good year for Nixon, business and science' (he was at least premature about Nixon), and a *New York Times* correspondent debated whether the decade should actually close at midnight on 31 December 1959 or 1960.[1] Taking 1 January 1961 as the beginning of the next decade seems most helpful, ushering in a new Democratic administration and a young president in the White House, the first to be born in the twentieth century as John F. Kennedy reminded voters. There was also some respite from cold war fears, with public opinion expressing the 'cautious hope' that Kennedy would 'find ways of easing East–West tensions', even though the Soviets seemed in triumphant mood at the close of 1960 and Washington was on the verge of severing diplomatic links with communist Cuba.[2]

One could make the case that the 1950s closed before the end of the calendar decade, perhaps in autumn 1957 (the year of McCarthy's death) with the launch of the Soviet satellite Sputnik 1 which NBC radio announced 'forevermore separated the old from the new' and the Little Rock Central High School controversy which ushered in the major phase of the civil rights movement.[3] Other world events suggest 1957 is a key year. Following the meeting in April 1955 of Asian and African states at the Bandung Conference in Indonesia, 1957 saw 'third world' countries emerge from the grip of colonialism when Ghana became the first African nation to declare its independence under the presidency of Kwame Nkrumah: an event celebrated by black thinkers Richard Wright and C. L. R. James as a moment of seismic global change. This sense of transition was also felt at home by contributors to the 'American Notebook' special issue of *Dissent* from summer 1957, including worries about an economic downswing and the prediction 'that American institutions will presently undergo tremendous dislocations and reorganizations of a more fundamental nature than anything since the seventeenth century'.[4]

If signs of social transition were emerging in 1957, then 1958 seems more significant for breaking new cultural ground in the US with the proliferation of drama Off Broadway, the flourishing of Beat writers on the West Coast and the renaissance in avant-garde performance and graphic art. When deciding on an early end for the decade the danger is simply to fold late 1950s culture into the pop art movement of 1959–62 and the cultural experimentation of the mid-1960s. But *Look* magazine was in no doubt that January 1960 marked the beginning of a new period, claiming that, although cold war fears had not evaporated, 'most Americans today are relaxed, unadventurous, comfortably satisfied with their way of life and blandly optimistic about the future'.[5] Arthur Schlesinger Jr wrote an article for *Esquire* in January 1960 in which he discerned a new 'sense of motion, of leadership, and of hope' in the nation, a sentiment that Kennedy himself echoed in his presidential debates with Nixon nine months later, attacking the political stasis of the 1950s and promising to get 'America moving again'. This sense of motion was not just at the high end of politics either. In January 1961 *Look* magazine ran another feature on 'The Explosive Generation' which detected that young people across the nation were shaking up the complacency of the 1950s: 'the tempo of history has been doubled and redoubled, and social changes that once took decades are now happening over night'.[6]

The historian Mark Lytle makes the case that the long 1960s began as early as 1954 'when the cold war consensus was at its peak' (and did not end, in Lytle's view, until Watergate in 1974), but it would seem that 1960 was merely a prelude to the symbolic beginning of the new decade in 1961.[7] Kennedy's Inaugural Speech looked to both past and future, marking 'an end, as well as a beginning – signifying renewal, as well as change'; a new beginning occurred when nineteen-year-old Charlayne Hunter became the first black woman to be accepted as a student at the University of Georgia in January 1961, followed by James Meredith the first black student at the University of Mississippi in October 1962 (after he had earlier being barred); and John Huston's film *The Misfits* marked a clear closure to the 1950s, with its triad of stars Clark Gable, Marilyn Monroe and Montgomery Clift making final screen appearances (Gable died before the film was released and the others were dead soon after) and filming the previous summer in the Nevada desert was very tense with the pending divorce of Monroe and screenwriter Arthur Miller.[8]

Two documents are often cited as marking the transition between the decades: Eisenhower's Farewell Address of 21 January 1961 and the Port Huron Statement on 15 June 1962 by the Students for Democratic Society (SDS) which had formed as a group in 1960. Both documents reappraise the previous decade but also help to mythologize 'the fifties', constructing a semi-fictional period marked by political balance for Eisenhower and social complacency for the SDS.

Eisenhower was in no doubt that his Farewell Address marked the close of the decade, beginning his speech with the line: 'We now stand ten years past the midpoint of a century . . .' His Address famously identified a 'military-industrial complex' and was fearful of the growth of a 'scientific-technological elite' heedless of the consequences of the development of nuclear weapons.[9] Eisenhower's implication here was that the previous decade had been a peaceful time, reinforced by making no direct mention of Korea or McCarthy or to recent US operations in Iran (1953), Lebanon (1958) and Haiti (1959). But he predicted new fears stemming from the relationship between science, technology and the military, with the suggestion that his administration had managed to contain these threats (even though the H-bomb was being developed under his presidency and over a hundred aboveground nuclear tests had taken place in the Nevada desert).[10] The bomb Eisenhower dropped in 1961 was quite different to the one tested in Eniwetok the year that he came into office, but it was almost as potent: he warned of impending catastrophe unless citizens remained alert, vigilant and wary of the misuse of power.

In contrast the Port Huron Statement characterized the 1950s as a time in which many students 'began maturing in complacency' and did not become politicized until late in the decade. The SDS stated that the 'human degradation, symbolized by the Southern struggle against racial bigotry, compelled most of us from silence to activism' and 'the enclosing fact of the Cold War, symbolized by the presence of the Bomb, brought awareness that we ourselves, and our friends, and millions of abstract "others" we knew more directly because of our common peril, might die at any time'.[11] The powerful Port Huron Statement chimed with C. Wright Mills's 'Letter to the New Left' from autumn 1960 to help mobilize grassroots energies, confirming the argument of the *Look* feature that a far-reaching power shift was occurring on college campuses across the nation – and beyond it, with Martinique psychiatrist Frantz Fanon sensing that a whole number of colonies were ready to spring free from the 'motionless' grip of their colonial masters.[12] The *Look* feature claimed that the maturing baby-boomers in the US were willing to strive for the 'unattainable' to avoid the 'unimaginable' of nuclear annihilation.

The early 1960s is a key moment for reassessing the previous decade, but the re-imagining of the 1950s was happening well before the decade was officially over, with critics on both the Right and Left deploring the complacency that Irving Howe had popularized in his essay 'The Age of Conformity'. This 'bleak atmosphere of con-formism' led to the launch of Howe's leftist (but anti-Stalinist) journal *Dissent* in 1954 and, on the other end of the political spectrum, a few months afterwards the right-winger William F. Buckley Jr founded the *National Review*.[13] Buckley deplored apathy on college campuses and his 1959 book *Up from Liberalism* laid the intellectual groundwork for the rise of the New Right in the guise of the Arizona Senator Barry Goldwater, the previously liberal actor Ronald Reagan, and the grass-roots organization Young Americans for Freedom.[14]

If some thinkers, writers and artists were probing the veneer of the 1950s before it was over, then the early 1960s saw the emergence of a number of critiques that became very familiar later in the decade. Betty Friedan's *The Feminine Mystique* and Sylvia Plath's *The Bell Jar* (both 1963) questioned dominant gender roles and Richard Yates's novel *Revolutionary Road* and Claes Oldenburg's 3D assemblages stripped away the sheen from consumer lifestyles. Perhaps the most influential critique of the 1950s was Michael Harrington's *The Other America: Poverty in the United States* (1962) which brought to the fore 'invisi-ble' unskilled workers, migrant farmhands, the elderly, ethnic minor-ities and 'all the others who live in the economic underworld of American life'.[15] Harrington's thesis was that, although the middle classes were prospering in the 1950s, poor communities were 'shabby and defeated' with towns and slums 'permeated with failure'. Such was the power of Harrington's critique – 'the new poverty is constructed so as to destroy aspiration; it is a system designed to be impervious to hope' – that many commentators believed it influenced Lyndon Johnson's anti-poverty campaigns of the mid-1960s.[16]

Naturalized images of mid-1950s culture were also being tested with only a few years hindsight. In 1960 filmmaker Kenneth Anger wrote *Hollywood Babylon*, his scandalous book on the seedy underside of the film industry, while Andy Warhol's mass-market silkscreen prints have often been interpreted as a simultaneous celebration and critique of the fame industry. Warhol's series of popular icons culminated in his exhibition in the Stable Gallery, New York, in November 1962, where his *Marilyn* diptych (in homage to the recent death of Marilyn Monroe) took its place beside images of mass production: *100 Soup Cans, 1000 Coke Bottles* and *100 Dollar Bills*. Monroe is made more enigmatic through Warhol's bold lines, but the humanity of the actress formerly known as Norma Jean Baker is also stripped bare, leaving a set of easily recognizable but alienating images in which cosmetically brightened hair, lips and eyebrows become the sole defining features.

Warhol was not alone in such pursuits and it is interesting that Monroe, following her mysterious death in August 1962, became a synecdoche of the previous decade. One example is Marty Greenbaum's artist's book *Park Place Position* (1962) which breaks a sequence of almost pure abstractions with a cut-out of Monroe, her head cocked over her right shoulder smiling seductively surrounded by a dark blue halo preserving her celebrity status, only for her right arm to be partially obscured by a piece of cellotape to which is attached some gold cord that twines randomly over this and the facing page. The line drawing of Monroe stands out starkly in the dense colours and textures that fill the two facing pages, with Greenbaum's use of crayon, charcoal and burnt page edges giving the book an unkempt and almost exhausted feel. Monroe's image is echoed in the stars that fill the page, the magazine cut-outs of angel's faces, a silhouetted angel made from foil, and a series of intersecting celestial circles, but these sit uncomfortably with signs of inclement weather and the handwritten words 'biRD FLIGHt'. Monroe is not just a dead icon here, or the celebrity image in Warhol's silkscreen prints; rather, she is part of the swirl of chaotic images that spiral away from meaning into a collage of social and cultural debris.[17]

The complexity verging on randomness of Greenbaum's collage is a useful metaphor for the 1950s: a decade that looks calm and uncomplicated from a distance, but at close range throws up a series of puzzling contradictions. This book has traced the theme of historical and cultural experience in and of the 1950s, but in the early twenty-first century a number of exhibitions, films and memoirs have renewed interest in the decade: fifty-year commemorations of *Brown* v. *the Board of Education* (2004), the polio vaccine (2005), the opening of Disneyland and McDonald's (both 2005) and the launch of Sputnik (2007), have renewed interest in the founding moment when the US 'first thought seriously of itself as the modern society'.[18]

Figure C.1 Seattle billboard celebrating fifty years since the first McDonald's restaurant opened, in Des Plaines, Illinois in 1955. © Martin Halliwell, 2005.

Nostalgia and Cultural Memory

In 1998 the journalist and long-term NBC anchorman Tom Brokaw popularized the phrase 'the greatest generation' to describe those born around 1920 who spent much of the 1940s in uniform. Brokaw hailed the men and women who fought in World War II as 'a generation birthmarked for greatness . . . of towering achievement and modest demeanor'.[19] Nostalgia for combat generations is nothing new and Brokaw's tribute to 'the greatest generation' carefully steers away from the devastating consequences of the dropping of the atom bomb over Hiroshima and the racism that Norman Mailer believed to be rife in Pacific combat during World War II (as depicted in his 1948 war novel *The Naked and the Dead*). Brokaw was twenty years younger than those he profiled in his book *The Greatest Generation* (1998) and he treats their 'tumultuous journey through adversity and achievement' with respect and admiration.[20]

One might expect that Brokaw would portray his own 'silent generation' that came of age in the 1950s as lacking the heroism of those who came before him, and he does not complicate his picture by looking at the difficulties that many World War II and Korean War veterans experienced in reintegrating into civilian society, as portrayed in

The Man in the Gray Flannel Suit and *The Blackboard Jungle*. Instead he acknowledges his debt to his elders, writing that 'they came home to resume lives enriched by the values they had defended' and stressing that his own life was blessed because of them: 'I am a child of the American men and women who . . . devoted their adult years to the building of modern America'.[21] Brokaw himself was born in 1940 in small-town South Dakota where he spent twenty-two years before moving in 1962 to work as a television journalist in Omaha after covering the 1956 election on the local radio station in Yankton. In his more recent memoir *A Long Way From Home* (2002), Brokaw notes that 'the prism through which you look back on your own life gives off a certain rosy tint', and he portrays his childhood in the 1950s as innocent and optimistic 'at a time when everything seemed possible in America'.[22]

Brokaw emphasizes in *A Long Way from Home* his fortune of being 'born in the right place at the right time' as the son of industrious hoteliers, and identifies his whiteness as a sign of privilege: 'as a young white male in the fifties, I was a member of the ruling class, however inadequate my qualifications or uncertain my prospects'.[23] His upbringing was very insular and his cultural engagement was limited to following the Brooklyn Dodgers through their run of World Series finals and his adolescent interest in beauty pageants. The young Brokaw listened to Elvis Presley, Chuck Berry and Pat Boone; some movies were shown locally (*Marty*, *The Seven Year Itch*, *Rebel without a Cause*); and he mentions Grace Metalious's controversial novel *Peyton Place*, but not whether he read it.[24] Perhaps to offset the whiteness of his world, Brokaw focuses one chapter on race, admitting that the civil rights struggle was far removed from his life ('on the issue of race we affected a certain moral superiority – or, in many instances, a benign indifference'), although the nearby Sioux reservation intrigued him (Indian history was not taught at his school) .[25] He even puts spin on his teenage ignorance of race issues, expressing gratitude that his 'formative years in the mostly white environment of the upper Midwest sharpened my sensibilities about the inequities and the complexities of race for the rest of my life', a concern that later informed his 1997 NBC documentary *Why Can't We Live Together?* focusing on the hidden racial rifts in suburbia.[26]

It is tempting to applaud Brokaw's picture of a decade of opportunities as the prize won by the generation that fought in World War II, but the result is that he brushes over many social and cultural complexities of the 1950s. Brokaw admits that 'it wasn't a perfect world, of course', but he fails to examine the causes and consequences of these imperfections. One has the impression reading Brokaw that had he examined the cultural contradictions of the 1950s without the filter of 'the greatest generation' that came before it, the 'prism' through which he looks would not be as rosy. His nostalgia stems from his sheltered experience of the 1950s, which Michael Kammen argues was a nostalgic decade and not the forward-looking one that the Year 2000 exhibition at the 1962 Seattle World's Fair might suggest (see Chapter 5). In exploring the nostalgia boom of the 1950s Kammen focuses on the triumphant liberation of the allies (many European communities in the US were in jubilant mood), the American Traditions Project 1957–9 (dedicated to dramatizing 'incidents illustrating how the good sense of Americans has prevailed in their daily lives'), and the re-launch of the *American Heritage* magazine in 1954 (promising readers 'a good deal of nostalgia' and an escape from commercialism).[27]

It is the legacy of two conservative periods, the 1980s and the 2000s, that has done most to resuscitate the 1950s as Brokaw's decade of 'broader horizons' and 'expanded rights', rather than the conformist and anodyne period pictured by the New Left in the 1960s, full of 'one-dimensional men' (Herbert Marcuse), frustrated housewives (Betty Friedan) and invisible minorities (Ralph Ellison). Some critics in the early 1960s who did not share the values of the student movement such as Barry Goldwater and Milton Friedman were keen to play up the traditionalism of the 1950s to offset what they saw as the pernicious effects of government intervention in the Roosevelt years.[28] The cold war was actually very good for conservatives, recruiting the likes of the previously liberal Ronald Reagan. 'By 1960 I had completed the process of self-conversion', Reagan claimed, turning away from big government towards the free enterprise that marked his eight years in office during the 1980s.[29]

The fact that the decade now has a rosy glow has been helped by attacks on the permissiveness of the 1960s by US and UK leaders George W. Bush and Tony Blair, both of whom were children of the 1950s at a time when Bush's grandfather Prescott Bush was Republican Senator for Connecticut (1952–63), despite his dubious connections to the eugenics movement during World War II. As Mark Lytle argues, the attempt to impeach Bill Clinton in 1998 over his affair with White House intern Monica Lewinsky and the Republican attacks in 2004 on Democratic presidential candidate John Kerry over his involvement in the Vietnam War (he was even dubbed 'Commie Kerry') can both be seen as assaults on the liberal version of the 1960s.[30] In fact, the conservative mood of the early twenty-first century has helped to reframe the 1950s as a time of social stability and good manners: a 'kinder, gentler' decade (as Mary Caputi calls it) where the carefree characters of George Lucas's film *American Graffiti* (1973) and the ABC sitcom *Happy Days* (1974–84) jostle with the heartland mentality evoked by Tom Brokaw and Hillary Clinton in their memoirs. Rather than the caustic tones of critic Eric Goldman in his scathing farewell to 'the stuffy decade' ('we live in a heavy, humourless, sanctimonious, stultifying atmosphere'), 'the fifties' have now been recreated as an optimistic, noble and prosperous decade.[31]

Michael Kammen argues that 'nostalgia is most likely to increase or become prominent in times of transition, in periods of cultural anxiety, or when a society feels a strong sense of discontinuity with its past'.[32] This explains why postwar nostalgia was prominent in the early 1970s (with the Vietnam War dragging on despite Nixon's election promise to withdraw troops), at the turn of the millennium when 'end of history' theories were common, and during the global tumult of the early twenty-first century following 9/11 and wars in Afghanistan and Iraq. Cultural historian Stephanie Coontz asserts that nostalgia for the 1950s is serious business, even though it should not be taken literally. She argues that many Americans are not really nostalgic for the insularity of the Levittown family, but seek a refuge from late-century concerns:

> the belief that the 1950s provided a more family-friendly economic and social environment, an easier climate in which to keep kids on the straight and narrow, and above all, a greater feeling of hope for a family's long-term future. The contrast between the perceived hopefulness of the fifties and our own misgivings about the future is key to contemporary nostalgia for the period.[33]

This view certainly informs Brokaw's perspective on the decade and has filtered down into popular memory, in contrast to more immediate problems of broken families, gun crime and urban governance in the late twentieth century.

The passing of a generation also feeds the kind of nostalgia evident in two recent music biopics: *Ray* (2004) and *Walk the Line* (2005). The films follow the careers of two major musicians of the late 1950s, Ray Charles and Johnny Cash, leading to Academy Awards for Jamie Foxx as Ray Charles and Reese Witherspoon as June Carter (Cash's singer partner, later his wife, and a member of the founding family of country music). Even though the films offer different racially inflected views of the postwar South, they both begin with traumatic childhood moments – Ray Charles watches his younger brother drown and Johnny Cash's brother is killed in a sawing accident – to explain the psychological complexity of the pair and the honing of their musical talents. In both films the serious study of postwar American culture is overshadowed by vibrant soundtracks and the mythical impact of the singers' lives.

Nostalgia for 'the fifties' certainly has its commercial side as evident in the 2006 Broadway revival of the 1954 musical *The Pajama Game* starring the Sinatraesque crooner Harry Connick Jr and Elvis Presley's home Graceland being made an Historic National Monument in March 2006. One positive outcome of this nostalgia has been the rediscovery of roots music. This has been aided by the Smithsonian Institute's repackaging of the Lomax recordings in the late 1990s, Bruce Springsteen's recording of an album of Pete Seeger songs *We Shall Overcome* (2006), and the efforts of music collector and producer T. Bone Burnett, who has now become the official consultant on a range of American films following the success of the bluegrass and old-time soundtrack for the Coen Brothers' film *O Brother, Where Art Thou?* (2000). The rediscovery of the Carter family, the bluegrass pioneer Earl Scruggs and the old-time legend Ralph Stanley (who has been 'on tour' since 1946) in the *O Brother* spin-off documentary *Down from the Mountain* (2000) and the long roots tradition profiled in the PBS documentary *The Appalachians* (2005) reveal the vitality of regional music in the post-World War II years often overlooked from a cold war perspective.[34] This renewed interest in regional cultures has helped to shift the emphasis away from the corporate and suburban Northeast which often dominates discussions of the 1950s to the outlying and patchwork cultures that the likes of Harry Smith, Pete Seeger, Jack Kerouac and Robert Frank were exploring at the time.

But, more often than not, the focus remains fixed on a decade dominated by a cold war agenda. This static image has been aided by the insistence of pundit Ann Coulter in her muckraking book *Treason: Liberal Treachery from the Cold War to the War on Terrorism* (2003) that McCarthy was wrongly vilified by liberals: 'in his brief ride across the landscape, Joe McCarthy . . . sacrificed his life, his reputation, his name. The left cut down a brave man, but not before the American people heard the truth'.[35] The likes of Coulter, Michelle Marvin and Rush Limbaugh on the Right have added their voices to 'the culture wars', in which conservatives and liberals slugged it out in the late

1980s and 1990s in a battle to define American cultural values, such as Allan Bloom's bold claim that McCarthyism 'had no effect whatsoever on [university] curriculum of appointments' in the 1950s.[36] More recently Coulter has tried to rescue the 'indispensable' McCarthy as a responsible conservative during the cold war but her primary goal is to attack what she calls 'liberal mythmaking' and 'liberal treachery'. Although Coulter is an extreme case, the problem with the culture wars is that, rather than creating a debate about the value and significance of the past, the warring factions (particularly on the Right, but also the likes of filmmaker Michael Moore on the Left) often resort to the kind of propaganda that recalls the anticommunist strategies of the 1950s, demonizing the opposition before accusing them of 'sedition and immorality'.[37] Nostalgia, then, is rarely innocent, especially when linked to claims of ownership over national identity.

There has been at least one nostalgia film about the 1950s for each decade since – *A Charlie Brown Christmas* (1965), *American Graffiti* (1973), *Back to the Future* (1985) and *Forrest Gump* (1994) – with critics divided on whether the Oscar-winning *Forrest Gump* provides a liberal appraisal of postwar history, or whether Forrest's homely values rooted in the South of the 1950s veil the kind of historical amnesia practised more explicitly in Ann Coulter's polemic. Another film that has much stronger liberal motivations in exploring the myths of the fifties is *Pleasantville* (1998), but even this does not entirely escape the nostalgic mode it sets out to critique. The film offers a neat allegory for the rise of McCarthyism by contrasting the black-and-white world of homely small-town America with the arrival of colour as a signifier of passion and political conviction.[38] Despite its experiments with colour, the film never quite escapes the simplicity of its central conceit of transporting two teenagers from the media-saturated 1990s into the anodyne TV-land of 1950s sitcoms in the mode of *The Adventures of Ozzie and Harriet*. It is precisely this 'Ozzie and Harriet' view of the decade that Stephanie Coontz argues lies at the heart of the culture wars between conservatives and liberals.[39]

Critical Interventions

A great deal of cultural attention in the early twenty-first century has focused on tributes to the personalities of the 1950s, as those of Tom Brokaw's generation face retirement and other prominent figures of the decade such as musicians Ray Charles and Johnny Cash, novelist Saul Bellow, playwright Arthur Miller, director Robert Wise, actors

Marlon Brando and Glenn Ford, artist Allan Kaprow, economist J. K. Galbraith and activists Rosa Parks and Coretta Scott King (widow of Martin Luther King Jr) have passed away. But there has also been a return to more searching interventions into the decade. These have ranged from reissues of classic 1950s texts, including *The Lonely Crowd* (reissued in 2001), *The Organization Man* (2002) and *The Man in the Gray Flannel Suit* (2005); the projected film re-make of the 1958 adaptation of Herman Wouk's bestseller *Marjorie Morningstar* (with Scarlett Johansson in line to play Natalie Wood's role as a Jewish girl caught between tradition and passion); neo-punk singer Pink's dramatic pop song 'Family Portrait' (2003) which uses the shadow of World War III to explore domesticity and the trauma of family separation; and a number of films that have unearthed neglected elements of 1950s culture.[40]

The mid-1980s saw musicians and writers drawing parallels to the 1950s as two key moments in the long cold war, which had become a reality again in 1983 with the launch of Ronald Reagan's Strategic Defensive Initiative. These renewed cold war fears are reflected in the former Police vocalist Sting's song 'Russians' (1986), with its explicit links between Khrushchev's earlier threat of to 'bury' the United States and Reagan's current promise to 'protect' US citizens.[41] But, despite the Star Wars initiative and the Doomsday Clock being reset at three minutes to midnight to reflect the renewed nuclear threats, the cold war was never as intense as it had been in the early 1950s, and the televised dismantling of the Berlin Wall on 7 November 1989 caught the public imagination as the most potent symbol of the end of communism.

Two months before the collapse of the Berlin Wall, in September 1989, the singer and one-time Levittown resident, Billy Joel, released his single 'We Didn't Start the Fire', with its breathless cavalcade of postwar culture: 'Rosenbergs, H-Bomb, Sugar Ray, Panmunjam / Brando, *The King and I*, and *The Catcher in the Rye*'.[42] Joel uses the Dylanesque patter technique of rhythmical listing to give historical momentum to the song. The narrative begins in 1949 and proceeds through the 1950s to Kennedy's assassination of 1963 before leaping ahead to the re-emergence of the cold war in the 1980s, prompting Joel's exasperated cry: 'what else do I have to say?' His invective is launched against national leaders (the names of Truman, Eisenhower and Stalin feature prominently and Nixon appears twice, once in his role in HUAC and then later as President), while the chorus suggests Joel's generation have been caught in the crossfire. Elsewhere on the 1989 *Storm Front* album Joel described himself as a 'cold war kid in

McCarthy time', extending his earlier evocations on *Nylon Curtain* (1982) which praises the blue-collar worker of suburban 'Allentown' and comradeship of Vietnam veterans in 'Goodnight Saigon'. *Nylon Curtain* was an attempt to write a song cycle about political disillusionment in the early 1980s, and turning forty prompted Joel in 1989 to give 'We Didn't Start the Fire' a broad historical sweep, following an alleged encounter with a high school pupil in which Joel's generation were accused of not having experienced history.[43]

Although there have been important historical reappraisals of the cold war from a transnational perspective, such as John Lewis Gaddis's *The Cold War* (2005), many recent cultural reflections on the 1950s have focused on social upheavals taking place on American soil. Most commentators agree that the film industry has recently come together to provide a left-liberal response to the more pernicious forces that George Bush's war on terrorism has spread at home (such as the Patriot Act with its resonances of covert cold war investigations) and is reinforced by a number of films that make parallels between the two periods, a trend underlined by actor/director George Clooney's speech at the 2006 Academy Awards, in which he revelled at being part of an industry self-consciously 'out of touch' with dominant social forces.

While Ann Coulter tries to rescue McCarthy and the Republican version of the fifties through polemic and browbeating, a number of recent films have re-investigated the relationship between past and present by entering into a debate about what cultural memory means. Whereas the historical critique in *Pleasantville* never quite reaches beyond its nostalgic framework, films such as *Far From Heaven* (2002), *Mona Lisa Smile* (2003), *Where the Truth Lies* (2005) and *Good Night, and Good Luck* (2005) are much more conscious of the decade's key pressure points. All four films can be read as an excavation of a decade that many in the film industry believe has been bleached of its complexity by conservatives claiming it as their own.

Two precedents for this critical approach are Peter Bogdanovich's film *The Last Picture Show* (1971) and David Lynch's *Blue Velvet* (1986) which, released at moments of great nostalgia for the 1950s, explore the emotional and physical cruelty that bubbles under seemingly wholesome relationships, while more recently dramatist Tony Kushner explores the Rosenberg case and political repression in his epic gay fantasia *Angels in America* (1992) and Robert Redford's *Quiz Show* (1997) revisits the big-money scandal that rocked the television networks back in 1958. Even more recently *Mona Lisa Smile* and *Far*

From Heaven examine the impact of enforced gender norms of the 1950s. As discussed in Chapter 5, *Mona Lisa Smile* contrasts a generation of college girls bred for conformity at Wellesley College with the free-thinking art teacher Katherine Ann Watson (Julia Roberts), who challenges their paint-by-numbers world with the complexities of Jackson Pollock's abstracts and prompts them to question the domestic seductions of the decade.

Far From Heaven also focuses on this ideal suburban world in leafy Connecticut where a picture-perfect house and the latest commodities appear to fulfil executive Frank Whittaker and housewife Cathy Whitaker (Dennis Quaid and Julianne Moore) – that is, until Cathy discovers her husband is gay. Todd Haynes's film deliberately deploys the iconography and domestic mise-en-scène of Douglas Sirk's 1950s melodramas, using widescreen, a heightened colour palette and deep focus to stunning effect, to explore what lies beneath the nostalgia for the decade. As a retelling of Sirk's melodrama *All That Heaven Allows* (1955), which investigates the implausibility of a New England romance across class lines, *Far From Heaven* adds the extra ingredient of race. Although racial restrictions of the mid-1950s (even in the Northeast) mean that Cathy and her black gardener Raymond Deagan's budding relationship is doomed, Raymond (Dennis Haysbert) acts as a catalyst to help Cathy to see beyond the limitations of her suburban dream-world. As Mary Caputi notes, the Sirkian references of *Far From Heaven* prove to be useful tools for enabling Haynes to get beyond the mythical construction of the decade and interrogate its 'inconsistencies, hypocrises, and internal confusions'.[44]

Compared to the lush cinematography of *Far From Heaven* the first few minutes of the docudrama *Good Night, and Good Luck* might lead the viewer to think that this is a nostalgic 'monochrome memory' of the 1950s. Evocative black-and-white cinematography offsets the soft jazz that plays at a CBS dinner party and the smoke spiralling from Edward Murrow's ubiquitous cigarette. The film explores the politics of broadcast journalism in the early days of television from a post-9/11 perspective, a period which left-liberal thinkers and journalists have dubbed 'The New McCarthyism'.[45] The central focus of *Good Night, and Good Luck* is Murrow's attempt to expose Joe McCarthy in the run up to the Army–McCarthy hearings of 1954. The fifty-year parallels are very subtle in the film, but network censorship following the Janet Jackson incident of February 2004 (see the Introduction) and the rhetoric of a divided nation following the November 2004 election

Figure C.2 Dennis Quaid and Julianne Moore in the domestic suburban idyll of *Far From Heaven* (Todd Haynes, 2002). © Killer Films/The Kobal Collection.

(with Democratic states threatening to secede after George W. Bush won a second term) suggest that the Murrow and McCarthy stand-off was a defining moment in the culture wars.

As director George Clooney and producer/writer Grant Heslov make clear, *Good Night, and Good Luck* is politically motivated, with Clooney seeing the *See It Now* broadcast on McCarthy as one of two defining moments in television history (the other being CBS anchorman Walter Cronkite's 'mired in stalemate' report on the Vietnam War in February 1968).[46] But Clooney and Heslov try hard not to indulge in a heroes-and-villains-style history lesson, in which Murrow (played by David Strathairn) would take the role of noble vigilante and McCarthy demonized as the 'buffoon assassin', as the *New York Post* had called him in the 1950s. Instead, the film makes clear that Murrow is in danger of losing his objectivity at times, while McCarthy is left to do his own damage by appearing as himself in extensive archival news footage. The film industry rarely portrays history without heroes, but director George Clooney's ensemble cast comes close, even though Clooney makes his intent obvious by appearing as Fred Friendly, Murrow's producer at CBS.[47]

Another contemporary film which explores the contours of post-World War II America is the Canadian director Atom Egoyan's

Figure C.3 David Strathairn as Edward Murrow in the CBS studio in *Good Night, and Good Luck* (George Clooney, 2005). © Warner Independent/2929 Prod/The Kobal Collection.

neo-noir *Where the Truth Lies*, adapted from the 2003 novel by Rupert Holmes. Rather than taking a retrospective look at the 1950s from the perspective of the present, the film is reminiscent of a Hitchcock thriller in its complex double-plotting and psycho-sexual intrigue. Egoyan's film follows Holmes's novel in setting the present in 1974 when a savvy young author Karen O'Connor (Alison Lohman) is commissioned to write an account of the comedy team Vince Collins and Lanny Morris (played by Colin Firth and Kevin Bacon), based loosely on the comic duo Dean Martin and Jerry Lewis. As a young girl growing up in the late 1950s O'Connor idolized the pair and actually appeared on one of their twenty-four-hour telethons to raise money for polio relief.

The film shuttles over fifteen years between the present (1974) and past (1959), with O'Connor playing detective in an attempt to discover the motivation behind the death of a student chambermaid Maureen O'Flaherty (Rachel Blanchard), an incident which marks the end of Morris and Collins's professional and personal relationship. While O'Connor is intent on gleaning Collins's side of the story, she receives regular written instalments from Morris that mythologize the late 1950s as a time of Rat Packers, debauchery and drug-taking: a hedonistic portrait of Morris which contrasts with the gentle man whom she meets by accident on a transcontinental flight in 1974 and whom she remembers from her childhood.

Where the film succeeds best is in drawing the viewer's attention to the constructed nature of memory, in which Morris's exaggerated stories of life on the road with his partner in 1959 are an elaborate cover-up for the events leading to the death of Maureen O'Flaherty. Sharing a similar theme to *Far From Heaven*, the repressed truth revolves around Collins's homosexual feelings for Morris, which the novel and film deliberately hide from the viewer until towards the end. The fact that O'Connor (a shadow-image of O'Flaherty) is caught up in a web of romance and intrigue with the two men implies that there can be no disinterested historical view; at one point in the novel O'Connor even admits: 'I had not had an extended conversation with anyone in the last twenty-four hours to whom I hadn't been lying . . . I wondered what it would be feel like to speak the truth'.[48] By pulling her into the midst of the dissembling world O'Connor has been commissioned to investigate, *Where the Truth Lies* implies that the 1950s is more deceptive and ambiguous a period than it first appears precisely because it seems so unproblematic on the surface.

The Cultural Legacy of the 1950s

One theme I have pursued through this book is the way in which cultural modernism was undergoing a transition in the 1950s. Partly shaped by the cold war climate and partly influenced by the growth of mass culture after the war, the book has argued that modernist currents run throughout the major cultural forms of the decade. One reason why on closer inspection the 1950s is such a difficult decade to comprehend is because of the instability of postwar modernism, representing an artistic retreat for some practitioners and a critical social tool for others. Much fifties nostalgia, such as travel writer Bill Bryson's light-hearted account of his midwestern childhood in *The Life and Times of the Thunderbolt Kid* (2006), feeds off the popular trends of the decade without looking closely at industrial forces (the paperback book market, broadcasting networks, advertising, private and public art patrons) and the more organic changes that gave rise to the blurring of genres in tragicomic fiction, mixed-mode performance and hybrid forms of music and art.

The contradictions of the 1950s become more evident when focusing on the interrelation of cultural forms, played out in the arena where forces of standardization (the *Billboard* Top 40, dead-centrist television programming, Levittown housing and corporate architecture) came into contact with cultures of hybridity (roots music, rock 'n' roll, avant-garde film and half-abstract art) as two antagonistic social trends.[49] Modernism is a limiting tool if used merely as a periodizing concept (ending in the United States some time between the 1930s and the 1960s), or closely linked to social progress and industrialization, or merely a label for erudite and difficult art. The institutionalization of modernist art in the late twentieth century, particularly the corporate sponsorship of avant-garde art, suggests that modernism is a dated concept ready to be consigned to history. But modernism still has its uses if it is taken as a modality that inflects cultural transitions in American life during the twentieth century. In fact, after the waning of critical interest in postmodernism in the mid-1990s, critics have extended the historical horizon of 'late modernism' to describe a long historical arc that includes cultural production after World War II.

If one view of postmodernism is a rapid recycling of past styles, then it is premised on a theory of late capitalism that replaces continuity with the relentless pace of the market. Fredric Jameson discusses the way in which modernism is bound up with both continuity and rupture; it rarely seeks a complete break with history, but rather tries to negotiate between present and past. Jameson claims that late modernism emerged as 'the survival and transformation of more properly modernist creative impulses after World War II' as evident in Jasper Johns paintings, Vladimir Nabokov's fiction and John Cage's musical performances; as such, Jameson argues late modernism is a distinctly North American form.[50] Rather than separating 'art' (good) from 'culture' (bad) as the Frankfurt School thinkers Adorno and Horkheimer attempted, Jameson looks back to art critic Clement Greenberg's realization that art and culture were increasingly entangled after the war (see Chapter 5) and the kind of mixed mode or maverick modernism that revived the avant-garde attempt to close the gap between art and life. There is a historical dimension here in that modernism implies a continual reassessment of the past in light of the ever-changing present. Looking simultaneously in two directions is precisely what Eisenhower and Kennedy did in their 1961 speeches and what, forty years later, is again evident in the cycle of fifties retro-films.

While the partisanship of the culture wars has distorted certain elements of 1950s culture, some recent critical interventions help to refocus attention on the material and historical fabric of mid-twentieth-century America. Rather than resorting to the heavy-handed *Pleasantville* trick of transplanting a 1990s character into a 1950s setting, these films offer more interesting narrative links from one moment to the other. For example, the retro-qualities of *Far From Heaven* may tempt the critic to discuss the film in terms of post-modern pastiche, but it can be better be positioned alongside *Where the Truth Lies* as investigative texts that work inside the frame of nostalgia to unearth hidden elements that would otherwise lie beyond cultural memory. This is not about appropriating the past to justify or condemn the present, but using culture as a critical tool that frees the viewer from believing that there can be only one authentic historical account.

Following in the wake of two experimental reworkings of the early 1950s, E. L. Doctorow's *The Book of Daniel* (1971) and Robert Coover's *The Public Burning* (1977) which tread the fine line between fact and fiction to examine the climate of distrust during the McCarthy and Rosenberg years, in *1959: A Novel* (1992) African American writer Thulani Davis turned her attention to a transitional year at the end of the decade. Telling the story of a rural community in Turner, Virginia, the novel begins with the death of Billie Holiday on 17 July 1959, itself a symbol of the close of the decade. The story follows twelve-year-old Willie Tarrant as she comes of age and slowly becomes aware of racial oppression in her hometown. But when eight black teenagers demand to be served in a local store five years after the formal end of segregation, Willie comes to realize that grassroots forces can be mobilized against those who wield power. The story charts Willie's rites of passage by offering a double movement into the future and past. She is inspired when she meets Martin Luther King and absorbs the political writings of James Baldwin, but Willie also discovers her family heritage when she reads her Aunt Fannie's diary that records the tribulations facing African Americans at the beginning of the century. This symbolic reaching in two directions is resonant of a mid-century tale, recalling Hannah Arendt's view of the postwar period as one caught between past and future.

Davis has been criticized for being too self-conscious in her novel of cultural and political awakening and for allowing the seams of the story to show through, but this appears to be precisely Davis's modernist intent.[51] *1959* is not straightforward historical storytelling, but an attempt to intervene in and to reconstruct the transition between the 1950s and 1960s in an honest way. The alternative strategy of hiding the seams of the story may imply an act of deception, transporting readers into the past without prompting them to ask questions about the purpose of historical construction. Davis's story of the late 1950s and early 1960s is one in which conflicting cultural pressures cannot be easily resolved, but it also reveals the possibility that personal reflection and collective action can come together in meaningful ways.

Although Willie spends much of her childhood and early adolescence watching television and listening to the radio, the act of engaging directly with culture (rather than casually consuming it) enables her to understand that history affects whole communities and not just individuals. Culture in this sense offers Willie an expanded field of experience, helping her to cultivate an awareness of the multiple intersections between art and politics and the complex relationships between national and local history. Like her earlier (but more naïve) white incarnation Frankie Addams in Carson McCullers' novella *The Member of the Wedding* growing up in the Deep South during World War II (see Chapter 1), Willie learns she must wear 'a mixture of old and new clothes' if she is to make a mark on the future.[52] Although history has been 'ripped up and set loose' in her Virginian town at the end of the 1950s, Willie learns the supreme lesson that if she listens very closely to the past then hidden stories will 'cling very close to [her] ear and tell softly what [she has] forgotten or never known'.[53]

Notes

Introduction

1. 'The Producers', *Variety* Cannes Conference Series, 15 May 2004.
2. Hillary Rodham Clinton, *Living History* (London: Headline, [2003] 2004), p. 1.
3. Lizabeth Cohen, *A Consumers' Republic: The Politics of Mass Consumption in Postwar America* (New York: Knopf, 2003), p. 7.
4. Fred Orton, 'Footnote One: The Idea of the Cold War', *Avant-Gardes and Partisans Reviewed*, ed. Fred Orton and Griselda Pollock (Manchester: Manchester University Press, 1996), p. 205.
5. See Eric F. Goldman, *The Crucial Decade: America 1945–1955* (New York: Knopf, 1956) and Hannah Arendt, *Between Past and Future: Eight Exercises in Political Thought* (New York: Penguin, [1968] 1978).
6. J. Ronald Oakley, *God's Country: America in the Fifties* (New York: Dembner Books, [1986] 1990), p. x.
7. Richard M. Fried, '1950–1960', in *A Companion to 20th-Century America*, ed. Stephen J. Whitfield (Oxford: Blackwell, 2004), p. 71.
8. Robert H. Bremner and Gary W. Reichard (eds), *Reshaping America: Society and Institutions, 1945–1960* (Columbus OH: Ohio State University Press, 1982), pp. ix–x.
9. Nixon and Khrushchev's 'kitchen debate' did not disguise the fact that cold war fears had started to mount again after the launch of Sputnik in 1957. In May 1959, for example, *Look* magazine claimed 'we are wide open to attack from Russian submarines' and that 'we have left a shocking hole in our defenses': J. Robert Moskin, 'The War We Are Not Ready to Fight', *Look* (26 May 1959), pp. 27–8.
10. William Childress, 'The Long March', in *Retrieving Bones: Stories and Poems of the Korean War*, ed. W. D. Ehrhart and Philip K. Jason (New Brunswick NJ: Rutgers University Press, 1999), p. 167.

11. Sylvia Plath, *The Bell Jar* (London: Faber, 1963), p. 234.

12. Thomas Hine, *Populuxe* (New York: Knopf, 1986), pp. 12, 15.

13. See Alice Jardine, 'Flash Back, Flash Forward: The Fifties, the Nineties, and the Transformed Politics of Remote Control', in *Secret Agents: The Rosenberg Case, McCarthyism and Fifties America*, ed. Marjorie Garber and Rebecca L. Walkowitz (New York: Routledge, 1995), pp. 107–23, and Mark Hamilton Lytle, *America's Uncivil Wars: The Sixties Era from Elvis to the Fall of Richard Nixon* (New York: Oxford University Press, 2006).

14. Lisle A. Rose, *The Cold War Comes to Main Street* (Lawrence KA: University Press of Kansas, 1999), p. 1.

15. See George F. Kennan, 'The Sources of Soviet Conduct', *Foreign Affairs*, 25 (4) (July 1947), pp. 566–82.

16. For Truman's Address before a Joint Session of Congress (12 March 1947), see http://usinfo.state.gov/usa/infousa/facts/funddocs/truman.txt. For Eisenhower's First Inaugural Address (20 January 1953), see http://www.bartleby.com/124/pres54.html.

17. Truman cited in Ernest W. Lefever, *America's Imperial Burden: Is the Past Prologue?* (Boulder CO: Westview Press, 1999), p. 73. Allen Hunter (ed.), *Rethinking the Cold War* (Philadelphia PA: Temple University Press, 1998), p. 2.

18. Norman Mailer, *Advertisements for Myself* (New York: Andre Deutsch, 1961), p. 259.

19. Henry F. May, *The End of American Innocence: A Study of the First Years of Our Own Time, 1912–1917* (London: Jonathan Cape, 1960), p. 30.

20. J. Edgar Hoover, *Masters of Deceit* (New York: Henry Holt, 1958), p. 168.

21. Theodor Adorno and Max Horkheimer, *Dialectic of Enlightenment* (London: Verso, [1944] 1979), pp. 120–1.

22. David M. Potter, *People of Plenty: Economic Abundance and the American Character* (Chicago: University of Chicago Press, 1954), p. 12.

23. Potter, *People of Plenty*, p. 77. Cohen, *A Consumers' Republic*, p. 119.

24. Cohen, *A Consumers' Republic*, p. 119.

25. Potter, *People of Plenty*, p. 188. For an exceptionalist reading of *People of Plenty*, see Paul Giles, *Virtual Americas: Transnational Fictions and the Transatlantic Imaginery* (Durham NC: Duke University Press 2002), pp. 162–3.

26. Vance Packard, *The Hidden Persuaders* (London: Penguin, [1957] 1960), p. 11.

27. Ibid., p. 12.

28. Ibid., p. 13.

29. Ibid., p. 37.

30. The Hudson advert is printed in *Time* (8 March 1948), 78, and the Roadmaster advert republished in Jim Heimann, *All-American Ads 50s* (Cologne: Taschen, 2002), pp. 184–5.

31. Other Hudson adverts capitalize on this language of pleasure: an advert for the Hudson Hornet of 1951 focuses on beauty, thrills, grace and luxury as well as its 'low upkeep cost and trouble-free operation': Heimann, *All-American Ads 50s*, p. 178.

32. Packard, *The Status Seekers* (London: Penguin, [1959] 1961), p. 15.

33. See Karal Ann Marling, *As Seen on TV: The Visual Culture of Everyday Life in the 1950s* (Cambridge MA: Harvard University Press, 1996), p. 228.

34. Theodor Adorno, *Minima Moralia*, trans. E. F. N. Jephcott (London: New Left Books, [1951] 1975), p. 65.

35. Speech give by Edward R. Murrow, RTNDA Convention, Chicago (15 October 1958): http://www.rtnda.org/resources/speeches/murrow. shtml.

36. Hugo Ernst, 'Labor Views the Campaigns', *The Nation* (10 May 1952), p. 447. For a more balanced contemporary view of McCarthy, see Dennis H. Wrong, 'Theories of McCarthyism – A Survey', *Dissent*, 1 (4) (autumn 1954), pp. 385–92.

37. Michael Paul Rogin, *The Intellectuals and McCarthy: The Radical Specter* (Cambridge MA: MIT Press, 1967), p. 3.

38. Ibid., p. 6.

39. C. Wright Mills, 'The Conservative Mood', *Dissent* 1 (1) (winter 1954), pp. 22–31, reprinted in *50 Years of Dissent*, ed. Nicolaus Mills and Michael Walzer (New Haven CT: Yale University Press, 2004), pp. 22–6.

40. Rogin, *The Intellectuals and McCarthy*, p. 218.

41. See Clement Greenberg, 'The Plight of Our Culture: Industrialism and Class Mobility' (1953), in *The Commentary Reader: Two Decades of Articles and Stories*, ed. Norman Podhoretz (New York: Atheneum, 1966) and Dwight Macdonald, 'Masscult & Midcult' (1960), *Against the Grain* (New York: Vintage, 1962), p. 50.

42. John Alsop cited in Goldman, *The Crucial Decade*, p. 222. See also Irving Howe's essay 'Stevenson and the Intellectuals', *Dissent* 1 (1) (winter 1954), 12–21.

43. Arthur Schlesinger Jr, 'The Highbrow in Politics', *Partisan Review*, 20 (March–April 1953), p. 165, cited in Richard Hofstadter, *Anti-Intellectualism in American Life* (New York: Vintage, 1962), p. 4.

44. Philip Wylie, *Generation of Vipers* (Normal IL: Dalkey Archive Press, [1955 edn] 1996), p. xviii.

45. Ibid., pp. 194, 316.

46. Norman Vincent Peale, *The Power of Positive Thinking* (New York: Simon & Schuster, [1952] 2000), p. xii.

47. Reinhold Niebuhr, *Pious and Secular America* (New York: Scribner's, 1958), p. 12.

48. Lewis Coser, 'Imperialism and the Quest for New Ideas', *Dissent*, 1 (1) (winter 1954), p. 9.

49. Martin Mayer, *Madison Avenue U.S.A.* (London: Penguin, [1958] 1961), p. 43.

50. Ibid., p. 44

51. John Kenneth Galbraith, *The Affluent Society*, 2nd edn (London: Penguin, [1958] 1970), p. 20.

52. Ibid., p. 14.

53. Ibid., p. 44.

54. See Ed Murrow's discussion with Robert Oppenheimer, broadcast on CBS (4 January 1955), and the debate between Nixon and Khrushchev (24 July 1959): www.cnn.com/specials/cold.war/episodes/14/documents/debate.

55. Galbraith, *The Affluent Society*, pp. 45, 279.

56. Ibid., p. 282.

57. Hofstadter, *Anti-Intellecualism in American Life*, p. 428.

58. Ibid., p. 3. Wylie, *Generation of Vipers*, p. xiv.

59. Wylie, *Generation of Vipers*, p. xiv.

60. Rogin, *The Intellectuals and McCarthy*, pp. 10–11.

61. Lewis Mumford, *Art and Technics* (New York: Columbia University Press, 1952), p. 11.

62. Trilling, *The Liberal Imagination* (Garden City NY: Anchor, [1950] 1957), pp. 95–6.

63. Philip Rahv and William Phillips (eds), *The New Partisan Review Reader, 1945–1953* (New York: Harcourt, 1953), p. vii.

64. Ibid., p. vii.

65. Trilling, 'Our Country and Our Culture' (1952), reprinted as *America and the Intellectuals*, *Partisan Review* Series, 4 (1953), p. 111.

66. Irving Howe, 'This Age of Conformity', *Partisan Review*, 21 (January–February 1954), pp. 7–33.

67. *America and the Intellectuals*, p. 81.

68. Ibid., pp. 82–3.

69. Norman Podhoretz, 'Intellectuals and Writers Then and Now', special issue of *Partisan Review* ('Our Country, Our Culture'), 69 (4) (Fall 2002), p. 507.

70. Nevada Senator George Malone, cited in *Edward R. Murrow: This Reporter* (Susan Steinberg, CBS, 1990).

71. George B. Leonard, Jr, 'Hawaii: State-to-Be Where Many Bloodlines Blend in Beauty', *Look* (12 May 1959), pp. 29–30.

72. See Richard Kuisel, *Seducing the French: The Dilemma of Americanization* (Berkeley CA: University of California Press, 1993), pp. 190–3.

73. Peter Coleman, *The Liberal Conspiracy: The Congress for Cultural Freedom and the Struggle for the Mind of Postwar Europe* (New York: Free Press, 1989), p. 56. Kevin Mattson, *When We Were Great: The Fighting Faith of Postwar Liberalism* (New York: Routledge, 2004), pp. 81–2.

74. Richard Pells, *Not Like Us: How Europeans Have Loved, Hated, and Transformed American Culture since World War II* (New York: Basic Books, 1997), p. 73.

75. Penny M. von Eschen, *Satchmo Blows Up the World: Jazz Ambassadors Play the Cold War* (Cambridge MA: Harvard University Press, 2004), p. 25.

76. See Sally B. Woodbridge, 'Visions of Renewal and Growth: 1945 to the Present', *Visionary San Francisco*, ed. Paolo Polledri (Munich: Prestel, 1990), pp. 119–32.

77. Ronald Oakley, *God's Country*, p. 10.

78. Stephanie Coontz, *The Way We Really Are* (New York: HarperCollins, 1997), p. 38.

79. David B. Bittan, 'Ordeal in Levittown', *Look* (19 August 1958), pp. 84–5. See Kenneth Jackson, *Crabgrass Frontier: The Suburbanization of the United States* (New York: Oxford University Press, 1985), p. 241, and Dolores Hayden, *Building Suburbia: Green Fields and Urban Growth, 1820–2000* (New York: Vintage, 2003), p. 135.

80. 'Levittown's Palimpsest' (14 January 2004): http://tigger.uic.edu/~pbhales/race.html

81. *In the Suburbs* is available as an extra on the DVD *The End of Surburbia: Oil Depletion and the Collapse of the American Dream* (Gregory Greene, 2004).

82. Cohen, *A Consumers' Republic*, p. 195. Cohen assesses that suburban populations rose 43 per cent from 1947 to 1953 while the general population only increased by 11 per cent.

83. 'Behind New York's Façade', *Look* (18 February 1958), p. 71.

84. See Robert A. M. Stern et al., *New York 1960: Architecture and Urbanism between the Second World War and the Bicentennial* (New York: Monacelli Press, 1997), pp. 13–46.

85. See Mark Luccarelli, *Lewis Mumford and the Ecological Region: The Politics of Planning* (New York: Guilford Press, 1995), pp. 190–1.
86. Mumford, *The City in History* (London: Penguin, [1961] 1966), p. 553.
87. Ibid., p. 554.
88. Ibid., p. 564.
89. Disney reputedly claimed in 1920 that 'one of these days I'm going to build an amusement park – and it's going to be clean': Charles Solomon, *Enchanted Drawings* (New York: Knopf, 1989), p. 191.
90. 'The Disneyland Story' (ABC, 27 October 1954), *Disneyland USA* DVD (Disney Enterprises Inc., 2000).
91. Robert De Roos, 'The Magic Worlds of Walt Disney', *National Geographic* (August 1963), reprinted in Eric Smoodin (ed.), *Disney Discourse: Producing the Magic Kingdom* (New York: Routledge, 1994), p. 50.
92. Comment by Bob Cummings in 'Dateline Disneyland' (ABC, 17 July 1955), *Disneyland USA* DVD.
93. For Disney's testimony to HUAC in 1947 and his conflict with his workers, see Marc Eliot, *Walt Disney: Hollywood's Dark Prince* (New York: Andre Deutsch, [1995] 2003).
94. Jean Baudrillard, *America* (London: Verso, [1986] 1989), p. 56.
95. Marling, *As Seen on TV*, p. 93.
96. Betty Friedan, *The Feminine Mystique* (New York: Dell, [1963] 1973), p. 16.
97. Steve Cohan, *Masked Men: Masculinity and the Movies in the Fifties* (Bloomington IN: Indiana University Press, 1997), p. 1.
98. Louis Lyndon, 'Uncertain Hero: The Paradox of the American Male', *Woman's Home Companion* (November 1956), pp. 41–3, 107.
99. William Attwood, 'Why Does He Work So Hard?', *Look* (4 March 1958), p. 74, cited in Cohan, *Masked Men*, p. 6
100. Although Alfred Kinsey's reports suggested that homosexuality was much more widespread than commonly thought, it was not until the end of the decade that sociologist Erving Goffman's study *The Presentation of Self in Everyday Life* (1959) offered a systematic challenge to the belief that homosexuality is a pathological condition.
101. See Glenna Matthews, *The Rise of Public Woman: Women's Power and Women's Place in the United States, 1630–1970* (Oxford: Oxford University Press, 1994).
102. See Eugenia Kaledin, *Mothers and More: American Women in the 1950s* (Boston MA: Twayne, 1984) and Joanne Meyerowitz (ed.), *Not June Cleaver: Women and Gender in Postwar America, 1945–1960* (Philadelphia PA: Temple University Press, 1994).

103. Allison Graham, *Framing the South: Hollywood, Television, and Race during the Civil Rights Struggle* (Baltimore MD: Johns Hopkins University Press, 2001), p. 18.

104. See the HBO film *The Notorious Bettie Page* (Mary Harron, 2005) for a retrospective view of the anti-pornographic hearings.

105. Ardis Cameron, 'Open Secrets: Rereading *Peyton Place*' (1998), in Grace Metalious, *Peyton Place* (London: Virago, 2002), p. xi.

106. Wini Breines, 'The "Other" Fifties: Beats and Bad Girls', *Not June Cleaver*, ed. Meyerowitz, pp. 382–408.

107. J. D. Salinger, *Franny and Zooey* (London: Penguin, [1961] 1964), p. 26.

108. *The Labor Movement: Beginnings and Growth in America* (Coronet Instructional Film, 1959) and *The Rise of Labor* (Encyclopedia Britannia Educational Corporation, 1968). Both films are held in the Moving Picture Reading Room, Library of Congress, Washington DC

109. Cohen, *A Consumers' Republic*, p. 164.

110. Patricia Bradley, *Mass Media and the Shaping of American Feminism, 1963–1975* (Jackson MI: University Press of Mississippi, 2003), pp. 11–17.

111. For a contextual reading of *On the Waterfront*, see Kenneth R. Hey, 'Ambivalence as a Theme in *On the Waterfront* (1954)', in *Hollywood as Historian: American Film in a Cultural Context*, ed. Peter Rollins (Lexington KY: University Press of Kentucky, 1983), pp. 159–89.

112. Ben Sidran, *Black Talk* (Edinburgh: Payback, [1971] 1995), pp. 116–60.

113. See, for example, Thomas Cripps, *Making Movies Black: The Hollywood Message Movie from World War II to the Civil Rights Era* (New York: Oxford University Press, 1993); Craig Werner, *A Change is Gonna Come: Music, Race and the Soul of America* (New York: Plume, 1999); and Brian Ward, *Radio and the Struggle for Civil Rights in the South* (Gainsville FL: University Press of Florida, 2004).

114. Richard H. King, *Race, Culture, and the Intellectuals, 1940–1970* (Baltimore MD: Johns Hopkins University Press, 2004), p. 125.

115. C. L. R. James, 'The Revolutionary Answer to the Negro Problem in the USA', *The C. L. R. James Reader*, ed. Anna Grimshaw (Oxford: Blackwell, 1992), pp. 182–9.

116. Walter A. Jackson, 'White Liberal Intellectuals, Civil Rights and Gradualism, 1954–60', in *The Making of Martin Luther King and the Civil Rights Movement*, eds Brian Ward and Tony Badger (Basingstoke: Macmillan, 1996), p. 96. See also Charles B. Turner Jr, 'The Black Man's Burden: The White Liberal', *Dissent* (Summer 1963), pp. 215–18.

117. Niebuhr, *Pious and Secular America*, p. 78.

118. Ralph Ellison's letter of 19 May 1954 is published by John F. Callahan, ' "American Culture is of a Whole": From the Letters of Ralph Ellison', *New Republic* (1 March 1999), pp. 38–9. James Baldwin, 'Down at the Cross', *The Fire Next Time* (London: Penguin, 1964), p. 74.

119. Sidney Poitier later starred as Justice Thurgood Marshall in the ABC show *Separate But Equal* (1991), a role for which he prepared by discussing the *Brown* ruling with the octogenarian Marshall. The ongoing cultural importance of *Brown* can be gauged by the number of historical reappraisals published around 2004 as well as numerous fifty-year exhibitions such 'With an Even Hand: Brown v. Board at Fifty' at The Library of Congress and 'Separate Is Not Equal' at the Museum of American History, Washington DC.

120. Daniel Bell, *The Cultural Contradictions of Capitalism* (New York: Perseus, [1973] 1996), p. 20.

121. Oakley, *God's Country*, p. x. Fried, '1950–1960', *A Companion to 20th-Century America*, p. 71.

1. Fiction and Poetry

1. For the transcript of Faulkner's Nobel Prize speech (10 December 1950), see http://www.mcsr.olemiss.edu/~egjbp/faulkner/lib_nobel.html

2. Stephen Spender, 'The Modernist Movement is Dead', *New York Times Book Review* (3 August 1952), pp. 1–2.

3. Leslie Fiedler, *Waiting for the End* (London: Penguin, 1964), p. 9.

4. Brooks Atkinson, 'At the Theatre', *New York Times* (6 January 1950), p. 26.

5. Morris Dickstein, *Leopards in the Temple: The Transformation of American Fiction, 1945–1970* (Cambridge MA: Harvard University Press, 2002), pp. x–xi.

6. Russell Lynes, 'High-Brow, Low-Brow, Middle-Brow', *Life* (11 April 1949), pp. 99–102.

7. Richard Chase, *The American Novel and Its Tradition* (New York: Anchor, 1957), p. 244.

8. Daniel Bell, *The End of Ideology: The Exhaustion of Political Ideas in the Fifties* (Cambridge MA: Harvard University Press, [1960] 1988), pp. 313–14. See also Bell, *The Cultural Contradictions of Capitalism* (London: Heinemann, [1976] 1979), pp. 33–84.

9. Dickstein, *Leopards in the Temple*, p. 20.

10. Vernon Shetley, *After the Death of Poetry: Poet and Audience in Contemporary America* (Durham NC: University of North Carolina Press, 1993), pp. 16–17.

11. Delmore Schwartz, 'Two Problems in Writing Poetry', in *Mid-Century American Poets*, ed. John Ciardi (New York: Twayne, 1950), p. 285.

12. Ibid., p. 283.

13. Censors in the late 1940s and early 1950s 'sought to purge the wire racks of lurid literature' when the House of Representatives appointed a Select Committee on Current Pornographic Materials (The Gathering Committee) to investigate editorial and marketing practices: Thomas L. Bonn, *UnderCover: An Illustrated History of American Mass Market Paperbacks* (London: Penguin, 1982), pp. 55–7.

14. Leslie Fiedler, 'The State of American Writing, 1948: Seven Questions', *Partisan Review*, 15 (August 1948), p. 875.

15. A report from 1950 revealed that in 1946 the Southeast and West Central regions (40.6 per cent of the population) had only 22.3 per cent of book sales, while the Northeast region (26.5 per cent of the population) had 42.4 per cent of sales, with 22.2 per cent of national sales in 1944 in New York State: Bernard Rosenberg and David Manning White (eds), *Mass Culture: The Popular Arts in America* (Glencoe IL: Free Press), p. 127.

16. Lowell, 'Memories of West Street and Lepke', *Life Studies*, p. 99.

17. Allen Ginsberg, 'America', *Howl and Other Poems* (San Francisco CA: City Lights, [1956] 1959), p. 39.

18. Norman Mailer, *Advertisements for Myself* (London: HarperCollins, [1961] 1994), p. 250.

19. Ibid., p. 291. For a response to Mailer's 'The White Negro', see Jane Hayman, 'The White Jew', *Dissent*, 8 (2) (spring 1961), pp. 191–6.

20. See Dwight D. Eisenhower, 'Farewell Address' (17 January 1961) and C. Wright Mills, 'The Structure of Power in American Society' (March 1958), in *Power in Postwar America*, ed. Richard Gillam (Boston MA: Little, Brown, 1971), pp. 157–9, pp. 52–62.

21. John Ciardi, *Mid-Century American Poets*, p. xi.

22. J. D. McClatchy (ed.), *The Vintage Book of Contemporary American Poetry* (New York: Vintage, 1990), p. xxiii. Ciardi, *Mid-Century American Poets*, p. xxiv. While postmodernism was not used as a common label until the 1980s (despite critics Leslie Fielder and Ihab Hassan using the term in the early 1970s), critics David Perkins and Paul Hoover view the divergent currents of 1950s poetry within an early postmodern paradigm.

23. Charles Olson, 'Projective Verse' (1950), *Collected Prose*, ed. Donald Allen and Benjamin Friedlander (Berkeley CA: University of California Press, 1997), pp. 239–49.

24. Michael McClure, *Simple Eyes and Other Poems* (New York: New Directions, 1994), p. viii.

25. McClure, 'Ode to Jackson Pollock' (1961), in *Postmodern American Poetry*, ed. Paul Hoover (New York: Norton, 1994), p. 256.

26. Thomas Mann, 'Past Masters' (1933), cited in William Van O'Connor, *The Grotesque: An American Genre* (Carbondale IL: Southern Illinois University Press, 1962), p. 5.

27. Saul Bellow, *The Adventures of Augie March* (London: Penguin [1953] 1984), p. 3.

28. Bellow, *Augie March*, p. 514.

29. Paul Bowles, *The Sheltering Sky* (London: Flamingo, [1949] 1993), p. 270.

30. Bernard Malamud, *The Assistant* (London: Penguin, [1957] 1992), p. 24.

31. Fielder, *Waiting for the End*, p. 103.

32. Elaine Tyler May, *Homeward Bound*, p. 50.

33. Josephine Hendin, *Vulnerable People: A View of American Fiction Since 1945* (Oxford: Oxford University Press, 1978), p. 88.

34. For a different gender slant on corporate life, see Catherine Gaskin, *Corporation Wife* (New York: Dell, 1960), dubbed 'the Peyton Place of the Corporation Town'.

35. Erica Arthur, 'Emasculation at Work: White-Collar Protest Fiction in the 1950s and 1990s', unpublished Ph.D. thesis (University of Nottingham, 2004), p. 112. See also Graham Thompson, *The Business of America* (London: Pluto, 2004), pp. 40–7.

36. Sloan Wilson, *The Man in the Gray Flannel Suit* (New York: Simon & Schuster, 1955), n. p.

37. Ibid., p. 22.

38. Ibid., p. 12.

39. Ibid., pp. 13–14.

40. Ibid., p. 69.

41. Ibid., p. 267.

42. Ibid., p. 272.

43. For a bleaker approach to white-collar work and suburban life, see Richard Yates's 1961 novel *Revolutionary Road*.

44. C. Wright Mills, 'The Structure of Power in American Society', in *Power in Postwar America*, ed. Richard Gillam, pp. 52–3.

45. Ibid., p. 62.

46. Lionel Trilling, *Freud and the Crisis of Our Culture* (Boston MA: Beacon, 1955), p. 17.

47. Trilling, *The Liberal Imagination* (Oxford: Oxford University Press, [1950] 1981), p. xv.

48. Trilling, *The Opposing Self* (London: Secker & Warburg, 1955) p. x.

49. David Castronovo dismisses *The Man in the Gray Flannel Suit* for having 'limited staying power' mainly because Tom and Betsy eventually

capitulate to their middle-class lifestyle. He argues that the novel 'no longer seem[s] to speak to our condition' in the twenty-first century, but this view only reinforces the perceived divide between popular and serious fiction: David Castronovo, *Beyond the Gray Flannel Suit* (New York: Continuum, 2004), pp. 9–10.

50. Salinger, *The Catcher in the Rye* (London: Penguin, [1951] 1958), p. 5.

51. Ibid., pp. 55, 220

52. Ibid., pp. 13, 17, 20, 186.

53. See Edgar Branch, 'Mark Twain and J. D. Salinger: A Study in Literary Continuity', *American Quarterly*, 9 (Summer 1957), pp. 144–58 and Jack Salzman (ed.), *New Essays on The Catcher in the Rye* (Cambridge: Cambridge University Press, 1991), pp. 8–9.

54. Salinger, *Catcher in the Rye*, p. 89.

55. Mary McCarthy argues that Salinger's fictional world is 'based on a scheme of exclusiveness' with 'characters divided into those who belong to the club and those who don't': Mary McCarthy, 'J. D. Salinger's Closed Circuit' (1962), in *The Writing on the Wall and Other Literary Essays* (New York: Harcourt Brace Jovanovich, 1970), p. 35

56. Sally Robinson, 'Masculine Protest in *The Catcher in the Rye*', in Sarah Graham, *J. D. Salinger's The Catcher in the Rye* (Londen: Routledge, 2007), p. 71.

57. Peter Shaw, 'Love and Death in *The Catcher in the Rye*', *New Essays on The Catcher in the Rye*, ed. Salzman, p. 99.

58. David Riesman, *The Lonely Crowd: A Study of the Changing American Character* (New Haven CT: Yale University Press, [1950] 2001), p. 305.

59. Salinger, *Catcher in the Rye*, p. 139. Mailer, *Advertisements for Myself*, p. 189.

60. Salinger, *Catcher in the Rye*, p. 220.

61. Marcus Cunliffe, *The Literature of the United States*, 4th edn (Harmondsworth: Penguin, 1986), p. 401.

62. Christopher Beach, *Twentieth-Century American Poetry* (Cambridge: Cambridge University Press, 2003), pp. 154–5.

63. Perkins, *A History of Modern Poetry: Modernism and After*, p. 331.

64. Edward Brunner, *Cold War Poetry: The Social Text in the Fifties Poem* (Urbana IL: University of Illinois Press, 2001), p. 13.

65. W. H. Auden, *Collected Shorter Poems, 1927–1957* (London: Faber, 1966), pp. 307–10.

66. Archibald MacLeish, 'To Face the Real Crisis: Man Himself', *New York Times* (25 December 1960), p. 5.

67. Louis Simpson, *A Revolution in Taste* (London: Macmillan, 1978), p. xvi.

68. Jeffrey Meyers (ed.), *Robert Lowell: Interviews and Memoirs* (Ann Arbor MI: University of Michigan Press, 1988), p. 86.

69. Elizabeth Bishop, 'Conversation' and 'At the Fishhouses', *The Complete Poems, 1927–1979* (New York: Farrar, Straus and Giroux, 1983), pp. 76, 64.

70. David Kalstone, *Five Temperaments* (New York: Oxford University Press, 1977), p. 12. Edward Brunner discusses the ways in which Bishop embeds uncertainty and absence in a particular poetic form such as the sestina: Brunner, *Cold War Poetry*, pp. 170–3.

71. Bishop, 'Gerard Manley Hopkins: Notes on Timing in his Poetry', *Vassar Review*, 23 (1934), 6–7, quoted in Longenbach, *Modern Poetry After Modernism*, p. 25.

72. Bishop, 'A Cold Spring', *The Complete Poems*, p. 55.

73. Mark Doty, 'The "Forbidden Planet" of Character: The Revolutions of the 1950s', in *A Profile of Twentieth-Century American Poetry*, ed. Jack Myers and David Wojahn (Carbondale IL: Southern Illinois University Press, 1991), p. 146.

74. Frank O'Hara, *Selected Poems*, ed. Donald Allen (London: Penguin, 1994), p. xiv.

75. Frank O'Hara, *The New American Poetry, 1945–1960*, ed. Donald Allen (Berkeley CA: University of California Press, [1959] 1999), p. 419.

76. O'Hara, *Selected Poems*, pp. 96, 146. Mark Ford (ed.), *The New York Poets: An Anthology* (Manchester: Carcanet, 2004), p. 49.

77. O'Hara, *Selected Poems*, p. 87.

78. M. L. Rosenthal, 'Poetry as Confession, *The Nation* (19 September 1959), p. 154. McClatchy (ed.), *The Vintage Book of Contemporary American Poetry*, p. xxvi.

79. Auden, *Selected Poems*, p. 297. Robert Lowell, *Life Studies* (London: Faber, 1959), p. 73.

80. Lowell, *Life Studies*, p. 78.

81. Ibid., p. 21.

82. Ibid., p. 101.

83. *Life Studies* can be seen to hover on the cusp of modernist and post-modernist aesthetics in shifting from 'the high-church values of Lowell's earlier work' in Part 1 'to the free verse anxieties of poems about his family and his mental collapse' in Part 4: Longenbach, *Modern Poetry after Modernism*, p. 5.

84. Allen Ginsberg, 'Notes Written on Finally Recording "Howl"', *Deliberate Prose* (London: Penguin, 2000), p. 229.

85. Cited in James Campbell, *This Is The Beat Generation: New York – San Francisco – Paris* (London: Secker & Warburg, 1999), p. 170.

86. William Carlos Williams, 'Howl for Carl Solomon', in Allen Ginsberg, *Howl and Other Poems* (San Francisco: City Lights Books, [1956] 1959), pp. 7–8.

87. Ginsberg, *Howl and Other Poems*, pp. 9, 20.

88. In 1950 Olson described a 'projective poet' as one who goes 'down through the workings of his own throat to that place where breath comes from, where breath has its beginning, where drama has to come': Olson, *Collected Prose*, p. 249.

89. Ginsberg, 'When the Mode of Music Changes the Walls of the City Shake', *Deliberate Prose: Selected Essays 1952–1995*, ed. Bill Morgan (London: Penguin, 2000), p. 247.

90. Marshall Berman uses Ginsberg's figure of Moloch to symbolize the devastation that urban planner Robert Moses caused to the Bronx after the war when he replaced the Grand Concourse with the Cross-Bronx Expressway: Berman, *All That's Solid Melts into Air* (New York: Penguin, [1982] 1988), pp. 290–311.

91. J. W. Ehrlich (ed.), *Howl of the Censor* (San Carlos CA: Nourse Pub. Co., 1961), p. 64.

92. Lawrence Ferlinghetti, 'This World', *San Francisco Chronicle* (19 May 1957), p. 5.

93. Malamud, *The Assistant*, p. 154.

94. For discussion of suburbia in *Goodbye, Columbus*, see Sanford Pinsker, *Jewish American Fiction, 1917–1987* (New York: Twayne, 1992), pp. 80–9.

95. William Burroughs, *Junky* (London: Penguin, [1953] 1977), p. xi.

96. Ibid., p. xvi.

97. Ibid., pp. 43, 28.

98. Timothy S. Murphy, *Wising Up the Marks: The Amodern William Burroughs* (Berkeley CA: University of California Press, 1997), p. 47.

99. Burroughs, *Junky*, p. 152.

100. John Clellon Holmes, 'This Is the Beat Generation', *New York Times* (16 November 1952), *Saturday Magazine*, pp. 10, 19–20.

101. Lizabeth Cohen, *A Consumers' Republic*, p. 307.

102. Jack Kerouac, *On the Road* (London: Penguin, [1957] 1972), p. 13.

103. Ibid., p. 14.

104. Ibid., p. 75.

105. Ibid., p. 118.

106. Ibid., p. 250.

107. Ibid., pp. 281–2.

108. Richard Wright, *White Man Listen!* (London: HarperCollins, [1957] 1995), p. xvi.

109. For discussion of Wright and Baldwin, see James Campbell, *Exiled in Paris: Richard Wright, James Baldwin, Samuel Beckett, and others on the Left Bank* (New York: Scribner's 1995) and Sarah Ralyea, *Outsider Citizens: The Remaking of Postwar Identity in Wright, de Beauvoir, and Baldwin* (London: Routledge, 2005).

110. Ralph Ellison, *Shadow and Act* (New York: Vintage, [1964] 1972), p. xviii.

111. Ibid., p. 26.

112. Ibid., p. 26.

113. Ellison, *Invisible Man* (London: Penguin, [1952] 1965), p. 10.

114. Ibid., p. 10.

115. In 1955 Ellison argued that there is 'no dichotomy between art and protest' and that without art protest novels can become very narrow and provincial: Ellison, 'The Art of Fiction: An Interview' (1955), *Shadow and Act*, p. 169.

116. Ibid., pp. 57–8.

117. Ellison, *Invisible Man*, p. 16.

118. Irving Howe, 'Black Boys and Native Sons', *Dissent* (Autumn 1963), pp. 353–68.

119. Saul Bellow, 'Man Underground', *Commentary* (June 1952), p. 609.

120. Howe, 'A Negro in America', *The Nation* (10 May 1952), p. 454. For Ellison's response to Howe's 'Black Boys and Native Sons', see 'The World and the Jug' (1964), in *Shadow and Act*, pp. 107–44.

121. Bellow, 'Man Underground', p. 609.

122. Ellison, *Invisible Man*, p. 464.

123. Ibid., p. 465.

124. Ellison, *Shadow and Act*, p. 177.

125. Dickstein, *Leopards in the Temple*, p. 15.

2. Drama and Performance

1. Arthur Miller, *The Crucible: Viking Critical Edition* (New York: Penguin, 1996), p. 157.

2. Miller, *The Crucible*, p. 160.

3. Miller, *Timebends: A Life* (London: Methuen, [1987] 1999), p. 262.

4. Steven Adler, *On Broadway: Art and Commerce on the Great White Way* (Carbondale IL: Southern Illinois University Press, 2004), p. 3.

5. Richard Schickel, *Intimate Strangers: The Culture of Celebrity* (New York: Doubleday, 1985), p. 99.

6. Arnold Aronson, *American Avant-Garde Theatre: A History* (London: Routledge, 2000), pp. 42–3.

7. Thomas P. Adler, *American Drama, 1940–1960: A Critical History* (New York: Twayne, 1994), p. ix.

8. See Foster Hirsch, *A Method to Their Madness: The History of the Actors Studio* (New York: Da Capo Press, 1984), pp. 124–69.

9. Miller, *Timebends*, p. 179.

10. Ibid., pp. 180–1.

11. Miller argued in 1957 that *Look Back in Anger* was 'the only modern English play' and quite unlike mainstream theatre in London: Charles Marowitz et al. (ed.), *New Theatre Voices of the Fifties and Sixties: Selections from Encore Magazine 1956–1963* (London: Eyre Methuen, [1965] 1981), pp. 247–8.

12. Brooks Atkinson, 'Theater: Tragic Journey', *New York Times* (November 8, 1956), p. 47.

13. Miller, *Plays: One* (London: Methuen, 1988), p. 49

14. Gerald Bordman, *American Muscial Theatre: A Chronicle*, 3rd edn (Oxford: Oxford University Press, 2002), p. 583.

15. David Savran, *Communists, Cowboys and Queers: The Politics of Masculinity in the Work of Arthur Miller and Tennessee Williams* (Minneapolis MN: University of Minnesota Press, 1992), p. 9.

16. R. Baird Shuman, *William Inge*, revised edn (New York: Twayne, 1989), p. 2.

17. William Inge, *Four Plays by William Inge* (New York: Grove Press, 1958), pp. 240, 283.

18. Ibid., p. 300.

19. Ibid., p. 240.

20. Ibid., p. viii.

21. Tennessee Williams, 'Williams: Person to Person', *New York Times* (20 March 1955), X1.

22. Williams, *The Rose Tattoo and Other Plays* (London: Penguin, 1976), pp. 113, 67.

23. Williams, 'On the "Camino Real"', *New York Times* (15 March 1953), X1, reprinted in Williams, *The Rose Tattoo and Other Plays*, p. 119.

24. Jan Balakian, '*Camino Real*: Williams's Allegory about the Fifties', in *The Cambridge Companion to Tennessee Williams*, ed. Matthew C. Roudané (Cambridge: Cambridge University Press, 1997), pp. 71–2.

25. Williams, *Four Plays by Tennessee Williams* (London: Secker & Warburg, [1945] 1974), p. ix.

26. Atkinson, 'Theater: Tennessee Williams' "Cat"', *New York Times* (25 March 1955), p. 18.

27. Miller, *Timebends*, p. 132.

28. Miller, *Plays: One*, p. 379.

29. Ibid., p. 51.
30. Ibid., p. 54.
31. Miller, *Echoes Down the Corridor: Collected Essays, 1944–2000* (London: Methuen, 2000), p. 287.
32. Miller, *The Crucible*, p. 8. See also Miller, 'Journey to "The Crucible"', *New York Times* (8 February 1953), p. X3.
33. Miller, *The Crucible*, p. 190.
34. Ibid., p. 160.
35. Miller, *Collected Plays* (New York: Viking, 1957), pp. 40–1.
36. Miller, *The Crucible*, p. 7. Miller, *Echoes Down the Corridor*, p. 287.
37. Miller, *The Crucible*, p. 94.
38. Ibid., p. 123.
39. Ibid., p. 144.
40. Bordman, *American Musical Theatre*, p. 634.
41. *Singin' in the Rain* was an original film musical and not adapted for Broadway until 1985, with a largely unknown cast and without box office success.
42. Richard Rodgers and Oscar Hammerstein II, 'About "The King and I"', *New York Times* (25 March 1951), p. 77.
43. Martin Gottfried, *Broadway Musicals* (New York: Harry Abrams, 1979), pp. 17–19.
44. Rodgers and Hammerstein, 'About "The King and I"', p. 77.
45. David H. Lewis, *Broadway Musicals: A Hundred Year History* (Jefferson NC: McFarland & Co, 2002), p. 62.
46. Kurt Gänzl, *The Encyclopedia of the Musical Theatre*, 2nd edn (New York: Schirmer, 2001), Vol 2, p. 1083.
47. Caren Kaplan, '"Getting to Know You": Travel, Gender, and the Politics of Representation in *Anna and the King of Siam* and *The King and I*', in *Late Imperial Culture*, ed. Román de la Campa et al. (London: Verso, 1995), pp. 44, 39.
48. Stephen Sondheim, *New York Times* (4 January 1976), D1, cited in Lewis, *Broadway Musicals*, p. 116.
49. Gottfried, *Broadway Musicals*, p. 197.
50. Michael Freedland, *Leonard Bernstein* (London: Harrap, 1987), p. 140.
51. Leonard Bernstein, 'Excerpts from A West Side Log', *Playbill* (25 September 1957): http://www.westsidestory.com/site/level2/archives/journal/excerpts.html
52. Langston Hughes, 'Why Ill Winds and Dark Clouds Don't Scare Negroes Much' (21 October 1953), in *Langston Hughes and The Chicago Defender*, ed. Christopher de Santis (Urbana IL: University of Illinois Press, 1995), p. 189.

53. Mordden, *Coming Up Roses*, p. 238.

54. Letter from William Inge to Edward Albee (13 August 1958), cited in Mel Gussow, *Edward Albee: A Singular Journey* (New York: Simon & Schuster, 1999), p. 97.

55. Richard Kostelantz, *The Theatre of Mixed-Means* (New York: R K Editions [1968], 1980), p. 3.

56. Allan Kaprow, 'Notes on the Creation of a Total Art' (1958), in *The Blurring of Art and Life*, ed. Jeff Kelley (Berkeley CA: University of California Press, 1993), p. 12. Langston Hughes, *The Langston Hughes Reader* (New York: George Braziller, 1981), p. 89.

57. Michael E. Rutenberg, *Playwright in Protest* (New York: DBS Publications, 1969), p. 8.

58. Edward Albee, 'Which Theater Is the Absurd One?', *New York Times Magazine* (25 February 1962), p. 64.

59. Albee, 'Which Theater Is the Absurd One?', p. 64.

60. Brian Way, 'Albee and the Absurd: *The American Dream* and *The Zoo Story*' (1967), reprinted in *Edward Albee*, ed. Harold Bloom (New York: Chelsea House, 1987), p. 9.

61. Albee, *The American Dream* and *The Zoo Story* (New York: Signet, 1961), p. 9.

62. Ibid., pp. 37, 42, 45.

63. Albee was unhappy that the Berlin production (directed by Walter Henn) was too physical early on and it cut Jerry's climactic speech about the zoo that links to the play's title: Albee to William Flanagan (13 October 1959), cited in Gussow, *Edward Albee*, pp. 112–13.

64. Albee, *The American Dream* and *The Zoo Story*, pp. 48–9.

65. Ibid., p. 49.

66. For the production of *The Zoo Story*, see Gussow, *Edward Albee*, pp. 93–118.

67. See Norma Jenckes, 'Postmodernist Tensions in Albee's Recent Plays', in *Edward Albee: A Casebook*, ed. Bruce J. Mann (New York: Routledge, 2003).

68. John A. Jackson, *Big Beat Heat: Alan Freed and the Early Years of Rock & Roll* (New York: Schirmer, 1991), pp. 45–6.

69. Alan Woll, *Black Musical Theatre: From Coontown to Dreamgirls* (Baton Rouge LA: Louisiana State University Press, 1989), pp. 210–17.

70. Woll, *Black Musical Theatre*, pp. 221–7.

71. Doris E. Abramson, *Negro Playwrights in the American Theatre, 1925–1959* (New York: Columbia University Press, 1969), p. 188. For discussion of William Branch and the development of the American Negro Theatre, see Errol G. Hill and James V. Hatch, *A History of*

African American Theatre (Cambridge: Cambridge University Press, 2003), pp. 351–73.

72. Margaret B. Wilkerson, 'From Harlem to Broadway: African American Playwrights at Mid-Century', in *The Cambridge Companion to American Women Playwrights*, ed. Brenda Murphy (Cambridge: Cambridge University Press, 1999), pp. 151–2. For a discussion of race and gender politics in Childress's 1950s drama, see La Vinia Delois Jennings, *Alice Childress* (New York: Twayne, 1955), pp. 18–55.

73. Lorraine Hansberry, 'An Author's Reflections: Willy Loman, Walter Lee and He Who Must Live', *Village Voice* (12 August 1959), pp. 7–8, reprinted in *Women in Theatre: Compassion and Hope*, ed. Karen Malpede (New York: Drama Book Publishers, 1985), p. 169.

74. Hansberry was self-critical about the overshadowing of Walter Lee Younger's aspirations by the family drama, claiming that 'he fails to dominate our imagination': Malpede (ed.), *Women in Theatre*, pp. 166–7. For the criticism that the play is not ethnically specific enough, see Harold Cruse, 'Lorraine Hansberry', *The Crisis of the Negro Intellectual* (New York: New York Review Books, [1967] 2005), pp. 267–84.

75. Hansberry, *A Raisin in the Sun*, Act I, Scene 1, in *Contemporary Black Drama: From* A Raisin in the Sun *to* No Place to Be Somebody, ed. Clinton F. Oliver and Stephanie Sills (New York: Scribner's, 1971), p. 56

76. Ibid., Act II, Scene 1, p. 87. This theme of getting bigger continues: when his son Travis declares he wants to be a bus driver, Walter claims that it is not a 'big enough' aspiration.

77. Hansberry, 'A Letter from Lorraine Hansberry on *Porgy and Bess*', *Theatre* (August 1959), p. 10.

78. Ossie Davis claimed that audiences overlooked the racial particularity of *A Raisin in the Sun* and 'kidnapped' it for its universal qualities: Ossie Davis, 'The Significance of Lorraine Hansberry', *Freedomways* (summer 1985), quoted in *A Raisin in the Sun* (New York: Modern Library, 1995), p. xix.

79. See Hansberry, *To Be Young, Gifted and Black: A Portrait of Lorraine Hansberry in Her Own Words*, ed. Robert Nemiroff (New York: Vintage, [1969] 1995) and her attack on 'the most fundamental illusion . . . that art is not, and *should* not and, when it is at its best, CANNOT possibly be social', in 'The Negro Writer and His Roots: Towards a New Romanticism', *Black Scholar* (March–April 1961), pp. 2–12.

80. Hansberry's interest in the African liberation movement is exemplified in *Les Blancs* (1964), her response to French writer Jean Genet's *Les Nègres* (1960). *A Raisin in the Sun* was turned into a musical *Raisin* in

1973; reprised in New York by the Roundabout Theatre in 1986; made
into an American Playhouse television production in 1989; and produced again on Broadway in 2004.

81. LeRoi Jones, *Dutchman* (1964), in *Contemporary Black Drama*, p. 230.
82. See Amiri Baraka, 'A Critical Reevaluation: A Raisin in the Sun's Ending
    Passion', in *A Raisin in the Sun* and *The Sign in Sidney Brustein's
    Window* (New York: Vintage, 1995), pp. 9–20. *Black Theatre
    Movement: A Raisin in the Sun to the Present* (Woodie King Jr, 1978).

3. Music and Radio

1. James Miller, *Almost Grown: The Rise of Rock and Roll* (London:
   Arrow, 1999), p. 56.
2. Susan Douglas, *Listening In: Radio and the American Imagination*
   (New York: Random House, 1999), p. 220.
3. Douglas estimates the growth of small radio stations increased by 500
   per cent between 1946 and 1950 taking the radio power base away from
   New York City and reflecting 'more local, grassroots influences':
   Douglas, *Listening In*, p. 225.
4. These figures derive from a *Time* magazine survey from December 1953,
   cited in Kathryn Alexander, 'The Status of Contemporary Black-
   Oriented Radio in the United States', unpublished Ph.D. thesis (New
   York University, 1981), pp. 106–10. Alexander links the rise of black
   radio to the growth of African Americans as a consumer group, taking
   figures from the 1957 *Radio and the Negro Market* which charted a dramatic growth in black employment, with income of $3 billion in 1940
   growing to $11 billion in 1950 and $16 billion in 1958.
5. Douglas, *Listening In*, p. 223.
6. Houston A. Baker Jr, *Blues, Ideology, and Afro-American Literature: A
   Vernacular Theory* (Chicago: University of Chicago Press, 1984), p. 3.
7. Ibid., pp. 6–7.
8. André Hodeir, *Jazz: Its Evolution and Essence* (New York: Grove Press,
   1956), p. 21.
9. Ibid., p. 35.
10. Ibid., p. 36.
11. Aaron Copland, *Music and Imagination* (Cambridge MA: Harvard
    University Press, 1952), pp. 57, 95.
12. Louis Armstrong, *Satchmo: My Life in New Orleans* (New York:
    Prentice-Hall, 1954), p. 1.
13. William Bruce Cameron, 'Is Jazz a Folk Art?', *The Second Line*, 9 (1–2)
    (January–February, 1958), p. 5.

14. Burl Ives, *The Burl Ives Song Book* (New York: Ballantine Books, 1953), p. x. Perhaps because Ives had left the folk community in 1952 his *Song Book* was savaged in the magazine *Sing Out!* for containing only two black songs and being insensitive to African American history: Irwin Silber, 'The Burl Ives Songbook', *Sing Out!*, 4 (2) (January 1954), p. 12.

15. For discussion of the Lomaxes' work for the Library of Congress and links to Roosevelt's New Deal see Benjamin Filene, *Romancing the Folk: Public Memory and American Roots Music* (Chapel Hill NC: University of North Carolina Press, 2000), pp. 133–51.

16. John and Alan Lomax, *Folk Song U.S.A.* (New York: Duell, Sloan & Pearce, 1947), p. vii.

17. Ibid., pp. vii–viii.

18. See David Hinckley, 'Patronage – or Pillage?', *New York Daily News* (28 July 2002), p. 16.

19. JoAnne Mancini, ' "Messin' with the Furniture Man": Early Country Music, Regional Culture, and the Search for an Anthological Modernism', *American Literary History*, 16 (2) (2004), p. 210.

20. Mancini, ' "Messin' with the Furniture Man" ', p. 228. For Alan Lomax's functionalist approach to folk music, see 'Folk Song Style: Musical Style and Social Context', *American Anthropologist*, 61 (6) (December 1959), pp. 927–54, reprinted in Alan Lomax, *Selected Writings 1934–1997*, ed. Ronald D. Cohen (New York: Routledge, 2003), pp. 139–72.

21. John & Alan Lomax, *Folk Song U.S.A.*, p. ix.

22. Robert Cantwell, *When We Were Good: The Folk Revival* (Cambridge MA: Harvard University Press, 1996), p. 165.

23. Ibid., p. 181.

24. *Songs for Political Action: Folkmusic, Topical Songs and the American Left, 1926–1953*, Disc 10: 'An Era Closes: 1949–1953' (Bear Family Records, 1996).

25. Irwin Silber, 'The Weavers – New "Find" of the Hit Parade', *Sing Out!*, 1 (9) (February 1951), p. 6. For a fuller discussion of the Weavers and the Red Scare, see Ronald D. Cohen, *Rainbow Quest: The Folk Music Revival and American Society, 1940–1970* (Amherst MA: University of Massachusetts Press, 2002), pp. 67–92.

26. Pete Seeger, *The Incompleat Folksinger*, ed. Jo Metcalf Schwartz (New York: Simon & Schuster, 1972), p. 22.

27. See the special issue of *Sing Out!* dedicated to Huddie Leadbelly, 2 (8) (February 1952).

28. Cantwell, *When We Were Good*, p. 180.

29. Editorial, 'The First Issue', *Sing Out!*, 1 (1) (May 1950), p. 1.

30. Seeger, *The Incompleat Folksinger*, p. 21.

31. 'How to Write a Song', *Sing Out!*, 1 (6) (October 1950), p. 6.

32. 'How to Write a Song', *Sing Out!*, 1 (7) (December 1950), p. 6.

33. Editorial, 'The Rosenbergs', *Sing Out!* 3 (11) (October 1953), p. 2.

34. Editorial, 'Folk-Singer Oscar Brand Joins Witch-Hunt Hysteria', *Sing Out!*, 2 (5) (November 1951), p. 2.

35. Editorial, 'The "Un-American" Subpoenas', *Sing Out!* 2 (9) (March 1952), p. 2. Editorial, 'The Time of the Lists', *Sing Out!* 4 (2) (January 1954), p. 2.

36. Editorial, 'The Time of the Lists', p. 11.

37. Irwin Silber's sleeve-notes for *American Industrial Ballads* (Smithsonian/Folkways Recordings, [1957] (1992).

38. Gillett, *The Sound of the City*, pp. 290–1.

39. See Alan Lomax, 'The "Folkniks" – and the Songs They Sing', *Sing Out!* 9 (1) (summer 1959), pp. 30–1, reprinted in Lomax, *Selected Writings 1934–1997*, pp. 195–7. Irwin Silber & David Gahr, 'Top Performers Highlight 1st Newport Folk Festival', *Sing Out!* 9 (2) (autumn 1959), pp. 21–4. The Newport Festival programme noted that 'the "progressive" influence in the folk music revival has all but disappeared, but it has left an ever growing body of enthusiasts devoting their time to recapturing the spirit of our traditional music': Billy Faier, 'Folk Music Today', *Newport Folk Festival: First Annual* (Newport RI, 11–12 July 1959). Seeger worried about large folk festivals; Alan Lomax dismissed the Newport Festival as a publicity stunt; and Oscar Brand argued that musical populists were ready to 'alter, subvert, emasculate, even deprecate the [folk] material if this will bring him money or power': Oscar Brand, *The Ballad Mongers: The Rise of the Modern Folk Song* (New York: Funk & Wagnalls, 1962), p. 222.

40. *Sing Out!* published thirteen songs by Bob Dylan between 1962 and 1964, but in a November 1964 article editor Irwin Silber wrote an open letter to Dylan expressing his concern that he had 'lost contact with the people', and that the 'paraphernalia of fame' and the 'American Success Machinery' were compromising his art: Silber, 'An Open Letter to Bob Dylan', *Sing Out!*, 14 (5) (November 1964), pp. 22–3.

41. The 1997 CD reissue of Smith's *Anthology of American Folk Music* contains two booklets: a reprint of Smith's original catalogue and a new booklet of essays, appreciations, and annotations from which this quotation comes: p. 3.

42. Mancini, ' "Messin' with the Furniture Man" ', p. 222.

43. Filene, *Romancing the Folk*, p. 115.

44. Filene, *Romancing the Folk*, pp. 115–16

45. Cantwell, *When We Were Good*, pp. 199–200.

46. Greil Marcus, 'The Old, Weird America', 1997 reissue booklet of *Anthology of American Folk Music*, pp. 5–6.

47. Reissue booklet of *Anthology of American Folk Music*, p. 37.

48. Bob Dylan, *Chronicles Volume One* (New York: Simon & Schuster, 2004), p. 73.

49. See John A. Jackson, *Big Beat Heat: Alan Freed and the Early Years of Rock & Roll* (New York: Schirmer, 1991), pp. 1–8. James Miller, *Almost Grown*, pp. 57–61.

50. For the effects of rock 'n' roll on British audiences, see Dominic Sandbrook, *Never Had It So Good* (London: Little, Brown, 2005), pp. 427–81.

51. Jackson, *Big Beat Heat*, pp. 22–3.

52. Douglas, *Listening In*, p. 231.

53. See Louis Cantor, *Wheelin' on Beale* (New York: Pharos, 1992), pp. 41–55; for a description of 'a typical fifties day' on WDIA, see pp. 111–36.

54. For further discussion of NBC trying to secure a black audience, see J. Fred MacDonald, *Don't Touch That Dial!: Radio Programming in American Life, 1920–1960* (Chicago: Nelson-Hall, 1979), pp. 364–8.

55. Gillett, *The Sounds of the City*, pp. 23–34.

56. Ibid., p. 34.

57. David Szatmary estimates that 20 per cent of record sales in 1956 and 1957 were from supermarkets: David Szatmary, *Rockin' in Time: A Social History of Rock-and-Roll* (New Jersey: Prentice-Hall, [1995] 2006), p. 25.

58. Jackson, *Big Beat Heat*, pp. 74–6.

59. Vance Packard cited in Szatmary, *Rockin' in Time*, p. 22.

60. Jackson, *Big Beat Heat*, pp. 95–8 and Szatmary, *Rockin' in Time*, pp. 22–3.

61. Figures from Parke Gibson's *$70 Billion in the Black* (New York: Macmillan, 1978), cited in Kathryn Alexander, 'The Status of Contemporary Black-Oriented Radio in the United States', pp. 103, 120.

62. Szatmary, *Rockin' in Time*, p. 22.

63. Cited by Peter Guralnick, *Last Train to Memphis: The Rise of Elvis Presley* (Boston MA: Little, Brown, 1994), p. 108.

64. Michael Bertrand, *Race, Rock and Elvis*, p. 27.

65. Louis Cantor, *Wheelin' on Beale*, p. 194.

66. Hanif Kureishi and Jon Savage (eds), *The Faber Book of Pop* (London: Faber, 1995), p. 85.

67. Szatmary, *Rockin' in Time*, pp. 48–50.

68. Charlie Gillett, *The Sound of the City: The Rise of Rock n Roll* (London: Souvenir, 1983), p. 28.

69. Nik Cohn, *A WopBopaLooBop A LopBamBoom* (London: Paladin, 1969), pp. 23, 25.

70. Nelson George links Norman Mailer's 'white negro' to the early Presley; the cutting of Presley's hair can be interpreted as 'bleaching' his musical persona and assimilation into the white mainstream: George, *The Death of Rhythm & Blues* (New York: Dutton), pp. 61–4.

71. Tony Russell, *Blacks, Whites and Blues* (London: Studio Vista, 1970), p. 102.

72. Angela Y. Davis, *Blues Legacies and Black Feminism: Gertrude 'Ma' Rainey, Bessie Smith, and Billie Holiday* (New York: Pantheon, 1998), pp. 181–97 and Hazel V. Carby's 'It Jus Be's Dat Way Sometime: The Sexual Politics of Women's Blues', *Radical America*, 20 (4) (June–July 1986), pp. 9–24. For discussion of Josh White and cultural activism in the 1940s, see Michael Denning, *The Cultural Front: The Laboring of American Culture in the Twentieth Century* (London: Verso, 1997), pp. 348–61.

73. Barbara Beeching, 'Paul Robeson and the Black Press: The 1950 Passport Controversy', *The Journal of African American History*, 87 (summer 2002), p. 345. David W. Stowe, 'The Politics of Café Society', *The Journal of American History*, 84 (March 1998), p. 1406.

74. Elijah Ward claims that Josh White's testimony 'showed a man doing his best to walk a narrow line between pride and capitulation': Elijah Ward, *Josh White: Society Blues* (Amherst MA: University of Massachusetts Press, 2000), p. 189. See also Ward's essay 'Josh White: Free and Equal Blues', *Josh White: Free and Equal Blues* (Rounder Records, 2001).

75. Seeger, 'The Purist vs. the Hybridist' (1957–58), *The Incompleat Folksinger*, pp. 174–5.

76. Cameron, 'Is Jazz a Folk Art?', *The Second Line* (1958), pp. 6–7.

77. Ibid., p. 8.

78. Ibid., p. 13.

79. Editorial, 'Crusaders for Jazz', *The Second Line*, 1 (9) (December 1950), p. 1.

80. Bruce Mitchell, 'The American Paradox', *The Second Line*, 2 (6) (June and July 1951), p. 1. George Frazier, 'A Tribute to Jazz, Ltd.', *The Second Line*, 3 (5/6) (May and June 1952), p. 8.

81. Azalea Stewart Thorpe, 'Enigma – Jazz – U.S.A.', *The Second Line*, 6 (11/12) (November and December 1955), p. 3.

82. Ellison, *Invisible Man*, p. 11.

83. For the 'cool tendency' in jazz, see Hodeir, *Jazz*, pp. 116–36.

84. Ben Sidran, *Black Talk* (Edinburgh: Payback Press, [1971] 1995), p. 125.

85. Ibid., p. 139.

86. Duke Ellington, 'The Race for Space' (1957), in *The Duke Ellington Reader*, ed. Mark Tucker (New York: Oxford University Press, 1993), p. 296.
87. Ibid., p. 296. For discussion of the 1958 re-recording of *Black, Brown and Beige* and for Ellington's utopian vision, see Graham Lock, *Blutopia: Visions of the Future and Revisions of the Past* (Durham NC: Duke University Press, 1999), pp. 108–18.
88. See David Sanjek, 'One Size Does Not Fit All: The Precarious Position of the African American Entrepreneur in Post-World War II American Popular Music', *American Music* (winter 1997), pp. 549–51.
89. Stowe, 'The Politics of Café Society', p. 1394.
90. Bert Stern, *Adventures* (Boston MA: Little, Brown, 1997), p. 13.
91. E. Richard Freniere, 'Plenty False Notes at the Festival', *The Second Line*, 10 (1–2) (January–February 1959), p. 3.
92. John S. Wilson, 'Newport Tribute Paid to Ellington', *New York Times* (4 July 1958), p. 16.
93. For Stern's 1962 photo-shoot of Monroe, see Norman Mailer, *Marilyn: A Biography* (New York: Grosset & Dunlap, 1973) and the Mailer-Monroe *Time* cover story (16 July 1973).
94. John Wilson claimed that stylistic distinctions were not as permeable as some musicians hoped: 'there was no more reason to have [Chuck] Berry at a jazz festival than there would to go to an opposite extreme, to have Mantovani': Wilson, 'Mahalia Jackson Star of Newport', *New York Times* (7 July 1958), p. 22.
95. See Craig Werner, *A Change is Gonna Come: Music, Race and the Soul of America* (New York: Plume, 1999), pp. 4–15. Reebee Garofalo argues that black music was out of step with the pace of civil rights activism in the late 1950s (he cites Chuck Berry's 1957 single 'School Days' which had little to do with the events in Arkansas Central High School that year), and did not catch up until the early 1960s with releases such as Martha and the Vandellas' 'Dancing in the Streets' (1963): Reebee Garofalo, 'The Impact of the Civil Rights Movement on Popular Music', *Radical America*, 21 (6) (November–December 1987), pp. 15–22.
96. John Wilson, 'A Jazz Festival that was not a Grab Bag', *New York Times* (13 July 1958), X7.

4. Film and Television

1. Christopher Anderson, *Hollywood TV: The Studio System in the Fifties* (Austin TX: University of Texas Press, 1994), p. 1.

2. Anderson, *Hollywood TV*, p. 2. Major studios such as Paramount wanted to make use of television but were restricted by the Federal Communications Commission which wished to protect television broadcasting from being owned by monopolies: Timothy R. White, 'Hollywood's Attempt at Appropriating Television: The Case of Paramount Pictures', in *Hollywood in the Age of Television*, ed. Tino Balio (Boston MA: Unwin Hyman, 1990), pp. 145–63.

3. Thomas Schatz, *The Genius of the System: Hollywood Film-making in the Studio Era* (London: Faber, [1989] 1998), p. 298.

4. Ibid., p. 412.

5. Gilbert Seldes, *The Great Audience* (New York: Viking, 1950), pp. 9–11.

6. Leon Shamroy, 'Filming *The Robe*' (1953), *Cinegrafie 16: CinemaScope, Larger than Life* (Bologna: Le Mani, 2003), p. 273.

7. John Belton, 'CinemaScope and the Widescreen Revolution', *Cinegrafie 16*, p. 246.

8. Quotation from *4-Track Magnetic Stereo and CinemaScope Demonstration Film* (1953).

9. For discussion of CinemaScope cartoons see Solomon, *Enchanted Drawings*, p. 170.

10. Belton, 'Glorious Technicolor', pp. 206–7. For animated experiments with CinemaScope and 3-D see Solomon, *Enchanted Drawings*, pp. 204–5.

11. William Hawes, *Live Television Drama, 1946–1951* (New York: McFarland, 2001), p. 2.

12. Erik Barnouw, *A History of Broadcasting in the United States, II: The Golden Web* (New York: Oxford University Press, 1968), p. 285.

13. 60 per cent of broadcasting revenue was made up from supermarket products such as food, toiletries, medication and cleaning products in 1950: Barnouw, *The Golden Web*, p. 277.

14. Kenneth Hey, '*Marty*: Aesthetics vs. Medium in Early Television Drama', in *American History/American Television: Interpreting the Video Past*, ed. John E. O'Connor (New York: Frederick Ungar, 1983), pp. 95–133.

15. Lynn Spigel, *Make Room for TV: Television and the Family Ideal in Postwar America* (Chicago: University of Chicago Press, 1992), p. 6.

16. Edward R. Murrow, quoted in Whitfield, *The Culture of the Cold War*, p. 155.

17. The host of *The Great Challenge*, journalist Howard K. Smith, had been named as a communist supporter early in the 1950s but had been protected as he was a United Press correspondent in London at the time.

The Great Challenge was welcomed by reviewers for bringing together 'the ideas of some of the most learned men of our time', but also criticised because its one-hour format did not allow discussion to develop much beyond generalities: see *New York Times* (26 May 1958), p. 51; (2 March 1959), p. 51; (30 May 1959), p. 51; (6 April 1959); p. 55 and (11 April 1960), p. 63.

18. Ella Taylor, *Prime-Time Families: Television Culture in Postwar America* (Berkeley CA: University of California Press, 1989), p. 22.

19. See Gorman and McLean, *Media and Society in the Twentieth Century*, pp. 128–31.

20. For further discussion of 'dead centrism', see Hey, '*Marty*: Aesthetics vs. Medium in Early Television Drama', pp. 97–8.

21. Gunther Anders, 'The Phantom World of TV', *Dissent*, 3 (1956), pp. 14–24, reprinted in *Mass Culture: The Popular Arts in America*, ed. Rosenberg and White, p. 360.

22. Ibid., p. 360. For a more recent discussion of domestic containment along these lines, see Elaine Tyler May, *Homeward Bound*, pp. 27–36.

23. Anders, 'The Phantom World of TV', p. 365.

24. Henry Rabassiere, 'In Defense of Television', *Dissent*, 3 (1956), 327–32, reprinted in *Mass Culture: The Popular Arts in America*, p. 370.

25. Ibid., p. 372.

26. Ibid., p. 373.

27. For the cultural impact and ideological implications of the McCarthy coverage, see Daniel J. Leab, '*See It Now*: A Legend Reassessed', *American History/American Television*, pp. 1–32 and Thomas Doherty, *Cold War, Cool Medium*, pp. 161–88.

28. On the relationship between children and television in the 1950s, see Spigel, *Make Room For TV*, pp. 50–60.

29. For further discussion of the *Twenty-One* scandal, see Maxene Fabe, *TV Game Shows* (New York: Doubleday, 1979). Redford's film *Quiz Show* emphasises Herb Stempel's feelings of anti-Semitism and Stempel's claim that on the show 'a Jew is always followed by a gentile, and the gentile always wins more'.

30. Christopher Beach, *Class, Language, and American Film Comedy* (Cambridge: Cambridge University Press, 2002), p. 3.

31. The African American scholar Henry Louis Gates Jr remembers growing up in West Virginia in the mid-1950s where he watched *Leave it to Beaver*, noting that it depicted a world of aspiration that was 'just out of reach' for a black kid: Henry Louis Gates Jr, *Colored People: A Memoir* (New York: Random House, 1994), p. 21.

32. Frances Gray, *Women and Laughter* (Charlottesville VA: University Press of Virginia, 1994), p. 42.

33. Ibid., p. 54.

34. For further discussion of NBC's attempt to gain an African American audience, see Thomas Cripps, 'Amos 'n' Andy and the Debate over American Racial Integration', *American History/American Television*, pp. 38–40.

35. Ibid., p. 50.

36. Taylor, *Prime-Time Families*, p. 26. Spigel, *Make Room For TV*, pp. 177–8.

37. Stefan Kafer, *Ball of Fire: The Tumultuous Life and Comic Art of Lucille Ball* (London: Faber, 2003), p. 148.

38. Spigel, *Welcome to the Dreamhouse: Popular Media and Postwar Suburbs* (Durham NC: Duke University Press, 2001), pp. 31–59.

39. See Thomas Schatz, 'Desilu, *I Love Lucy*, and the Rise of Network TV', in *Making Television: Authorship and the Production Process*, ed. Robert J. Thompson & Gary Burns (New York: Praeger, 1990), pp. 117–35. David Marc & Robert J. Thompson, *Prime Time, Prime Movers* (Boston MA: Little, Brown, 1992), pp. 28–9.

40. For further discussion of Ball, Arnaz and the HUAC hearings, see Doherty, *Cold War, Cool Medium*, pp. 52–9 and Kanfer, *Ball of Fire*, pp. 152–3, 167–70.

41. Lori Landay, *Madcaps, Screwballs, and Con Women: The Female Trickster in American Culture* (Philadelphia PA: University of Pennsylvania Press, 1998), p. 155.

42. Ibid., pp. 173–7.

43. Jacques Rivette, 'Notes sur une révolution', *Cahiers du Cinéma*', 54 (Christmas 1955), reprinted in *Cahiers du Cinéma: The 1950s: Neo-Realism*, ed. Jim Hillier (Cambridge MA: Harvard University Press, 1985), p. 94.

44. Rivette, 'Notes on a Revolution', p. 97.

45. Jonathan Rosenbaum (ed.), *Rivette: Texts and Interviews* (London: British Film Institute, 1977), p. 50.

46. François Truffaut, 'L'Admirable Certitude', *Cahiers du Cinéma*, 46 (April 1955), reprinted in *Cahiers du Cinéma*, ed. Jim Hillier, p. 108.

47. Eric Rohmer, *The Taste for Beauty*, trans. Carol Volk (Cambridge: Cambridge University Press, 1989), p. 140.

48. Ibid., p. 146.

49. Jon Halliday (ed.), *Sirk on Sirk* (London: Faber, 1997), pp. 97, 105.

50. V. F. Perkins, 'The Cinema of Nicholas Ray', in *Movies and Methods*, ed. Bill Nichols (Berkeley CA: University of California Press, 1976),

p. 255. Geoff Andrews argues that *Bigger Than Life* replaces horizontal compositions with diagonals as the protagonist becomes more unstable: Geoff Andrews, *The Films of Nicholas Ray* (London: BFI, 2004), pp. 103–9

51. Jeremy G. Butler, '*Imitation of Life* (1934 and 1959): Style and the Domestic Melodrama', *Imitation of Life*, ed. Lucy Fischer (New Brunswick NJ: Rutgers University Press, 1991), p. 299. Stephen Handzo, 'Imitations of Lifelessness: Sirk's Ironic Tearjerker', *Bright Lights Film Journal* (18 March 1997), p. 1.

52. Doherty, *Cold War Cool Medium*, p. 26.

53. For fuller discussion of this shift in studio production, see David Bordwell et al., *The Classical Hollywood Cinema*, pp. 330–5.

54. Richard Dyer, *Heavenly Bodies: Film Stars and Society* (London: BFI, 1987), p. 21.

55. Ibid., pp. 34–8.

56. Sarah Churchwell, *The Many Lives of Marilyn Monroe* (London: Granta, 2004), p. 51.

57. Richard Schickel, *Intimate Strangers: The Culture of Celebrity* (New York: Doubleday, 1985), p. 91.

58. For interracial relationships in Hollywood, see Donald Bogle, *Bright Boulevards, Bold Dreams: The Story of Black Hollywood* (New York: Ballantine, 2005), pp. 318–26.

59. See Phil Stern, *Phil Stern's Hollywood: Photographs 1940–1979* (New York: Alfred A. Knopf, 1993).

60. Samantha Barbas, *Movie Crazy: Fans, Stars, and the Cult of Celebrity* (London: Palgrave, 2001), p. 121.

61. Ibid., p. 127.

62. Robert Osborne, *Academy Awards Illustrated* (Hollywood CA: Marvin Miller, 1965), p. 186.

63. Sarah Churchwell agrees with Richard Dyer that Monroe's 'popularity was such that, with the new widescreen process, she was heralded as Hollywood's defence against the incursions of television': Churchwell, *The Many Lives of Marilyn Monroe*, p. 65.

64. Schatz, *The Genius of the System*, pp. 440–62.

65. Alfred Hitchcock, 'Direction' (1937), in *Hitchcock on Hitchcock*, ed. Sidney Gottlieb (London: Faber, 1997), p. 257.

66. Hitchcock, 'On Style' (1963), in *Hitchcock on Hitchcock*, p. 289.

67. John Belton, ed., *Alfred Hitchcock's Rear Window* (Cambridge: Cambridge University Press, 2000), p. 1.

68. Eric Rohmer and Claude Chabrol, *Hitchcock: The First Forty-Four Films* (Oxford: Roundhouse, 1979), p. 125.

69. For an extended treatment of the cinematic language of *Rear Window*, see Steven DeRosa, *Writing with Hitchcock* (New York: Faber, 2001), pp. 223–35.

70. Sarah Street, ' "The Dress Had Told Me": Fashion and Femininity in *Rear Window*', *Alfred Hitchcock's Rear Window*, ed. Belton, p. 102.

71. Belton, ed., *Alfred Hitchcock's Rear Window*, p. 7.

72. Gina Marchetti, *Romance and the "Yellow Peril": Race, Sex, and Discursive Strategies in Hollywood Fiction* (Berkeley CA: University of California Press, 1993), p. 110.

73. Douglas Brode notes that *On the Waterfront* paved the way for other films to deal realistically with working-class jobs such as *Edge of the City* and *Slaughter on Tenth Avenue* (both 1957): Douglas Brode, *Lost Films of the Fifties* (New York: Citadel, 1991), p. 229.

74. The studio Paramount put up resistance to *Carrie* despite the film making Carrie Meeber more conventional than in Dreiser's novel. Even so, one critic saw the film as a sign that the modernists had taken over Hollywood: Manny Farber, 'Films', *The Nation* (17 May 1952), p. 485.

75. Bosley Crowther, 'Unlimited Humanity', *New York Times* (27 January 1952), p. X1.

76. Susan Courtney, *Hollywood Fantasies of Miscegenation: Spectacular Narratives of Gender and Race, 1903–1967* (Princeton NJ: Princeton University Press, 2005), p. 195.

77. Ibid., p. 196.

78. Andrea Meneghelli, 'The Wounds of Civilization: Lionel Rogosin and "Come Back, Africa" ', *Cinegrafie*, 18 (Bologna: Le Mani, 2005), 356–64.

79. The dubious quality of Elvis movies after *Jailhouse Rock* (1957) helps to explain why youth films tended towards the anodyne. Some films continued to explore young adulthood in interesting ways, though, addressing sexual magnetism in *Young and Dangerous* (1957) and what is depicted as the nihilism and criminality of Beat culture in the Canadian film *The Bloody Brood* (1959), but both films end by re-establishing moral order.

80. Eisenhower pledged $3 million to address the problems of delinquency in 1955 and Benjamin Fine claimed that 'we must recognize that juvenile delinquency is not a passing phenomenon – it is not a flying saucer observed by a few – but a dark and all too real facet of our modern way of life, distressing to all of us': Benjamin Fine, *One Million Delinquents* (London: Victor Gollancz, 1956), p. 29.

81. Robert M. Lindner, *Rebel without a Cause: The Hypnoanalysis of a Criminal Psychopath* (New York: Grune & Stratton, 1944), p. ix.

82. Ibid., pp. 13, 2.

83. Ibid., p. 2.
84. One key tension in the film is between youthful rock 'n' roll and the 1940s swing music of maths teacher Joshua Edwards (Richard Kiley), whose records are destroyed by his class: Lester J. Keyser and Andre H. Ruszowski, *The Cinema of Sidney Poitier* (San Diego CA: Barnes & Co., 1980), p. 31.
85. Paul Goodman, *Growing Up Absurd* (New York: Vintage, 1960), p. 20.
86. See, for example, Bosley Crowther, 'The Exception or the Rule?', *New York Times* (27 May 1955), p. X1. The reactions in the British press were equally negative: see Editorial, ' "Jungle" Appalls Critics in Britain', *New York Times* (18 September 1955), p. 69.
87. Cited in Jackson, *Big Beat Heat*, p. 95.
88. For a more detailed account of its initial reception, see Aram Goudsouzian, *Sidney Poitier: Man, Actor, Icon* (Chapel Hill NC: University of North Carolina Press, 2004), pp. 108–11.
89. Ibid., p. 103.
90. Penelope Huston argues that *The Blackboard Jungle* adopts a 'hit and run technique': 'after launching . . . a formidable attack on a section of the American educational system, the film slides off into some facile melodramatics': cited in Kreidl, *Nicholas Ray*, p. 159.
91. Goudsouzian, *Sidney Poitier*, pp. 104, 106.

5. The Visual Arts beyond Modernism

1. Clement Greenberg, 'Avant-Garde and Kitsch', *Partisan Review*, 6 (5) (1939), reprinted in *Art and Culture* (London: Thames & Hudson [1961] 1973), pp. 11–12. This essay and 'Towards a Newer Laocoon' (1940) are reproduced with contextual commentary in Francis Frascina, ed., *Pollock and After* (London: Routlege, [1985] 2000), pp. 50–109.
2. Mary Caputi, *A Kinder, Gentler America: Melancholia and the Mythical 1950s* (Minneapolis MN: University of Minnesota Press, 2005), p. 43.
3. Francis V. O'Connor, *Jackson Pollock* (New York: Museum of Modern Art, 1967), p. 79.
4. Clement Greenberg, ' "American-Type" Painting' (1955) and 'Jackson Pollock's New Style' (1952), *The Collected Essays and Criticism, 3: Affirmation and Refusals, 1950–1956*, ed. John O'Brian (Chicago: University of Chicago Press, 1993), pp. 235, 106.
5. Clement Greenberg, 'The Plight of Our Culture' (1953), *Collected Essays, 3*, p. 137.
6. Greenberg, 'The European View of American Art' (1950) and 'Feeling is All' (1952), *Collected Essays, 3*, pp. 62, 103.

7. For a discussion of Norman W. Lewis, see Romare Bearden and Harry Henderson, *A History of African-American Artists* (New York: Pantheon, 1993), pp. 316–27. African American artists did not group together in the fight for civil liberties until 1963 with the formation of the interracial Spiral group in Greenwich Village: ibid., pp. 400–3.

8. Charlotte Streifer Rubinstein, *American Women Artists* (Boston MA: G. K. Hall, 1982), pp. 268–305.

9. Ann Gibson, *Abstract Expressionism: Other Politics* (New Haven CT: Yale University Press, 1997), p. xxiii.

10. Ibid., p. xxii.

11. Cara Greenberg, *Mid-Century Modern: Furniture of the 1950s* (New York: Harmony, 1984), p. 25.

12. Ibid., pp. 45–9.

13. Barbara Haskell, *Blam! The Explosion of Pop, Minimalism, and Performance 1958–1964* (New York: Whitney Museum of American Art, 1984), p. 12.

14. The Pope labelled all abstract art 'profane' and 'sterile' because it does not help 'men to know each other' and bring them nearer God: 'Pope Condemns Art in Abstract Forms', *New York Times* (6 September 1950), p. 32. Jane de Hart Mathews, 'Art and Politics in Cold War America', *The American Historical Review*, 81 (4) (October 1976), p. 781. Another important but more anecdotal work from the early 1970s is Dore Ashton, *The New York School: A Cultural Reckoning* (Berkeley CA: University of California Press, 1972).

15. Mathews, 'Art and Politics in Cold War America', p. 780.

16. The joint Museums' Manifesto was reported as 'Museums Demand Freedom for Arts', *New York Times* (28 March 1950), p. 33.

17. Guilbaut, *How New York Stole the Idea of Modern Art*, p. 190.

18. Jean Baudrillard, 'Hot Painting: The Inevitable Fate of the Image', in *Reconstructing Modernism*, ed. Guilbaut, p. 23.

19. Ibid., p. 24.

20. Guilbaut, *How New York Stole the Idea of Modern Art*, p. 6.

21. Greenberg, *Art and Culture*, p. 195.

22. The most complete reproduction of Hofmann's paintings can be found in James Yohe, ed., *Hans Hofmann* (New York: Rizzoli, 2002).

23. Hans Hofmann, 'The Object in the Visual Arts' (1951), in Helmut Friedel and Tina Dickey, *Hans Hofmann* (New York: Hudson Hills Press, 1997), p. 92.

24. Hofmann, 'The Color Problem in Pure Painting – Its Creative Origin', *Arts and Architecture* (February 1956), p. 34, reprinted in Wight, *Hans Hofmann*, p. 56.

25. Stuart Preston, 'Abstract in Tenor', *New York Times* (18 November 1951), p. X9.
26. Hofmann cited in William C. Seitz, *Hans Hofmann* (New York: Museum of Modern Art, [1963] 1972), p. 14.
27. William S. Rubin, *Frank Stella* (New York: Museum of Modern Art, 1970), p. 7.
28. Interview with Frank Stella in the documentary *Hans Hofmann: Artist/Teacher Teacher/Artist* (US, Amgott Productions, 2002). Mondrian's influence can also be detected in Hofmann's work such as his series of geometric paintings from 1958, *Abstract Euphony*, *Pastorale*, *Equipoise* and *Equinox*: Yohe, ed., *Hans Hofmann*, pp. 186–9.
29. Robert Pincus-Witten, 'The Black and Metallic Paintings', *Frank Stella: Black and Metallic Paintings 1959–1964* (New York, Gagosian Gallery, 1990).
30. Frank Stella cited in Rubin, *Frank Stella*, pp. 46–7.
31. Guilbaut, *How New York Stole the Idea of Modern Art*, p. 174.
32. Rubin, *Frank Stella*, p. 149.
33. Serge Guilbaut, ed., *Reconstructing Modernism: Art in New York, Paris, and Montreal 1945–1964* (Cambridge MA: MIT Press, 1990), p. xiii.
34. Howard Devree, ' "Anonymous" Art', *New York Times*, X13.
35. See Lois Fichner-Rathus, 'Abstract Expressionism', *The Dada/Surrealist Heritage*, ed. Sam Hunter (Williamstown MA: Sterling & Francine Clark Art Institute, 1977), p. 9.
36. Mathews, 'Art and Politics in the Cold War', p. 785.
37. Timothy J. Clark, 'Jackson Pollock's Abstraction', in *Reconstructing Modernism*, ed. Guilbaut, p. 180.
38. For discussion of San Francisco painters in the 1950s, see Caroline A. Jones, *Bay Area Figurative Art, 1950–1965* (Berkeley CA: University of California Press, 1990). See also Greenberg, 'Jackson Pollock's New Style' (1952), *Collected Essays, 3*, p. 106.
39. Howard Devree, 'Current Extremes', *New York Times* (24 April 1955), p. X9.
40. For discussion of Rauschenberg's abstract paintings, see Helen Molesworth, 'Before *Bed*', *Robert Rauschenberg*, ed. Branden W. Joseph (Cambridge MA: MIT Press, 2002), pp. 75–91.
41. In 1959 Rauschenberg claimed: 'painting relates to both art and life. Neither can be made. (I try to act in that gap between the two)': *Sixteen Americans*, ed. Miller, p. 58.
42. Leo Steinberg, 'Reflections on the State of Criticism' (1972), in *Robert Rauschenberg*, ed. Joseph, p. 28.

43. Lawrence Alloway et al, *Modern Dreams: The Rise and Fall and Rise of Pop* (New York: The Institute for Contemporary Art, 1988), p. 89.

44. Claes Oldenburg, 'I am for an art . . .', (1961), in *Modern Dreams*, p. 105.

45. 'His Heart Belongs to Dada', *Time* (4 May 1959), p. 53.

46. Leo Steinberg, *Jasper Johns* (New York: George Wittenborn, 1963), p. 10.

47. Mark Rosenthal, '*Dancers on a Plane* and other stratagems', *Dancers on a Plane: Cage – Cunningham – Johns* (New York: Knopf, 1990), p. 117.

48. Christel Hollevoet (ed.), *Jasper Johns: Writings, Sketchbook Notes, Interviews* (New York: Museum of Modern Art, 1996), p. 81.

49. Hollevoet, ed., *Jasper Johns*, p. 82.

50. Fred Orton, *Figuring Jasper Johns* (London: Reaktion, 1994), p. 112.

51. Max Kozloff, 'American Painting During the Cold War', *Artforum*, 11 (9) (May 1973), p. 51.

52. Jasper Johns in a BBC interview with David Sylvester (10 October 1965), cited in Marco Livingstone (ed.), *Pop Art: An International Perspective* (London: Royal Academy of Arts, 1991), p. 48.

53. For discussion of the 1954 Flag Day context, see Orton, *Figuring Jasper Johns*, pp. 101–3.

54. Morey Engle, *Denver Comes of Age* (Boulder CO: Johnson Books, 1994), p. x.

55. For developments in photojournalism in the 1950s, see Marianne Fulton, *Eyes of Time: Photojournalism in America* (Boston MA: Little, Brown, 1988), pp. 175–88. See also John Howard Griffin, *Black Like Me* (New York: Signet 1962).

56. For photographs accompanying these essays, see *W. Eugene Smith: Photographs 1934–1975*, eds Gilles Mora and John T. Hill (London: Thames & Hudson, 1998), pp. 128–63.

57. Mora and Hill (eds), *W. Eugene Smith*, pp. 276–80. For Smith discussing his *Life* assignments, see Eugenia Parry Janis and Wendy MacNeil (eds), *Photography within the Humanities*, (Danbury NH: Addison House, 1977), pp. 96–109.

58. *Robert Capa Photographs* (New York: Aperture, 1996), pp. 145–87.

59. Alan Trachtenberg, 'Picturing History in the Morgue', *The Tumultuous Fifties*, ed. Douglas Dreishpoon and Alan Trachtenberg (New Haven CT: Yale University Press, 2001), p. 22.

60. Aaron Siskind published his first book of photography in 1959 aged 56. For a collection of his images, see James Rehm, *Aaron Siskind* (London: Phaidon, 2003).

61. Jonathan Spaulding, *Ansel Adams and the American Landscape* (Berkeley CA: University of California Press, 1995), pp. 64, 81.

62. Ansel Adams, *Examples: The Making of 40 Photographs* (New York: Little, Brown, 1976), pp. 17, 100.

63. Ibid., p. 54.

64. For discussion of Adams's relationship to the postwar art movements, see Spaulding, *Ansel Adams and the American Landscape*, pp. 256–61.

65. Edward Steichen, 'Freedom and the Artist' (1963), in *Edward Steichen: Selected Texts and Bibliography*, ed. Ronald J. Gedrim (New York: G. K. Hall, 1996), p. 98.

66. *The Family of Man* (New York: Museum of Modern Art, [1955] 1986), p. 5.

67. Jonathan Green, *American Photography: A Critical History 1945 to the Present* (New York: Harry Abrams, 1984), p. 37. Donna Haraway, *Modest_Witness@Second_Millennium* (New York: Routledge, 1997), p. 243.

68. Interview with Robert Frank, in *Photography within the Humanities*, ed. Janis and MacNeil, p. 54.

69. Robert Frank, 'A Statement', *U.S. Camera Annual* (New York: U.S. Camera Publishing, 1958), p. 115.

70. Janis and MacNeil (eds), *Photography within the Humanities*, p. 54.

71. Peter Bunnell, *Degrees of Guidance* (Cambridge: Cambridge University Press, 1993), p. 74.

72. Tod Papageorge, *Walker Evans and Robert Frank: An Essay on Influence* (New Haven NJ: Yale University Art Gallery, 1981), p. 1.

73. Green, *American Photography*, p. 81.

74. Janis and MacNeil (eds), *Photography within the Humanities*, pp. 53, 55.

75. For the development of Frank's aesthetics, see Sarah Greenough et al., *Robert Frank: Moving Out* (Zuirch: Scalo, 1994).

76. Robert Frank, 'I'd Like to Make a Film . . .', *Robert Frank* (New York: Pantheon, 1974), n. p.

77. Frank, 'I'd Like to Make a Film . . .', n. p.

78. For Frank's political photography, see Barbara Tannenbaum, ed., *Robert Frank and American Politics* (Akron OH: Akron Art Museum, 1985).

79. Susan Sontag, 'In Memory of Their Feelings', *Dancers on a Plane: Cage – Cunningham – Johns*, p. 13.

80. For discussion of Black Mountain College and Rutgers University, see Geoffrey Hendricks (ed.), *Critical Mass: Happenings, Fluxus, Performance, Intermedia and Rutgers University 1958–1972* (New Brunswick NJ: Rutgers University Press), pp. 11–19.

81. Jonas Mekas, 'Movie Journals', *Film Culture: Expanded Arts*, 43 (winter 1966), pp. 10–11.

82. Allan Kaprow, 'Notes on the Creation of a Total Art' (1958), in *The Blurring of Art and Life*, ed. Jeff Kelley (Berkeley CA: University of California Press, 1993), p. 12.

83. Jonas Mekas, 'Movie Journals', *Film Culture: Expanded Arts*, 43 (winter 1966), pp. 10–11.

84. Jonas Mekas, 'Movie Journal', *Village Voice* (16 September 1959), reprinted in *Wide Angle* 19 (2) (April 1997), p. 120.

85. Dwight Macdonald, 'Some Animadversions on the Art Film', *Esquire* (April 1962), reprinted in *Wide Angle*, 19 (2) (April 1997), p. 156. Founder of Cinema 16, Amos Vogel replied to Macdonald's criticisms: Amos Vogel, 'Riposte from Cinema 16', *Esquire* (September 1962), reprinted in *Wide Angle*, 19 (2) (April 1997), p. 162.

86. Mekas, 'A Call for a New Generation of Film-makers', *Film Culture*, 19 (1959), reprinted in *Film Culture Reader*, ed. P. Adams Sitney (New York: Praeger, 1970), pp. 73–4.

87. See Stan Brakhage's portrait of Marie Menken in *Film at Wit's End: Eight Avant-Garde Filmmakers* (New York: McPherson & Co, 1989), p. 41. It is worth noting that Mekas, Menken and Fluxus artist George Maciunas were all of Lithuanian extraction.

88. See Amy Taubin, 'Beginnings, Continuations, Renewals: Robert Frank's personal New American Cinema', *Frank's Films: The Film and Video Work of Robert Frank*, ed. Brigitta Burger-Utzer and Stefan Grissemann (Zurich: Scalo, 2003), pp. 88–101.

89. Bruce Conner quoted in *Bruce Conner Drawings 1955–1972* (San Francisco: The Fine Arts Museum of San Francisco, 1974), n. p.

90. Peter Boswell, 'Bruce Conner: Theater of Light and Shadow', *2000 BC: The Bruce Conner Story Part II* (Minneapolis MN: Walker Art Center, 2000), pp. 28–33. For a discussion of *A Movie* as cultural criticism, see also in the same volume Bruce Jenkins, 'Explosion in a Film Factory: The Cinema of Bruce Conner', pp. 187–94.

91. Anthony Reveaux, *bruce conner* (St Paul MN: Film in the Cities, 1981), p. 1.

92. For the first statement of The New American Cinema Group from summer 1961, see Sitney, ed., *Film Culture Reader*, pp. 79–83.

93. See Harold Rosenberg, 'The American Action Painters', *Art News*, 51 (December 1952), p. 22, cited in Hannah Higgins, *Fluxus Experience* (Berkeley CA: University of California Press, 2002), p. 106.

94. Simon Anderson, 'Fluxus Publicus', in *In the Spirit of Fluxus*, ed. Janet Jenkins (Minneapolis MN: Walker Art Center, 1993), p. 40.

95. Stephen C. Foster, 'Historical Design and Social Purpose: A Note on the Relationship of Fluxus to Modernism', in *The Fluxus*

Reader, ed. Ken Friedman (Chichester: Academy Editions, 1998), pp. 166–71.

96. Fluxus chronologies differ: some go back to 1957 and 1959; others as far as the early 1950s such as in *Critical Mass*, pp. 181–97; and others do not begin until 1960, such as the detailed one in *The Fluxus Reader*, pp. 257–82.

97. La Monte Young, *An Anthology* (New York: Young & Mac Low, 1963; 2nd edn, 1970), n. p.

98. Earle Brown, 'Notes, Thoughts and Assorted Material from Notebook' (1952–3), *An Anthology*, n. p.

99. Kostelanetz, *The Theatre of Mixed Means*, p. 288.

100. The focus on science came increasingly to the fore, with local newspapers stressing the World's Fair's aim to celebrate Seattle's history as well as Alaskan and Pacific Rim cultures as late as 1958. See 'The Century 21 Exposition: the 1962 Seattle World's Fair: Scrapbooks', compiled by Edward E. Carlson, vols 1–5 (1962), held in the Special Collections division, Allen Library, University of Washington, Seattle WA.

101. *Century 21 Exposition* (Seattle WA: Century 21 Exposition, Inc., 1959), n. p.

102. *Seattle World Fair* (Seattle WA: Acme, 1962), p. 8.

103. *Century 21 Exposition*, p. 17.

104. 'Seattle's Art Explosion', *New York Herald Tribune* (22 April 1962), p. 1. 'Art at Seattle Offers Year's Most Important Coast Show', *Los Angeles Times* (13 May 1962), p. 14.

105. Emily Genauer, 'Seattle's Art Explosion', p. 7.

106. Cited in Murray Morgan, *Century 21: The Story of the Seattle's World Fair, 1962* (Seattle WA: Acme Press, 1963), p. 15.

107. *The Seattle Times*, 19 April 1987, p. A10. *The Seattle Post-Intelligencer*, p. A5.

Conclusion

1. Gay Talese, 'Hindu Astrologer of Broadway Peeks Into the Future', *New York Times* (31 December 1959), p. 10. Diogenes, 'End of a Decade', *New York Times* (1 January 1960), p. 18.

2. 'Enter 1961: Report on World Mood', *New York Times* (1 January 1961), p. E1.

3. Cited in Paul Dickson, *Sputnik: The Shock of the Century* (New York: Berkeley Books, 2001), p. 1.

4. Harvey Wheeler, 'Danger Signals in the Political System', *Dissent*, 4 (3) (summer 1957), p. 310.

5. William Atwood, 'How America Feels as we Enter the Soaring Sixties', *Look* (5 January 1960), p. 12.

6. Arthur Schlesinger Jr, 'The New Mood in Politics', *The Politics of Hope* (Boston MA: Houghton Mifflin, 1962), p. 93. George B. Leonard Jr, 'Youth of the Sixties . . . The Explosive Generation', *Look* (3 January 1961), p. 16.

7. Mark Hamilton Lytle, *America's Uncivil Wars: The Sixties Era from Elvis to the Fall of Richard Nixon* (New York: Oxford University Press, 2006), p. 7.

8. Laurence Goldstein argues that *The Misfits* is a film all about endings and Monroe's death in 1962 'provided the absolute closure of fatality the film seemed to summon from the depths of the American experience': Goldstein, '*The Misfits* and American Culture', in *Arthur Miller's America: Theater and Culture in a Time of Change*, ed. Enoch Brater (Ann Arbor MI: University of Michigan Press, 2005), p. 110.

9. While Eisenhower is often credited with the idea of the 'industrial-military complex' there are precedents: 'the marriage of the military machine with the research scientist has . . . been unexpectedly happy . . . It is largely because of technology and science that the military leaders have come to exercise greater influence in American government and industry than ever before in peace time': Edward Speyer, 'Scientists in the Bureaucratic Age', *Dissent*, 4 (4) (Autumn 1957), p. 402.

10. The powerful documentary *Why We Fight* (Eugene Jarecki, 2006) uses Eisenhower's Farewell Address as its starting point to argue that his fears about the military-industrial complex are being realised in the early twenty-first century. For a discussion of *Why We Fight* and other recent anti-war films such as *Fahrenheit 9/11*, see James Wolcott, 'Through a Lens Darkly', *Vanity Fair* (February 2006), pp. 88–94.

11. Port Huron Statement by the Students for a Democratic Society (15 June 1962), in *Takin' it to the Streets*, ed. Alexander Bloom and Wini Breines (Oxford: Oxford University Press, 1995), pp. 61–74. See also C. Wright Mills's 'Letter to the New Left', New Left Review, 5 (September–October 1960), reprinted in *Takin' it to the Streets*, pp. 75–81.

12. Frantz Fanon, *The Wretched of the Earth*, trans. Constance Farrington (London: Penguin, [1961] 1967), p. 40.

13. 'A Word to Our Readers', *Dissent*, 1 (1) (winter 1954), p. 3.

14. In *Up From Liberalism* Buckley tried to distance himself from McCarthy, but nevertheless credited McCarthy for bringing 'liberalism to the boil': William F. Buckley Jr, *Up From Liberalism* (New Rochelle NY: Arlington House, [1959] 1968), p. 39. For the rise of the New Right,

see John A. Andrew III, *The Other Side of the Sixties: Young Americans for Freedom and the Rise of Conservative Politics* (New Brunswick NJ: Rutgers University Press, 1997), pp. 5–31.

15. Michael Harrington, *The Other America: Poverty in the United States* (New York: Macmillan, 1962), p. 2.

16. Ibid., p. 10.

17. Marty Greenbaum, *Park Place Position* (1962) held in the Joan Flasch Artists' Book Collection, John M. Flaxman Library, The Art Institute of Chicago. For a similar set of defamiliarizing techniques focusing on Marilyn Monroe, see Bruce Conner's avant-garde film *Marilyn Times Five* (14 mins, 1973).

18. Anthony Woodiwiss, *Postmodernity USA: The Crisis of Social Modernism in Postwar America* (London: Sage, 1993), p. 15.

19. Tom Brokaw, *The Greatest Generation* (New York: Random House, 1998), p. 11.

20. Ibid., p. 12.

21. Ibid., p. 389. Brokaw, *The Greatest Generation Speaks: Letters and Reflections* (Norwalk CT: Easton Press, 1999), p. xix.

22. Tom Brokaw, *A Long Way from Home: Growing Up in the American Heartland* (New York: Random House, 2002), pp. ix–x.

23. Ibid., pp. x, 176.

24. Ibid., pp. 144–5.

25. Ibid., p. 188.

26. Ibid., p. 206.

27. Michael Kammen, *Mystic Chords of Memory: The Transformation of Tradition in American Culture* (New York: Knopf, 1991), pp. 544, 539.

28. See Barry Goldwater, *Conscience of a Conservative* (Washington DC: Regnery Gateway, [1960] 1990) and Milton Friedman, *Capitalism and Freedom* (Chicago: University of Chicago Press, [1962] 2002).

29. Andrew E. Busch, *Reagan's Victory: The Presidential Election of 1980 and the Rise of the Right* (Lawrence KS: University Press of Kansas, 2005), p. 21. Ronald Reagan, *An American Life* (New York: Simon & Schuster, 1992), p. 134.

30. Mark Hamilton Lytle, *America's Uncivil Wars*, p. x.

31. Eric F. Goldman, 'Good-By to the Fifties – and Good Riddance', *Harper's*, 220 (January 1960), p. 27.

32. Kammen, *Mystic Chords of Memory*, p. 618.

33. Coontz, *The Way We Really Were*, p. 34.

34. See *Down from the Mountain* (Nick Doob, Chris Hegedus and D. A. Pennebaker, 2000) and the three-part PBS broadcast *The Appalachians* (Mari-Lynn Evans, 2005).

35. Ann Coulter, *Treason: Liberal Treachery from the Cold War to the War on Terrorism* (New York: Three Rivers Press, 2003), p. 71.

36. Allan Bloom, *The Closing of the American Mind* (New York: Simon & Schuster, 1987), p. 324. Bloom argues that the student movement of the 1960s 'bankrupted' the university system in the US, arguing that it created too much permeability between universities and social movements rather than bastions of academic thought: p. 334.

37. Richard Bolton, ed., *Culture Wars* (New York: New Press, 1992), p. 15.

38. For a persuasive reading of *Pleasantville*, see Paul Grainge, '*Pleasantville* and the Textuality of Media Memory', *Memory and Popular Film*, ed. Paul Grainge (Manchester: Manchester University Press, 2003), pp. 202–19.

39. Stephanie Coontz, *The Way We Never Were: American Families and the Nostalgia Trap* (New York: HarperCollins, 1992), pp. 23–41.

40. Pink, 'Family Portrait', *Missundaztood* (Arista, 2001).

41. Sting, 'Russians', *Dream of the Blue Turtles* (A&M, 1985).

42. Billy Joel, 'We Didn't Start the Fire', *Storm Watch* (Columbia, 1989).

43. In its tone of exasperation, 'We Didn't Start the Fire' is closer to the culture of unease in the 1950s than to the focused protest of the 1960s. There are obvious educational dangers in Joel's foreshortening of history, but it is interesting that many high school and college classes have used the lyrics from 'We Didn't Start the Fire' to interrogate postwar history.

44. Caputi, *A Kinder, Gentler America*, p. 114.

45. See E. J. Dionne Jr, 'The New McCarthyism', *The Washington Post* (28 June 2005), p. A15 and William Watson, 'The New McCarthyism', *National Post* (4 November 2005), p. 19. For a discussion of parallels between 1954 and 2004, see Haynes Johnson, *The Age of Anxiety: From McCarthyism to Terrorism* (New York: Harcourt, 2005), pp. 495–507.

46. See the DVD Companion Piece to *Good Night, and Good Luck* (Warner Bros, 2005).

47. Not surprisingly Ann Coulter attacks Ed Murrow and Fred Friendly as bad researchers and status seekers: Coulter, *Treason*, pp. 63, 97.

48. Rupert Holmes, *Where the Truth Lies* (New York: Random House, 2004), p. 274.

49. Matei Calinescu argues that the relationship in the twentieth century between 'two bitterly conflicting modernities' – social modernism and aesthetic modernism – has been 'irreducibly hostile, but not without allowing and even stimulating a variety of mutual influences in their rage for each other's destruction': Matei Calinescu, *Five Faces of Modernity* (Durham NC: Duke University Press, 1987), p. 41.

50. Jameson, *A Singular Modernity: Essay on the Ontology of the Present* (London: Verso, 2002), pp. 168, 197.
51. Gloria T. Hull, 'Review of *1959: A Novel*', *Women's Review of Books*, 9 (May 1992), p. 6.
52. Thulani Davis, *1959: A Novel* (London: Penguin, 1993), p. 274.
53. Ibid., p. 3.

Bibliography

General

James Baldwin, *Notes on a Native Son* (London: Penguin, [1955] 1995).

Erik Barnouw, *A History of Broadcasting in the United States* (New York: Oxford University Press, 1966–70), 3 volumes.

James Baughman, *The Republic of Mass Culture: Journalism, Filmmaking, and Broadcasting in America since 1941*, 2nd edn (Baltimore MD: Johns Hopkins University Press, 1997).

Daniel Bell, *The End of Ideology: On the Exhaustion of Political Ideas in the Fifties* (New York: Macmillan, 1961).

Paul S. Boyer, *By the Bomb's Early Light: American Thought and Culture at the Dawn of the Atomic Age* (New York: Pantheon, 1985).

Wini Breines, *Young, White, and Miserable: Growing Up Female in the Fifties* (Boston MA: Beacon, 1992).

Robert H. Bremner and Gary W. Reichard (eds), *Reshaping America: Society and Institutions, 1945–1960* (Columbus OH: Ohio State University Press, 1982).

Tom Brokaw, *A Long Way from Home: Growing Up in the American Heartland* (New York: Random House, 2002).

William F. Buckley Jr, *Up From Liberalism* (New Rochelle NY: Arlington House, [1959] 1968).

Richard Butsch, *For Fun and Profit: The Transformation of Leisure into Consumption* (Philadelphia PA: Temple University Press, 1990).

Mary Caputi, *A Kinder, Gentler America: Melancholia and the Mythical 1950s* (Minneapolis MN: University of Minnesota Press, 2005).

Paul Carter, *Another Part of the Fifties* (New York: Columbia University Press, 1983).

David Caute, *The Dancer Defects: The Struggle for Cultural Supremacy During the Cold War* (Oxford: Oxford University Press, 2003).

George Chauncey, *Gay New York* (New York: Basic Books, 1994).

Noam Chomsky et al., *The Cold War and the University: Toward an Intellectual History of the Postwar Years* (New York: New Press, 1997).

Alison J. Clarke, *Tupperware: The Promise of Plastic in 1950s America* (Washington DC: Smithsonian Institution Press, 1999).

Lizabeth Cohen, *A Consumers' Republic: The Politics of Mass Consumption in Postwar America* (New York: Knopf, 2003).

Peter Coleman, *The Liberal Conspiracy: The Congress for Cultural Freedom and the Struggle for the Mind of Postwar Europe* (New York: Free Press, 1989).

Stephanie Coontz, *The Way We Never Were: American Families and the Nostalgia Trap* (New York: HarperCollins, 1992).

Stephanie Coontz, *The Way We Really Are* (New York: HarperCollins, 1997).

Robert J. Corber, *Homosexuality in Cold War America* (Durham NC: Duke University Press, 1997).

Pete Daniels, *Lost Revolutions: The South in the 1950s* (Chapel Hill NC: University of North Carolina Press, 2000).

Michael Denning, *The Cultural Front: The Laboring of American Culture in the Twentieth Century* (New York: Verso, 1997).

John Patrick Diggins, *The Proud Decades: America in War and Peace, 1941–1960* (New York: Norton, 1988).

Dwight D. Eisenhower, *Mandate for Change, 1953–1956* (New York: New American Library, 1963).

Ralph Ellison, *Shadow and Act* (New York: Vintage, [1964] 1972).

Robert S. Ellwood, *The Fifties Spiritual Marketplace: American Religion in a Decade of Conflict* (New Brunswick NJ: Rutgers University Press, 1997).

Robert S. Ellwood, *1950: Crossroads of American Religious Life* (Louisville KY: Westminster John Knox Press, 2000).

Penny M. von Eschen, *Satchmo Blows Up the World: Jazz Ambassadors Play the Cold War* (Cambridge MA: Harvard University Press, 2004).

Leslie Fiedler, *An End to Innocence* (Boston MA: Beacon Press, 1955).

Douglas Field (ed.), *Cold War Culture* (Edinburgh: Edinburgh University Press, 2004).

Christopher Finch, *Walt Disney's America* (New York: Abbeville, 1978).

John M. Findlay, *Magic Lands: Western Cityscapes and American Culture after 1940* (Berkeley CA: University of California Press, 1992).

Joel Foreman (ed.), *The Other Fifties: Interrogating Midcentury American Icons* (Urbana IL: University of Illinois Press, 1997).

Stephen Fox, *The Mirror Makers: A History of American Advertising and Its Creators* (New York: Vintage, 1985).

Betty Friedan, *The Feminine Mystique* (New York: Dell, [1963] 1973).

John Kenneth Galbraith, *The Affluent Society* (Boston MA: Houghton Mifflin, 1958).

Herbert J. Gans, *The Levittowners: Ways of Life and Politics in a New Suburban Community* (New York: Pantheon, 1967).

James Gilbert, *A Cycle of Outrage: America's Reaction to the Juvenile Delinquent in the 1950s* (New York: Oxford University Press, 1986).

James Gilbert, *Men in the Middle: Searching for Masculinity in the 1950s* (Chicago: University of Chicago Press, 2005).

Richard Gillam (ed.), *Power in Postwar America* (Boston MA: Little, Brown, 1971).

Eric F. Goldman, 'Good-by to the Fifties – and Good Riddance', *Harper's*, 220 (January 1960), pp. 27–9.

Eric F. Goldman, *The Crucial Decade: America 1945–1955* (New York: Knopf, 1956).

Paul Goodman, *Growing Up Absurd* (New York: Vintage, 1960).

David Halberstam, *The Fifties* (New York: Villard, 1993).

Martin Halliwell, *The Constant Dialogue: Reinhold Niebuhr and American Intellectual Culture* (Lanham MD: Rowman & Littlefield, 2005).

Michael Harrington, *The Other America: Poverty in the United States* (New York: Macmillan, 1962).

Jeffrey Hart, *When the Going Was Good! American Life in the Fifties* (New York: Crown, 1982).

M. J. Heale, *American Anticommunism: Combating the Enemy Within, 1830–1970* (Baltimore MD: Johns Hopkins University Press, 1990).

Cyndy Hendershot, *Anti-communism and Popular Culture in Mid-Century America* (New York: McFarland & Co, 2003).

Margot Henriksen, *Dr Strangelove's America: Society and Culture in the Atomic Age* (Berkeley CA: University of California Press, 1997).

Thomas Hine, *Populuxe* (New York: Knopf, 1986).

Richard Hofstadter, *Anti-Intellectualism in American Life* (New York: Vintage, 1962).

J. Edgar Hoover, *Masters of Deceit* (New York: Henry Holt, 1958).

Irving Howe, 'This Age of Conformity', *Partisan Review*, 21 (January–February 1954), pp. 7–33.

Irving Howe, *A Margin of Hope: An Intellectual Autobiography* (New York: Harcourt Brace Jovanovich, 1982).

Allen Hunter (ed.), *Rethinking the Cold War* (Philadelphia PA: Temple University Press, 1998).

Andreas Huyssen, *After the Great Divide: Modernism, Mass Culture and Postmodernism* (London: Macmillan, 1986).

Kenneth L. Jackson, *Crabgrass Frontier: The Suburbanization of the United States* (New York: Oxford, 1985).

Marty Jezer, *The Dark Ages: Life in the United States, 1945–1960* (Boston MA: South End, 1982).

Haynes Johnson, *The Age of Anxiety: From McCarthyism to Terrorism* (New York: Harcourt, 2005).

Eugenia Kaledin, *Mothers and More: American Women in the 1950s* (Boston MA: Twayne, 1984).

Michael Kazin and Joseph A. McCartin (eds), *Americanism: New Perspectives on the History of an Ideal* (Chapel Hill NC: University of North Carolina Press, 2006).

Richard H. King, *Race, Culture, and the Intellectuals, 1940–1970* (Baltimore MD: Johns Hopkins University Press, 2004).

Christopher Lasch, 'The Cultural Cold War: A Short History of the Congress for Cultural Freedom', in *Towards a New Past: Dissenting Essays in American History*, ed. Barton J. Bernstein (New York: Pantheon, 1968), pp. 322–59.

George Lewis, *The White South and the Red Menace: Segregationists, Anticommunism, and Massive Resistance, 1945–1965* (Gainsville FL: University of Florida Press, 2004).

Peter Lewis, *The Fifties* (New York: J. B. Lippincott, 1978).

W. T. Lhamon Jr, *Deliberate Speed: The Origins of a Cultural Style in the American 1950s* (Washington DC: Smithsonian Institution Press, 1990).

Ronnie Lipschutz, *Cold War Fantasies: Film, Fiction and Foreign Policy* (Lanham MD: Rowman & Littlefield, 2001).

George Lipsitz, *Class and Culture in Cold War America: 'A Rainbow At Midnight'* (South Hadley MA: Bergin & Garvey, 1982).

Mark Hamilton Lytle, *America's Uncivil Wars: The Sixties Era from Elvis to the Fall of Richard Nixon* (New York: Oxford University Press, 2006).

Dwight Macdonald, *Against the Grain* (New York: Vintage, 1962).

Norman Mailer, *Advertisements for Myself* (London: Flamingo, [1959] 1994).

Karal Ann Marling, *As Seen on TV: The Visual Culture of Everyday Life in the 1950s* (Cambridge MA: Harvard University Press, 1996).

Martin E. Marty, *Modern American Religion, 3: Under God Divisible, 1941–1960* (Chicago: University of Chicago Press, 1996).

Kevin Mattson, *When America Was Great: The Fighting Faith of Postwar Liberalism* (New York: Routledge, 2004).

Elaine Tyler May, *Homeward Bound: American Families in the Cold War Era* (New York: Basic Books, [1988] 1999).

Lary May, ed., *Recasting American Culture and Politics in the Age of the Cold War* (Chicago: University of Chicago Press, 1989).

Martin Mayer, *Madison Avenue U.S.A.* (London: Penguin, [1958] 1961).

Michael Medred, *Hollywood vs. America: Popular Culture and the War on Traditional Values* (New York: HarperCollins, 1992).

Thomas Meehan, 'Must We Be Nostalgic About the Fifties?', *Horizon* 14 (winter 1972), pp. 4–17.

Joanne Meyerowitz (ed.), *Not June Cleaver: Women and Gender in Postwar America, 1945–1960* (Philadelphia PA: Temple University Press, 1994).

Douglas T. Miller and Marion Nowak, *The Fifties: The Way We Really Were* (Garden City NY: Doubleday, 1977).

C. Wright Mills, *White Collar* (New York: Oxford University Press, [1951] 2002).

C. Wright Mills, *The Power Elite* (New York: Oxford University Press, 1956).

C. Wright Mills, 'Letter to the New Left', *Power, Politics, and People* (New York: Oxford University Press, 1963), pp. 247–59.

Lewis Mumford, *Art and Technics* (New York: Columbia University Press, 1952).

George H. Nash, *The Conservative Intellectual Movement in America: Since 1945* (New York: Basic Books, 1976).

Reinhold Niebuhr, *Pious and Secular America* (New York: Scribner's, 1958).

J. Ronald Oakley, *God's Country: America in the Fifties* (New York: Dembner, 1990).

William O'Neill, *American High: The Years of Confidence, 1945–1960* (New York: Free Press, 1986).

Vance Packard, *The Hidden Persuaders* (London: Penguin, [1957] 1960).

Vance Packard, *The Status Seekers* (London: Penguin, [1959] 1961).

James T. Patterson, *Brown v. Board of Education: A Civil Rights Milestone and its Troubled Legacy* (New York: Oxford University Press, 2002).

Richard H. Pells, *The Liberal Mind in a Conservative Age: American Intellectuals in the 1940s and 1950s*, 2nd edn (Middletown CT: Wesleyan University Press, 1989).

Richard H. Pells, *Not Like Us: How Europeans Have Loved, Hated, and Transformed American Culture since World War II* (New York: Basic Books, 1997).

Brenda Gayle Plummer, *Rising Wind: Black Americans and U.S. Foreign Affairs, 1935–1960* (Chapel Hill NC: University of North Carolina Press, 1996).

Richard Polenberg, *One Nation, Divisible: Class, Race, and Ethnicity in the United States Since 1938* (London: Penguin, 1980).

David M. Potter, *People of Plenty: Economic Abundance and the American Character* (Chicago: University of Chicago Press, 1954).

Diane Ravitch, *The Troubled Crusade: American Education, 1945–1980* (New York: Basic Books, 1983).

George A. Reisch, *How the Cold War Transformed Philosophy of Science* (Cambridge: Cambridge University Press, 2005).

David Riesman, *The Lonely Crowd: A Study of the Changing American Character* (New Haven CT: Yale University Press, [1950] 2001)

Michael Paul Rogin, *The Intellectuals and McCarthy* (Cambridge MA: Harvard University Press, 1967).

Lisle A. Rose, *The Cold War Comes to Main Street: America in 1950* (Lawrence KA: University Press of Kansas, 1999).

Bernard Rosenberg and David Manning White (eds), *Mass Culture: The Popular Arts in America* (Glencoe IL: Free Press, 1957).

Harold Rosenberg, *Discovering the Present: Three Decades in Art, Culture and Politics* (Chicago: University of Chicago Press, 1973).

Arthur Schlesinger Jr, *The Politics of Hope* (Boston MA: Houghton Mifflin, 1963).

Laura Shapiro, *Something for the Oven: Reinventing Dinner in 1950s America* (New York: Viking, 2004).

Mark Silk, *Spiritual Politics: Religion and America Since World War II* (New York: Simon & Schuster, 1988).

Lynn Spigel, *Welcome to the Dreamhouse: Popular Media and Postwar Suburbs* (Durham NC: Duke University Press, 2001).

Lionel Trilling, *The Liberal Imagination* (Garden City NY: Anchor, [1950] 1957).

Lionel Trilling, *Freud and the Crisis of Our Culture* (Boston MA: Beacon, 1955).

Dan Wakefield, *New York in the Fifties* (New York: Houghton Mifflin, 1992).

Carol A. B. Warren, *Madwives: Schizophrenic Women in the 1950s* (New Brunswick NJ: Rutgers University Press, 1991).

James Wechsler, *The Age of Suspicion* (New York: Random House, 1953).

Robert Whitaker, *Mad in America: Bad Science, Bad Medicine, and the Enduring Treatment of the Mentally Ill* (London: Perseus, 2002).

Stephen J. Whitfield, *The Culture of the Cold War* (Baltimore MD: Johns Hopkins University Press, 1990).

Stephen J. Whitfield (ed.), *A Companion to 20th-Century America* (Oxford: Blackwell, 2004).

William H. Whyte, *The Organization Man* (London: Penguin, [1955] 1960).

Lawrence S. Wittner, *Cold War America: From Hiroshima to Watergate* (New York: Praeger, 1974).

Richard Wright, *White Man Listen!* (London: HarperCollins, [1957] 1995).

Philip Wylie, *Generation of Vipers* (Normal IL: Dalkey Archive Press, [1955 edn] 1996).

Howard Zinn, *Postwar America: 1945–1971* (Indianapolis IN: Bobbs-Merrill, 1973).

Fiction and Poetry

Houston Baker, *Blues, Ideology and Afro-American Literature* (Chicago: University of Chicago Press, 1984).

Bernard Bell, *The Afro-American Novel and its Tradition* (Amherst MA: University of Massachusetts Press, 1987).

Malcom Bradbury, *The Modern American Novel* (Oxford: Oxford University Press, [1983] 1993).

James E. Breslin, *From Modern to Contemporary: American Poetry 1945–1965* (Chicago: University of Chicago Press, 1984).

Edward Brunner, *Cold War Poetry: The Social Text in the Fifties Poem* (Urbana IL: University of Illinois Press, 2001).

James Campbell, *This is the Beat Generation: New York – San Francisco – Paris* (London: Secker & Warburg, 1999).

David Castronovo, *Beyond the Gray Flannel Suit: Books from the 1950s that Made American Culture* (New York: Continuum, 2004).

Ann Charters (ed.), *The Penguin Book of the Beats* (London: Penguin, 1992).

Richard Chase, *The American Novel and Its Tradition* (New York: Anchor, 1957).

John Ciardi (ed.), *Mid Century Poets* (New York: Twayne, 1950).

Michael Davidson, *Guys Like Us: Citing Masculinity in Cold War Poetics* (Chicago: University of Chicago Press, 2004).

Morris Dickstein, *Leopards in the Temple: The Transformation of American Fiction, 1945–1970* (Cambridge MA: Harvard University Press, 2002).

Mark Doty, 'The "Forbidden Planet" of Character: The Revolutions of the 1950s', in *A Profile of Twentieth-Century American Poetry* (Carbondale IL: Southern Illinois University Press, 1991), pp. 131–57.

W. D. Ehrhart and Philip K. Jason (eds), *Retrieving Bones: Stories and Poems of the Korean War* (New Brunswick NJ: Rutgers University Press, 1999).

Leslie Fiedler, *Waiting for the End* (London: Penguin, 1964).

Daniel Galloway, *The Absurd Hero in American Fiction* (Austin TX: University of Texas Press, 1970).

Donald B. Gibson, *Five Black Writers: Essays on Wright, Ellison, Baldwin, and Le Roi Jones* (New York: New York University Press, 1970).

Allen Ginsberg, *Deliberate Prose: Selected Essays, 1952–1995*, ed. Bill Morgan (London: Penguin, 2000).

Robert von Hallberg, *American Poetry and Culture, 1945–1980* (Cambridge MA: Harvard University Press, 1985).

Louis Harap, *In the Mainstream: The Jewish Presence in Twentieth Century American Literature, 1950s–1980s* (New York: Greenwood Press, 1987).

Josephine Hendon, *Vulnerable People: A View of American Fiction Since 1945* (Oxford: Oxford University Press, 1978).

John Clellon Holmes, 'This Is the Beat Generation', *New York Times* (16 November 1952), Saturday Magazine, pp. 10, 19–20.

Irving Howe, 'Black Boys and Native Sons', *Dissent* (autumn 1963), pp. 353–68

Langston Hughes, *Good Morning Revolution: Uncollected Social Protest Writings*, ed. Faith Berry (New York: Lawrence Hill, 1973).

M. Thomas Inge et al., *Black American Writers* (New York: St. Martin's, 1978).

David Kalstone, *Five Temperaments* (New York: Oxford University Press, 1977).

Frederick Karl, *American Fictions, 1940–1980* (New York: Harper and Row, 1983).

Alan Nadel, *Containment Culture: American Narratives, Postmodernism and the Atomic Age* (Durham NC: Duke University Press, 1995).

Lisa Phillips, *Beat Culture and the New America 1950–1965* (New York: Whitney Museum, 1995).

Sanford Pinsker, *Jewish-American Fiction, 1917–1987* (New York: Twayne, 1992).

Norman Podhoretz, *Doings and Undoings: The Fifties and After in American Writing* (London: Rupert Hart-Davis, 1965).

Sarah Ralyea, *Outsider Citizens: The Remaking of Postwar Identity in Wright, de Beauvoir, and Baldwin* (London: Routledge, 2005).

Walter B. Rideout, *The Radical Novel in the United States, 1900–1954* (Cambridge MA: Harvard University Press, 1956).

Thomas Schaub, *American Fiction in the Cold War* (Madison WI: Wisconsin University Press, 1991).

David Seed, *American Science Fiction and the Cold War* (Edinburgh: Edinburgh University Press, 1999).

Mark Shechner, *After the Revolution: Studies in the Contemporary Jewish-American Imagination* (Bloomington IN: Indiana University Press, 1987).

Tony Tanner, *City of Words: American Fiction 1950–1970* (London: Jonathan Cape, [1971] 1979).

Graham Thompson, *The Business of America: The Cultural Production of a Post-War Nation* (London: Pluto, 2004).

Drama and Performance

Doris E. Abramson, *Negro Playwrights in the American Theatre, 1925–1959* (New York: Columbia University Press, 1969).

Steven Adler, *On Broadway: Art and Commerce on the Great White Way* (Carbondale IL: Southern Illinois University Press, 2004).

Thomas P. Adler, *American Drama, 1940–1960: A Critical History* (New York: Twayne, 1994).

Arnold Aronson, *American Avant-Garde Theatre: A History* (London: Routledge, 2000).

C. W. E. Bigsby, *A Critical Introduction to Twentieth-Century American Drama*, Vol. 2 (Cambridge: Cambridge University Press, 1984).

C. W. E. Bigsby, *Modern Amerian Drama 1945–1990* (Cambridge: Cambridge University Press, 1992).

P. Biner, *The Living Theatre* (New York: Horizon Press, 1972).

Gerald Bordman, *American Muscial Theatre: A Chronicle*, 3rd edn (Oxford: Oxford University Press, 2002).

Enoch Brater (ed.), *Arthur Miller's America: Theater and Culture in a Time of Change* (Ann Arbor MI: University of Michigan Press, 2005).

Harold Cruse, *The Crisis of the Negro Intellectual* (London: Granta, [1967] 2005).

Martin Gottfried, *Broadway Musicals* (New York: Harry Abrams, 1979).

'Lorraine Hansberry: Art of Thunder, Vision of Light', special issue of *Freedomways: Quarterly Review of the Freedom Movement*, Vol. 19 (1979).

Mary Emma Harris, *The Arts at Black Mountain College* (Cambridge MA: Harvard University Press, 1987).

Geoffrey Hendricks (ed.), *Critical Mass: Happenings, Fluxus, Performance, Intermedia and Rutgers University 1958–1972* (New Brunswick NJ: Rutgers University Press).

Errol G. Hill and James V. Hatch, *A History of African American Theatre* (Cambridge: Cambridge University Press, 2003).

Caren Kaplan, '"Getting to Know You": Travel, Gender, and Politics of Representation in *Anna and the King of Siam* and *The King and I*', in *Late Imperial Culture*, ed. Roman de la Cámpa et al. (London: Verso, 1995), pp. 33–52.

Allan Kaprow, *Assemblage, Environments and Happenings* (New York: Harry N. Abrams, 1966).

Richard Kostelantz, *The Theatre of Mixed-Means* (New York: R K Editions [1968], 1980).

Abe Lauffe, *Broadway's Greatest Musicals* (New York: Funk & Wagnalls, 1977).

S. W. Little, *Off Broadway: The Prophetic Theater* (New York: Coward, McCann & Geoghegan, 1972).

Karen Malpede (ed.), *Women in Theatre: Compassion and Hope* (New York: Drama Book Publishers, 1985).

Arthur Miller, *Timebends: A Life* (London: Methuen, [1987] 1999).

Ethan Mordden, *Coming Up Roses: The Broadway Musical in the 1950s* (New York: Oxford University Press, 1998).

Brenda Murphy (ed.), *The Cambridge Companion to American Women Playwrights* (Cambridge: Cambridge University Press, 1999).

Gerald Nachman, *Seriously Funny: The Rebel Comedians of the 1950s and 1960s* (New York: Pantheon, 2003).

Mariellen R. Sandford (ed.), *Happenings and Other Acts* (London: Routledge, 1995).

R. Baird Shuman, *William Inge*, revised edn (Boston MA: Twayne, 1989).

John Tytell, *The Living Theatre: Art, Exile, and Outrage* (New York: Grove Press, 1995).

David Walsh and Len Platt, *Musical Theater and American Culture* (Westport CT: Praeger, 2003).

J. Charles Washington, 'A Raisin in the Sun Revisited', *Black American Literature Forum* 22 (1) (spring 1988), pp. 109–24.

Alan Woll, *Black Musical Theatre: From* Coontown *to* Dreamgirls (Baton Rouge LA: Lousiana State University Press, 1989).

Music and Radio

Oscar Brand, *The Ballad Mongers: The Rise of the Modern Folk Song* (New York: Funk & Wagnalls, 1962).

Robert Cantwell, *When We Were Good: The Folk Revival* (Cambridge MA: Harvard University Press, 1996).

Samuel Charters, *The Poetry of the Blues* (New York: Avon, 1970).

Ronald D. Cohen, *Rainbow Quest: The Folk Music Revival and American Society, 1940–1970* (Amherst MA: University of Massachusetts Press, 2002).

Nik Cohn, *A WopBopaLooBop A LopBamBoom* (London: Paladin, 1969).

Aaron Copland, *Music and Imagination* (Cambridge MA: Harvard University Press, 1952).

Angela Y. Davis, *Blues Legacies and Black Feminism: Gertrude 'Ma' Rainey, Bessie Smith, and Billie Holiday* (New York: Pantheon, 1998).

R. Serge Denisoff, *Great Day Coming: Folk Music and the American Left* (Urbana IL: University of Illinois Press, 1971).

Susan J. Douglas, *Listening In: Radio and the American Imagination* (New York: Random House, 1999).

Philip H. Ennis, *The Seventh Stream: The Emergence of Rock'n'Roll in American Popular Music* (Hanover NH: Wesleyan University Press, 1992).

Penny M. von Eschen, *Satchmo Blows Up the World: Jazz Ambassadors Play the Cold War* (Cambridge MA: Harvard University Press, 2004).

Benjamin Filene, *Romancing the Folk: Public Memory and American Roots Music* (Chapel Hill NC: University of North Carolina Press, 2000).

Peter Fornatale and Joshua E. Mills, *Radio in the Television Age* (Woodstock NY: Overlook Press, 1984).

Reebee Garofalo, 'The Impact of the Civil Rights Movement on Popular Music', *Radical America*, 21 (6) (November–December 1987), pp. 15–22.

Nelson George, *The Death of Rhythm & Blues* (New York: Dutton, 1989).

Charlie Gillett, *The Sound of the City: The Rise of Rock and Roll* (London MA: Souvenir, [1970] 1983).

Peter Guralnick, *Last Train to Memphis: The Rise of Elvis Presley* (Boston MA: Little, Brown, 1994).

Michele Hilmes, *Hollywood and Broadcasting: From Radio to Cable* (Urbana IL: University of Illinois Press, 1990).

Michele Hilmes, *The Nation's Voice: Radio in the Shaping of American Culture* (Minneapolis: University of Minnesota Press, 1997).

John A. Jackson, *Big Beat Heat: Alan Freed and the Early Years of Rock and Roll* (New York: Schirmer Books, 1991).

Graham Lock, *Blutopia: Visions of the Future and Revisions of the Past* (Durham NC: Duke University Press, 1999).

Alan Lomax, *Selected Writings 1934–1997*, ed. Ronald D. Cohen (New York: Routledge, 2003).

J. Fred MacDonald, *Don't Touch That Dial! Radio Programming in American Life 1920–1960* (Chicago: Nelson-Hall, 1979).

JoAnne Mancini, ' "Messin' with the Furniture Man": Early Country Music, Regional Culture, and the Search for an Anthological Modernism', *American Literary History*, 16 (2) (2004), pp. 208–37.

Greil Marcus, *Mystery Train: Images of America in Rock and Roll* (London: Penguin 1991).

James Miller, *Almost Grown: The Rise of Rock and Roll* (London: Arrow, 1999).

Richard A. Reuss and Joanne C. Reuss, *American Folk Music and Left-Wing Politics, 1927–1957* (London: Scarecrow Press, 2004).

Tony Russell, *Blacks, Whites and Blues* (London: Studio Vista, 1970).

Timothy Scheurer, *American Popular Music: Volume 2, The Age of Rock* (Bowling Green OH: Bowling Green Popular Press, 1989).

David Szatmary, *Rockin' in Time: A Social History of Rock-and-Roll* (New Jersey: Prentice-Hall, [1995] 2006).

Nicholas E. Tawa, *A Most Wondrous Bubble: American Art Composers, Their Music, and the American Scene, 1950–1985* (Westport CT: Greenwood Press, 1987).

Steven C. Tracy, *Write Me a Few Lines: A Blues Reader* (Amherst MA: University of Massachusetts Press, 1999).

Brian Ward, *Radio and the Struggle for Civil Rights in the South* (Gainsville FL: University Press of Florida, 2004).

Elijah Ward, *Josh White: Society Blues* (Amherst MA: University of Massachusetts Press, 2000).

Craig Werner, *A Change is Gonna Come: Music, Race and the Soul of America* (New York: Plume, 1999).

Film and Television

Christopher Anderson, *Hollywood TV: The Studio System in the Fifties* (Austin TX: University of Texas Press, 1994).

Kent Anderson, *Television Fraud: The History and Implications of the Quiz Show Scandals* (Westport CT: Greenwood Press, 1978).

Geoff Andrews, *The Films of Nicholas Ray* (London: BFI, 2004).

Helen Baehr and Gillian Dyer (eds), *Boxed In: Women On and In Television* (London: Pandora, 1986).

Tino Balio (ed.), *Hollywood in the Age of Television* (Boston MA: Unwin Hyman, 1990).

Erik Barnow, *Tube of Plenty: The Evolution of American Television* (New York: Oxford University Press, 1982).

Michael Barrier, *Hollywood Cartoons: American Animation in its Golden Age* (Oxford: Oxford University Press, 2003).

Jeanine Basinger, *A Woman's View: How Hollywood Spoke to Women, 1950–1960* (London: Chatto & Windus, 1993).

James Baughman, *The Republic of Mass Culture: Journalism, Filmmaking, and Broadcasting in America since 1941*, 2nd edn (Baltimore MD: Johns Hopkins University Press, 1997).

Christopher Beach, *Class, Language, and American Film Comedy* (Cambridge: Cambridge University Press, 2002).

John Belton, *American Cinema/American Culture* (New York: McGraw Hill, 1994).

John Belton (ed.), *Alfred Hitchcock's Rear Window* (Cambridge: Cambridge University Press, 2000).

Nancy E. Bernhart, *U.S. Television News and Cold War Propaganda, 1947–1960* (Cambridge: Cambridge University Press, 1998).

Peter Biskind, *Seeing is Believing: How Hollywood Taught us to Stop Worrying and Love the Fifties* (New York: Pantheon, 1983).

William Boddy, *Fifties Television: The Industry and its Critics* (Urbana IL: University of Illinois Press, 1990).

Leo Bogart, *The Age of Television: A Study of Viewing Habits and the Impact of Television on American Life* (New York: Frederick Ungar, 1956).

Douglas Brode, *The Films of the Fifties* (New York: Citadel, 1976).

Douglas Brode, *Lost Films of the Fifties* (New York: Citadel, 1991).

Jackie Byars, *All That Hollywood Allows: Re-Reading Gender in 1950s Melodrama* (Chapel Hill NC: University of North Carolina Press, 1991).

Harry Castleman and Walter J. Podrazik, *Watching TV: Four Decades of American Television* (New York: McGraw Hill, 1982).

Larry Ceplair and Steven Englund, *The Inquisition in Hollywood: Politics in the Film Community* (Garden City NJ: Anchor Press, 1980).

Sarah Churchwell, *The Many Lives of Marilyn Monroe* (London: Granta, 2004).

David Cochran, *American Noir* (Washington DC: Smithsonian Institute, 2000).

Steven Cohen, *Masked Men: Masculinity and the Movies in the Fifties* (Bloomington IN: Indiana University Press, 1997).

Susan Courtney, *Hollywood Fantasies of Miscegenation: Spectacular Narratives of Gender and Race, 1903–1967* (Princeton NJ: Princeton University Press, 2005).

Thomas Cripps, *Making Movies Black: The Hollywood Message Movie from World War II to the Civil Rights Era* (New York: Oxford University Press, 1993).

Ronald L. Davis, *Celluloid Mirrors: Hollywood and American Society Since 1945* (Forth Worth TX: Harcourt Brace, 1997).

Thomas Doherty, *Teenagers and Teenpics: The Juvenilization of American Movies in the 1950s* (Boston MA: Unwin Hyman, 1988).

Robert J. Donovan & Scherer, *Unsilent Revolution: Television News and American Public Life* (Cambridge: Cambridge University Press, 1992).

Andrew Dowdy, *'Movies are Better than Ever': Wide-Screen Memories of the Fifties* (New York: Morrow, 1973).

Richard Dyer, *Heavenly Bodies: Film Stars and Society* (London: BFI, 1987).

Maxene Fabe, *TV Game Shows* (Garden City NY: Doubleday, 1979).

Peter Fornatale and Joshua E. Mills, *Radio in the Television Age* (Woodstock NY: Overlook Press, 1984).

Sidney Gottlieb (ed.), *Hitchcock on Hitchcock* (London: Faber, 1997).

Aram Goudsouzian, *Sidney Poitier: Man, Actor, Icon* (Chapel Hill NC: University of North Carolina Press, 2004).

Allison Graham, *Framing the South: Hollywood, Television, and Race During the Civil Rights Struggle* (Baltimore MD: Johns Hopkins University Press, 2001).

Paul Grainge (ed.), *Memory and Popular Film* (Manchester: Manchester University Press, 2003).

Jon Halliday, (ed.), *Sirk on Sirk* (London: Faber, 1997).

William Hawes, *Live Television Drama, 1946–1951* (Jefferson NC: McFarland, 2001).

Jim Hillier (ed.), *Cahiers du Cinéma: The 1950s: Neo-Realism* (Cambridge MA: Harvard University Press, 1985).

Mark Jancovich, *Rational Fears: American Horror in the 1950s* (Manchester: Manchester University Press, 1996).

James Joslyn and John Pendleton, 'The Adventures of Ozzie and Harriet', *Journal of Popular Culture*, 7 (summer 1973), pp. 23–41.

Stefan Kafer, *Ball of Fire: The Tumultuous Life and Comic Art of Lucille Ball* (London: Faber, 2003).

John Francis Kreidl, *Nicholas Ray* (Boston MA: Twayne, 1977).

Nina C. Leibman, 'Leave Mother Out: The Fifties Family in American Film and Television', *Wide Angle* 10 (4) (1988), pp. 24–41.

Nina C. Leibman, *Living Room Lectures: The Fifties Family in Film and Television* (Austin TX: University of Texas Press, 1995).

Jon Lewis, *The Road to Romance and Ruin: Teen Films and Youth Culture* (New York: Routledge, 1992).

Fred J. MacDonald, *One Nation Under Television: The Rise and Decline of Network Television* (New York: Pantheon, 1990).

Fred J. MacDonald, *Blacks and White TV: African Americans in Television since 1948* (Chicago: Nelson-Hall, 1992).

Gina Marchetti, *Romance and the "Yellow Peril": Race, Sex, and Discursive Strategies in Hollywood Fiction* (Berkeley CA: University of California Press, 1993).

Steve Neale, *Genre and Hollywood* (London: Routledge, 1999).

Bill Nichols (ed.), *Movies and Methods* (Berkeley CA: University of California Press, 1976).

John E. O'Connor (ed.), *American History/American Television* (New York: Frederick Ungar, 1983).

Terence Pettigrew, *Raising Hell: The Rebel in the Movies* (NY: St. Martin's, 1986).

Leonard Quart and Albert Auster, *American Film and Society Since 1945* (Praeger, 1991).

Robert Ray, *A Certain Tendency of the Hollywood Film, 1930–1980* (Princeton: Princeton University Press, 1998).

Peter Roffman and Jim Purdy, *The Hollywood Social Problem Film: Madness and Despair from the Depression to the Fifties* (Bloomington IN: Indiana University Press, 1981).

Michael Rogin, *Blackface, White Noise: Jewish Immigrants in the Hollywood Melting Pot* (Berkeley CA: University of California Press, 1996).

Martha Saxon, *Jayne Mansfield and the American Fifties* (Boston MA: Houghton Mifflin, 1975).

Nora Sayre, *Running Time: Films of the Cold War* (New York, 1982).

Thomas Schatz, *The Genius of the System: Hollywood Film-making in the Studio Era* (London: Faber, [1989] 1998).

Ed Sikov, *Laughing Hysterically: American Screen Comedy of the 1950s* (New York: Columbia University Press, 1994).

Lynn Spigel, *Make Room for TV: Television and the Family Ideal in Postwar America* (Chicago: University of Chicago Press, 1992).

Ella Taylor, *Prime Time Families: Television Culture in Postwar America* (Berkeley CA: University of California Press, 1989).

Visual Arts

Lawrence Alloway et al., *Modern Dreams: The Rise and Fall and Rise of Pop* (New York: The Institute for Contemporary Art, 1988).

Brigitta Burger-Utzer and Stefan Grissemann (ed.), *Frank's Films: The Film and Video Work of Robert Frank* (Zurich: Scalo, 2003).

Mary Ann Caws, *Robert Motherwell: With Pen and Brush* (London: Reaktion, 2003).

Diana Crane, *The Transformation of the Avant-Garde: The New York Art World, 1940–1985* (Chicago: University of Chicago Press, 1987).

David Craven, *Abstract Expressionism as Cultural Critique* (Cambridge: Cambridge University Press, 1999).

Ashton Dore, *The New York School: A Cultural Reckoning* (Berkeley CA: University of California Press, 1973).

Peter Dormer, *Design Since 1945* (London: Thames & Hudson, 1993).

Erika Doss, *Benton, Pollock and the Politics of Modernism: From Regionalism to Abstract Expressionism* (Chicago: University of Chicago Press, 1991).

Douglas Dreishpoon and Alan Trachtenberg (ed.), *The Tumultuous Fifties* (New Haven CT: Yale University Press, 2001).

Francis Fascina (ed.), *Pollock and After: The Critical Debate* (New York: Harper & Row, 1985).

B. H. Friedman, *Jackson Pollock: Energy Made Visible* (London: Weidenfeld & Nicolson, 1973).

Ken Friedman (ed.), *The Fluxus Reader* (Chichester: John Wiley, 1998).

Marianne Fulton, *Eyes of Time: Photojournalism in America* (Boston MA: Little, Brown, 1988).

Ann Gibson, *Abstract Expressionism: Other Politics* (New Haven CT: Yale University Press, 1997).

Jonathan Green, *American Photography: A Critical History, 1945 to the Present* (New York: Abrams, 1984).

Cara Greenberg, *Mid-Century Modern: Furniture of the 1950s* (New York: Harmony, 1984).

Clement Greenberg, *The Collected Essays and Criticism, 3: Affirmation and Refusals, 1950–1956*, ed. John O'Brian (Chicago: University of Chicago Press, 1993).

Serge Guilbaut, *How New York Stole the Idea of Modern Art: Abstract Expressionism, Freedom and the Cold War* (Chicago: University of Chicago Press, 1983).

Serge Guilbaut (ed.), *Reconstructing Modernism: Art in New York, Paris, and Montreal 1945–1964* (Cambridge MA: MIT Press, 1990).

James Guimond, *American Photography and the American Dream* (Chapel Hill NC: University of North Carolina Press, 1991).

Ann Hammond, *Ansel Adams: Divine Performance* (New Haven CT: Yale University Press, 2002).

David Hanks et al., *High Styles: Twentieth-Century American Design* (New York: Whitney Museum of American Art, 1985).

Barbara Haskell, *Blam! The Explosion of Pop, Minimalism, and Performance 1958–1964* (New York: Whitney Museum of American Art, 1984).

Marika Herskovic (ed.), *American Abstract Expressionism of the 1950s* (New York: New York School Press, 2003).

Hannah Higgins, *Fluxus Experience* (Berkeley CA: University of California Press, 2002).

Christel Hollevoet (ed.), *Jasper Johns: Writings, Sketchbook Notes, Interviews* (New York: Museum of Modern Art, 1996).

David Hopkins, *After Modern Art, 1945–2000* (London: Thames & Hudson, 2000).

Robert Hughes, *American Visions* (London: Harvill, 1997).

Sam Hunter (ed.), *The Dada/Surrealist Heritage* (Williamstown MA: Sterling & Francine Clark Art Institute, 1977).

Lesley Jackson, *The New Look: Design in the Fifties* (London: Thames & Hudson, 1991).

Eugenia Parry Janis and Wendy MacNeil (ed.), *Photography within the Humanities* (Danbury NH: Addison House, 1977).

Janet Jenkins (ed.), *In the Spirit of Fluxus* (Minneapolis MN: Walker Art Center, 1993).

Jill Johnson, *Jasper Johns: Privileged Information* (London: Thames & Hudson, 1996).

Caroline A. Jones, *Bay Area Figurative Art, 1950–1965* (Berkeley CA: University of California Press, 1990).

Branden W. Joseph, *Robert Rauschenberg* (Cambridge MA: MIT Press, 2002).

Wendy Kozol, *Life's America: Family and Nation in Postwar Photojournalism* (Philadelphia PA: Temple University Press, 1994).

Max Kozloff, 'American Painting During the Cold War', *Artforum*, 11 (9) (May 1973), pp. 43–54.

Ellen G. Landau (ed.), *Reading Abstract Expressionism: Context and Critique* (New Haven CT: Yale University Press, 2005).

Karal Ann Marling, *As Seen on TV: The Visual Culture of Everyday Life in the 1950s* (Cambridge MA: Harvard University Press, 1996).

Jane De Hart Mathews, 'Art and Politics in Cold War America', *American Historical Review*, 81 (October 1976), pp. 762–878.

Dorothy C. Miller (ed.), *Sixteen Americans* (New York: Museum of Modern Art, 1959).

Robert Motherwell, *The Collected Writings of Robert Motherwell*, ed. Stephanie Terenzio (Berkeley: University of California Press, [1992] 1999).

Michael O'Pray, *Avant-Garde Film: Forms, Themes and Passions* (London: Wallflower, 2003).

Fred Orton, *Figuring Jasper Johns* (London: Reaktion, 1994).

Miles Orvell, *American Photography* (London: Thames & Hudson, 2003).

Stephen Polcari, *Abstract Expressionism and the Modern Experience* (Cambridge: Cambridge University Press, 1991).

Bryan Robertson, *Jasper Johns* (London: Arts Council, 1978).

Deidre Robson, *Prestige, Profit and Pleasure: The Market for Modern Art in New York in the 1940s and 1950s* (New York: Garland, 1995).

William S. Rubin, *Frank Stella* (New York: Museum of Modern Art, 1970).

Eric Sandeen, *Picturing an Exhibition: The Family of Man and 1950s America* (Albuquerque NM: University of New Mexico Press, 1995).

Jonathan Spaulding, *Ansel Adams and the American Landscape* (Berkeley CA: University of California Press, 1995).

Sidra Stich, *Made in the USA: An Americanization in Modern Art: The 50s and 60s* (Berkeley CA: University of California Press, 1987).

David Sylvester, *Interviews with American Artists* (London: Chatto & Windus, 2001).

Barbara Tannenbaum (ed.), *Robert Frank and American Politics* (Akron OH: Akron Art Museum, 1985).

Alan Trachtenberg, *Reading American Photographs* (New York: Hill & Wang, 1989).

Patricia Vettel-Becker, *Shooting from the Hip: Photography, Masculinity and Postwar America* (Minneapolis MN: University of Minnesota Press, 2005).

Daniel Wheeler, *Art Since Mid-Century: 1945 to the Present* (Englewood Cliffs NJ: Prentice-Hall, 1991).

Frederick S. Wight, *Hans Hofmann* (Berkeley CA: University of California Press, 1957).

Deborah Willis (ed.), *Picturing Us: A History of Black Photography* (New York: The New Press, 1994).

James Yohe (ed.), *Hans Hofmann* (New York: Rizzoli, 2002).

Audio-Visual Sources

American Visions Series (PBS, US, 1997).

Anthology of American Folk Music (Folkways, Smithsonian Institute, [1952] 1997).

The Atomic Café (Kevin Rafferty, Jayne Loader and Pierce Rafferty, US, 1982).

Black Theatre Movement: A Raisin in the Sun to the Present (Woodie King Jr, US, 1978).

By Brakhage: An Anthology (Stan Brakhage, Criterion Collection, US, 2003).

Classic Commercials (St Laurent, Quebec: Madacy Entertainment, 2002).

The Cry of Jazz (Edward O. Bland, US, 1959).

Disneyland USA (Disney Inc., US, 2001).

The End (Christopher Maclaine, US, 1953; Arthouse Inc., 1996).

Eyes on the Prize Series (Boston MA, Blackside Inc., US, 1988–90).

Hans Hofmann: Artist/Teacher Teacher/Artist (Amgott Productions, US, 2002).

The Honeymooners: "Classic 39" Episodes (CBS/Paramount, US, 2003).

I Love Lucy: The Complete First Season (Paramount, US, 2003).

Jazz on a Summer's Day (Bert Stern, US, 1959).

Pull My Daisy (Robert Frank and Alfred Leslie, G-String, US, 1959).

1950s TV's Greatest Comedies (Falcon Picture Group, US, 2002).

The Sid Caesar Collection (New Video Group, US, 2005).

Songs for Political Action: Folkmusic, Topical Songs and the American Left, 1926–1953 (Bear Family Records, 1996).

Index